Intoxication

Intoxication and Society

Problematic Pleasures of Drugs and Alcohol

Edited by

Jonathan Herring
Professor of Law, University of Oxford

Ciaran Regan
Professor of Neuropharmacology, University College Dublin

Darin Weinberg
Reader in Sociology, University of Cambridge

Phil Withington
Professor of Early Modern History, University of Sheffield

First published 2013 by
PALGRAVE MACMILLAN

Palgrave Macmillan in the UK is an imprint of Macmillan Publishers Limited, registered in England, company number 785998, of Houndmills, Basingstoke, Hampshire RG21 6XS.

Palgrave Macmillan in the US is a division of St Martin's Press LLC, 175 Fifth Avenue, New York, NY 10010.

Palgrave Macmillan is the global academic imprint of the above companies and has companies and representatives throughout the world.

Palgrave® and Macmillan® are registered trademarks in the United States, the United Kingdom, Europe and other countries

ISBN: 978–1–137–00832–9 hardback
ISBN: 978–1–137–00834–3 paperback

This book is printed on paper suitable for recycling and made from fully managed and sustained forest sources. Logging, pulping and manufacturing processes are expected to conform to the environmental regulations of the country of origin.

A catalogue record for this book is available from the British Library.

A catalog record for this book is available from the Library of Congress.

10 9 8 7 6 5 4 3 2 1
22 21 20 19 18 17 16 15 14 13

Printed and bound in Great Britain by
TJ International, Padstow

Contents

Section 2   *Spatial Politics*

Section 3   *Culture and Practice*

Notes on Contributors

Angus Bancroft works in sociology at the University of Edinburgh. His research has focused on a range of issues including deviance and pathology, drug problems and families, and the culture of public problems. He has written *Drugs Intoxication and Society* (2009 Cambridge: Polity Press) and, with Ralph Fevre, *Dead White Men and Other Important People: Sociology's Big Ideas* (2011 Basingstoke: Palgrave Macmillan).

Virginia Berridge is director of the Centre for History in Public Health at the London School of Hygiene and Tropical Medicine, University of London. She has published widely on substance use policy and history – alcohol, illicit drugs and smoking – as well as on public health policy. She is a partner in the History and Policy initiative.

Alan Bogg, University of Oxford, received his undergraduate and graduate education in Oxford, being awarded his BA in law (first class) in 1997. Thereafter, he was awarded the degrees of BCL (first class) and DPhil. Following a period as a lecturer at the University of Birmingham, Alan returned to Oxford in 2003 to take up his fellowship at Hertford College. Alan's research focuses predominantly on theoretical issues in domestic, European and international labour law and criminal law. His book, *The Democratic Aspects of Trade Union Recognition* (2009 Oxford: Hart Publishing) was awarded the Society of Legal Scholars Peter Birks' Prize for Outstanding Legal Scholarship in 2010.

James Brown is based in the Faculty of History, University of Oxford, where he manages the research project 'Cultures of Knowledge: An Intellectual Geography of the Seventeenth-Century Republic of Letters'. He is interested in the social and cultural history of seventeenth-century England. His doctoral thesis, a case study of public houses in Southampton, was confirmed at the University of Warwick in 2008. He has published on public houses as sites of surveillance and on the manufacture of beer in urban communities, and has co-edited a collection of essays on the history of identity documentation. He is currently co-editing a volume on the intellectual geography of early modern Europe.

David Clemis is associate professor of early modern history and former chair of the Department of General Education at Mount Royal University, Calgary, Canada. His research focuses on understandings of alcohol intoxication and conceptions of craving, habit and addiction in the seventeenth and eighteenth centuries. This work explores the writings of medical, legal and moral authorities, as well as sources of popular thought. It is part of a wider interest and ongoing research into the history of understandings of moral agency, cognition and personal identity in 'the British enlightenment'.

Karen D Ersche, University of Cambridge, is a psychologist who is interested in the effects of chronic drug use on brain function and the question of how occasional drug use turns into addiction in some people. Her aim is to better understand what renders some people vulnerable for developing dependence while others remain resilient to the addictive effects of drugs. Her research therefore aims to elucidate the neurobiological substrates of vulnerability and resilience for drug dependence. She hopes that this knowledge will help to develop more efficient strategies for the prevention and treatment of addiction. A secondary research aim of her work is to understand the effects of addictive drugs such as cocaine and heroin on general health, well-being and on processes such as ageing. She believes that a better understanding of the underlying mechanisms involved in drug addiction will provide a solid basis for the development of efficient therapeutic interventions while helping reducing the widespread stigma attached to people who have become dependent on drugs.

Shaun French is lecturer in economic geography at the University of Nottingham. He has research interests in geographies of money and finance and, in particular, geographies of biofinancialization, financial subjectification, and the politics of financial exclusion. He is co-editor of *Key Methods in Geography* (2012 London: Sage) and has published widely in journals such as *Environment and Planning, Society and Space, British Journal of Politics and International Relations* and *Transactions of the Institute of British Geographers*.

Jonathan Herring is a fellow in law at Exeter College, Oxford University, and professor of law at the Law Faculty, Oxford University. He has written on family law, medical law, criminal law and legal issues surrounding old age. He has written over 40 books including: *Older People in Law and Society* (2009 Oxford: Oxford University Press); *European Human Rights and Family Law* (2010 Oxford: Hart Publishing) (with Shazia Choudhry); *Medical Law and Ethics* (2010 Oxford: Oxford University Press); *Criminal Law* (7th edn 2011 Basingstoke: Palgrave Macmillan); *Criminal Law* (4th edn 2012 Oxford: Oxford University Press); *Great Debates in Criminal Law* (2nd edn 2012 Basingstoke: Palgrave Macmillan) and *Family Law* (4th edn 2011 Harlow: Pearson).

James Kneale is a senior lecturer in geography at University College London. A cultural and historical geographer, his research focuses on spaces of drink in Britain from the nineteenth century to the present day. He has published on drinking places and on the spatial imaginaries of temperance and alcohol policy, as well as writing with Shaun French on actuarial calculations of risk attributed to drinking and other 'lifestyle' factors. Most recently he has been working on the history of temperance life insurance between 1840 and 1911, a topic that combines commercial, moral and medical constructions of risk and responsibility. He has also published on geographies of literature.

Arlie Loughnan is a senior lecturer at the University of Sydney. She is a graduate of the University of Sydney (BA Hons 1, LLB Hons 1), New York University Law School (LLM) and London School of Economics (PhD). Her research concerns criminal law and the criminal justice system, with a focus on the relationship between legal doctrines, practices, institutions and knowledge. Her particular interests are constructions of criminal responsibility and non-responsibility, the interaction of legal and expert medical knowledges and the historical development of the criminal law. Her book, *Manifest Madness: Mental Incapacity in Criminal Law*, was published by Oxford University Press in 2012.

Ciaran Regan is professor of neuropharmacology at University College Dublin. His main area of research relates to understanding mechanisms of brain structural change that contribute to the formation of long-term memory and their potential as novel drug targets. His work has been recognised by the award of several honours including the Conway Medal of the Royal Academy of Medicine in Ireland and the Royal Irish Academy Medal for achievement in pharmacology and toxicology. He is a Fellow of the World Academy of Art and Science and a Member of the Royal Irish Academy. His book, *Intoxicating Minds* (2001 New York: Columbia University Press) has contributed to popularising science for the general reader on the role of mind-altering drugs in society.

Craig Reinarman is professor of sociology and legal studies at the University of California, Santa Cruz. He has also served as a visiting professor at the University of Amsterdam and the University of Utrecht in the Netherlands. His research has centered on cultures of drug use and the politics of drug law. He has been the principal investigator on research grants from the US National Institute on Drug Abuse. He is the author of *American States of Mind: Political Beliefs and Behaviour* (1987 New Haven: Yale University Press) and co-author of *Cocaine Changes: The Experience of Using and Quitting*, with D Waldorf and S Murphy (1991 Philadelphia: Temple University Press) and *Crack in America: Demon Drugs and Social Justice*, with H G Levine et al. (1997 Berkeley: University of California Press).

Cathy Shrank is professor of Tudor and Renaissance literature at the University of Sheffield. Her research focuses on sixteenth and early seventeenth-century literature. Her publications are mainly on sixteenth-century literature, particularly before Shakespeare, and in 2004 she published *Writing the*

Nation in Reformation England, 1530–1580 (Oxford: Oxford University Press). *The Oxford Handbook of Tudor Literature, 1485–1603*, co-edited with Mike Pincombe, was published in 2009 by Oxford University Press.

Darin Weinberg is a fellow of King' College Cambridge and a reader in the Department of Sociology at Cambridge University. He received a BA in sociology and communications from the University of California, San Diego, in 1984, an MSc in social philosophy from the London School of Economics in 1985, and a PhD in sociology from the University of California, Los Angeles, in 1998. In 2011 Darin won the Melvin Pollner Prize in Ethnomethodology from the American Sociological Association's Section on Ethnomethodology and Conversation Analysis and the Outstanding Article Award from the Social Problems Theory Division of the Society for the Study of Social Problems. His research focuses primarily on the practical purposes to which concepts of addiction, mental illness and learning disability are applied in various historical and contemporary contexts. He has co-authored *Talk and Interaction in Social Research Methods* (2006 London: Sage) and written *Of Others Inside: Insanity, Addiction, and Belonging in America* (2005 Philadelphia: Temple University Press).

Rebecca Williams holds a CUF lectureship at Oxford University, in association with Pembroke College. Rebecca was previously a fellow of Robinson College, Cambridge, having done her PhD at Birmingham. Rebecca's principal teaching interests are criminal law and public law. Her book *Unjust Enrichment and Public Law: A Comparative Study of England, France and the EU* was published by Hart Publishing in 2011.

Phil Withington is professor of early modern history at the University of Sheffield. He has published on the history of citizenship, popular politics, urbanization, intoxication and sociability and is currently researching the history of intoxicants in early modern Britain. His books include *The Politics of Commonwealth: Citizens and Freemen in Early Modern England* (2005 Cambridge: Cambridge University Press) and *Society in Early Modern England: the Vernacular Origins of Some Powerful Ideas* (2012 Cambridge: Polity Press).

1
Starting the Conversation

Jonathan Herring, Ciaran Regan, Darin Weinberg
and Phil Withington

Introduction

Substances that alter the mental and physiological state of the person – here termed *intoxicants* – are a modern obsession. Debates over licensing and 'binge drinking'; the categorization and policing of 'addictive' substances; the rights and wrongs of smoking in 'public' places; the relationship between intoxicants and notions of the self; the aesthetic and symbolic significance of intoxicants: all testify to the central place of intoxicants in contemporary society. They also demonstrate that the problem of intoxication transcends the boundaries of any single academic discipline. It is trans-historical and trans-cultural and also traverses the divide between the natural and social sciences since the physical characteristics and effects of intoxicants only take on significance within particular social contexts. For example, modern concepts of 'addiction' depend as much on medical and legal discourses as on a substance's molecular structure; 'taste' is something learnt, practised and displayed as well as biologically embedded; and the meaning and significance of substances are always representational as well as innate. Likewise, the peculiar relationship between intoxicants and medicine clearly illustrates how the history of medicine is integral to the history of societies (and vice versa). New intoxicants commonly derive their initial legitimacy from medical theory and practice. This was true for tobacco in the sixteenth century and cocaine in the nineteenth century.

This book canvasses these various dimensions of intoxication in a single volume and provides readers with a more panoramic understanding of the dynamic relationship between intoxicants and society than is normally available in studies rooted in a particular disciplinary framework. It is our hope that by bringing together multiple perspectives on the study of intoxication we might begin to foster a richer and more inclusive dialogue regarding the causes, characteristics and consequences of intoxicant use in modern

1

societies. More specifically, we hope that by bringing together discussions of the medical, historical, legal and cultural aspects of intoxication this volume will serve to facilitate some intellectual bridge-building between these research domains. How and to what extent have law and public policy development been responsive to ascendant cultural images of intoxication, to the commerce and politics of intoxicants in particular communal spaces, or to medical discoveries regarding their nature and effects on how humans function? In what ways has medical expertise regarding addiction and intoxication itself been shaped not only by scientific discoveries but by the cultural and institutional contexts within which it has been forged? How have the experiences of intoxication, intoxicants and/or our capacities to control their use been governed not only by anatomy and physiology but by cultural beliefs and social practices? Taken together the chapters comprising this book encourage a more robust appreciation for the complex interactions that have and continue to transpire between the legal, political, cultural and scientific legacies.

Before developing these themes, it is important to be clear about what we mean by intoxication and intoxicants. Intoxicants are typically known by the more pejorative synonym drugs, which are substances with distinct chemical properties and physical and psychological effects. Some are distinguished by the fact that they act on the central nervous system and may be used to change thoughts, feelings, perceptions, or behaviour. Drugs are used in religious ceremonies, as medical treatments, for fun and recreation; they can cause disease, they can lead to vice and crime. Some are also known as 'drugs of abuse', a social description rather than a pharmacological property, because, when used freely, their effects are considered dangerous enough to create a health hazard and/or social problem. Among them are the opiates heroin and morphine, the stimulants nicotine, amphetamine and cocaine, and sedatives like the barbiturates and alcohol. Morphine is a powerful medicine yet, in certain contexts, its procurement can be associated with crime and it is certainly not considered to be a drug for recreation. Alcohol, self-prescribed, is fun unless you use too much, and then it can lead to physical illness and addiction. Caffeine is a utilitarian drug used to wake us in the morning and stave off fatigue during the day. Caffeine is available to all; coffee may not be advisable for children but caffeine is contained in the majority of their favoured carbonated drinks. The problem that has eluded contemporary society is how to keep these categories separate. Society's response to the use and control of these recreational drugs, particularly over the twentieth century, might best be described in terms of their historical antecedents rather than logic. Despite little being known of the pharmacology of these substances, our legislators have often based their opinions on personal agendas and the inflation of their institutions, often disingenuously.

Surprisingly, as a general rule, alcohol being an exception, a single common thread exists – the drug laws of all nations are similar, despite some variations in severity (Bakalar and Grinspoon, 1984).

What follows highlights some of the key themes to emerge from the chapters. It will then provide a background to the ways in which medicine, history, sociology and law have approached intoxication, before concluding with a discussion of the benefits of undertaking such an interdisciplinary examination of the topic.

Some key themes

One of the striking features of this volume is that it combines essays by 'experts' in particular fields of knowledge – law, psychology, neuroscience – with papers which seek to contextualize and interrogate the very basis of 'expertise'. This combination of perspectives has been deliberate and we regard it as one of the primary virtues of the collection. However, we also acknowledge that this combination requires us to speak explicitly to what many might take to be an intrinsic theoretical tension. Historically, it has been common practice to assume that by subjecting expert authority to socio-historical analysis one must inevitably debunk its claims to validity. The production of valid knowledge, it is said, must wholly transcend the myriad social forces at work both within and beyond the confines of the laboratory, library, or consulting room lest it be reduced to mere ideology. How, then, can we endorse broadly social constructionist orientations to the rise and legitimation of various sorts of legal, sociological, historical and/or medical expertise regarding intoxication and addiction without inevitably discrediting or at least casting suspicion upon the legitimacy of such claims to expertise? Put simply, we view this putative tension between socio-historically explaining and epistemologically honouring claims to expertise as a false and pernicious one. We summarily reject the argument that by socially situating and explaining the production and consumption of expert knowledge one thereby demonstrates its falsity. Because the conduct and evaluation of expertise are themselves intrinsically social accomplishments, there can be no reasonable alternative for experts but to attend and seek to respond competently to the specific social conditions that surround their enterprise. Hence, illuminating exactly what those social conditions are and how they have influenced the formation of expertise in any given instance does not and cannot of itself undermine the authority of that expertise.

Expert knowledge is always forged under distinctive economic, political, cultural and institutional circumstances, all of which may impact upon its character and reception. Improving our understanding of these circumstances actually promotes (rather than prevents) a more discerning capacity to assess the distinctive value and comparative merits of divergent knowledge claims. Far from undermining the quest for truth, efforts to unpack and explain the socio-historical conditions that have given rise to particular understandings of intoxication only serve to better highlight the distinctive value these understandings have had for those who develop or adopt them. As noted above, intoxication has received a great deal of sustained scholarly attention from a variety of different disciplines, all of which shine light upon different facets of the phenomenon. By attending to the social conditions under which they have been developed and put to practical use we become better equipped to consider these discourses. This is true not only in terms of the esoteric standards of their practitioners but, more broadly, as citizens with a shared stake in putting knowledge of various sorts to use to foster the well-being of our societies and to solve the problems we must collectively confront.

The courtroom is a good example of these tensions at work. The court is often faced with the defendant's account of his or her intoxicated behaviour; the account of an expert medical witness; the 'common sense' understanding of intoxication of the jury or the judge; and the broader social policies. All of these must be fitted within the standard legal framework for assessing guilt or innocence. The legal chapters of this book argue that those involved in the legal process manage this 'fitting' with only limited success. Standard legal doctrines of responsibility under the law do not accord with the accounts of intoxication brought by the defendant or medical expertise. The law ends up making what from a medical or philosophical point of view might appear grossly simplistic assumptions about notions of responsibility. Lawyers might point out the restrictions of what can be accepted and understood as evidence in a courtroom. These are inevitably limited in terms of time, money and understanding. However, the danger is that the further the law's approach matches the scientific understanding or the understanding of the person in the street, the more its own credibility and legitimacy comes under strain.

Another feature that makes this collection distinctive is its attention to the present and the past. Though our foci have been more or less confined to the English-speaking world, contributions run the gamut from the early modern era through to the present time. It is our hope that by juxtaposing past and present, the volume will encourage readers to appreciate more fully the extent to which contemporary concerns surrounding intoxication often have remarkably enduring roots in the past. For example, though we periodically read in the popular press of the growing tendencies of modern societies to foster drug epidemics, a survey of history reveals that such moral panics are hardly unique to the twenty-first century. Such knowledge discourages rash judgments regarding the causes of drug use in contemporary societies or the gravity of its consequences. It also promotes a more rational, wide-ranging and balanced consideration of not only the causes and consequences of the use of drugs itself, but the causes and consequences of our sometimes rather irrational opinions and public policy responses to drug use. Attention to history also allows us to identify more effectively what is distinctive about more recently emergent intoxication practices and to think more carefully about the myriad factors that might have influenced their emergence.

The issue of responsibility is a theme which runs through the legal and medical chapters in particular. Responsibility arises for lawyers in two senses. The first is the extent to which a person is responsible for becoming intoxicated in the first place. Some addicted defendants in particular have plausible claim to lack responsibility for their intoxication, although as the chapter by Alan Bogg and Jonathan Herring demonstrates, in fact the law is very reluctant to accept that addiction removes responsibility. Karen Ersch's chapter could be used to question the law's reluctance to see addiction as blame-reducing. Her study of brain scans demonstrates that the brains of addicts are distinct from the brains of non-addicts. Although what such scans cannot tell us is the relevance of these to moral accountability. It is notable that the law takes it for granted that being intoxicated is something for which one should be held to account. It is assumed to be a 'blameworthy' state to be in, something that Phil Withington's chapter, for example, demonstrates has not always been the case (especially not for lawyers themselves).

The second issue of responsibility for lawyers is the extent to which an intoxicated person is responsible for his or her actions. Rebecca Williams' chapter highlights the difficulty the law experiences in accounting for this. Frankly fictional devices are used to reach what is regarded as the acceptable result that intoxicated defendants are criminally responsible for the harms they cause. A more nuanced view of the impact of intoxication could be provided by detailed study of science, as Ciaran Regan's chapter indicates. One gets the impression the law feels more at home with the certainties produced by its fictions, than with the ambiguities revealed by science. Of course, the law here is not operating simply as a reflection of sound knowledge, but in response to political and social forces. The law is best understood as a response to the fear of the intoxicated, rather than a genuine attempt to assess responsibility.

Having highlighted some of the key characteristics of the volume, the remainder of this introduction provides some disciplinary context for the individual chapters which follow. The next section looks at history and intoxication and is followed by sections on sociology, law and science.

Intoxication and history

The thematic organization of this volume reflects, in many respects, some of the key preoccupations of the historiography on intoxication in the

Anglo-American world. It should be noted that the term historiography is here used in a broad sense to describe a range of scholarly literatures which, while taking 'the past' as their primary unit of study, nevertheless focus on very different kinds of processes and phenomena, and so also belong to other disciplinary traditions. Thus the historical contributions to *Intoxication and Society* include examples of the history of medicine and public policy, historical geography and social history, and cultural and literary history.

The diverse historical repertoire suggested by these labels reflects the obvious but sometimes forgotten fact that it is not just nations, politics, or social classes which have a history. So, too, do 'experts' and the traditions of knowledge which define them (such as doctors, lawyers, clerics, scientists); the institutions, ideologies and procedures responsible for governance; the language and metaphors by which we perceive and describe ourselves and our worlds; and the very streets, buildings and social practices which shape our daily lives. As we assembled this volume of essays it became clear that intoxication belongs to all of these histories: that, indeed, it is to this messy, multidimensional past that we owe our messy, multidimensional present. The realisation is important if only because modern commentators on intoxication – in particular scientists, medics and lawyers – often seem to regard themselves as operating in an historical vacuum. A vacuum in which the modern problem of intoxication is without antecedents and the epistemological and institutional resources used to deal with the problem are *not* themselves the product of historical developments and processes. One contention of this book is that nothing could be further from the truth; that, indeed, it is only by unearthing intoxication's deeply intertwined historical roots that we can even begin to understand the confusing canopy of the present.

The chapters by David Clemis and Virginia Berridge are a case in point. In commenting on the relationship between intoxication and medical expertise they draw on two perennial and related concerns of the history of medicine and public policy. Clemis deals primarily with the state of *discursive* play during the eighteenth century – how medical writers conceptualized and wrote about drunkenness for the reading public, and the nature of the intellectual traditions upon which they drew. Berridge in turn focuses on some of the *institutional politics* of medical provision and practice into the twentieth century, highlighting the importance of both informal networking and organizational adroitness on the part of individuals in determining official attitudes and treatments. The two approaches are neither mutually exclusive nor chronologically specific: eighteenth-century medicine was characterized by institutional politicking just as twentieth-century medicine has been marked by striking discursive contests and developments. With more space the volume would have teased out these connections synchronically. When taken together, what the chapters of Clemis and Berridge nicely highlight are the interlocking factors which determine the capacity of 'experts' both to inform public attitudes and shape the policies of those wielding political power and resources.

In the first instance, experts must claim and enjoy authority over some kind of knowledge which is recognized as indubitable, revered as specialist, or manages to be both. Clemis argues, for example, that for much of the eighteenth century medical attitudes towards intoxication continued to be predicated on Renaissance assumptions about the body derived from the classical tradition, primarily the writings of Galen (for an outline of humoral theory see Shrank below). Over the preceding centuries classical theories had been woven into vernacular practice, and medical writers accordingly viewed intoxication in 'common-sense' terms: their statements carried authority because they reproduced an established and widely held orthodoxy. It was only in the second half of the eighteenth century that a new medical perspective on drunkenness began slowly to develop, one which was eventually to transform medical experts from the guardians of the commonplace to masters of an altogether more esoteric, neurological knowledge which only they could comprehend and legitimately apply. Indubitable orthodoxy thus became specialist learning, which over time would become indubitable in its own right. The issues they raise are picked up again in the chapter by Arlie Loughnan, who analyses the approach of lawyers to expertise in the courtroom. Interestingly, she emphasizes the role played by the expertise of the layperson, the general knowledge of the ordinary person, in the development of the law and the response of the courts.

The chapter by Berridge reminds us, secondly, that discursive trends such as these cannot be treated in a social vacuum, certainly if we are interested in the impact of ideas on social life. Berridge argues that experts are political animals and that their influence is not accidental, nor a consequence of the inherent veracity of their approach. Rather it is the result of contingency, circumstance and power. In order to exert public influence, doctors and scientists of different stripes need to cultivate personal networks and relationships, colonize existing institutions, and develop their own organizational resources, be it through the organs of the 'state', private corporations, or charitable foundations. It is by these means that experts influence both policy makers and 'public opinion' more generally. Berridge underestimates, perhaps, the levels of institutional politics before the nineteenth century (early modern physicians and apothecaries were quite as monopolistic as modern psychiatrists and pharmacologists). However, what she powerfully demonstrates is the formation of *new* networks and organizations after 1870 which provided the infrastructures to inculcate and implement precisely the kind of discursive developments with which Clemis concludes his chapter. It is to this period of discursive and institutional fecundity that our contemporary culture of

medical expertise – with its sponsorship of psychiatric and psychopharmacological treatments and its proximity both to the state and the pharmaceutical
industry – can be traced.

The chapters by James Brown and by Shaun French and James Kneale
consider a different, though related, aspect of the history of intoxication.
They draw on a tradition of 'new social history' and social geography which,
since the spread of sociological and anthropological methodologies in the
1960s, has looked to recover the everyday social practices and experiences
of ordinary people. Within this historiography, drinking was quickly recognized as an important, indeed perennial, aspect of popular culture; so, too,
the attempts by those with political authority to control and police popular
drinking habits. The chapters by Brown and French and Kneale accordingly
examine how and by whom the consumption of alcohol was regulated (as
it were) 'on the ground'. More to the point, both chapters consider modes
of regulation – at once communal and personal – before the emergence of
the modern bureaucratic state. Brown focuses on the later sixteenth and
seventeenth centuries, painstakingly analysing the local legal records of
Southampton in order to recreate the regulatory culture of a small but busy
English port. French and Kneale turn their attention to the United Kingdom
Temperance and General Provident Institution (UKT&GPI), an extremely
successful Victorian company which, from its establishment in the 1840s,
developed a national network of offices selling life insurance.

Although a period of 200 years separates the events described by the chapters, the stories they tell resonate with each other in important respects. First,
both depict the development of new procedures for regulating consumption. Brown describes the moment in which licensing first became an instrument of English governance. From 1552, national legislators identified the
alehouse as a potentially disorderly drinking space, and in a sequence of
parliamentary Acts required local magistrates to decide who should and
should not be allowed to sell ale within their communities. The procedure
described by French and Kneale centred on the individual rather than the
community: from 1841, the managers of the UKT&GPI invited prospective customers to purchase life assurance policies on the understanding
that they 'entirely abstain from intoxicating beverages'. Second, both chapters describe the capacity for meaningful social organization and the exercise of public power outwith the infrastructures of the bureaucratic state.
Brown describes a national polity largely dependent on the co-operation
of locally situated magistrates – in this instance the corporate governors
of Southampton. This urban oligarchy exercised considerable civic authority, with licensing becoming an important weapon in their governmental
armoury by the seventeenth century. However, Brown also finds that a medieval institution, the court leet, remained an important means of association

for urban householders below the level of the civic elite; that, indeed, it was this ostensibly declining institution which was most vociferous in agitating for a stricter licensing policy after 1600. French and Kneale demonstrate, in turn, the importance of voluntary associations – or what contemporaries termed 'societies' – in shaping public behaviour during the Victorian era. Insurance companies were one such kind of association: national corporations which demanded certain kinds of behaviour on the part of members in return for financial security. Temperance societies were another, and in the early days of UKT&GPI membership of a 'total-abstinence society' was a prerequisite of life assurance.

A third issue raised by both chapters is the social identity of those most invested in regulating drinking practices. Brown makes clear that in early modern Southampton it was not the urban elites who looked to use the licence aggressively, in order to delimit and police alehouses, but rather the more humble shopkeepers and tradesmen whom contemporaries tended to describe as the 'middling sort'. French and Kneale likewise point out that the moving spirits of UKT&GPI were drawn from the Victorian middle class: the society was established by Robert Warner, a young tradesman who worked (and eventually ran) the family business of bell-founders, and its executive committee was full of respectable craftsmen, manufacturers, traders and professionals. These members of the seventeenth-century 'middling sort' and nineteenth-century 'middle class' acted, finally, against the backdrop of considerable ideological upheaval. The national legislation against drunkenness originated with the Edwardian Reformation and by the seventeenth century the alehouse had become a deeply symbolic and contested space for reformers ('puritans') and their opponents. Although Brown does not explore whether the court leet in Southampton was used to pursue an ideological agenda, it is clear that in other places reformatory ideology and aggressive licensing were closely linked. The temperance origins of UKT&GPI are, of course, explicit; that temperance advocated abstinence or moderation on moral and social rather than medical grounds is also well known. In this sense it is no coincidence that Robert Warner was a Quaker or that his company's underlying financial logic, and indeed success – that teetotallers lived longer than drinkers, and so paid into their insurance policy for longer – flew in the face of accepted medical wisdom.

These chapters show that historians have long recognized the importance of intoxicants to the histories of medical expertise and social regulation. Indeed, so important are these historiographical traditions to our understanding of intoxicants that it could easily be assumed that it is only in the medical, moral and regulative realms that the significance of intoxication lies. The chapters by Cathy Shrank and Phil Withington suggest otherwise. Shrank writes from the perspective of a literary historian in order to examine discourses of intoxication in English Renaissance textual culture. She finds that motifs and references to intoxication were pervasive: that, indeed, English writers in the sixteenth and seventeenth centuries may well have been as obsessed with intoxication as writers and other cultural producers in the twenty-first century (cf. Smyth, 2004). Shrank argues that this obsession was predicated on a humoral conception of the person and the eternal conflict between 'reason' (in the sense of rationality) and the 'passions' (in the sense of bodily responses and appetites). Within this framework (which is also described by Clemis) intoxication amounted to the loss of reason and an imbalance of humours: it was a mental and physiological condition in which the passions – fear, lust, greed, anger and so on – swamped the person. The excessive consumption of alcohol could obviously lead to this kind of state, and in this sense the ubiquity of the language of intoxication is testimony to the popularity of medical texts and writings. Shrank suggests, however, that this is by no means the whole story. In the first instance, discourses about intoxication were not limited to excessive drinking. Rather intoxication as a state of being was also a feature of other kinds of 'madness'. It was deployed to understand political tyranny, whereby the passions of the tyrant overwhelmed their rational faculties. It also characterized religious error and misplaced zeal. In both instances, the language of intoxication was not so much metaphorical as analytical: it explained the ostensibly inexplicable. In the second instance, Shrank argues that for many early modern moralists the best means of combatting intoxication was not, in fact, self-control and discipline, as Stoicism taught. Rather it was more effective to fight fire with fire, or to be more precise, passion with passion. People did not necessarily moderate their behaviour on account of reason. They did, however, respond to fear. Some of these themes find echoes in the legal chapters. As Rebecca Williams describes in her chapter, the law feels a strong urge to blame those, while intoxicated, who harm others but struggles to fit this within an orthodox account of the law's understanding of responsibility for one's actions. This is all the more apparent in cases of addiction when, as Alan Bogg and Jonathan Herring discuss, the law struggles with allocating the appropriate level of blame, if any, to defendants intoxicated as a result of addiction.

The chapter by Withington is also concerned with the centrality of intoxication to Renaissance culture. Whereas Shrank focuses on its disruptive qualities, Withington looks at how intoxication was actively valorised by England's educated elites – not least the future lawyers, physicians, clerics and magistrates who attended the universities and Inns of Court in ever increasing numbers between the 1560s and 1640s. Drawing on the work of literary and cultural historians, Withington argues that the very same class of men who were ostensibly responsible for reforming the drinking habits of the wider populace were also in the vanguard of developing new conventions and aesthetics of sociability – conventions which placed especial emphasis on drinking, often to excess. He argues that the fetish for 'wit', 'good fellow-ship' and 'toasting' displayed in Renaissance texts corresponded with the way educated men were increasingly expected to behave in practice. Far from becoming the preserve of poorer, less educated groups, as social historians have tended to imply, intoxication was reinvented from the later sixteenth century as an integral component of Renaissance masculine identity. It might well be argued that this process of cultural appropriation, whereby one gener-ation adapts or rejects the social rituals and habits of their predecessors, has continued ever since.

Sociology

Sociological research on intoxication began in earnest with the publication of Alfred Lindesmith's classic social psychological study of opiate addiction (Lindesmith, 1938). In this study Lindesmith noted that those who had been administered sufficient opiates in medical settings to become physically dependent rarely became addicted whereas those who acquired their drugs on the streets were much more prone to do so. He argued this was due to the fact that, unlike street users, medical patients tended not to know their symptoms of opiate withdrawal for what they were and hence did not seek to alleviate these symptoms through further opiate use. Lindesmith thereby introduced the idea that the meanings people confer upon drug effects are crucial determinants of how those effects are experienced and, in turn, how people behaviourally respond to them. This idea was expanded upon by Howard Becker (1953; 1967) who argued that not only withdrawal symptoms but the whole range of psychoactivity attributed to drugs is also inevitably mediated by the symbolic interpretations that actors confer upon them. Though the Lindesmith/Becker claim that the meaning of addiction and intoxication is inevitably embodied in *linguistic or symbolic representations* of these experiences has been criticized, the insistence that meaning plays a crucial role in shaping the experience of intoxication and drug-seeking behaviour remains axiomatic in sociological research on these phenomena (cf. Weinberg, 1997; 2002).

A second major branch of sociological research looks at the role of the state and, more specifically, criminalization in shaping various dimensions of the relationship between drug use and society. For instance, Lindesmith (1965) argued that it was the criminalization of opiate use that pressed drug users into a range of other forms of criminality and immorality rather than their intrinsic propensity toward criminality and immorality that led them into drug use. While this insight might strike us as rather obvious today, it was very much at odds with prevailing expert opinion in Lindesmith's day which overwhelmingly tended to cast drug addicts as psychopaths and degenerates for whom very little hope or compassion was warranted. Lindesmith's work in this regard along with that of Lemert (cf. 1951; 1962; 1967), Becker (1953) and Duster (1970) contributed to the rise of the societal reaction or labelling theory of deviance which came to prominence in the 1960s and 1970s and was profoundly influential in the sociological study of drugs and drug users.

Societal reaction theorists often focused on the roles played by official agents of social control in not only formally responding to drug use but, more broadly, in fostering definitions of it that stigmatize and otherwise marginalize drug users. They highlighted the important fact that if particular definitions of drug use and drug users become hegemonic in a given society it is usually because these definitions have been promoted by people who possess sufficient power to enforce these definitions over others. In time, societal reaction theory expanded beyond the early focus on public policy makers and official agents of social control to the wider socio-historical contexts within which they work. Valuable work has been done on the political and socio-cultural processes through which moral sentiments contrary to the use of drugs spread through societies and generated public interest and anxieties about drugs in the first place (cf. Gusfield, 1986 [1963]; Reinarmann and Levine, 1997). This research highlights the varieties of activity undertaken by private citizens prior, and usually as a necessary precursor, to official state responses to drug use.

Gusfield's (1986 [1963]) pioneering work introduced the importance of cultural status and symbolism as political variables independent of economic class. He showed how a moral movement founded by what he called the 'New England Federalist "aristocracy"' (Gusfield 1986 [1963], p. 5) to promote their own Protestant values and thusly defend their declining status in American society came to resonate with the status concerns of a number of disparate social groups during the middle and late nineteenth century. The use of alcohol and one's opinions about it came to serve as symbolic markers of one's affiliations in cultural battles pitting Protestant and Catholic, native against immigrant, rural dweller against urbanite, and middle class against both lower and upper class. Levine (1978) has argued that the temperance movement, though it focused only on alcohol, presaged much of the subsequent thinking on drugs as social problems. He suggests the rise of the temperance movement was symptomatic of a larger cultural revolution that swept Europe and America in the eighteenth and nineteenth centuries. This cultural revolution demanded heightened levels of self-control, individualism and accountability to the demands of a capitalist economy, all of which were found incompatible with certain patterns of heavy alcohol use. According to Levine, the political and economic changes that characterized this era provided the context in which temperance ideology, and in particular the notion of addiction, could take root and appear reasonable to large numbers of people.

Social movement research is immensely illuminating and helps to situate the meaning of drug use in the wider context of Western historical development. However, as Gusfield himself has noted, casting one's explanations at too general a level of analysis can also miss the extent to which history and culture are subject to important local variations. Hence, Gusfield (1991, p. 408) has called for 'a microhistorical approach that specifies time, space, and group'. This advice was anticipated in a number of important ways by sociologists who employed ethnographic methods to explore the local variations according to which drugs users formed subcultures. Developing upon Finestone's (1957) classic study of 'the cat' as an ideal typical urban Black heroin user, Sutter (1966; 1969) was among the first to argue that drug users could not be subsumed under a single subculture or characterological type:

> Any attempt to describe or analyse the phenomenon of street level drug use in terms of a cultural system must account for different types of users, must grasp the nature of this selective process, and must recognize that worlds of drug use are subject to great fluctuations over time. (Sutter, 1969, p. 803)

In his own work, Sutter distinguished between 'dope fiends', 'righteous dope fiends', 'hard players', 'easy players', 'mellow dudes', 'crystal freaks', 'weed heads', 'pill freaks', 'acid freaks', 'garbage junkies', 'winos', as well as distinguishing between various attitudes and identities that issued from the ways in which drug users acquire money to support their drug use. Sutter made a powerful case for the diversity of drug-using careers on the 'street scene' and made generalization regarding deviant drug users or drug cultures seem a rather complicated, if not wholly spurious, endeavour. Later ethnographic accounts have tended toward a recognition of diversity and shied away from generic statements about drug users and their cultures. Studies have focused on the argot of certain groups of drug users (cf. Preble and Casey, 1969; Iglehart, 1985), various settings of drug use or drug-related activity (cf. Spradley, 1970; Williams, 1989; 1992; Bourgois, 1998; Measham, 2004) and/or the pre-eminent norms and practices characteristic of different drug and alcohol-using subcultures (cf. Agar, 1973; Cavan 1966; Johnson et al., 1985; Anderson, 2009; Bourgois and Schonberg 2009).

In addition to addressing the distinctive language, settings, norms and practical activities of various groups of drug users, ethnographic studies have often also drawn upon the concept of career to both illuminate and emphasize the development and evolution of drug-use patterns over the course of an individual's biography (cf. Rubington, 1967; Coombs, 1981). Whereas thinking in terms of setting specific language, norms and activities allows ethnographers to locate the meaning of drugs, their effects and the circumstances of their use in social *space*, the notion of career allows ethnographers to organize the meanings they find attendant to drug use along a *temporal* dimension. For example, some ethnographers have found it useful to distinguish between the kinds of issues that draw people into experimentation with drug use and the kinds of issues that lead to ongoing and/or destructive drug involvements. Studies of active heroin users (cf. Finestone, 1957; Sutter, 1966; Feldman, 1968; Waldorf, 1973; Rosenbaum, 1981), for example, have often distinguished between the motivations of initiates to heroin use on the one hand and the motivations of users once they have become physiologically tolerant to the drug. Waldorf et al. (1991) provide a nuanced appreciation of the patterns that mark different people's careers of cocaine involvement. Others have used the notion of career to highlight the role of labelling in maintaining people in drug-using identities and/or lifestyles (cf. Ray, 1961; Stephens, 1991). Adler (1993) looked at the careers through which drug dealers passed on their way into and out of smuggling and the upper echelons of the drug-selling world. Johnson and his colleagues (1985) analysed the economic careers of heroin users. Rosenbaum (1981) offered the important, and as yet under-appreciated, theoretical insight that the careers of heavy drug users often produce a vicious spiral of reduced options that goes well beyond the deleterious consequences of heavy drug use itself. Important work using the concept of career has also been done by ethnographers who have investigated how people move out of their putatively problematic patterns of drug use. Rudy (1986) and Denzin (1993) provided insights into the recovery careers of former alcoholics in Alcoholics Anonymous. Biernacki (1986) and Waldorf (1970; 1983) have richly detailed the careers former heroin addicts have taken on their way to recovery without treatment.

Perhaps the most radically sociological research on drugs, their use and effects hails from the school of thought known as social constructionism. Emerging from earlier research in labelling theory and social movement research, social constructionism carries forward the thesis that the meaning of drug use and drug-induced experience is influenced by social processes to suggest that the very reality of these phenomena cannot be meaningfully dissociated from the social contexts within which they are found in any given instance. Hence authors like Room (1985) have argued that addiction is an intrinsically culture-bound phenomenon – that it is unintelligible outside the nexus of cultural practices and beliefs within which it takes place (see also Levine, 1978; Keane, 2002; Reinarman, 2005; Weinberg, 2005). Excellent social constructionist studies have also been done on the influence of addiction science in modern history (and the influence of modern history on addiction science) (cf. Acker, 2002; Gomart, 2002; Campbell, 2007). Using a social constructionist frame, Conrad and Schneider (1992) demonstrated the social struggles attendant to the rise of medical jurisdiction, or the 'medicalization', of opiate addiction and alcoholism. Reinarman and Levine (1997) have investigated why and how crack cocaine emerged as a public problem despite limited hard evidence to support the hyperbolic claims routinely found in the popular press and public policy circles. These studies are only a small sample of the work that has been, and is continuing to be, done on the social construction of drug problems and drug experiences more generally.

Law

Historians and sociologists have clearly spent much time and effort thinking about intoxication. If official statistics are anything to go by then lawyers should do the same (Alcohol Concern, 2005; Home Office, 2009; National Health Service (NHS), 2010):

- alcohol-related crime costs the UK £7.8 billion a year and costs the NHS £2.7 billion;
- 45 per cent of victims of violent crime believe their attackers were intoxicated;
- 58 per cent of rapists were intoxicated;
- 37 per cent of domestic violence offenders were drunk;
- 88 per cent of criminal damage cases involved a drunk offender;
- in 2008, 6769 people in England and Wales died from causes directly linked to alcohol consumption.

Yet, despite the prevalence of intoxicated crime, intoxication has attracted relatively little attention from academic criminal lawyers. In part this is because (as Rebecca William's chapter in this volume illustrates) the law is riddled with complexity. But it is a source of some embarrassment: the law on intoxication does not sit comfortably with the general principles underpinning the criminal law.

The response of the criminal law to intoxication has been twofold. First, there have been laws prohibiting the state of intoxication itself. In 1606 an Act (4 Jac. c. 5) was passed seeking to stamp out the 'odious and loathsome sin of drunkenness' describing it as 'the root and foundations of many other enormous sins, as...murder, swearing, fornication, adultery and such like, to the...disabling of divers workmen and the general impoverishing of many good subjects, abusively wasting the good creatures of God'. The current formulation, being drunk and disorderly in a public place (s. 91, Criminal Justice Act 1967), has a very different focus. The current law sees the problem of drunkenness not in moral wrongness, but in terms of its impact on public order. This shift in focus sits with current thinking around the function of criminal law, which is that it should seek to protect the public from harms, rather than seeking to impose moral values on the public. It is to stop people being devils, rather than changing them into angels. It is interesting, however, that being disorderly itself is not an offence, only when it is combined with drunkenness. Perhaps this captures a perception that drunken disorderliness is more disturbing of the peace than sober disorderliness. That might be because intoxication is seen as a source of unpredictable behaviour and therefore frightening. Whether there is any justification for such a fear may well be questioned.

The main focus of the criminal law is on drunken defendants who commit criminal offences. To understand the approach of the courts it is necessary to appreciate the law's general approach to the mental elements of an offence. To be guilty of a crime, at least serious crimes, it must be shown that the defendant intended to cause a harm or was reckless as to causing the harm. The law is recent years has generally adopted a subjective approach. This means, as Lord Steyn explained in *R v G and R* [2003] (para. 55): 'It is generally necessary to look at the matter in the light of how it would have appeared to the defendant.' Hence the straightforward approach is that intention requires evidence that the defendant aimed to produce a result and recklessness requires evidence that the defendant foresaw the risk of a harm, but nevertheless decided to take that risk. Defendants are not taken to have foreseen a harm simply because a reasonable person in their shoes would have foreseen it; nor intended it because a reasonable person would have intended it.

Although a subjective approach is taken, where a risk is obvious a defendant is going to face an uphill task persuading a jury that he or she did not see the risk. The difficulty is that in the case of an intoxicated defendant such a claim in eminently plausible. At least it is sufficient to mean a jury may not be persuaded beyond reasonable doubt that the defendant foresaw the risk. The logical conclusion would be that intoxicated defendants could escape liability. Not on the basis that they were intoxicated, but on the basis that they lacked the necessary mental state. Yet Lord Bridge in *G and R* [2003] (para. 36) stated:

> one instinctively recoils from the notion that a defendant can escape the criminal consequences of his injurious conduct by drinking himself into a state where he is blind to the risk he is causing to others.

Hence the dilemma for the criminal law. How can the law hold onto the principle that defendants are only to blame for the consequences of their acts that they have foreseen and yet justify convicting defendants who were intoxicated at the time of their offence?

Of course there is no difficulty in cases where despite the intoxication the defendant has the necessary *mens rea*. Then the courts simply say 'a drunken intent is nevertheless still an intent' (*R v Sheehan and Moore* [1975]). The difficulty arises in cases where because of the drunkenness the defendant does not see the results of their actions. In such cases, we have the infamous *Majewski* rules. These are explained in detail in Rebecca Williams' chapter. In short they mean a voluntarily intoxicated defendant is treated as being reckless. As she explains, various lines of argument have been adopted to explain why such a defendant is reckless in accordance with the ordinary subjective principles of recklessness (e.g. that by getting drunk a defendant takes the risk of becoming intoxicated and thereby the risk that they might commit an offence). None of these are really convincing. It may be more honest that they are in place because they are seen to promote 'law and order' and 'to protect the public' (Law Commission, 2009). The Law Commission (1995, para. 314) seeks to justify this approach by saying: 'The real reason for punishing is the outrage that would quite reasonably be felt if serious injury caused to an innocent person by a drunk were to go unpunished.' Hence, the embarrassment for criminal lawyers mentioned earlier. The argument that this defendant should be guilty because the public think he or she should be guilty is a pretty weak one, even for a lawyer!

The law's response to intoxication reflects broader social understandings and attitudes about it. The criminal law has never seen intoxication as a 'defence'. Indeed, quite the opposite: it is regarded as inculpatory. This means that a defendant who might otherwise be able to rely on a defence that he or she failed to see the risk of harm will nevertheless be found reckless where the reason for that failure is the intoxication. Jeremy Horder (1993) has argued that the current law takes an 'office Christmas Party' view of the impact of alcohol, exemplified by Glanville Williams' (1983, p. 464) description of alcohol's effect:

> [Alcohol's] apparently stimulating effect is due solely to the fact that it deadens the higher control centres...so weakening or removing the inhibitions that normally keep us within the bounds of civilised behaviour. It also impairs perception, reasoning, and the ability to foresee consequences.

As Jeremy Horder (1993) points out, in earlier times a rather darker understanding of intoxication was accepted. Alcohol distorted moral control over a person's actions. Hale (undated, p. 32), writing in the seventeenth century, saw intoxication as creating a 'Phrenzy'. He argued that it could cause madness and thereby base a claim for acting involuntarily. Later cases seemed to develop this notion that intoxication could cause a loss of capacity. In 1849 in *R v Monkhouse*, Colderidge J explained that the key question for the jury was whether the defendant was 'rendered by intoxication entirely incapable of forming the intent charged...it is not enough that he was excited or rendered more irritable, unless the intoxication was such as to prevent his restraining himself from committing the act in question'. Links were thereby drawn between intoxication and the defence of insanity. German law still adopts such an approach with intoxication placed alongside mental illness as a basis for denying the capacity for committing the crime (Fletcher, 2000). However, the German law then goes on to make it a specific offence to commit a crime while intoxicated. The focus of the punishment, however, moves from liability for the offence itself, to liability for getting intoxicated. In its current form in English law intoxication is not regarded as a kind of lack of capacity, but at most a removal of inhibitions.

As to this last point, the case of *R v Kingston* (1994) illustrates the issues well. A defendant who admitted having paedophilic tendencies was given a cup of coffee by a man seeking to blackmail him. Unknown to the defendant it had been spiked with a disinhibiting drug. He was led to a room where there was a child whom he assaulted. Although Kingston accepted he was aware of what he was doing, he argued that the drug had removed his inhibitions. Without it he would simply have walked away. The House of Lord's reluctance to allow a defence was based on the fact he had the *mens rea* and therefore was guilty. This is markedly different from the understanding of intoxicating 'Phrenzy' which produces a madness. While not explicitly putting it in these terms, their Lordships may have seen the intoxication as allowing the defendant's true character to emerge. Critics of the decision argue the opposite: namely that the defendant's true character was revealed by his normal approach to sexual temptations, that is, to walk away from them. The intoxication led him to act 'out of character' (Sullivan, 1994). In *Kingston* we see the inconsistency with the law's approach. With voluntary intoxication the law is treating the defendant who fails to see the risk as responsible for their original choices and not able to hide behind 'the person intoxication has made them'; while in cases of involuntary intoxication they must be responsible for the 'person intoxication has made them' because that reflects their true character.

The law places much weight on the distinction between voluntary and involuntary intoxication. Although not as much as might be expected. It is interesting to see how this concept is understood in the law. It is assumed that those who take illegal drugs or alcohol and then become intoxicated are voluntarily intoxicated. The harshness of this approach is demonstrated by *R v Allen* [1988] where the defendant took what he believed was a low alcohol drink, but in fact had strong alcohol content. Because he knew that he was taking alcohol he was deemed voluntarily intoxicated. The assumption that anyone taking any amount of alcohol or illegal drugs is automatically voluntarily intoxicated is questionable. The *Allen* ruling would seem to imply that a defendant whose beer was spiked with spirits leading to intoxication would be voluntarily intoxicated. It may well be that the strict approach of the courts is taken because they are aware that otherwise trials would become over-complicated by arguments about the extent to which a defendant was aware of the alcoholic content of the drinks.

Another aspect of the harshness of the law's approach to the distinction between voluntary and involuntary is the reluctance of the courts to accept an argument that the defendant's addiction was involuntary. As the chapter in this book by Alan Bogg and Jonathan Herring illustrates, the courts will only accept that a defendant's addiction to intoxicants meant that their intoxication was involuntary in the most exceptional of cases.

We can see, therefore, in the law's response to intoxication a reflection of broader social and political responses to the subject. Fears of drunkenness as a source of public disorder; perceptions that intoxication reflects moral failure; arguments over whether intoxication reveals 'true character' or creates a form of madness, all find themselves played out in the criminal law. Appropriately enough, the law fails to find any kind of coherent or logical approach to the issues. It stumbles through them in a somewhat confused way!

Scientific expertise

The most important justification for strict legal and social controls on drugs is dependency and addiction. It provides the best reason for saying that the drug user is not free, and anyone exposed to the drug may lose personal freedom. The idea of classifying drug abuse as a disease was introduced in the eighteenth century, but this remained to be ratified by the American Medical Association until 1958. This ratification did not arise from any new scientific knowledge; indeed it may be argued that we know little more in that sense than we did two centuries ago. The concept that alcohol addiction might be a disease had to be presaged by the failure of Prohibition in the United States (1920–1933). A more decisive turning point, however, was the founding of Alcoholics Anonymous (1935), an organization that viewed alcoholism as a progressive disease and not a moral failing. Increasing recognition of the serious withdrawal symptoms, such as convulsions and delirium, further reinforced the idea that the pharmacological action of alcohol induced both a state of craving and an inability to abstain. In the early 1950s, the World Health Organization (WHO) attempted to conceptualize the phenomenon of addiction as being the direct consequence of specific substances. By 1964, WHO had replaced the term addiction with drug dependence and, in a major change in 1969, stated that compulsive behaviour, and not physical dependence, was its defining characteristic. The final WHO terminology of dependence syndrome was adopted in 1998 (Mann et al., 2000; Gilson, 2010). This coincided with a period of intense neurobiological research, notably by George Koob and colleagues in the United States, which suggested that alcohol dependence was an aberration of the normal homeostatic state of the body arising from alcohol-induced loss of brain excitatory neurotransmission and a corresponding increase in the activity of the inhibitory system (Koob and LeMoal, 2001).

The notion that drugs of abuse might alter the balance of chemical neuro-transmission in the brain by acting through defined cell-surface receptors on neurons had its origins in the late nineteenth century. The German scientist Paul Erhlich (1854–1915) introduced the term 'receptor' to describe sites on the cell to which drugs bind to signal change in cellular metabolism. This idea was supported by the Cambridge physiologist John Newport Langley (1852–1925) who elaborated a key concept – the binding and affinity of a drug to a specific receptor signalled change in metabolic effect. Langley termed this agonist action as drug efficacy. Alfred Joseph Clark (1885–1941), a pharmacologist working at University College London, added the final touch to this concept by demonstrating that the relationship between drug dose and response could be described by a mathematical equation. The basic mechanism by which drugs could have lasting effects on the body, the dose-response, was now in place (Flower, 2002). The human fate of addiction could no longer be considered to be passively determined by genetic constitution. Environmental stimuli, such as continued exposure to drugs of abuse, had the potential to differentially regulate gene expression and lead to altered bodily states. The public authority of the scientist on mechanisms of addiction could now flow from expertise.

As twenty-first-century society moved further towards professional hegemony in the regulation and control of drugs, knowing more seems to have become associated with the right and power to further legislate. Yet all scientific statements and laws have a single common characteristic: they are 'true' or 'false'. This imposes a significant limitation on the types of questions that can be answered by scientists and the authority of their knowledge (Shapin, 2008). There cannot be immoral science anymore more than there can be scientific morals. The physicist and Nobel Laureate Richard Feynman (1918–1988) has said: 'As far as I know in the gathering of scientific evidence, there doesn't seem to be anywhere, anything that says whether the Golden Rule is a good one or not.' Do ethics and science share the same domain?

This question is never better illustrated than by scientific definitions and attitudes towards addiction. Nineteenth-century physicians clearly recognized alcohol addiction to be an uncontrollable craving for alcohol. They distinguished it from alcoholism, however, by pathological change as might be observed in the liver of such individuals. In this manner they adhered to the definitions provided by Giovanni Morgagni in *De Sedibus et Causis Morborum*, his classic work published in 1761. Little changed until the mid-1940s when Morton Jellinek published a paper on 'Phases in the drinking history of alcoholics' (Jellinek, 1946). In this paper, he described alcoholism as a disease, a category reserved for those individuals who exhibited tolerance, withdrawal symptoms and either 'loss of control' or 'inability to abstain' from alcohol. Importantly, Jellinek considered features of the disease, such as inability to abstain and loss of control, to be shaped by cultural factors and that prevention or treatment of alcoholism would require complex cultural, political and economic issues to be addressed.

In parallel with Jellinek's remarkable insight, a flurry of activity presaged the contemporary view of addiction being a disease that could be medically treated or at least controlled to some extent. In the early 1890s, the frequency of relapse to drug use in individuals addicted to narcotic drugs led to the establishment of clinics that could legally provide heroin and morphine as maintenance therapy. The clinics failed dismally, as they did not lead to abstinence, and they were eventually closed by a legal interpretation of the 1914 Harrison Act, an Act which controlled the production, importation and distribution of opiates. Medical personnel could no longer provide maintenance therapy to addicts, a prohibition that lasted from the early 1920s until 1965. Vincent Dole and Marie Nyswander then made a simple but critical observation. They discerned that long-term maintenance was virtually impossible using short-acting narcotics but that it could be achieved with narcotics that had a long duration of action (Dole and Nyswander, 1965). By using methadone, a synthetic opiate with a duration of action averaging 24 to 36 hours, as compared to 10 minutes for heroin, they could block the euphoria experienced by injecting heroin. We now know methadone, being a partial agonist, exerted very little effect on the brain opiate receptors but blocked the action of morphine or heroin, which are full agonists with very strong effects. Dole and Nyswander, however, did not arrive at the idea of using methadone on a receptor-based theory of pharmacology, they relied on a metabolic theory developed mainly by Vincent Dole (Dole and Nyswander, 1967). He argued that as individuals became addicted to narcotics they 'underwent a permanent metabolic change', a state not unlike that for which a diabetic requires insulin.

Harry Collier, an English pharmacologist, had a different view to the metabolic hypothesis proposed by Dole. He suggested the effect of addictive drugs to be mediated by a cell receptor-based mechanism (Collier, 1965), a speculation that was most sophisticated. In essence, he maintained that the continued presence of a drug acting on specific receptors in the brain caused an adaptive change in the numbers of those receptors and that this effect caused tolerance to the drug. Secondly, and as a consequence of the increased number of receptors, removal of the drug allowed the physiological effects of the natural transmitter acting on the receptor to have a greater functional impact and that this change caused the drug withdrawal syndrome. Truly, this was a most remarkable insight. It was a flight of genius that pre-empted our current concepts of drug action and the mechanisms of addiction.

In 1973, Candace Pert and Solomon Snyder demonstrated the existence of opiate receptors in the brain. At that time the analgesic action of the opiate drugs was well known and their relative potencies in relieving pain had been established. Pert and Snyder selected naloxone for their studies as this potently blocks the analgesic actions of other opiates, such as morphine and heroin, and therefore might be expected to bind with great avidity to the putative opiate receptors in the brain (Pert and Snyder, 1973). Secondly, they attached a radioactive tracer to naloxone and used the labelled drug to directly measure its affinity for the brain receptors. Finally, they used other opiate drugs to competitively displace the radioactive naloxone from the brain receptors to show that its binding was specific to the site at which the other opiates mediated their action. Of particular interest was the finding that the avidity of morphine for the opiate receptor was much greater than that of methadone, an observation that predicted its addicting potential. John Hughes and Hans Kosterlitz, working in Aberdeen, subsequently identified the brain's natural neurotransmitter for the opiate receptor to be a family of small peptides, chains of amino acids linked together (proteins are very long peptides) that they termed enkephalins (Hughes et al., 1977). The brain system upon which addicting narcotic drugs exerted their action had been described. More importantly, this work had been carried out against the backdrop of the Nixon presidency; a time of tumultuous social change in the USA with political and military problems in Vietnam and the identification of drug-related problems as one of the contributing sources of the crises facing the government. The funding paradigms supporting the science of addiction had been born.

This demonstration of opiate receptors and their transmitters in the brain fuelled optimism that addiction could be understood at the molecular level. The receptor sites of action for most drugs of abuse have now been identified and this feat of molecular biology has allowed such drugs to be classified according to their action. This was a significant advance as drugs of abuse had previously been classified according to their physiological or psychological actions – stimulants or sedatives. Secondly, the idea that drugs of abuse impacted on normal brain neurotransmission, which is a highly controlled process, further reinforced the idea of addictive substances altering 'homeostatic' balance and this facilitated an understanding of the extremes of perception and behaviour observed in addicts.

Developments in the elucidation of molecular mechanisms for the action of drugs of abuse were paralleled by an increasing interest in the motivational and behavioural consequences of drugs of abuse and their relationship to states of addiction. Progress in this domain stemmed from a paper published by James Olds and Peter Milner in 1954 in which they described a phenomenon by which direct electrical stimulation of certain brain areas in rats evoked very specific behavioural effects (Olds and Milner, 1954). In order to receive such stimulations, Olds and Milner observed that animals would readily approach a circumscribed part of their environment. Clearly, these animals actively sought the rewarding properties of these electrical stimulations. Secondly, Olds and Milner found that animals would learn to perform a task, such as pressing a lever, in order to receive further stimulations – certain behaviours could be reinforced. Thus, the terms 'reward' and 'reinforcement' have very different meanings. Reward refers to the idea of pleasure and is used to describe those stimuli that are actively sought out by animals and humans. The term 'reinforcement' has its antecedents in the work of Edward Thorndike (1874–1949). He had observed that certain events strengthen a preceding stimulus response. As in the work of Olds and Milner, electrical stimulation 'reinforced' the lever-press task. This was Thorndike's connectionist hypothesis, an idea later significantly reworked by the psychologist Burrhus Frederic Skinner (1904–1990). He used the term 'operant conditioning' to describe this phenomenon.

Subsequent work demonstrated the ventral tegmental area in the midbrain to be the primary region responding to intracranial self-stimulation. This area connects to the nucleus accumbens by neuronal fibres that use dopamine as their chemical neurotransmitter. From this anatomical observation, the idea evolved that dopamine regulated the response to all of our natural biological rewards, such as food and sex (Stellar and Stellar, 1985). The role of dopamine in motivational processes of reward and reinforcement was established by demonstrating that drugs that mimic its action (agonists) increase the rewarding value of intracranial self-stimulation. Drugs of abuse were also found to augment the rewarding and reinforcing effects of intracranial self-stimulation and this effect showed a good correspondence with their abuse potential (Kornetsky et al., 1979). Eventually, using a technique known as microdialysis, increased dopamine overflow in the accumbens was observed to occur following administration of either amphetamine, cocaine, morphine, nicotine and alcohol and this outflow was accompanied by behavioural reinforcement (DiChiara and Imperato, 1988). The focal point of reward and reinforcement for drugs of abuse was now firmly linked to activation of the midbrain dopamine neurons (Koob and Bloom, 1988).

Further progress on understanding the role of dopamine in the neurocircuitry of the addicted state was only made possible by the significant advances achieved in the technology of brain imaging. These techniques specifically advanced our capability of relating brain structure to function in conscious subjects. The methods rely largely on indices of blood flow as measured using radioactive tracers (such as positron emission tomography (PET)) or radio signals that differ according to the composition of tissue and allow provision of detailed images of different brain regions (magnetic resonance imaging (MRI)). Functional MRI (fMRI) measures the change in magnetic fields associated with the ratio of oxygenated to deoxygenated haemoglobin and thus can be used to visualize neural activities with high spatial and temporal resolution.

These imaging techniques have been widely embraced by neuroscientists as a means of understanding the neural mechanisms that mediate phenomena ranging from cognition to consciousness to the pondering of complex ethical conundrums. Critics of these imaging techniques have been most vociferous in their condemnations, deriding them as 'mind-reading' or 'neophrenology'. These extreme positions arise frequently from a poor understanding of the capabilities and limitations of these imaging techniques. The overarching assumption in these imaging techniques is that the mind can be divided into modules and that their individual activities can be imaged. The concern with this viewpoint is that unified brain function does not operate by the activity of individual components. Another concern is that these imaging methods rely largely on indices of blood flow which is a surrogate signal for the activity of a heterogeneous group of neurons. Notwithstanding these concerns, the imaging techniques employed would appear to measure change in functional activity in defined populations of neurons because these changes concur with outcomes from decades of study relating discrete lesions and electrophysiological recordings to function (Logothetis, 2008).

Using PET studies in particular, the overwhelming conclusion is that drugs of abuse, when evaluated in humans, produce significant increases in dopamine in the nucleus accumbens (ventral striatum) and that this is associated with the subjective perception of the drugs being rewarding (Volkow et al., 2009). Imaging has also allowed Volkow and colleagues to suggest the key circuits disrupted in states of addiction and to relate this to impaired dopamine function (Volkow et al., 2012). These circuits include a disrupted reward system in the nucleus accumbens, loss of control over motivation in areas of the prefrontal cortex, and impaired memory and learning in subcortical structures termed the hippocampus and amygdala. In essence, Volkow and colleagues view addiction as a state of disease that centres on disrupted function in the prefrontal cortex that, in turn, leads to loss of inhibitory control and appropriate decision-making in drug addicts. Further, they believe this gives rise to addicts requiring immediate reward of the drug and experiencing loss of control over their intake. Finally, Volkow and colleagues consider that the greatest problem facing drug addicts is their lack of awareness of the disease and the need of therapeutic intervention. Elucidating the neurocircuitry underlying this dysfunctional insight of addicts is the goal they now aim to achieve (Goldstein et al., 2009).

Learning from interdisciplinarity

This book is meant to start conversations rather than offer definitive and conclusive remarks. Juxtaposing such a range of methodologies and disciplinary approaches is risky, in the sense that it can tend to incoherence; but it is also rewarding, revealing the multidimensionality and deep complexity of the problem in hand. The chapters which follow accordingly show how intoxication figures in various aspects of social life. Whereas some of our contributors focus on the changing structures and/or activities of the state in regulating intoxicants at different stages of the modern era, or to the specific legal issues that have arisen with respect to this regulation, others look at the rise and institutionalization of various medical and/or otherwise expert discourses. Some attend to the characterization of intoxication in the popular press, highlighting the extent to which the media have shaped both popular and expert opinion. We look to the indigenous cultures of intoxicant users themselves to demonstrate how less formalized or explicitly codified beliefs and cultural conventions have affected the use and effects of intoxicants, whether or not those effects are considered problematic. We also consider the nexus between individual and society, and the ways in which, for example, ideas about addiction are bound up with the rise of the liberal model of the individual as a rational self-governing agent, or how such ideas are put to practical use during the ongoing conduct of social interaction.

The net result is a volume that resolutely rejects simplistic reductions of drug use or drug problems to any one particular explanatory framework. Physicians may believe addicts to be patients, yet it is politicians who decide how drugs will be controlled and the availability of addiction treatment policies. The criminal justice system struggles with the admission of neuroscientific evidence and determining the law-relevant mental states of defendants and witnesses. Historians have recorded and transcribed the rise of addiction as a medical and scientific field but are suspicious of reductive methodologies which ignore all that cannot be studied in terms of chemical neurotransmission (Courtwright, 2012). Others consider addiction to be a social construction or behaviour, a term both scientifically and philosophically flawed, a concept built around a range of prejudices (Kushner, 2010). Most importantly, perhaps, addiction is often viewed as a moral outrage, a pleasure-oriented behaviour that is out of control, leads to personal and social harms, and requires robust policing and firm punishment. If this simplistic and prejudicial perspective drives media campaigns about excessive or addictive consumption, then it sits awkwardly alongside the papers here. For all their disciplinary differences, the contributors demonstrate that intoxication is a high-stakes game about our understanding of human behaviour, motivation and pleasure and the policies we should adopt to regulate them. This is true at once historically, sociologically, legally and scientifically. They also suggest that, whatever the difficulties of interdisciplinary debate, it is better to work with rather than against each other. The importance of the subject demands it.

Acknowledgments

The editors would like to thank the Wellcome Trust and the Cambridge Socio-Legal Group for supporting the discussions out of which this volume of essays developed.

Bibliography

Acker, C (2002) *Creating the American Junkie* (Baltimore MD: Johns Hopkins University Press)

Adler, P (1993) *Wheeling and Dealing: An Ethnography of an Upper-Level Drug Dealing and Smuggling Community* (New York: Columbia University Press)

Agar, M (1973) *Ripping and Running: A Formal Ethnography of Urban Heroin Addicts* (New York: Seminar Press)

Alcohol Concern (2005) *Alcohol and Crime* (London: Alcohol Concern)

Anderson, T (2009) *Rave Culture: The Alteration and Decline of a Philadelphia Music Scene* (Philadelphia PA: Temple University Press)

Bakalar, J B and L Grinspoon (1984) *Drug Control in a Free Society* (Cambridge: Cambridge University Press)

Becker, H (1953) 'Becoming a Marijuana User' **59** *American Journal of Sociology* 235–42

Becker, H (1967) 'History, Culture, and Subjective Experience: An Exploration of the Social Bases of Drug-Induced Experiences' **8** *Journal of Health and Social Behavior* 162–76

Biernacki, P (1986) *Pathways From Heroin Addiction: Recovery Without Treatment* (Philadelphia PA: Temple University Press)

Bourgois, P (1998) 'Just Another Night in a Shooting Gallery' **15**(2) *Theory, Culture and Society* 37–66

Bourgois, P and J Schonberg (2009) *Righteous Dopefiend* (Berkeley CA: University of California Press)

Campbell, N (2007) *Discovering Addiction* (Ann Arbor MI: University of Michigan Press)

Cavan, S (1966) *Liquor License: An Ethnography of Bar Behavior* (Chicago IL: Aldine Publishing Company)

Collier H (1965) 'A General Theory of the Genesis of Drug Dependence by Induction of Receptors' **205** *Nature* 181–2

Conrad, P and J Schneider (1992) *Deviance and Medicalization: From Badness to Sickness* (Philadelphia PA: Temple University Press)

Coombs, R (1981) 'Drug Abuse as Career' (Fall) *Journal of Drug Issues* 369–87

Courtwright D (2012) 'Addiction and the Science of History' **107** *Addiction* 486–92

Denzin, N (1993) *The Alcoholic Society: Addiction and Recovery of the Self* (New Brunswick NJ: Transaction Publishers)

Di Chiara, G and A Imperato (1988) 'Drugs Abused by Humans Preferentially Increase Synaptic Dopamine Concentrations in the Mesolimbic System of Freely Moving Rats' **85** *Proceedings of the National Academy of Sciences of the United States of America* 5274–8

Dole, V and M Nyswander (1965) 'A Medical Treatment for Diacetylmorphine (Heroin) Addiction' **193** *Journal of the American Medical Association* 646–50

Dole, V and M Nyswander (1967) 'Heroin Addiction – A Metabolic Disease' **120** *Archives of Internal Medicine* 19–24

Duster, T (1970) *The Legislation of Morality: Law, Drugs and Moral Judgment* (New York: The Free Press)

Feldman, H (1968) 'Ideological Supports to Becoming and Remaining a Heroin Addict' **9**(2) *Journal of Health and Social Behavior* 131–9

Finestone, H (1957) 'Cats, Kicks, and Color' **5**(1) *Social Problems* 3–13

Fletcher, G (2000) *Rethinking Criminal Law* (Oxford: Oxford University Press)

Flower, R (2002) 'A Long Engagement' **415** *Nature* 587

Gilson, A (2010) 'The Concept of Addiction in Law and Regulatory Policy Related to Pain Management' **26** *Clinical Journal of Pain* 70–7

Goldstein, R, A Craig, A Bechara, H Garavan, A Childress, M Paulus and N Volkow (2009) 'The Neurocircuitry of Impaired Insight in Drug Addiction' **13** *Trends in Cognitive Sciences* 372–80

Gomart, E (2002) 'Towards a Generous Constraint: Freedom and Coercion in French Addiction Treatment' **24**(5) *Sociology of Health and Illness* 517–49

Gusfield, J R (1986 [1963]) *Symbolic Crusade: Status Politics and the American Temperance Movement* (Urbana IL: University of Illinois Press)

Gusfield, J R (1991) 'Benevolent Repression: Popular Culture, Social Structure, and the Control of Drinking' in S Barrows and R Room (eds), *Drinking: Behavior and Belief in Modern History* (Berkeley CA: University of California Press)

Hale (undated), *History of the Pleas of the Crown*

Home Office (2009) *Alcohol-Related Crime* (London: Home Office)

Horder, J (1993) 'Pleading Involuntary Lack of Capacity' *Cambridge Law Journal* 296

Hughes J, H W Kosterlitz and T W Smith (1977) 'The Distribution of Methionine Enkephalin and Leucine Enkephalin in the Brain and Peripheral Tissues' **61** *British Journal of Pharmacology* 639–47

Iglehart, A (1985) 'Brickin' It and Going to the Pan: Vernacular in the Black Inner-City Heroin Users' Lifestyle' in B Hanson, G Beschner, J M Walters and E Bovelle (eds), *Life with Heroin: Voices from the Inner City* (Lexington MA: Lexington Books)

Jellinek, E M (1946) 'Phases in the Drinking History of Alcoholics' **7** *Quarterly Journal of Studies on Alcohol* 1–88

Johnson, B D, P Goldstein, E Preble, J Schmeidler, D Lipton, B Spunt and T Miller (1985) *Taking Care of Business: The Economics of Crime by Heroin Abusers* (Lexington MA: Lexington Books)

Keane, H (2002) *What's Wrong With Addiction?* (New York: New York University Press)

Koob, G and F E Bloom (1988) 'Cellular and Molecular Mechanisms of Drug Dependence' **242** *Science* 715–23

Koob, G and M LeMoal (2001) 'Drug Addiction, Dysregulation of Reward, and Allostasis' **24** *Neuropsychopharmacology* 97–129

Kornetsky, C, R U Esposito, S McLean and J O Jacobson (1979) 'Intracranial Self-Stimulation Thresholds: A Model for the Hedonic Effects of Drugs of Abuse' **36** *Archives of General Psychiatry* 289–92

Kushner, H I (2010) 'Toward a Cultural Biology of Addiction' **5** *BioSocieties* 8–24

Law Commission (1995) *Legislating the Criminal Code, Intoxication and Criminal Liability* Report 229 (London: Law Commission)

Law Commission (2009) *Intoxication and Criminal Liability* Report 314 (London: Law Commission)

Lemert, E M (1951) *Social Pathology: A Systematic Approach to the Theory of Sociopathic Behavior* (New York: McGraw-Hill Book Company)

Lemert, E M (1962) 'Alcohol, Values, and Social Control' in D Pittman and C Snyder (eds), *Society, Culture, and Drinking Patterns* (New York: John Wiley & Sons)

Lemert, E M (1967) *Human Deviance, Social Problems, and Social Control* (Englewood Cliffs, NJ: Prentice-Hall)

Levine, H G (1978) 'The Discovery of Addiction: Changing Conceptions of Habitual Drunkenness in America' **39**(1) *Journal of Studies on Alcohol* 143–74

Lindesmith, A (1938) 'A Sociological Theory of Drug Addiction' *American Journal of Sociology*, 43:593–609

Lindesmith, A (1965) *The Addict and the Law* (Bloomington IN: Indiana University Press)

Logothetis, N K (2008) 'What We Can Do and What We Cannot Do With fMRI' **453** *Nature* 869–78

Macmillan, M (2002) *An Odd Kind of Fame: Stories of Phineas Gage* (Cambridge MA: MIT Press)

Mann, K, D Hermann and A Heinz (2000) 'One Hundred Years of Alcoholism: The Twentieth Century' **35** *Alcohol & Alcoholism* 10–15

Measham, F (2004) 'Play Space: Historical and Socio-Cultural Reflections on Drugs, Licensed Leisure Locations, Commercialisation and Control' **15** *International Journal of Drug Policy* 337–45

National Health Service (2010) *Statistics on Alcohol: England 2010* (London: NHS)

Olds, J and P Milner (1954) 'Positive Reinforcement Produced by Electrical Stimulation of Septal Area and Other Regions of Rat Brain' **47** *Journal of Comparative Physiological Psychology* 419–27

Pert, C B and S H Snyder (1973) 'Opiate Receptor: Demonstration in Nervous Tissue' **179** *Science* 1011–14

Preble, E and J J Casey (1969) 'Taking Care of Business: The Heroin User's Life on the Street.' **4** *International Journal of the Addictions* 1–24

Ray, M (1961) 'The Cycle of Abstinence and Relapse Among Heroin Addicts' **9**(2) *Social Problems* 132–40

Reinarman, C (2005) 'Addiction as Accomplishment: The Discursive Construction of Disease' **13**(4) *Addiction Research and Theory* 307–20

Reinarman, C and H Levine (eds) (1997) *Crack in America* (Berkeley CA: University of California Press).

Room, R (1985) 'Dependence and Society' **80**(2) *British Journal of Addiction* 133–9

Rosenbaum, M (1981) *Women on Heroin* (New Brunswick NJ: Rutgers University Press)

Rubington, E (1967) 'Drug Addiction as a Deviant Career' **2** *International Journal of the Addictions* 3–20

Rudy, D R (1986) *Becoming Alcoholic: Alcoholics Anonymous and the Reality of Alcoholism* (Carbondale IL: Southern Illinois University Press)

Shapin, S (2008) *The Scientific Life* (Chicago IL: University of Chicago Press)

Smyth, A (2004) '"It Were Far Better Be a Toad, or a Serpent, than a Drunkard": Writing about Drunkenness' in A Smyth (ed.), *A Pleasing Sinne: Drink and Conviviality in 17th-Century England* (Woodbridge: Boydell & Brewer)

Spradley, J P (1970) *You Owe Yourself a Drunk: An Ethnography of Urban Nomads.* (Boston MA: Little, Brown & Company)

Stellar, J R and E Stellar (1985) *The Neurobiology of Motivation and Reward* (New York: Springer-Verlag)

Stephens, R C (1991) *The Street Addict Role: A Theory of Heroin Addiction* (Albany NY: State University of New York Press)

Sullivan, G (1994) 'Involuntary Intoxication and Beyond' *Criminal Law Review* 272

Sutter, A G (1966) 'The World of the Righteous Dope Fiend' **2**(2) *Issues in Criminology* 177–223

Sutter, A G (1969) 'Worlds of Drug Use on the Street Scene' in D Cressey and D Ward (eds), *Delinquency, Crime, and Social Process* (New York: Harper & Row)

Volkow N D, J S Fowler, G J Wang, R Baler and F Telang (2009) 'Imaging Dopamine's Role in Drug Abuse and Addiction' **56** (Suppl. 1) *Neuropharmacology* 3–8

Volkow N D, G J Wang, J S Fowler and D Tomasi (2012) 'Addiction Circuitry in the Human Brain' **52** *Annual Review of Pharmacology and Toxicology* 321–36

Waldorf, D (1970) 'Life Without Heroin: Some Social Adjustments During Long Periods of Voluntary Abstention' **18**(2) *Social Problems* 228–43

Waldorf, D (1973) *Careers in Dope* (Englewood Cliffs NJ: Prentice-Hall)

Waldorf, D (1983) 'Natural Recovery from Opiate Addiction: Some Social Psychological Processes of Untreated Recovery' **13** *Journal of Drug Issues* 237–80

Waldorf, D, C Reinarman and S Murphy (1991) *Cocaine Changes: The Experience of Using and Quitting* (Philadelphia PA: Temple University Press)

Weinberg, D (1997) 'Lindesmith on Addiction: A Critical History of a Classic Theory' **15**(2) *Sociological Theory* 150–61

Weinberg, D (2002) 'On the Embodiment of Addiction' **8**(4) *Body and Society* 1–19

Weinberg, D (2005) *Of Others Inside: Insanity, Addiction and Belonging in America*. (Philadelphia PA: Temple University Press)

Williams, G (1983) *Textbook of Criminal Law* 2nd edn (London: Stevens)

Williams, T (1989) *The Cocaine Kids: The Inside Story of a Teenage Drug Ring* (Reading: Addison-Wesley)

Williams, T (1992) *Crackhouse: Notes from the End of the Line* (Reading: Addison-Wesley)

Cases

R v Allen [1988] Crim LR 698

R v G and R [2003] UKHL 50

R v Kingston [1994] UKHL 9

R v Monkhouse (1849) 4 Cox CC 55

R v Sheehan and Moore [1975] 1 WLR 793

Legislation

Act 1606 4 Jac. c. 5

Criminal Justice Act 1967

Harrison Act 1914

Section 1
The Formation of 'Expertise'

2
Medical Expertise and the Understandings of Intoxication in Britain, 1660 to 1830

David Clemis

In 1785 the clergyman William Paley listed the 'bad effects' of 'the mischief of drunkenness'. He observed how:

1. It betrays most constitutions either into extravagancies of anger, or sins of lewdness.
2. It disqualifies men for the duties of their station, both by the temporary disorder of their faculties, and at length by a constant incapacity and stupefaction.
3. It is attended with expences, which can often be ill spared.
4. It is sure to occasion uneasiness to the family of the drunkard.
5. It shortens life. (Paley, 1791, vol. 2, p. 245)

That Paley should write about drunkenness was by no means unusual: then as now, the perceived ubiquity of chronic drinking prompted public commentary from various perspectives. His list hints at the variety of discourses by which drunkenness was conceptualized and the kinds of commentators, or experts, with some authority over these discourses: moralists, political economists, social commentators, medical men. Work on the nature of public debate in the period suggests that this expertise was deployed by particular interests, usually on an episodic basis, in the name of the political or reforming agendas of individuals or factions. At times, such episodes might develop into 'moral panics', in which concerns about drinking temporarily animated the press (Dillon, 2002; Warner, 2002; Nicholls, 2009, pp. 43–8).

On these and other occasions moralists and medical writers were not only the most prominent authorities on drunkenness but also the most likely to provide the most convincing analyses of its nature, causes and cures. And although moralists dealt with the soul and medics with the body, for much of the eighteenth century both took the condition of chronic drinking to be essentially a matter of moral judgment and agency. The pre-eminence of moralistic perspectives on drunken behaviour and chronic drinking remained until developments in the medical understandings in neurology made it possible for physicians to claim that they could understand and treat these matters. Yet even when doctors would eventually claim expertise in the matter of chronic drinking, it did not follow that moralists became irrelevant. Instead, as medical understandings of chronic drinking became more compelling, moralists adjusted their sphere of expertise. This entailed adopting the new medical understandings to reinforce moralists' especial concern: the promotion of personal and social action to redeem the drunkard and repair his or her damage to the community.

In seeking the roots of modern medical understandings of alcoholism, many historians accept the essential position of Joseph Hirsh that Thomas Trotter, in 1788, and Benjamin Rush, in 1785, offered the first elaborated conceptions of the 'disease concept of alcoholism' (Hirsh, 1949, p. 230). Harry Gene Levine notes that 'it is in the writings of Benjamin Rush that we find the first clearly developed modern conception of alcohol addiction' and it was Rush who 'organized the developing medical and common-sense wisdom into a distinctly new paradigm' (Levine, 1978, p. 151). Critics of this view suggest that Rush had many antecedents, and that the modern conception of addiction and alcoholism developed gradually over the course of the eighteenth century (Porter, 1985, pp. 385–96; Warner, 1994, pp. 685–91; Ferentzy, 2001, p. 363; Porter, 2003, pp. 398–9; Nicholls, 2009, pp. 64–6). In either scenario, the shift from drunkenness as vice to drunkenness as disease is central. It follows that, over the course of the eighteenth century, the locus of expertise shifted from the moralist to the physician.

This chapter argues that a specific medical expertise with respect to chronic drinking indeed emerged in the later eighteenth century. It did so because of particular developments in neurological theory, which encouraged chronic drinking to be approached without reference to moral agency and the language of sin and vice. This did not preclude, however, moralists making use of these new medical perspectives. Medical expertise did not simply supplant moral expertise. Rather, new thinking about the mind, body and nerves prompted a reconfiguration of the respective spheres of medical and moral authorities on the matter of chronic drinking.

Eighteenth-century physicians inherited, and in certain respects sustained, ideas about how alcohol affected the body from classical medicine, in particular Galen and his Renaissance translators (Porter, 2003, pp. 48–61; Shorter, 2006, pp. 107–8; Lindemann, 2010, pp. 84–120). These notions were rooted in a 'humoral' conception of the body, and their survival is evident in medical writing about drunkenness before the 1780s. Such writings were usually engaged in the exhaustive cataloguing of illnesses, symptoms and remedies.

Discussions of drunkenness focused on the condition of the body's systems and organs once wine or spirituous liquor had been imbibed. Such discussions were usually in the context of medical writers' passion for nosology – the classification of diseases – normally through comparison of the symptoms of various afflictions. These medical writers were interested in drunkenness because it produced symptoms like those of other conditions such as delirium or coma. Reflection on the effects of drinking on the body illuminated how the body's systems worked and, by inference, the character and possible causes of illnesses resembling drunkenness. As in previous centuries, eighteenth-century medical writers also showed considerable interest in the therapeutic use of beer, ale, wine and spirits. In terms redolent of the humoral model, most eighteenth-century physicians relied on what they took to be the stimulating effects of such drinks to restore the body's balances (Short, 1727, pp. 4–5; Thomson, 1782, pp. 32–3; Bell, 1791, p. 32; Porter, 2003, pp. 235–6; Curth and Cassidy, 2004, p. 144).

Until the last decades of the eighteenth century, medical expertise on drunkenness largely consisted of nosology and humoral diagnostics. Medical writings seldom addressed the problem of why alcohol produced certain behaviour; nor was there much interest in how drinking became habitual. That is not to say questions about the cognitive capacity and moral agency of drunkards, or why people became chronic drinkers, were not asked. However, those issues were taken up by moralists, the clergy and occasionally jurists, but seldom physicians. When physicians engaged these questions it was not from what we might regard as pathological or diagnostic perspectives systematically linked to their wider understanding of the body. Instead, medics adopted the moral and spiritual language utilized by moralists in their understandings of chronic drinking and drunken behaviour.

That such a distinct medical perspective on chronic drinking and drunkenness did not emerge, or rather, that the moral and the medical were not distinguished, likely owes much to wider ideas about the relation of mind and body. These writers did not readily disentangle the body, mind and soul; or rather, they attached such primacy to the soul that discussions of purely medical aspects of drunkenness and habitual drinking could never be seen as determining the moral agency of the drunkard. To assert that psycho-chemical agents exist, that they can change behaviour, engender habits and become, in a modern sense, addictive requires either the body, mind, or self to constitute a material unity, or that they are so configured that the material condition of the body is determinative of the mind and, especially, of the moral self. Few in the seventeenth and early eighteenth centuries would have accepted such notions. Although humoral theory posited a mind–body equilibrium that could be altered by particular foodstuffs and medicinal agents, the causes of chronic drinking were not explained in these terms. The Galenist

linking of the mind and body was largely understood in terms of states of
mind, emotions, or levels of consciousness that might be altered by dietary or
medicinally driven changes in the humoral balance. But a moral judgment,
such as choosing to drink persistently, was not seen as a necessary function of, or determined by, material, causative agents. Put simply, the causes
and remedies for chronic drinking were not a subject for medical expertise,
because chronic drinking was not seen as a disease. Certainly, alcohol affected
the body and it might alter states of mind or stimulate particular emotional
states. And, while the proximate cause might be a humoral imbalance or a
stimulation of animal spirits, the initial cause was the decision to start and to
keep drinking. Although various senses of addiction had been current since
the sixteenth century (Oxford English Dictionary, 2011), neither Galenists
nor the emerging scientific 'medical mechanists' (Porter, 1995, p. 58) could
provide a compelling explanation of why people became chronic drinkers,
nor had they reliable prescriptions that would medically end the inclination
to drink. Thus, for much of the eighteenth century, physicians were unlikely
to see chronic drinking as a medical issue. In so far as drunkenness might be
cast as a health matter, it was within the context of 'spiritual or moral health'
and so lay within the clergyman's or moralist's sphere of expertise.

In trying to understand the particular interest of eighteenth-century medical writers in the effects of alcohol, together with why they did so little to
diagnose or publish therapies to alleviate chronic drinking, we must be careful not to suggest that the moral implications of drinking and the bodily
consequences of doing so might not be discussed together. When reciting the
symptoms of drunkenness, many medical writers moved easily to a moralist's perspective. In his 1650 description of drunkenness, Humphrey Brooke
makes no distinctions between physiology, matters of character and capacity
for social engagement:

> Resolutions of the Nerves, Cramps and Palsies. Inflation of the
> Belly and Dropsies, Redness and Rheums in the Eyes, Tremblings
> in the Hands and Joynts. Inclination to Feavers and the Scurvy.
> Sicknesses at Stomack and sowre Belchings. A furious and unman-
> ageable Disposition to Lust. A Subjection to all the Passions, Decay
> of Memory, and Understanding. Loss of Credit and Reputation. An
> unfitness for Business, and Dispatch of Affairs. An easy Discovery
> of all Secrets. (Brooke, 1650, pp. 137–8)

His ascriptions of the causes of these afflictions are not medical:

> These and many more are the bitter Fruits that grow upon that
> unhappy Tree: God having wisely annexed to every Evil its insep-
> arable Inconvenience: Every Vice hath its Sting, and every Vertue

its Recompense; two Paths he hath made the streight and crooked, and given commands that we should walk in the one, and eschew the other; the first leads to Felicity, the last to Misery, and Man hath Understanding and Freedom, to know and chuse the best, and consequently himself only too blame, if he prefer the worst. (Brooke, 1650, pp. 138–9)

This assertion of the drunkard's full moral agency is a consistent theme in such writings throughout the seventeenth and eighteenth centuries. It accords with moralists' assertions that drinking was a sin in itself and was the cause of greater sin. This spiritual message was embedded within of a medical metaphor in the title of a 1712 moralist tract: *An Antidote against Drunkenness*:

Drunkenness destroys the Soul in Two Ways, First, By exposing it to Eternal Damnation, as being in itself a great Vice, and damnable Sin. Secondly, By being the Occasion of many other Sins, which have the same Dismal Effect. (Anon., 1712, p. 47)

Throughout the eighteenth century, medical men were frequent advocates of this recurrent moral theme. James Stonhouse, a man of considerable medical education who had practised medicine for 20 years in Northampton and subsequently wrote the statutes for the Salisbury Infirmary (Berry, 2011) held that drunkenness was a sin quite simply because of the Biblical injunctions against it:

... for St. Paul expressily affirms, that Drunkards shall not inherit the Kingdom of God, I Cor. vi. 10. ... By all these Considerations you are most earnestly intreated to examine into the State of your Soul; and, for the Time to come, conscientiously to avoid both the Drink, the Company, and the Occasion, which would tempt, or lead you to this Vice... (Stonhouse, 1774, p. 11)

Physicians, writing in a moralist idiom, joined clerics in offering the public much guidance on the peril of drunkenness. Through the era of the Gin Acts (1729–1751) they prescribed reason and sound judgment as the means of controlling the base appetites of the body and resisting the temptations of alcohol:

Therefore the only way to avoid being Drunk is to exercise your intellects, and the Faculties of your Mind, especially your Memory; to remind you of the Filthy Discourses, and Sights, which you have heard, seen or read of Drunkenness, as also of the Madness and Follies, committed [by] Lewd and Debauch'd Persons, in their Excesses of Drinking, and by Drunkards, the Ruin and Destruction

of their Bodies, Goods, and Estates, and the Danger of their Souls
Emanently pursuing. (Anon., 1712, p. 27)

The emphasis here on reason and judgment is important. Reformers and
moralists frequently likened the habitual drunkard to a slave, captured and
reduced by his persistent intoxication. But this should not be mistaken for
the modern language of addiction: one is enslaved by drink as one might be
enslaved by any sin. The cause of one's fallen condition was the failure of
one's own moral judgment.

Amidst these persistent moral and spiritual pronouncements, some eighteenth-century physicians began to think differently about the mind in
general and the nature of insanity in particular. In doing so they laid the
essential foundations for conceptions of drunkenness and habitual drinking that would stand quite apart from the conventional moralist perspective. This would not be fully realized until the nineteenth century, but the
key enabling ideas emerged out of Enlightenment medicine. Historians have
noted that well into the Enlightenment era three rival models of understanding the natural world were in play. It is generally held, however, that by 1660
both Aristotelian scholasticism, once entrenched in the universities, and the
hermitic, neo-platonic world view developed in the Renaissance, were giving
way to the new science based on observation, mathematical description and
principles of regularity (Porter, 2000, pp. 138–9; Reill, 2003, pp. 25–6). With
respect to medicine in early eighteenth-century Britain, however, such developments were much less obvious. In particular, elements of Galenic medicine
persisted even as physicians followed the models of Harvey and Newton.

Indicative of this persistence is the influential Hermann Boerhaave
(1668–1738), a Dutch anatomist and medical teacher whose works were
known throughout Europe. He is associated with the 'iatromechanical' medical theorists, much influenced by Newtonian mechanics. Boerhaave's account
of the body is one of a complex hydraulic system in which the correct balance
of vascular fluids was the key to good health (Cunningham, 1990; Porter,
2006, p. 143; Lindemann, 2010, p. 106). For Boerhaave, and his many British
followers, alcohol or 'spirit of wine' disturbed the balance of blood within the
vascular system. In what he describes as the third and most severe degree of
drunkenness, Boerhaave notes that sleep and apoplexy follow:

> from the Spirit of Wine mixing with the Blood, and as a Body
> extremely volatile soon flying to the Head more than any other
> Part, where it expands the cortical Substance more than Medulla
> is capable of supporting. For such is the Nature of inflammable
> Spirits that they neither coagulate the Blood in the Vessels, nor
> do they arrive into the Vessels with their full Power, but insin-
> uating into the smallest Vessels, they disturb the Motion of the

Humours, which causes a Delirium. (Boerhaave, 1742–1746, vol. 4, pp. 322–3)

Others followed Boerhaave in retaining an element of Galenic humours within a mechanical, vascular conception of the body. Robert James held that fermentation changes vegetable juices 'from their relaxing, resolving, and saporceous [agreeably tasting], refrigerating, and for the most Part purging Quality, into one that corroborates, thickens the Humours, dries, and heats' (James, 1743–1745, vol. 1, s.v. 'Alcohol').

These vascular models of the body placed great importance on temperature, the action of fibres and animating spirits. Moderate drinking was thought to stimulate the body and enliven the drinker, while excess drinking threw the body off balance. In 1727 Thomas Short, a physician practising in Sheffield, described the matter in this way:

> When drunk they [i.e. malt liquor and wine] heat the Body...it generaly stimulates the Solids, and by consequence, accelerates the Circulation of the Fluids...
>
> If a Man continues to drink more after he is heated, it raises in him a Briskness and Vivacity greater than usual; i.e. it increases the Circulation of the Blood over the whole Body, and the Subtilization of the Spirits of the Liquor thereby make its finest parts run with greater Velocity over the Glands of the Brain; and cause a fuller Repletion of the Tubes with animal Juices, which flow plentifully into the Fibris of the Muscles. Hence a stronger Disposition in the Person to Action, Motion, and Pleasure.
>
> If the Man has not Power to refrain from Drinking, he will be intoxicated, or become drunk, i.e. his Vessels will be fill'd and distended with Fluids, so that the Balance of Nature betwixt Solids and Fluids will be overcome...Serious heart and brain damage can follow because those organs abound with capillaries that, having been so distended as to have their Tone weaken'd, and by frequent Debauches be destroy'd. The results can be loss of memory, palsy, loss of appetite, indigestion, tremors, apoplexy, convulsions, &c. (Short, 1727, pp. 4–6)

Well into the eighteenth century, many medical men believed that a key feature of their expertise lay in the art of prescribing 'spirit of wine' (only occasionally referred to as 'alcohol') with the aim of stimulating the circulation and rectifying imbalances of fluids caused by various afflictions. Thomas Short believed that, through fermentation, malt liquor consisted of 'such minute Particles, as some of them are instantly able to enter, and pass the delicate Tubes [of the vascular system]; afford animal Spirits and nervous Juices; and so relieve the weak, faint, weary and exhausted, almost that very

Moment they are swallowed down' (Short, 1727, p. 16). In dealing with gout, Peter Shaw recommended:

> A Medicine...that will promote all Secretions, and Excretions, add to the Vital force of the Heart, and enable it to give an Impulse to the Blood, and whirl it briskly throu' its Canals, preserve its Mixture and Uniformity, and keep it from falling into Heterogeneous Concretions...And that Wine will perform all this, I suppose is already prov'd beyond reasonable exception. (Shaw, 1724, p. 33)

An enthusiast for the curative properties of wine, Shaw recommended wine for what he called 'the Hippo [hypochondria] and Hystrical Disease', a disorder that 'principally resides in the Fancy, but owes its Origin to some Disorder in the animal Oeconomy' due to 'obstructed Perspiration' and hence an imbalance in the body's fluids. As this was an affliction that 'chiefly affects those who employ their Minds much more than their Bodies', Shaw recommended 'the Use of Wine duly proportion'd to the Case, and accompanied with proper Exercise and chearful Conversation' as the best cure (Shaw, 1724, pp. 41–2).

Shaw was entirely typical in holding to Galen's notions of the unity of the body, mind and soul and assuming that wine could remedy the weakened spirit or the uncongenial personality. He approvingly quotes a writer he believes to be Galen:

> 'Tis also an acknowledged Truth, that 'Wine seasonably drank, cures the Distempers of the Soul, makes the Miser liberal, the cruel Man compassionate, the envious kind; and melts the proud haughty Spirit into a wonderful Softness and Complacence; that it makes a Lamb of a Lion, and changes a Vulture to a Dove, purifying and transforming Souls into a Temper wholly divine: So that in short there's no living unless we sometime with this Fluid give Nature a new Ferment to rouze her from her Lees. (Shaw, 1724, p. 17)

Shaw does not see this as merely cheering patients up by getting them drunk. He faults Mandeville (1730) for the medicinal misuse of wine in a course of treatment of which 'he seems to think chiefly lies in hitting the Humour of his Patients, falling in with all he says, and diverting him from the Thoughts of espoused Distemper' (Shaw, 1724, p. 41). Rather, one ought to use alcohol to restore the balances that engender health and happiness.

Physicians were not alone in prescribing the use of alcohol to restoring all manner of physical and mental imbalances. Clerics also recommended the use of spirits in cases of ill-humour, or what might today be called depression. The author of *An Antidote against Drunkenness*, although concerned about excessive drunkenness, certainly recommended drinking in some cases:

> When a Poor Wretch is in Danger to Perish for want of Necessary Supports of Life, or is oppress'd with Grief or Sorrow, or is in any other deplorable Condition; then bring forth Wine in Plenty, and set it before such a Disconsolate Person, let him drink freely, till he hath cheared his Heart, and raised his drooping Spirits, and be able to think of something else, besides his Poverty and Misery; nay, till he be so Merry, as quite to forget the Cares and wearisome Labour it brings upon him. (Anon., 1712, pp. 94–5)

Despite concerns with the impairment of reason and the unleashing of the appetites of the body (see above), this moralist clearly endorsed the use of alcohol to alter mood and restore the balance of the personality. And he cites Scripture to validate his view:

> To be always Serious is to keep the Bow constantly Bent, which is not Prudence, being inconsistent with the Laws of Nature, Art and Reason. For such Bow so kept, loseth its natural Force, and the Spring that Nature endow'd it with, by a perverse, contrary usage, becomes Dull and Flat, and Useless; so Men's Spirits kept always to one Pitch will grow Flat, Dull and Unthoughtful; whereas, Wine and Strong Drink, moderately taken, have diverse contrary Effects; all which tend to the Good of our Natures, and Improvement of our Reason; and as the Royal Psalmist saith, Amongst all the Creatures God hath made, [he] Early yieldeth the Vine, which maketh glad the Heart of Man. (Anon., 1712, p. 95)

While physicians joined moralists in advising of the benefits of drinking, they based their prescriptions on Galen and his successors rather than biblical authority or 'common sense'. In this way their knowledge was corroborative rather than uniquely specialist. They likewise shared in the moral understanding of chronic drinking. General conceptions of the mind and body precluded enquiries into the nature of chronic drinking in neurological terms. As long as the ultimate causes of intoxication and the inclination to chronic drinking were located beyond the reach of the physician's enquiries – that is in the soul – doctors could not provide expertise. In such circumstances, moralists – including physicians assuming a moralistic perspective – would continue to provide the authoritative understanding and judgments of drunken behaviour and chronic drunkards. Nevertheless, conceptions of the body, typified in the thinking of Boerhaave, with its systematic, mechanistic character, did prompt further developments in medical thinking that would eventually enhance the place of medical expertise with respect to the nature and problems of chronic drunkenness.

David Hartley's *Observations on Man* (Hartley, 1749) was crucial in this respect. Hartley developed a new neurophysiology that superseded the Galenism in the views of Boerhaave and his adherents. For Hartley, the nerves were not ducts in which animal spirits flowed. Rather they were composed of minute particles whose movements were governed by the principles of Newtonian physics. From John Locke, Hartley derived a theory of sensations and ideas for which he provided a materialist account. Once generated through perception, ideas are conveyed and persist through vibrations of the nerves. The relationship and coherence of ideas in consciousness was explained through processes of association that were driven by pleasure or pain (Hartley, 1749, vol. 1, pp. 25–63, 74–102).

The effect of alcohol was explained thus:

> The common and immediate effect of wine is to dispose to joy, i.e. to introduce such kinds and degrees of vibrations into the whole nervous system or into the separate parts thereof as are attended with a moderate continued pleasure. This it seems to do chiefly by impressing agreeable sensations upon the stomach and bowels which are thence propagated into the brain continue there, and also call up the several associated pleasures that have been formed from pleasant impressions made upon the alimentary duct or even upon any of the external senses. (Hartley, 1749, vol. 1, p. 393)

Both Hartley's general theory and his particular account of the effects of alcohol were of considerable influence by the later eighteenth century (Robinson, 1995, pp. 249–51; Allen, 1999, pp. 2–14; Porter, 2003, p. 360). The stimulation of nerves and the pleasure or pain resulting would feature in many medical accounts of the nature of drunkenness. For example, Erasmus Darwin's *Zoonomia* (1796) explained how alcohol produces pleasurable feelings and at the same time suppresses volition by its action on the nerves. Darwin writes that 'the ardent spirit produced in fermentation ... [is] so agreeable to the nerves of the stomach, that, taken in a small quantity, they instantly pacify the sense of hunger'. This internal stimulation engenders a pleasure that renders the drinker inattentive to the external stimuli of the world, and so they succumb to 'reveries of imagination' and are inclined to sleep. But, in the 'noise, light, and business' that accompany such social occasions, drinkers manage to carry on imbibing, which has the effect of producing 'irritative movements' so that the nerves 'of the stomach are excited into greater action than is natural'. In this state, Darwin says, 'pleasure is introduced in consequence of these increased motions from internal stimulus'. This pleasure obviates any desires and creates an absence of pain. The effect of that is to suppress volition which, Darwin says, is driven by the pursuit of pleasure or the aversion of pain. This weakened volition may extend from such matters as willing the muscles to focus the eyes – hence the drunkard's blurred vision – to the initiation of much more sophisticated acts and judgments (Darwin, 1796, vol. 1, pp. 75, 244–8, 252, 420).

Darwin's account of intoxication was not without its critics. Some suggested that Darwin's views were speculative and required empirical verification. The controversial Edinburgh physician, Thomas Brown, also faulted elements of Darwin's reasoning (Brown, 1798, pp. 418–24). Nevertheless, Darwin's account of drinking was influential and, although he did not address whether drunken behaviour or chronic drinking should be understood in medical terms, his discussion of intoxication and volition was suggestive.

Two years after the publication of *Zoonomia*, John Coakley Lettsom published an important tract intended for a popular audience but clearly informed by his experience as physician of sufficient status to have successfully founded the Medical Society of London in 1773. Lettsom adhered to the views of many moralists in *Hints Respecting the Effects of Hard Drinking*. It was a cautionary work utilizing a physician's witness of the physical suffering of drunkards in an effort to help people to choose not to drink habitually. Yet in it we can a see a significantly different conception of chronic drinking that suggests the moral agency of the drunkard was much diminished by drinking itself. For that reason, Lettsom notes that the moral choice must be made before becoming a regular drunkard, because once ensnared in the habit of drinking, it was nearly impossible to give up: 'whilst it insinuates its deleterious influence, it leads on its votaries, till it becomes almost as fatal to retreat, as to proceed' (Lettsom, 1798, p. 4).

Hints was influenced by Hartley and Darwin. The damage of nerves and the subversion of volition through excessive pleasurable stimulation led Lettsom to observe:

> Painful indeed is this truth, that when the indulgence in spirituous liquors is rendered habitual, it is extremely difficult to overcome. Although the miserable object is persuaded that it clouds his reason, debilitates his mental as well as corporeal faculties, debars him of all cheerful gratifications annexed to health and virtue; yet so excessive are the debility and tremors of the body – and so horrid is the despondency of the mind after the exhilarating effects of these liquors have subsided, that without a perseverance in determined efforts to vanquish this habit, a repetition of the delusive poison will be indulged, till resolution is too transient and weak to enable the victim to stop at the precipice, which terminates his painful existence. (Lettsom, 1798, pp. 17–18)

Lettsom suggests that long-time drinkers have the possibility of escaping this habit by a very gradual reduction in the quantities of alcohol consumed. He warns that too rapid a leaving off of drinking will not allow the body to adjust, and the person risks sinking into 'irretrievable debility' (Lettsom, 1798, p. 17). Lettsom implies that the dependence of the body could be greater than the individual's moral agency. He is not espousing a modern theory of addiction here, but it is a characterization of drunkards' experiences that resonated with subsequent medical thinkers.

Hartley and Lettsom both suggest the possibility of an entirely materialist account of drunken behaviour and habitual drinking – one that imputed little or no real moral agency to drunkards and conceptualized these matters entirely in physiological terms. Yet no such view appears to have been articulated before the end of the eighteenth century. Reflecting more widely on the understandings of insanity and the workings of the mind in general in this period, Roy Porter has argued that this is because the philosophical sensationalism of Hartley and his followers was fundamentally epistemological in its aims, and 'it by no means automatically followed that such inquirers needed or wanted to translate understanding of mental operations into the language of bio-medicine (Porter, 1995, p. 72). Indeed, that conceptual leap may not have been obvious and, for devout Christians like Hartley and Lettsom, it would not have been attractive. Thorough-going materialism had its advocates in France such as Julien Offray de La Mettrie (1709–1751) and Paul-Henri Thiry, Baron d'Holbach (1723–1789); but such ideas gained little currency among the leading members of the British medical community. Although the period's empirical spirit had enlarged the spheres open to explanation in material terms, it had hardly eradicated mind/body dualism. And, there was a further barrier to the provision of a completely materialistic account of the nature of drunkenness and habitual drinking. Physicians were simply unable to provide sufficiently comprehensive accounts of the nature of alcohol and the mechanism of habitual drinking in material terms. Indeed, the preliminary matter of the composition of alcohol was not established by Antoine Lavoisier until 1781 and its chemical formula was not described until 1808 by Nicolas-Théodore de Saussure.

Porter has argued that in the face of this paucity of useful knowledge of material substances and processes, the only possibility for a modern medicalization of chronic drinking lay through the development of a science of mind: psychology (Porter, 1995, p. 73). Porter has further suggested that William Cullen's conception of insanity and nervous diseases was important in this regard because, while it was founded on the prevailing views derived from Hartley, it offered a new approach which did not depend on resolving the inadequacies of purely materialistic accounts (Porter, 2003, pp. 311–12). Cullen rooted his conception of insanity in Hartley's notions of the origins of ideas in sensations, which were then processed by the irritation of the nerves – a neurophysiologi-cal process. The association of ideas in the mind, however, was a mental proc-ess. Madness, delirium and other disorders arose when there was a defect in a neurological process – a 'morbid organic affection...in some part of the brain', and/or an 'usual and commonly hurried association of ideas' – a defect of the mental process (Cullen, 1793, vol. 2, pp. 258–9, 272). It was this mental proc-ess gone wrong – the defective association of ideas – which would be the object of study in the new science of mind. It was no longer thought necessary to develop a complete account of the neurophysiological processes that were the site of the mind. The systematic observation and study of the patterns of these defective associations of ideas would be enough to allow insight into mental process affording diagnostic and clinical responses.

Cullen was not particularly engaged by problems relating to the nature of drunkenness or habitual drinking. Like many of his predecessors, Cullen found drunkenness of interest because it presented symptoms that were comparable to fevers, delirium and other morbid conditions. He nevertheless offered a model for the extension of this wider analysis of mental conditions to understandings of drunkenness, making it possible to see drunkenness in terms of a defective mental process – as a kind of disease. Given Cullen's influence as leading professor of medicine at Edinburgh, it seems likely that his work was an important step in establishing a medical understanding of chronic drunkenness that rendered considerations of moral agency irrele-vant. This would be a key step in establishing the authority of modern medi-cal expertise (Bynum, 2004).

Cullen's innovation is particularly evident in the writings of Thomas Trotter who, along with Benjamin Rush, is regarded by some as being the first to conceive of drunkenness in purely modern medical terms (Porter, 1985, pp. 385–96; Sournia, 1993; Warner, 1994, pp. 685–91; Ferentzy, 2001, p. 363; Porter, 2003, pp. 400–1). Trotter's notion of the origins of habitual drinking in 'the physical influence of custom confirmed into habit interwoven with the actions of our sentient system and reacting on our mental part' (Trotter, 1804, p. 3) is highly resonant with Cullen's explanation of insanity in terms that rely on both neurophysiological elements and the association of ideas in mind. This is further evident in Trotter's observation that, when dealing with the habitual drunkard, '[i]t is to be remembered that a bodily infirmity is not the only thing to be corrected. The habit of drunkenness is a disease of the mind. The soul itself has received impressions that are incompatible with its reasoning powers.' (Trotter, 1804, p. 172) Trotter's description of his approach is reminiscent of that of later psychologists:

> This disease, I mean the habit of drunkenness, is like some other
> mental derangements; there is an ascendancy to be gained over
> the person committed to our care which, when accomplished,

brings him entirely under our controul. Particular opportunities are therefore to be taken, to hold up a mirror as it were, that he may see the deformity of his conduct, and represent the incurable maladies which flow from perseverance in a course of intemperance. There are times when a picture of this kind will make a strong impression on the mind; but at the conclusion of every visit, something consolatory must be left for amusement, and as food for his reflections. (Trotter, 1804, p. 174)

In 1834 the Glaswegian physician, Robert MacNish, similarly wrote that in dealing with 'the habit of drunkenness…we have not only to contend against the cravings of the body, but against those of the mind; and in struggling with the body, we are, in reality, carrying on a combat with nature herself' (MacNish, 1834, p. 147). Also like Trotter, MacNish denied the relevance of moralists' assertions about nature and causes of drunkenness:

Moral lectures do not come within the scope of a medical treatise, and seem to be of little [vii] use at any time in terrifying drunkards from the continuance in their destructive vice. A much more effectual weapon for this purpose is a faithful representation of the effects of habitual intoxication on the human frame…Drunkenness debases and brutifies the intellect so much, that neither moral nor religious considerations have any great effect upon it. (MacNish, 1834, pp. vii–viii)

Trotter and MacNish rejected moralist claims to authority in dealing with drunkenness, instead identifying it as a subject in which the physician's expertise was most relevant. Before the 1780s such claims would have been difficult. The causes of drunkenness were attributed to the choices people made. Chronic drinking was the repetition of the same sinful decision or the indulgence in the same vice by a character that was so immorally inclined. To make drunkenness and habitual drinking objects of medical expertise, they had to be cast as phenomena amenable to physicians' methods. Through the innovations of Hartley, Cullen and others, it became possible to reconceive of mental processes such that drunkenness was not simply a sin or the by-product of an unfortunate moral disposition, but rather a state of the nervous system and a quality of mental processes that might eventually be explained and potentially acted upon. Chronic drinking could be understood, not as the indulgent choice of those inclined to vice, but rather in terms of a diseased mind whose process of choice-making had been made defective by the mutually reinforcing interaction of mistaken ideas, destructive habits and neurophysiological damage. These were matters which physicians could study and speak about with authority – when the public eventually concurred on the nature of the problem.

While this might have been the path by which Trotter and MacNish reached their confident assertions of the pre-eminence of medical expertise in questions relating to alcohol, the moralists hardly went away. Indeed, as suggested in the studies of Brian Harrison and James Nicholls (Harrison, 1994, p. 90; Nicholls, 2009, pp. 96–106), the early nineteenth-century temperance movements were driven by those whose claims to understanding were far more often rooted in Scripture than neurophysiology or new sciences of the mind. In 1828 the great campaigner for political and moral reform William Cobbett, wrote:

> drunkenness is a man's own act; an evil deliberately sought after; an act of violence wilfully committed against reason, against nature, against the word and in the face of the denunciations of God; and that, too, without the smallest temptation, except from the vicious appetite which the criminal himself voluntarily created. (Cobbett, 1823, p. 28)

Nevertheless, as unrealistic as the hopes of Trotter and MacNish were for the primacy of the medical expert, the scope of medical authority on matters relating to drinking had considerably changed since the early eighteenth century. Medical understandings, for physicians at least, were distinct from moral perspectives; and the problem of chronic drinking could be addressed in neurophysiolgical terms without reference to moral agency. The testimony of medical authorities accordingly became an important part of nineteenth-century temperance campaigns (Harrison, 1994, pp. 2, 88). In 1818, the *Annuals of Philosophy* announced a temperance talk by a clergyman who promised to consider both morals and medicine. The citation of notable medical experts was important for the speaker's credibility:

> The Rev. J. Yates MA is about to publish four Discourses on the Effects of drinking Spirituous and other intoxicating Liquors. This work is designed to serve as a popular and practical treatise combining powerful persuasives derived from the influence of spirituous liquors upon the morals and the understanding with an accurate description of their effects upon the bodily frame in compiling which the author has availed himself of the opinions and testimonies of Drs. Willan, Lettsom, Heberden, Linnaeus, Rush, Trotter, Beddoes, Aikin, and various other writers. (Anon., 1818, p. 75)

Compared to those practising in the previous century, early nineteenth-century medical experts had much more to say about drunkenness. More to the point, they did so in terms that were distinctively their own.

Bibliography

Abel, E L (2001) 'Gin Lane: Did Hogarth Know about Fetal Alcohol Syndrome?' 36(2) *Alcohol and Alcoholism* 131–4

Oxford English Dictionary (2011), available at http://library.mtroyal.ca:2142 /view/Entry/2179?redirectedFrom=addiction, s.v. 'addiction'

Allen, R C (1999) *David Hartley on Human Nature* (Albany NY: State University of New York Press)

Andrews, J and A Scull (2001) *Undertaker of the Mind: John Monro and Mad-Doctoring in Eighteenth-Century England* (Berkeley CA: University of California Press)

Anon. (1712) *An Antidote against Drunkenness: Being the Drunkard's Looking Glass: In a Philological, Philosophical, Theological Discourse on the Excessive Use of Strong Drink. By a Young Gentleman* (London)

Anon. (1735) 'Reasons for Promoting the British Distillery...' in T Robe (ed.), *A Collection of Political Tracts* (London: T Cooper)

Anon. (1818) in T Thomson (ed.), *Annuals of Philosophy or Magazine of Chemistry, Mineralogy, Mechanics, Natural History of Agriculture and the Arts* (London), p. 75

Bell, J (1791) *An Inquiry into the Causes which Produce, and the Means of Preventing Diseases Among British Officers, Soldiers, and Others in the West Indies. Containing Observations on the... Action of Spirituous Liquors on the Human Body; on the Use of Malt Liquor, and on Salted Provisions* (London)

Berry, A (2011) 'Stonhouse, Sir James, Seventh and Tenth baronet (1716–1795)' in *Oxford Dictionary of National Biography*, online edn (Oxford: OUP), available at http://0-www.oxforddnb.com.aupac.lib.athabascau.ca/view /article/26582

Boerhaave, H (1734) *Dr Boerhaave's Elements of Chymistry* 2nd edn (London: printed for J Wilford, behind the Chapter-House in St Paul's Church-Yard)

Boerhaave, H (1742–1746) *Dr Boerhaave's Academical Lectures on the Theory of Physic*, 4 vols (London)

Brooke, H (1650) *Ugieine or A Conservatory of Health. Comprized in a Plain and Practicall Discourse Upon the Six Particulars Necessary to Mans Life*, MB (London: Printed by R W for G Whittington, and are to be sold at the Blew-Anchor in Cornhill, near the Exchange)

Brown, T (1798) *Observations on the Zoonomia of Erasmus Darwin, MD* (Edinburgh)

Bynum, W F (2004) 'Cullen, William (1710–1790)', *Oxford Dictionary of National Biography*, online edn (Oxford: OUP), available at www.oxforddnb.com. aupac.lib.athabascau.ca/view/article/6874

Cobbett, W (1828) *Twelve Sermons, on 1. Hypocrisy and Cruelty. 2. Drunkenness, etc.* (London)

Cullen, W (1793) *First Lines of the Practice of Physic*, 2 vols (New York)

Cunningham, A (1990) 'Medicine to Calm the Mind: Boerhaave's Medical System, and Why it was Adopted in Edinburgh' in *Medical Enlightenment of the Eighteenth Century* (Cambridge: Cambridge University Press)

Curth, L H and T M Cassidy (2004) '"Health, Strength and Happiness": Medical Constructions of Wine and Beer in Early Modern England' in A Smyth (ed.), *A Pleasing Sinne. Drink and Conviviality in 17th-Century England* (Woodbridge, Suffolk: D S Brewer)

Darwin, E (1796) *Zoonomia; or the Laws of Organic Life*, 2 vols (London)

Dillon, P (2002) *The Much-Lamented Death of Madam Geneva* (London: Review)

Ferentzy, P (2001) 'From Sin to Disease: Difference and Similarities Between Past and Current Conceptions of Chronic Drunkenness' **28**(3) *Contemporary Drug Problems* 363–90

Gonson, Sir J (1728) *The Charge of Sir John Gonson Knt to the Grand Jury of the Royalty of the Tower of London, and Liberties and Precincts thereof* (London)

Harrison, B (1994) *Drink and the Victorians: The Temperance Question in England, 1815–1872* 2nd edn (Keele: Keele University Press)

Hartley, D (1749) *Observations on Man, His Frame, His Duty, and His Expectations*, 2 vols (London)

Hirsh, J (1949) 'Enlightened Eighteenth Century Views of the Alcohol Problem' **4**(2) *Journal of the History of Medicine and Allied Sciences* 230–6

James, R (1743–1745) *A Medicinal Dictionary: Including Physic, Surgery, Anatomy, Chymistry, and Botany*, 3 vols (London)

Lettsom, J C (1798) *Hints Respecting the Effects of Hard Drinking* (London)

Levine, H G (1978) 'The Discovery of Addiction: Changing Conceptions of Habitual Drunkenness in America' **39** *Journal of Studies in Alcohol* 143–74

Lindemann, M (2010) *Medicine and Society in Early Modern Europe* 2nd edn (Cambridge: Cambridge University Press)

MacNish, R (1834) *The Anatomy of Drunkenness* 5th edn (Glasgow: W R M'Phun)

Mandeville, B (1730) *A Treatise of the Hypochondriack and Hysterick Diseases in Three Dialogues* (London: printed for J Tonson in the Strand)

Nicholls, J (2003) 'Gin Lane Revisited: Intoxication and Society in the Gin Epidemic' **7**(2) *Journal for Cultural Research* 125–46

Nicholls, J (2008) 'Vinum Britannicum: the "drink question" in Early Modern England' **22**(2) *Social History of Alcohol and Drugs* 190–208

Nicholls, J (2009) *The Politics of Alcohol. The History of the Drink Question in England* (Manchester: Manchester University Press)

Paley, W (1791) *The Principles of Moral and Political Philosophy*, 2 vols (London)

Pitcairn, A (1727) *The Whole Works of Dr Archibald Pitcairn, Published by Himself. Wherein Are Discovered, the True Foundation and Principles of the Art of Physic* (London: printed for E Curll in the Strand, J Pemberton in Fleet-Street, and W and J Innys at the West-End of St Paul's)

Porter, R (1985) 'The Drinking Man's Disease: the Pre-History of Alcoholism in Georgian Britain' **80** *British Journal of Addiction* 385–96

Porter, R (1990) 'Introduction' in J C Sournia, *A History of Alcoholism*, N Hindley and G Stanton (trans.) (London: Basil Blackwell)

Porter, R (1995) 'Medicine and Human Science in the Enlightenment' in C Fox, R Porter and R Wokler (eds), *Inventing Human Science. Eighteenth Century Domains* (Berkeley CA: University of California Press)

Porter, R (1999) 'Medicine' in I McCalman (ed.), *An Oxford Companion to the Romantic Age: British Culture 1776–1832* (Oxford: Oxford University Press)

Porter, R (2000) *Enlightenment: Britain and the Creation of the Modern World* (London: Penguin Books)

Porter, R (2001) *Bodies Politic. Disease, Death, and Doctors in Britain, 1650–1900* (Ithaca NY: Cornell University Press)

Porter, R (2003) *Flesh in the Age of Reason* (London: Penguin Books)

Porter, R (2006) 'Medical Science' in R Porter (ed.), *The Cambridge History of Medicine* (Cambridge: Cambridge University Press)

Reill, P H (2003) 'The Legacy of the Scientific Revolution' in D C Lindberg and R L Numbers (eds), *The Eighteenth Century* vol. 4, R Porter (ed.), *The Cambridge History of Science* (Cambridge: Cambridge University Press)

Robinson, D N (1995) *An Intellectual History of Psychology* (Madison WI: University of Wisconsin Press)

Shaw, P (1724) *The Juice of the Grape: or, Wine Preferable to Water. A Treatise, Wherein Wine is Shewn to be the Grand Preserver of Health, and Restorer in Most Diseases* (London)

Short, T (1727) *Vinum Britannicum: or, an Essay on the Properties and Effects of Malt Liquors. Wherein is Considered, in What Cases and to What Constitutions* (London)

Shorter, E (2006) 'Primary Care' in R Porter (ed.), *The Cambridge History of Medicine* (Cambridge: Cambridge University Press)

Stonhouse, J (1774) *Admonitions Against Drunkenness, Swearing and Sabbath-Breaking* (Bristol)

Smyth, A (ed.) (2004) *A Pleasing Sinne: Drink and Conviviality in Seventeenth-Century England* (Cambridge: D S Brewer)

Sournia, J C (1990) *A History of Alcoholism*, Nick Hindley and Gareth Stanton (trans.) (London: Basil Blackwell)

Thomson, A (1782) *An Enquiry into the Nature, Causes, and Method of Cure, of Nervous Disorders. In a Letter to a Friend* 2nd edn (London)

Trotter, T (1804) *An Essay, Medical, Philosophical, and Chemical, on Drunkenness and its Effects on the Human Body* (London: T N Longman and O Rees)

Warner, J (1994) '"Resolved to Drink No More": Addiction as a Preindustrial Construct' **55** *Journal of Studies on Alcohol* 685–91

Warner, J (2002) *Craze. Gin and Debauchery in an Age of Reason* (New York: Four Walls Eight Windows)

White, J (2003) 'The "Slow but Sure Poyson": The Representation of Gin and its Drinkers, 1736–1751' **42** *Journal of British Studies* 35–64

Wilson, T (1736) *Distilled Spirituous Liquors the Bane of the Nation* (London: J Roberts)

Wright, J P (1991) 'Boerhaave on Minds, Human Beings and Mental Diseases' **20** *Studies in Eighteenth Century Culture* 289–302

3
The Expertise of Non-Experts: Knowledges of Intoxication in Criminal Law

Arlie Loughnan

Introduction

In the current era, the law governing how intoxication affects criminal liability is notorious for its complexity and technicality. The law prescribes when evidence of an individual's intoxication – by alcohol or any other drug – can be introduced in court to show that he or she did not have the mental element or *mens rea* of the offence. In England and Wales, when such evidence can be introduced is determined by two factors: how the person became intoxicated and the kind of criminal offence they are alleged to have committed. In relation to the way in which the person became intoxicated, a distinction is drawn between self-induced, voluntary or advertent intoxication, on the one hand, and involuntary or inadvertent, intoxication on the other. The legal approach to evidence of voluntary intoxication – the type of intoxication at issue in the vast majority of cases – varies according to the type of offence with which an individual is charged. The *Majewski* rule (named after the House of Lords' decision from which it came – *DPP v Majewski* [1977]) provides that voluntary intoxication may be used to prove that an individual did not form the requisite *mens rea* for what have been known as offences of 'specific intent' (a category that roughly correlates with more serious offences – see Horder, 1995; Williams, Chapter 14 in this volume). By contrast, in relation to a residual category of offences of 'basic intent', the individual's voluntary intoxication cannot be taken into account when determining whether he or she formed the mental state required for conviction. Evidence of involuntary intoxication may be adduced in relation to both specific intent and basic intent offences (see *R v Kingston* [1995]).

In the years since the formulation of the *Majewski* rule, confusion and controversy have been overlaid onto the complexity and technicality of the law. The confusion relates to the distinction between basic intent and specific intent, which Alan Norrie labels a 'distinction without a real difference' (Norrie, 1990, p. 172). Although the development in case law since *Majewski* has determined whether particular criminal offences are specific intent or basic intent offences, the rigidity of an offence-by-offence approach to intoxicated offending has created its own problems (see *R v Heard* [2007]). Recently, the Law Commission for England and Wales dismissed as 'unhelpful' the view that all offences could be categorized as either basic intent or specific intent offences (Law Commission, 2009, para. 2.22 and Part 2 more generally). While acknowledging that the terms specific intent and basic intent are 'ambiguous, misleading and confusing', the Law Commission nonetheless stated that, when properly understood, they refer to genuinely different mental or fault elements for criminal offences and maintained that evidence of intoxication should only be able to be adduced in relation to some offences and not others (paras 1.28 and 3.33–4; see paras 3.46–52 for the Law Commission's specific recommendations). These comments seem to signal the ongoing relevance of the basic intent/specific intent distinction for the law of intoxication.

The controversy stalking the law on intoxication arises because, at the point of intersection of voluntary intoxication and basic intent, the law derogates from standard principles of criminal liability. As it excludes an ingredient of the fact scenario – self-induced intoxication – from the adjudication process, the *Majewski* rule excludes certain intoxicated offenders from the subjectivist conception of criminal liability (see Dingwall, 2007). This subjectivist conception holds that the cardinal mental state or fault element in the criminal law of the current era is subjective fault, where an individual is judged according to what they knew, perceived or intended at the time of the offence (see Lacey, 2001; Norrie, 2001). This derogation from principle in the law on intoxication is thought to be justified on public policy grounds: as the Law Commission stated, 'the particular case of harm or damage caused by an intoxicated person [is thought to] demand a departure from those [standard] principles' of liability (Law Commission, 1995, para. 1.1).

Some critical purchase on this state of affairs is provided by an examination of the historical development of this part of the criminal law. In this chapter, I focus on the development of the law over the nineteenth century. I take this focus because it is in this period that it is possible to detect the appearance of the modern legal approach to intoxicated offending, and also because this is the period in which the modern organization of knowledge developed (see Burke, 2000). Bringing these contemporaneous developments into the same scholarly frame, an examination of this period provides the key to understanding the knowledge practices underpinning the current criminal law on intoxication. Having built up a picture of the development of the law and changes in knowledges of intoxication in the second and third sections of this chapter, in the final section, I suggest one way in which lay knowledge of intoxication may be approached by scholars – as the expertise of non-experts.

Although not typically considered by legal scholars, an examination of knowledge practices relating to intoxicated offending provides insights into the law. Such an approach sheds an alternative light on the law which is usually analysed, by criminal law scholars, either from a legalistic perspective, on the one hand, or a policy perspective, on the other (see e.g. Dimock, 2011, and Mackay, 1995, respectively). There is a wealth of scholarship on knowledge, spread across philosophy, sociology and law, among other disciplines, and the study of knowledge practices has been approached in different ways. With the confines of this chapter in mind, the approach taken here is a modest one. Knowledge is approached as what, in the context of a discussion of historical knowledge, Michael Bentley has usefully called 'paradigms of what was and what was not to count as worth knowing' (Bentley, 2005, p. 175). The reference to paradigms indicates that what counts as knowledge – and who counts as knowers – changes across time and space. This means that the linked concepts the study of knowledge practices often conjures up – such as authority and legitimacy – must be understood as both dynamic and contingent.

The formalization of the law on intoxicated offending over the nineteenth century

In the early modern era, the advent of mass intoxication had produced new subjects of law – individuals who were 'in liquor' at the time of their offence – but it did not immediately produce new legal concepts. From the first decades of the nineteenth century, informal practices around intoxicated offending began a process of development via which a distinct law on intoxication, recognizable in the current era, would be created. The development of the law on intoxication was part of a broader movement toward the 'factualization' of fault in criminal law, a process by which individual mental states came to be amenable to investigation in the courtroom, and crucial in the development of modern structures of criminal responsibility (see Lacey, 2001, p. 268; see also Farmer, 1997). As Nicola Lacey argues, between the eighteenth and twentieth centuries the English criminal process was marked 'by a broad movement from ideas of responsibility as founded in character to conceptions of responsibility as founded in capacity' (Lacey, 2001, p. 250). These changes were themselves premised on changing knowledge practices, specifically the development of psychological knowledges concerning the link between mind and body, which I discuss below.

Reflecting initial uncertainty about the way in which intoxication affected criminal liability, the first half of the nineteenth century was marked by inconsistent legal approaches to intoxicated offending (Smith, 1981, p. 85; McCord, 1990, p. 376). In these decades, some judges made 'cautious concessions to the new [social] tolerance' for alcohol (Walker, 1968, p. 178), while other judges denied the exculpatory effect of intoxication. The decision of *Grindley* is evidence of a generous approach: Justice Holroyd held that, although intoxication could not excuse, if the material question was (as in the case of murder) whether an act was premeditated or done with a 'sudden heat and impulse', intoxication could be taken into account (*R v Grindley* (1819), cited in *DPP v Beard* [1920], at 495). This direction was disapproved in the 1835 decision of *Carroll*, in which the court took a more stringent line. In *Carroll*, Justice Park concluded that drunkenness was not relevant to the question of intention. Reviewing earlier case law, Justice Park stated that 'there would be no safety for human life if [*Grindley*] was to be considered as law' (*R v Carroll* (1835), at 146). The rule in *Carroll* was itself overruled in *Cruse* in 1838, where the court held that intoxication was relevant to the question of intention: Justice Patterson directed the jury that, although drunkenness is no excuse for crime, it is often of very great importance in cases where liability rests on a question of intention (*R v Cruse* (1838), referred to in *DPP v Beard* [1920], at 497). The inconsistent judicial approaches to intoxicated offending that marked the initial development of the law prefigured the development of the dual meaning of intoxication for the criminal law that would emerge by the end of the century – as both exculpatory abnormality and morally culpable conduct – and I return to this point below.

Something of the uncertainty surrounding the relationship between intoxication and criminal liability was resolved in the middle of the century. In a way that appears to reflect the rise of a capacity conceptualization of criminal fault at this time, intoxication came to be conceptualized as affecting an individual's *capacity* to form intent. The idea that intoxication could lead to incapacity to form intent can be traced to the decision of *Monkhouse* in 1849. In *Monkhouse*, Justice Coleridge referred to the 'general rule' (now defunct) that juries are to presume a man to do what is the natural consequence of his act, and then stated that if an individual is proved to have been intoxicated, the question becomes 'was he rendered by intoxication entirely incapable of forming the intent charged'? In *Monkhouse*, the court instructed the jury that intoxication could not be considered unless it was 'such as to prevent [the individual] restraining himself from committing the act in question, or to take away from him the power of forming any specific intention' (*R v Monkhouse* (1849), cited in *DPP v Beard* [1920], at 497–8). No definition of specific intention was provided by the court in *Monkhouse* or in subsequent cases. From this point onwards, the term specific intent was used, but it was not used in all cases of intoxication, nor used consistently (Gough, 1996, p. 343) – there was no indication in the case law as to how offences involving specific intention were to be identified, other than by 'judicial designation' (Smith, 1998, p. 241). Over time, the law on intoxicated offending has come to centre on this notion of specific intent, which has taken on the character of a rule or doctrine, rather than a principle (see Horder, 1995).

In the twentieth century, the relationship between intoxication and fault was further elaborated via the notion of specific intent. In this period, specific intent was invested with a distinct, technical meaning, and came to denote the intent required for an offence, over and above the intent to do the particular physical act that forms the external component of the offence (see *R v Hatton* [2006]; *R v Heard* [2007]). In *Beard's Case*, the court stated that, where a 'specific intent is an essential element in the offence, evidence of a state of drunkenness rendering the accused incapable of forming such an intent should be taken into consideration' in determining where he or she had in fact formed intent (*DPP v Beard* [1920] at 499). In reaching this conclusion, the court criticized the earlier decision of *Meade* (*R v Meade* [1909]) for connecting exculpatory intoxication with the ability to foresee consequences (*DPP v Beard* [1920] at 504–5). The *Beard* approach to intoxication, fault and specific intent was adopted in subsequent appellate judgments. In *Bratty v Attorney-General for Northern Ireland* [1963], Lord Denning stated *obiter* that if a 'drunken man is so drunk that he does not know what he is doing, he has a defence to any charge…in which a specific intent is essential' (at 410). Similarly, in *Attorney-General for Northern Ireland v Gallagher* [1963], Lord Denning stated that 'if a man is charged with an offence in which a specific intention is essential…then evidence of drunkenness which renders him incapable of forming that intention, is an answer' (at 381).

Why did the law on intoxicated offending come to centre on this notion of specific intent? One dimension of the explanation becomes evident when the law on intoxication is situated in the broader context of the development of the criminal law over the nineteenth century. The development of a legal entity of intoxication in this period may be interpreted as one instance of broader processes by which criminal law principles and practices more generally solidified into the form they take in the current era. On this account, which I refer to as the formalization account, the discrete and technical rules that have come to comprise legal doctrines in the current era are regarded as specific instances of a wider trend by which the flexible and overtly moral–evaluative aspect of the early modern criminal law has gradually given way to rigid processes and precise rules (see Loughnan, 2012). The formalization of the criminal law (evident in the 'factualization' of *mens rea*, for instance) was connected to the formalization of both criminal trial process and the administration of the law (through institutions such as the police and prisons) (on which see, generally, Farmer, 1997).

In relation to intoxication, prompted by the formalization of other parts of the criminal law, including the law of insanity, this process of formalization meant that the parameters of the law were gradually defined and limited and intoxication (emerging as a 'doctrine of imputation'[1]) came to be understood as a discrete and circumscribed component of the criminal law corpus. Viewed in light of this idea of formalization, it becomes clear that the notion of specific intent came to be central to the law on intoxicated offending because the notion permitted a principled way of circumscribing the exculpatory effect of intoxication and dealing with intoxicated individuals in special ways, without impinging on the more general principles of liability held up as applicable to all (Gough, 1996, p. 344). As Stephen Gough argues, the doctrine of specific intent worked to distinguish certain kinds of offences – those that specifically required intent – from the general milieu, which merely required 'malice', effectively a negligence standard that intoxication would not negate (Gough, 1996, p. 344).

The second dimension of the explanation for the centrality of specific intent in the law of intoxication becomes evident when the broader knowledge practices impacting on the development of the criminal law are taken into account. To foreshadow the fuller discussion contained in the next part of the chapter, there are two points I wish to make here. First, while specific intent refers to an individual or subjective mental state, it actually rests on a generalized construction of the altered capacities of intoxicated individuals. In referring to capacity to form intent, specific intent collapses a question of fact (did the individual form the requisite intent?) into the question of capacity (was the individual capable of forming the requisite intent?) (see Gold, 1976–1977, p. 42). The second point I wish to make here relates to the type of knowledge that underpins the law on intoxicated offending: I suggest that it is lay or non-expert knowledge of intoxication. As I discuss below, the notion of specific intent – with its in-built assumption that intoxication affects 'higher order' thinking – is a product of lay beliefs about intoxication. Similarly, the residual and oppositional notion of basic intent – which is presumed to denote a part of mental processes unaffected by intoxication – is also a product of lay beliefs about intoxication. I return to each of these points below.

Before turning to discuss the development of knowledge practices on intoxication, it is worth noting that this formalization account of change over time contrasts with the usual story told about the appearance of a

---

1   As Paul Robinson writes, doctrines of imputation impute missing offence elements, providing an 'alternative means of holding the individual liable as if the required elements were satisfied' (see Robinson, 1997, p. 67; see also Simester, 2009, p. 3).

recognizable legal entity of intoxication over these decades. The usual story is one of judicial efforts to ameliorate the harshness of the prohibition on taking intoxication into account for the purposes of conviction. This judicial clemency account has a wide currency among legal actors and academics (see e.g. *DPP v Majewski* [1977], at 471 per Lord Elwyn-Jones LC and at 496 per Lord Edmund-Davies; Smith, 1998, pp. 100–2 respectively). By this account, the case law from *Grindley* in 1819 onwards represents judicial 'mitigation of the severity of the common law' (Court of Appeal decision of *Majewski* per Lawton LJ, extracted in *DPP v Majewski*, at 452). But the premise of this account of the development of the law – the 'severity' of the common law – does not withstand close inspection. While intoxication did not constitute a formal plea to a criminal charge, it was grounds for informal exculpation – acting as an ingredient in some acquittals, and also operating to reduce sentence or as a basis for recommendations to mercy (see Loughnan, 2012). As Wiener argues with regard to homicide, intoxication became *less* not more likely to be admitted as an excuse or a mitigating factor over the nineteenth century. Indeed, according to Wiener, in assault trials at the end of the nineteenth century, drunkenness became primarily an aggravating rather than mitigating factor (Wiener, 2004, p. 258). Thus, rather than mitigating the 'severity of the common law', nineteenth century judges seem to have had a role in tightening up the availability of intoxication as evidence for use in avoiding a conviction or in mitigation.

The development of expert and non-expert knowledges of intoxication

The emergence of the modern approach to knowledge practices provided the backdrop against which the legal developments, canvassed above, unfolded. This was itself part of a profound reorganization of elite knowledges that took place over the nineteenth century. In the decades from 1800, the generalized social concern about widespread alcohol consumption that had appeared by the end of the 1700s was amplified and elaborated by the development of a set of expert knowledges about alcohol. While, in the eighteenth century, individuals such as clergymen had claimed authority on the matter of drunkenness, such authority was derivative of generalized spiritual or moral claims made over individuals (see Clemis, Chapter 2 in this volume). The decades from the start of the nineteenth century saw a range of individuals, with divergent claims to authority, proffer something of a knowledge on intoxication specifically. Each of these specialists promulgated a depiction of intoxication – by alcohol, and to a much lesser extent, by drugs such as opium – as a genuine object of expertise, about which it was possible to offer intelligible explanations about cause and effect.

The appearance of expert knowledges specifically relating to alcohol consumption and its effects in the nineteenth century was a component of a larger intellectual history of changing knowledge practices across the century (see Collini, 1991; Burke, 2000). On the level of elite knowledges, this development encompassed new objects of knowledge, and spawned new specializations and new intellectual-cum-social groups or 'knowledge associations' (see Daunton, 2005). These new specializations and associations were marked by permeable intellectual and social borders, and conflict and contestation meant that their particular configuration was in flux over the course of the century (see Bynum, 1994). Reflecting its place in a wider if loose alliance of knowledges about public health and public order which arose in the Victorian era, the burgeoning expert or specialist knowledge about intoxication encompassed bureaucratic or administrative, scientific and medical, as well as an emergent psychiatric, knowledge. This latter type of knowledge – which focused on the effect of alcohol on individuals (the point of concern shared by the criminal law) – was one particular subset of this diffused expert knowledge about intoxication.

Among medical and psychiatric experts, historical studies indicate that a variety of attitudes and beliefs about drunkenness abounded. These attitudes can be usefully divided into two broad categories. One set of expert attitudes regarding drunkenness held that it was a matter of individual choice and was thus within an individual's control. This attitude was given additional impetus by the temperance movement. As Martin Wiener has noted, the temperance movement was 'probably the single most powerful and widespread social "cause" of the century', 'deeply coloring accepted notions of social respectability' (Wiener, 2004, p. 255). The new 'respectability' insisted upon 'duty and the ability of men to maintain self-management, an insistence that fit ill with drunkenness' (Wiener, 2004, p. 261). Wiener points to judicial statements condemning intoxication and suggests that, although these sorts of statements had been made in court before, in the second half of the nineteenth century, they were enforced in a novel way (Wiener, 2004, p. 260). This declining tolerance for intoxication and the interpersonal violence it was believed to cause is also evident in the increase in the prosecution and punishment of public drunkenness and drunken killings in the second half of the century (Wiener, 2004, p. 256). At the same time, an excuse based on intoxication was becoming less likely to prevent a murder conviction, although it continued to be taken into account as a mitigation of punishment in non-capital offences (Smith, 1998, p. 341).

The second set of expert attitudes about drunkenness depicted intoxicated individuals as suffering from what Wiener has referred to as 'diminished responsibility for drink' (Wiener, 1990, p. 295). This latter set of attitudes, which arose at the end of the nineteenth century, was accompanied by a 'less autonomous image of drunkards', meaning that individuals were not wholly culpable for their condition (Wiener, 1990, p. 294). This set of attitudes fed the growing approval of medical treatment for drunkenness apparent in the last decades of the century, although, as historians have noted, this treatment was in truth moral or disciplinary rather than medical (see Johnstone, 1996). An illustration of this set of attitudes is provided by the inebriates legislation, which was enacted towards the end of the century. The Habitual Drunkards Act 1879 ('An Act to Facilitate the Control and Cure of Habitual Drunkards') applied to a person who 'by reason of habitual intemperate drinking of intoxicating liquors' was 'at time dangerous to himself or herself or to others, or incapable of managing himself or herself and his or her affairs'. Those classed as 'habitual drunkards' could choose to go to asylums, but, once there, could be detained against their will and forced to undergo a course of treatment (Valverde, 1998, pp. 77–8). The 1879 Act was followed by the Inebriates Act 1898, which adopted the Latinate term 'inebriates' as a substitute for the morally laden reference to 'habitual drunkards' (Wiener, 1990, p. 297). Under the 1898 Act, judges could sentence 'habitual inebriates' to detention in inebriate reformatories for up to three years, in addition to any other punishment that might be imposed (Ajzenstadt and Burtch, 1990, p. 138). As has been pointed out by several writers, this legislation applied to a subset of those who drank to excess and who formed a particular locus for medical expertise, but it is indicative of a broader problematizing of alcohol consumption at this juncture (see Johnstone, 1993; Valverde, 1997).

The persistence of the idea of individual culpability for drunkenness within a discourse of diminished responsibility for drink is the key to the dual meaning of intoxication in criminal law – as exculpatory abnormality and morally culpable conduct – which emerged by the end of the century. In criminal law schemas, intoxication is understood as a species of mental incapacity and the doctrine encodes an idea of the abnormality of an intoxicated individual. The construction of abnormality and its pejorative connotations are evident, for instance, in *Majewski*, where Lord Elwyn-Jones referred to an individual who 'consciously and deliberately takes alcohol and drugs...in order to escape from reality...and thereby *disables* himself from taking the care he might otherwise take' (*DPP v Majewski* [1977], at 471 (emphasis added)). Alongside exculpatory abnormality, the legal entity of intoxication encodes an idea of intoxication as morally culpable conduct. This is evident in the way in which intoxication has been quarantined from the law on automatism (which relates to unwilled or unconscious conduct) – on the basis that individuals seeking to rely on intoxication to defeat a criminal charge are not wholly free from fault. Elsewhere, I suggest that, in the current era, these two different meanings given to intoxication are suspended in a fine balance in criminal law and process (see Loughnan, 2012).

The two sets of expert attitudes toward drunkenness were not mutually exclusive. As Mariana Valverde has written, both popularly and medically, inebriety was regarded as a 'hybrid object' – 'part vice, part disease' (Valverde, 1998, p. 51). Valverde argues that the hybrid status of intoxication meant that it was easily assimilated into the late Victorian branch of evolutionary science, degeneration theory in which 'bodily features were moralized and moral vices were blamed for causing physical degeneration' (Valverde, 1998, p. 51). In Valverde's words, there was a 'sort of refusal to medicalise' intoxication, based on the idea that doctors should not waste their time with 'social misfits' (Valverde, 1998, pp. 49–50). Valverde suggests that efforts to medicalize habitual drunkenness or alcoholism (via diagnostic entities such as 'moral insanity' and 'dipsomania') were not successful because the courts and ordinary people believed that 'heavy drinkers, if they really tried, could stop their destructive behaviour' (Valverde, 1998, p. 2).

In part because of the idea that expert medical professionals were thought to be wasting their time with 'social misfits', and in part because of the ubiquity of alcohol consumption, intoxication did not become exclusively the subject of expert knowledge in the nineteenth century. Particularly when compared with the development of expert medical knowledge about insanity by the same time, knowledge of intoxication and its effects on individuals remained intelligible to non-specialists. As a result, the development of a medical and psychiatric expertise about the effect of intoxication on individuals went only some way towards covering the field of knowledge practices. But, over and above this, the rise of expert or specialized knowledges about intoxication in this period had a profound effect – it *produced* a lay knowledge of intoxication. With the rise of an expert knowledge, the knowledge ordinary people had regarding intoxication must be seen in a different light. It was only as a result of the cleaving out of a set of expert knowledges from an undifferentiated general, common or everyday knowledge about intoxication that it became possible to talk of a lay or non-expert knowledge of intoxication – of alcohol and by analogy with alcohol.

The term lay knowledge is here used to denote a form of collective knowledge, and is intended to be a broad and flexible construct, capturing the socially ratified attitudes and beliefs about intoxication held by non-specialists. This type of knowledge is best conceptualized (and labelled) lay because it exists in contradistinction with expert or specialized knowledge such as medical knowledge.[2] As a non-expert form of knowledge, lay knowledge of

---

2   Lay knowledge is distinct although related to lay evaluation (archetypally, the role of the jury in a serious criminal trial) because it refers to the kind of knowledge enlisted in legal practices as opposed to the actions of particular actors (see, for discussion, Lacey, 1993, pp. 635–6). Elsewhere, I suggest that legal actors, including judges, are lay when it comes to understanding intoxication, although they are in different subject positions when compared with jurors (see Loughnan, 2012).

intoxication is both unsystematized and synthetic in that it is made up of different sources of understanding, such as suspicions and religious or other beliefs (and includes knowledge that has entered the common domain from specialized arenas). Of course, the content of the attitudes and beliefs comprising lay knowledge of intoxication is something of a black box. As Valverde has written of what she calls the 'common knowledge' of alcohol held by inspectors, patrons, licensees and hospitality staff, it has few intrinsic features (Valverde, 2003, p. 171).[3] Lay knowledge can be distinguished by its formal qualities – as with Valverde's category, 'common knowledge', lay knowledge is qualitative, non-scientific and non-numerical (Valverde, 2003, p. 171). Referring back to the approach taken to knowledge in this chapter (as 'paradigms of what was and was not to count as worth knowing'), lay knowledge encompasses experiential or first-hand knowledge (of alcohol, for instance), but extends beyond this empirical base to include general convictions held and assumptions made by non-experts. The term lay knowledge is used here not with a view to investigating its content but with the aim of conceptualizing it in order to be able to see what role it plays in criminal law.

Understood in this way, both lay and expert knowledge of intoxication is implicated in the evaluation and adjudication processes in criminal law. As foreshadowed above, the broader context of knowledge of intoxication is relevant to the criminal law in two ways. First, and as mentioned above, although specific intent refers to an individual or subjective mental state, it actually rests on a generalized construction of the altered capacities of intoxicated individuals. In this respect, specific intent is similar to the since-altered rule that an individual is presumed to have intended the probable consequences of his or her acts. Indeed, as Keith Smith suggests, the 'underlying rationale' of specific intent offences may be seen as 'derivative' of this rule (Smith, 1998, p. 241). Thus, specific intent can be analysed in the same way as this presumption of probable consequences. Here, analysis developed by Lacey is helpful. As Lacey argues in relation to the presumption of probable consequences, the rise of psychological knowledge altered the conditions under which criminal law decision-making would be legitimate. In Lacey's analysis, the presumption of probable consequences provided a solution to 'the problem of knowledge co-ordination', allowing courts to refer to a

---

3 Mariana Valverde has written extensively about the types of knowledges implicated in alcohol licensing laws (see e.g. Valverde, 1997; 1998; 2003; see also Levi and Valverde, 2001). In this body of work, Valverde examines the construction of a 'common knowledge' about alcohol possessed by untrained persons – knowledge that is simultaneously beyond the bounds of any one individual yet within the sphere of common sense. For Valverde, the idea that publicans, patrons, licensees and hospitality staff have the necessary knowledge to enact licensing laws – the 'logic of licensing' – finds its historical roots in eighteenth-century police science, a type of administrative knowledge, rather than a scientific knowledge of alcohol that developed subsequently.

defendant's 'interior mental world' without requiring close investigation of that world (Lacey, 2001, p. 370).

The second way in which the broader context of knowledges of intoxication is relevant to the criminal law relates to lay knowledge of intoxication – it is this type of knowledge that underwrites the technical legal form taken by the law on intoxicated offending. The legal approach to the way in which intoxication affects individuals is based on beliefs held on 'physiological grounds' and informed by either 'the personal experience of judges or folk wisdom or a combination of the two' (McCord, 1990, pp. 384, 378). As mentioned above, the notion of specific intent – with its attendant implication that intoxication affects 'higher order' thinking – is a product of lay knowledge of intoxication. In Valverde's words, the distinction between 'two modes of consciousness/volition' – specific intent and basic intent – translates into the 'lofty language of legal doctrine' the common-sense, everyday views of the effects of alcohol on humans (Valverde, 1998, p. 196). Similarly, the residual and oppositional notion of basic intent – which is presumed to denote a mental process that is unaffected by intoxication – is a product of lay beliefs about intoxication. According to Valverde, lay opinion holds that 'people who are very drunk cannot form "higher" thoughts or complex intentions, but that they are capable of, and indeed particularly susceptible to, more "impulsive" acts' (Valverde, 1997, pp. 258–9; see also McCord 1990, p. 384). As these comments suggest, the precision and technicality of the intoxication law is underwritten by a more open-textured lay knowledge of intoxication.

Approaching lay knowledge of intoxication in criminal law

The formalization of informal legal practices relating to intoxicated offending over the nineteenth century (and continuing into the twentieth century) marked the formation of a discrete and recognizable legal entity of intoxication. The technical and complex rules now governing intoxicated offending, canvassed at the outset of this chapter, have their genesis in this period. In particular, the notion of specific intent, on which the current law centres, can be traced to the nineteenth century. Despite its apparent precision, the law on intoxicated offending depends on an open-textured lay knowledge of intoxication. Lay knowledge about intoxication was created out of a body of common knowledge at the same time as a set of expert knowledges about alcohol and its effects developed in the nineteenth century. Bringing these contemporaneous nineteenth-century developments together provides the key to understanding modern knowledge practices implicated in the criminal law of intoxication. In this final section of the chapter, I suggest one way in which lay knowledge of intoxication may be usefully approached by scholars – as a form of expertise: the expertise of non-experts.

Approaching lay knowledge of intoxication as a form of expertise seems, at first blush, counter-intuitive. Lay knowledge of intoxication is here (and, indeed, in legal practice) defined by its position in opposition to expert or elite knowledges. As a matter of legal technicalities relating to rules of evidence, lay knowledge of intoxication is not treated as expert knowledge, unlike, say, a chemist's understanding of the pharmacological properties of LSD or the likely effect of mixing barbiturates and alcohol (see *R v Lipman* [1970] and *Majewski* [1977], respectively). Nor can lay knowledge of intoxication act as leverage or generate social capital in legal practices, in the manner of forms of professionalized knowledge (see Valverde, 2003, p. 172). Nonetheless, there seems to be value in approaching lay knowledge as a type of expertise – the expertise of non-experts. The value of this approach to the study of lay knowledge of intoxication arises in part because it helps to account for the fact that it has something of an ineffable independence in law, and is accorded significant power in legal practices. In addition, approaching lay knowledge of intoxication as a form of expertise provides a means of thinking anew about this part of criminal law, in that it demands a certain scholarly repositioning, and takes us some way toward grasping the power of lay knowledge in criminal law.

There seem to be three advantages to be derived from approaching lay knowledge of intoxication as a form of expertise. The first is that such an approach invites scholars to think of it as a distinct entity – more than a mere amorphous background – which is then deployed, in different ways, in legal practices. This approach renders this type of knowledge amenable to socio-legal study – without overwhelming or evacuating the legal entity of intoxication but, equally, without reducing lay knowledge to an amorphous mass. This approach helps to grasp the way in which this type of knowledge is taken seriously, as the basis of lay evaluation of claims based on intoxication. Because the question of whether a defendant formed the requisite *mens rea* for an offence committed while intoxicated is a question of fact, the jury has a potentially significant role in relation to intoxicated offending. And it is well-recognized that intoxication coincides with offending behaviour in more instances than it is raised by defence counsel to imply doubt about the prosecution case (in those cases where the defendant has been charged with a specific intent offence). Raising intoxication may not be a good defence strategy because it can open the defendant up to a negative evaluation by the jury, and an evaluation that is informed by the lay knowledge of the jurors. Reflecting on the strategies employed by defence counsel, it is possible to see the on-the-ground significance of lay knowledge of intoxication, and to identify a reason for taking it seriously.

A second advantage arising from approaching lay knowledge as a form of expertise is that this approach has the advantage of denaturalizing the knowledge paradigms used in criminal law. The constitution of lay knowledge of intoxication as an expertise is a product of legal processes and produced within the legal context, for criminal legal purposes. Thus, it is not just, as Valverde has argued in relation to pub licensing, that, in a world where there has been a 'huge explosion of highly technical knowledges', there are still spaces where other knowledges govern (Valverde, 2003, p. 163), but rather that, at least in criminal law practices concerning intoxicated offending, a division between lay and expert knowledges is not a natural one – rather, it is contingent and continuously constructed in and through legal practices. Recognizing this opens the way for an appreciation of the dynamism of knowledge practices in law, sensitizing scholars to change and continuity over time.

A third advantage of approaching lay knowledge as a form of expertise is that such an approach exposes the significance of rhetorical invocation of lay knowledge of intoxication – what is done by references to what we all know, what is thought to be common-sensical about intoxication. These rhetorical references do more than reference a distinct type of knowledge – they conjure it up, and in doing so, preserve jury autonomy and police the boundary of lay evaluation. An illustration of this role of lay knowledge of intoxication is provided by judicial references to jury autonomy in evaluating defendants' claims about intoxication. A recent example of such a rhetorical reference is provided by the 1981 decision of *Lawrence,* in which Lord Hailsham commented *obiter* that 'since the days of Noah, the effects of intoxication have been known to induce the state of mind described in English as recklessness, and not to inhibit it, and for that matter to remove inhibitions in the field of intention and not to destroy intention' (*R v Lawrence* [1981], at 530). This comment invokes a timeless 'truth' about intoxication, something known and evident to all. Specifically, Lord Hailsham's comment suggests that, as a matter of common knowledge, intoxication may affect the mind to the extent of recklessness (where recklessness is understood either in a legal or a popular way), but not disturb intention.

This comment hints at the role that lay knowledge of intoxication has come to play in the criminal law in the current era. Elsewhere, I argue that lay knowledge of intoxication plays a threefold part in the current law on intoxicated offending – to forestall certain arguments about what is known and not known about alcohol. As lay knowledge underpins the legal rules comprising the intoxication law, it sustains the complex and technical rules that make it up, serving to connect the general or objective (what everyone knows or is assumed to know) and the particular or subjective (what the individual knows). In this way, lay knowledge of intoxication forms a bridge linking intoxication law with the dominant subjective principles of *mens rea* or fault, and enmeshing the moral–evaluative with the descriptive, obscuring the former beneath the latter (see further Loughnan, 2012).

Conclusion

Scientific and allied knowledges (such as medical and forensic knowledges) have dominated scholarship on the parts played by extra-legal knowledges in legal practices. In the bulk of existing studies, lay or non-expert knowledge is largely eclipsed. Lay knowledge of intoxication (but also of other social objects) seems to be dismissed as a kind of generalized and nebulous knowledge background, against which more particular issues for determination (such as those discussed by experts) are foregrounded. Yet, it seems clear that extra-legal knowledges interact in the criminal law context in various ways, and what has been called the 'epistemological heterogeneity' of legal discourse extends further than just to other expert knowledges (Valverde, 2005, pp. 420, 423). Taking lay knowledge of intoxication seriously – and approaching it as the expertise of non-experts – assists in understanding the complexity of knowledge practices in criminal law. Approaching lay knowledge of intoxication as the expertise of non-experts is a useful way of restoring this non-elite form of knowledge to a prominent place, and provides a means by which it can be studied by socio-legal and other scholars. This effort might then be described as a contribution to a larger politics of knowledge in criminal law, a project that would require consideration of both expert or elite knowledges and non-expert and unsystematized knowledges.

Bibliography

Ajzenstadt, M and B Burtch (1990) 'Medicalization and Regulation of Alcohol and Alcoholism: The Professions and Disciplinary Measures' **13** *International Journal of Law and Psychiatry*, 127–47

Bentley, M (2005) 'The Evolution and Dissemination of Historical Knowledge' in M Daunton (ed.), *The Organisation of Knowledge in Victorian Britain* (Oxford: Oxford University Press for British Academy)

Burke, P (2000) *A Social History of Knowledge: From Gutenberg to Diderot* (Cambridge: Polity Press)

Bynum, W F (1994) *Science and the Practice of Medicine in the Nineteenth Century* (Cambridge: Cambridge University Press)

Collini, S (1991) *Public Moralists: Political Thought and Intellectual Life in Britain, 1850–1930* (Oxford: Clarendon Press)

Daunton, M (2005) 'Introduction' in M Daunton (ed.), *The Organisation of Knowledge in Victorian Britain* (Oxford: Oxford University Press for British Academy)

Dingwall, G (2007) 'Intoxicated Mistakes and the Need for Self-Defence' **70**(1) *Modern Law Review* 127–38

Dimock, S (2011) 'What are Intoxicated Offenders Responsible For?' **5** *Criminal Law and Philosophy* 1–20

Gough, S (1996) 'Intoxication and Criminal Liability: The Law Commission's Proposed Reforms' **112** *Law Quarterly Review* 335–51

Farmer, L (1997) *Criminal Law, Tradition and Legal Order: Crime and the Genius of Scots Law 1747 to the Present* (Cambridge: Cambridge University Press)

Gold, A D (1976–1977) 'An Untrimmed "Beard": The Law of Intoxication as a Defence to a Criminal Charge' **19** *Criminal Law Quarterly* 34–85

Horder, J (1995) 'Sobering Up? The Law Commission On Criminal Intoxication' **58**(4) *Modern Law Review* 534–46

Johnstone, G (1996) 'From Vice to Disease? The Concepts of Dipsomania and Inebriety, 1860–1908' **5** *Social & Legal Studies* 37–56

Lacey, N (2001) 'Responsibility and Modernity in Criminal Law' **9**(3) *Journal of Political Philosophy* 249–76

Lacey, N (1993) 'A Clear Concept of Intention? Elusive or Illusory?' **56**(5) *Modern Law Review* 621–42

Levi, R and M Valverde (2001) 'Knowledge On Tap: Police Science and Common Knowledge in the Legal Regulation of Drunkenness' **26**(4) *Law & Social Inquiry* 819–46

Loughnan, A (2012) *Manifest Madness: Mental Incapacity in Criminal Law* (Oxford: Oxford University Press)

Mackay, R (1995) *Mental Condition Defences in the Criminal Law* (Oxford: Clarendon Press)

McCord, D (1990) 'The English and American History of Voluntary Intoxication to Negate Mens Rea' **11** *Journal of Legal History* 372–95

Norrie, A (1990) *Law, Ideology and Punishment: Retrieval and Critique of the Liberal Idea of Criminal Justice* (London: Kluwer Academic Publishers)

Norrie, A (2001) *Crime, Reason and History: A Critical Introduction to Criminal Law* (London: Butterworths)

Robinson, P (1997) *Structure and Function in Criminal Law* (Oxford and New York: Clarendon Press)

Simester, A P (2009) 'Intoxication is Never a Defence' *Criminal Law Review* 3–14

Smith, R (1981) *Trial by Medicine: Insanity and Responsibility in Victorian Trials* (Edinburgh: Edinburgh University Press)

Smith, K (1998) *Lawyers, Legislators and Theorists: Developments in English Criminal Jurisprudence 1800–1957* (Oxford: Clarendon Press)

Valverde, M (2005) 'Authorizing the Production of Urban Moral Order: Appellate Courts and Their Knowledge Claims' **39**(2) *Law and Society Review* 419–56

Valverde, M (2003) *Law's Dream of Common Knowledge* (Princeton: Princeton University Press)

Valverde, M (1998) *Diseases of the Will: Alcohol and the Dilemmas of Freedom* (Cambridge: Cambridge University Press)

Valverde, M (1997) '"Slavery From Within": The Invention of Alcoholism and the Question of Free Will' **22**(3) *Social History* 251–68

Walker, N (1968) *Crime and Insanity in England vol. 1: The Historical Perspective* (Edinburgh: Edinburgh University Press)

Wiener, M (1990) *Reconstructing the Criminal: Culture, Law and Policy in England, 1830–1914* (Cambridge: Cambridge University Press)

Wiener, M (2004) *Men of Blood: Violence, Manliness and Criminal Justice in Victorian England* (Cambridge: Cambridge University Press)

Cases

Attorney-General for Northern Ireland v Gallagher [1963] AC 349

Bratty v Attorney-General for Northern Ireland [1963] AC 386

DPP v Majewski [1977] AC 443

DPP v Beard [1920] AC 479

R v Carroll (1835) 7 C & P 145

R v Cruse (1838) 8 C & P 541

R v Grindley (1819) 1 C & M 8

R v Hatton [2006] 1 Cr App R 16

R v Heard [2007] 3 WLR 475

R v Kingston [1995] 2 AC 355

R v Lawrence [1981] 2 WLR 524

R v Lipman [1970] 1 QB 152

R v Meade [1909] 1 KB 895

R v Monkhouse (1849) 4 Cox CC 55

Legislation

Habitual Drunkards Act 1879 (60 & 61 Vict. c. 60)

Inebriates Act 1898

Reports

Law Commission (2009) *Intoxication and Criminal Liability* Report No 214.

Law Commission (1995) *Legislating the Criminal Code: Intoxication and Criminal Liability* Report No 229.

4
Intoxicants: The Formation of Health Expertise in the Twentieth Century

Virginia Berridge

Introduction

Intoxicants is a broad term. This chapter will examine, under that heading, three sets of substances: drugs which are categorized as illicit; alcohol; and tobacco. It will focus on the formation of expertise in health – in the UK, but also with cross-national reference. In the first decades of the twenty-first century, we are very used to expertise in these areas. Health and substance use is a matter of media interest. Talking heads appear on television: Professor David Nutt is sacked as chair of the Advisory Council on the Misuse of Drugs (ACMD). Back in the nineteenth century, however, where this story starts, there were no networks of interest like these. If we parachute back to, say, 1850, then the sources of expertise for all three substances would have been lay people in the community, or perhaps the local druggist or pharmacist who would have been accustomed to sell all three substances over the counter (Berridge, 1999). But there was also a substantial and dominant non-medical, non-professional arena of competence – beer-house keepers or publicans for alcohol; tobacconists; and home remedies and patent medicines for opium and other drugs. How did we get from there to here? In this chapter, I argue that patterns of expertise have been of central importance in defining how the substances are seen and how they are dealt with. Scientific concepts and approaches are obviously important – but these gain their significance through the 'players', the dominant medico-scientific interest groups who support them. Networks and teams of players have risen and fallen and formed alliances around key concepts. The decades since the mid-nineteenth century show expertise emerging for alcohol and drugs (substances which have tended to operate in tandem), which I term the *psychiatric model*, and for tobacco separately where *public health* was the initial route to expertise. This chapter argues that, more recently, those historic models of public health and psychiatry have formed new alliances and new forms of science-based expertise have emerged, potentially unifying the field even further.

1870s–1920s: the emergence of medical expertise for drugs and alcohol

Historically, a medical model of expertise emerged for alcohol and for drugs in the last half of the nineteenth century. Disease models and the notion of treatment were newly apparent for the substances at this time and doctors campaigned, both in the USA and in the UK, for their acceptance and for the involvement of the state in treatment systems. The focus was the concept of inebriety (addiction as a word and a concept came later in the period around the time of the First World War) where the main concern was with alcohol. Inspired in part by the temperance movement, the main aim was to divert 'habitual drunkards' out of the 'revolving door' of prison and into treatment: the rationale was that drinkers were diseased and therefore amenable to treatment. Inebriety was classified according to the intoxicating agent: tippling laudanum was covered, but not injectable drugs. The main aim of reformers was, through legislation, to set up a state-funded system of reformatories which would treat inebriates. Various Acts were passed in the UK, in 1879, 1888 and 1898 but their implementation was blighted by financial battles between the Home Office and the local authorities that were charged with funding the measures. The legislation fell into disuse before the First World War and, in the USA and Germany, the popularity of the idea had also peaked before 1914. In the Nordic countries, interest peaked later, from 1910 to 1935 (Berridge, 2004).

From the point of view of expertise, however, this period was important in establishing an embryonic group of doctors with a clear interest in inebriety/ addiction. Many were temperance supporters and some, such as Norman Kerr, the President of the Society for the Study of Inebriety, and others in the society, which was the main UK professional body (established in the 1880s), were medical officers of health. Lobbying through their professional organization the British Medical Association (BMA) gave them experience of interaction with the state.

The importance of alcohol within the alliance with drugs diminished during and after the First World War. The centrality of alcohol to the war effort, embryonic nationalization of the drinks trade, the establishment of the Central Control Board, and restrictions on pub opening hours, were paralleled by a programme of scientific research funded through the newly established Medical Research Council (MRC), subsequently published as *Alcohol and the Human Organism*. These developments showed the incursion of new forms of expertise – primarily physiology – and the beginnings of state funding of science. After the war, however, the central war-time structures were not maintained and both temperance and alcohol as an issue declined in the inter-war years. Research on alcohol tended to focus on work discipline and industrial efficiency (Greenaway, 2003; Berridge, 2011).

The alliance of disease treatment and the state, emergent before 1914, was most strongly and significantly marked in the case of drugs. There, war and the peace settlement had brought into being a system of international control of drugs. This was the outcome of US-inspired policy manoeuvres in the Far East since the early 1900s and also the tactics of the pharmaceutical companies. The end product was that, in the 1920s, most countries, especially in Europe and the USA, aligned legislation to fit the new international reporting and control requirements. The USA and the UK provide contrasting case studies of what happened to medical expertise. The USA established a system of prohibition in which the role of medical expertise was downgraded, even criminalized. The 1914 Harrison Narcotics Act was interpreted to make the prescription of drugs to addicts illegitimate and criminal (Musto, 1999). In the UK, the opposite happened, although not without a struggle: a hybrid medico-penal system emerged. The control of drugs was the responsibility of the Home Office, which had also managed the inebriates Acts before the First World War. Attempts by the newly established Ministry of Health (1919) to exert control were brushed aside and the task, in the view of Sir Malcolm Delevingne, under-secretary responsible for drugs at the Home Office, was simply 'stamping out addiction' in the way the Americans were doing it (Berridge, 2005).

Delevingne wanted an authoritative statement that the prescription of drugs to addicts was not legitimate medical practice. But to obtain this, he had to turn to the medical profession and to the central state agency, the Ministry of Health, to arbitrate on what was indeed legitimate. Doctors in the UK had established greater leverage with the state than their colleagues in the US system. In Britain, his initiatives led to the establishment in 1924 of the Departmental Committee on Morphine and Heroin Addiction as a Ministry of Health committee. This move brought the ministry into an important mediating role. It might not have been the lead department, but it was a major link to doctors in practice and its regional medical officers had already been involved in dealing with cases of doctor addicts. It was a medical civil servant in the ministry, Dr E W Adams, secretary to the committee, who drafted its report and set the tenor of the response. Adams was concerned to protect disease views of addiction and a doctor's professional status. Thus, he wrote:

> If the addict is unwilling to enter into the relationship of patient to
> physician, but admits that he is merely coming to obtain supplies

of a drug which he cannot otherwise get, then it is the clear duty
of the doctor to refuse the case. But if the habitué desires treatment as a sick person for the relief of his pathological condition,
the physician must be allowed to use his discretion ... (Ministry of
Health, 1923)

Adams' views were supported by leading members of the committee. Its chair
was Sir Humphrey Rolleston, president of the Royal College of Physicians
and an exponent of disease views. Another member, Professor W E Dixon,
reader in pharmacology at Cambridge, had written forcibly in *The Times* in
opposition to attempts to foist the American model of drug control on British
doctors. A dissenting voice to their views came from Sir William Willcox,
adviser to the Home Office, and from a group of prison medical officers. Their
addict clientele were distinctively different from the middle-class, often medically connected, patients seen by the other members of the committee. The
end result was an official statement that the long-term prescription of drugs
to addicts for the purposes of treating their addiction was legitimate medical
practice, a statement of principle often referred to as the 'British system' of
drug control which is still revered in the more liberal wing of the drug arena
today. The International Harm Reduction Association, for example, gives an
annual Rolleston prize.

In reality, the report symbolized an alliance between medical profession
and state, but with the Home Office as well as the Ministry of Health. David
Downes long ago called this a 'system of masterly inactivity in the face of a
non existent problem' (Downes, 1988). Medical expertise was established but
within a framework of criminal justice. Doctors kept control of their patients
who, in turn, accepted their definition of expertise. If the problem of who
was perceived to be addicted had been different, then the solution might well
have been different as well.

If we look back on the development of health expertise for our two
substances, alcohol and drugs, by the inter-war period, a number of features
can be noted. The role of doctors and notions of disease and treatment had
become established for both, although more obviously for drugs than for alcohol. But the earlier connection with temperance and with public health as a
form of medical expertise had been largely lost. Rolleston and his peers were
consultants and did not operate at the public health local government level.
The emergent speciality was that of mental health: but the institutional solution, the inebriates asylum, was no longer an option in the inter-war period.
Mental health in general was moving away from institutions towards a focus
on a middle-class clientele, a model which drugs fitted well. The membership
of the Rolleston Committee, although medical, showed the heterogeneity of
medical interest in this area, but the language and focus of the report foreshadowed the subsequent dominance of psychiatry.

1960s: psychiatry ascendant for drugs and alcohol

The dominance of psychiatry came ultimately with the establishment of the National Health Service (NHS) in 1948 and the emergence of a new policy lobby for treatment among doctors. The alcohol and drug-related developments were separate but there were some clear commonalities across the substances. The role of psychiatry as the central health discipline; the establishment of specialist hospital-based treatment; the idea of addiction as disease; and the role of the newly established World Health Organization (WHO) were important in both spheres.

In Britain, the disease concept of alcoholism was discovered, or rather rediscovered, in the late 1940s. At WHO, alcohol was included in the terms of reference of its expert committee on mental health which met for the first time in 1949. This period of interest coincided with collaboration between a British psychiatrist, Dr G R Hargreaves, the head of the WHO Mental Health Unit and E M Jellinek, a scientist and scholar who had established his reputation at Yale. There, he had been influenced by the 'new scientific approach' to alcohol which was emergent in post-prohibitionist America. There a new model, influenced by social science, also filtered into the understanding of alcoholism. At the international level, WHO was also important in establishing internationally recognized disease classifications for the condition of addiction (Thom, 1999).

This international dimension interacted with the domestic situation in the UK. Here the post-war period saw the growth of an initial, or perhaps revived, 'policy community' (the term used in political science to encompass networks of expertise which straddle interests within and outside government) around alcohol, which resulted in 1962 in a memorandum issued by the Ministry of Health, *The Hospital Treatment of Alcoholism* (see Thom, 1999). This community was primarily hospital-based, reliant on the specialist model developed by the psychiatrist Max Glatt at Warlingham Park Hospital in Surrey, where group therapy initiatives developed into a separate group for alcoholics. Glatt was a refugee from Nazi Germany and an outsider in policy terms. But his influence came through T P Rees, superintendent at Warlingham and a member of ministry advisory committees. He promoted Glatt's membership of the BMA/Magistrates Committee (1958–1961), which was credited with stirring the ministry into action. Within the ministry, insider links were also developing with a civil servant, Richard Philippson, who had special responsibility for alcohol from the early 1960s. Glatt's specialist model won approval rather than advice from the better known D L Davies, Dean of the Institute of Psychiatry, a far more prestigious figure. But Davies considered that alcoholics did not need separate treatment and his research results were largely ignored. The Glatt model offered, as Betsy Thom (1999) has argued, a chance for the ministry to be seen to take action rather than the Davies model, which simply offered more of the same, with no particular alcohol-focused intervention.

Specialist treatment was a far from consensual option in the field at the time and there were soon moves to modify it. Nor did the treatment cater for the full range of drinkers seeking help. The advent of Alcoholics Anonymous (AA), coming from the USA in the 1940s, and the involvement of the British voluntary sector in dealing with chaotic street drinkers underlined the limitation of the specialist option. Its impact was confined in the main to males of higher social status. But the 1962 Ministry of Health memorandum did mark the consolidation of psychiatry as the dominant medical discipline within the field.

The same pattern is observable for drugs where key changes also took place in the 1960s. Here, as with the Rolleston report, the changes were much discussed subsequently, in particular the replacement of the general practitioner (GP), sometimes in private practice, as the main locus of expertise, by a psychiatric specialist hospital-based system. Concern was expressed in the late 1950s and early 1960s about the operation of the GP system. One doctor in particular, Lady Isabella Frankau, working in Harley Street, was prescribing large amounts of heroin and cocaine to addicts. In 1962, she prescribed a total of 6 kilograms (600,000 tablets) of heroin. On one occasion, she prescribed 9 grams (900 tablets) of heroin to an addict and gave the same patient a further 6 grams (600 tablets) three days later to replace pills lost in an accident. Frankau and a small number of other doctors working in NHS general practice were thought to be overprescribing heroin and other drugs to addicts. Concern within the Ministry of Health, and the rising numbers of addicts (although these were still very small) led to the reconvening in 1964 of the Interdepartmental Committee on Heroin Addiction (the Brain Committee) under chair Sir Russell Brain, a neurologist and former president of the Royal College of Physicians. Brain had chaired a previous committee on the same subject which had reported in 1961 and had reaffirmed the Rolleston position (Mold, 2008).

The Brain report (see Mold, 2008), which was published in 1965, saw the establishment of specialist treatment centres (Drug Dependence Units (DDUs)) under psychiatric leadership and the removal of responsibility for prescription from the GP. Doctors outside the DDUs were still able to prescribe heroin for pain relief but not for patients who were addicted to the drug. The change in the balance of expertise was dependent on a new view of addiction and its treatment. No longer was this simply an issue between the individual doctor and patient, but it also assumed a clear social dimension as well. The committee recommended that those seeking treatment for addiction be notified to a central authority, as was the case for infectious disease. But in this case, the central authority was the Home Office, not the Ministry of Health, thus reaffirming the medico-penal concordat contained within policy since the 1920s. The definition of addiction itself changed to encompass a view of social infection – 'for addiction is a socially infectious condition and its notification may offer a means for epidemiological assessment and control' (see Mold, 2008). Clinics were to control the spread of addiction into the wider population and also treat the individual addict. Here was an emergent alliance between older and newer forms of public health and psychiatric concepts.

The operation of these DDU clinics has been controversial. The chief drugs inspector at the Home Office, Bing Spear, felt that the GP system could have been reformed not removed. His writings show hostility to the 'psychiatric mafia', largely connected with the Maudsley Hospital in London, which came to dominate drug treatment (Spear, 2005). In the 1970s, the clinics shifted, in a controversial move, from prescribing heroin to prescribing methadone, a synthetic substitute, a move justified by research published after most specialists had made the change. The impact of such changes on the growth of an illicit market for heroin in the 1970s has been debated. From the point of view of changing patterns of expertise, it is notable that a small group of London-based psychiatrists could, through consensus among its members, make significant decisions about prescribing and access to drugs without reference to other authority. The division between NHS and private practice, where drugs were more easily available, developed during this period (Mars, 2005).

To sum up, approaches to both drugs and alcohol developed as specialist psychiatric enclaves during the immediate post-war decades. But there were also interesting indications of an awareness of emergent public health approaches via epidemiology and also elements of the older public health model were there, in particular in the provision for notification for drugs. This was not because public health as a profession was involved in the drugs issue. Public health expertise was at a low ebb in the 1960s after the establishment of the NHS, which was based on the specialist hospital model. Reorganization in the 1970s had further diminished the influence of the public health profession. What was represented for drugs and alcohol was rather the post-war emphasis on the hospital system, the integration of mental health services into the NHS and the rise of psychiatry and of social psychiatry, with international links. Such was the psychiatric model of expertise for drugs and alcohol by the 1960s.

1950s and 1960s: tobacco and public health epidemiology

Let us turn now from the above two intoxicants and look at tobacco. This substance initially took a completely different route in terms of expertise.

Sometimes mentioned alongside alcohol in the nineteenth century, then it did not fall within the public health/inebriety model nor within the later psychiatric model. It developed within a new public health model after the Second World War with a different form of science and a different set of experts (Berridge, 2007).

The key event scientifically was the 'discovery' of the relationship between smoking and lung cancer published in the *British Medical Journal* in 1950 by Sir Austin Bradford Hill and Richard Doll. Hill and Doll were a statistician and an epidemiologist. Their work was symbolic of a new source of expertise in medicine in the post-war world and a reorientation of public health. A new style of investigation through cohort studies and the rise of the 'risk factor', looked at long-term risk of poor health rather than immediate infection with disease. This change of focus was allied to a change in patterns of disease – from infectious to chronic – in the post-war years. Discussion turned to diseases of affluence or longevity such as cancer or heart disease, rather than those of poverty and disadvantage. The whole field of public health was in a state of flux at this time. The confident expectation of public health professionals, the medical officers of health, that they would be the lynch pins of the new NHS through a local-government-based health system had not proved to be the case. Public health academics, wedded to the ideas of social medicine, developed a reorientation of their ideas at this time through a focus on lifestyle, on individual behaviour and the psychology of the individual. Smoking and tobacco was the emergent issue which epitomized those new directions and new forms of expertise.

The membership of the first Royal College of Physicians (RCP) committee on smoking which reported in 1962 gives an indication of emergent public health expertise. It was stimulated quietly by public health interests within government, in particular the Deputy Chief Medical Officer George Godber who was frustrated by lack of Ministry of Health action. The committee's secretary was Charles Fletcher who had impeccable medical connections and was committed to communicating with the public about medicine through the media. Guy Scadding and Jerry Morris, social medicine doctors, were committee members, together with Aubrey Lewis of the Institute of Psychiatry. The focus was on risk and communicating it to the public. In an interview, Morris later recalled how they had tried to find a medical officer of health with an interest in smoking and failed (Berridge, 2007). The committee's work focused on consumer issues on advertising and the role of the media. Health economics as a central public health discipline was still somewhat in the future and so it was the social medicine pioneer Jerry Morris who was active throughout the life of the committee, himself investigating consumer expenditure and the role of tobacco advertising. Aubrey Lewis was not on the committee to promote a specialist psychiatric model of disease but rather to investigate the role of school-based health education and psychology. Treatment and hospital-based models were far from the new public health expertise. In fact, when Doll was later appointed to a Regius professorship at Oxford there was relief that he would not need consultant hospital beds. From the initial RCP reports in 1962 and 1971 (Berridge, 2007) and the formation of Action on Smoking and Health (ASH) in the same year can be dated the public heath model based on a range of disciplines from epidemiology to economics and psychology, allied with science-based media-focused activism. This model became the dominant one within the public health field, not just for smoking, during the 1970s and 1980s.

1970s and 1980s: the public health model for drugs and alcohol

This 'new public health model' also began to gain influence within the psychiatric model for drugs and alcohol in the 1970s (Berridge, 2007). Key crossover issues were the rise of 'whole population' theories of risk for alcohol consumption; the psychologically-based concept of dependence as a replacement for that of addiction; the growing psychiatric interest in epidemiology as a research tool; and parallel adoption of these ideas in the drugs field.

The French statistician Sully Ledermann had argued in the 1950s that there was a relationship between average per capita alcohol consumption and levels of alcohol misuse in a population (Berridge, 2007). This attracted little attention at the time but in the 1970s it became central to what was termed a new public health approach to alcohol. This chimed also with population theories articulated by epidemiologists such as Geoffrey Rose in the public health field. A new policy community was led by psychiatrists but it also took on board civil servants, the alcohol voluntary sector, the police and the law. Internationally, this approach was articulated through the famous alcohol 'purple book' (the colour of its cover) *Alcohol Control Policies in Public Health Perspective* which was published in 1975 and jointly authored from the Finnish Foundation for Alcohol Studies, the Addiction Research Foundation in Toronto, and WHO Regional Office for Europe (Thom, 1999). Led by Kettil Bruun, a Finnish sociologist, and with a mix of social science and medical disciplines among its authors, the report cemented an alliance between psychiatry and a wider range of disciplines. Its influence can still be seen in the near present through the recent *Alcohol and the Public Good* and *Alcohol: No Ordinary Commodity*, produced by some members and descendants of the original team (Berridge, 2001).

In Britain, these ideas were presented in key reports to government in the late 1970s but did not find political approval with the change of government from Labour to Conservative in 1979. At the same time, the WHO-legitimated new concept of 'dependence' brought psychologists and psychiatrists into closer relationships, even at one stage drawing tobacco and smoking within the purview of the psychiatric model. At the Addiction Research Unit at the Institute of Psychiatry, established in 1967 with MRC funding, programmes of drugs, alcohol and tobacco research were under psychiatric leadership with a clear role for psychology.

The epidemiological model of research also permeated the alcohol and drugs field, in part because of the 'whole population' model for alcohol but also because of the interest of leading psychiatrists in US research where epidemiology was strong. The drugs field was not immune. The Brain Committee's concept of the potential 'social infection' of drug addiction proposed epidemiological assessment and control. Brain's formulation significantly encapsulated older traditions of public health – infection and notification – with newer ones – risk, epidemiology and the whole population. Surveys of drug users in local areas also marked this period.

To sum up then, the psychiatric and public health models moved closer together in the 1970s for our chosen substances. But the professional groupings were still distinct. Psychiatrists were the lead figures for alcohol and drugs. The tobacco field did not embrace psychiatry. In fact the psychiatrist Michael Russell, who ran the smoking programme at the Institute of Psychiatry's Addiction Research Unit, was an unpopular figure in public health smoking circles because of his advocacy of 'dependence' as a concept and harm reduction, using nicotine, as a strategy. The public health smoking field was wedded to individual self-help, behavioural modification and abstention as the aim.

Expert committees and policy communities

Expertise and its relationship to the state had been a continuing theme since the late nineteenth century. In the 1970s, however, significant developments occurred which institutionalized arrangements and cemented a policy community. From the 1960s, doctor civil servants within the Ministry of Health had continuing responsibility for these areas and provided an important conduit of expertise into government. In the 1970s, formal expert committees were set up in line with more general developments in the role of scientific expertise within government. All three substances had their relevant committees: an Advisory Committee on Alcoholism; the ACMD; and the Independent Committee on Smoking and Health (ISCSH) for tobacco (Berridge, 1997). Only the ACMD, with a statutory basis in the 1971 Misuse of Drugs Act, secured long-term purchase within policy making. Its scientific membership, working in tandem with medical civil servants within the Ministry (later Department) of Health, saw a series of reports produced in the 1980s which had a significant impact on policy. Its report in 1982 on *Treatment and Rehabilitation* was credited with establishing a more community-based approach to services (see Berridge, 1996). In 1988, its part one report on *AIDS and Drug Misuse* was important in securing official political commitment to harm reduction in services for drug users. For smoking, however, the fate of the ISCSH was less secure. The policy community was more fragmented between public health anti-industry interests and scientists who wanted an accommodation with industry: the ISCSH did not develop to form a statutory committee for tobacco control as ministers such as David Owen had intended. The Advisory Committee on Alcoholism was also short-lived.

1990s onward: new disciplines and crossing boundaries

From the 1980s and 1990s, the blurring of the boundaries between the public health and psychiatric models of expertise outlined above, which started in the 1970s, has continued. But some new areas of expertise have been emergent and potentially dominant. The concept of 'problem use' began to be applied both to alcohol and to drugs in the 1980s and epitomized the widening policy community round these substances, including the voluntary sector and the commitment to more community-based approaches. The addict or the drug dependent was replaced by this 'problem' term in official reports, although views of disease remained much stronger in the US context. For drugs, the coming of HIV/AIDS underpinned pre-existing objectives of harm reduction but also was seen to bring into being a 'new public health' approach to drugs. In reality, as we have seen, the public health model had a longer history for drugs. The membership of the ACMD expanded during the 1980s to include statisticians, sociologists, psychologists and others, thus underlining the changing pattern of expertise. It was in this way that the rapprochement of public health and psychiatry developed.

Discourse and expertise for tobacco also became more closely aligned with drugs and also, to some degree, alcohol. This was not through the psychiatric route but through the rise of the concept of addiction, which had been applied to both drugs and alcohol but was then revised. The concept of addiction had, in contrast, never been central to tobacco discourse. There was a potential conflict over what the model implied for the public health approach. One interviewee (a psychologist) summed up the conflict between public health and psychiatric models. It was a matter of what the concept implied and also the institutional professional location of the message:

> By establishing the efficacy of nicotine replacement we're moving towards the public health model of brief interventions in primary care. That's a more acceptable message that has filtered

> through...Nicotine is less acceptable. People found it difficult
> to accept it as a form of drug addiction. They felt it was counter
> productive to label it as an addiction because it absolved people
> from responsibility...the association with the Maudsley was a
> problem – it wasn't a mental health issue. (quoted in Berridge,
> 2007, p. 272)

In the 1990s the rise of the 'new' arena of psychopharmacology and the re-importation of these ideas from the USA, gave them a new life in the smoking arena. Psychopharmacology, of course, was not new in the UK or elsewhere but the importation of ideas from the USA was a new development. Here was a new form of expertise coming from a new location and this gave the concept greater purchase.

The public discussion of the concept of addiction for smoking has been dominated by a 'heroes and villains' tale of a 'hidden concept' concealed by the duplicity of the tobacco industry. That is part of the US story but, in reality, the 'rise of addiction' as a key concept for smoking was a much more complex affair. It should also be seen as central to the strategies of different interest groups and the scientific concepts they did or did not choose to adopt (Berridge, 2007). Habit, dependence and addiction were concepts which the public health field had considered and largely rejected in the 1960s and 1970s; they were seen to have no legitimacy in the context of strategies of self-control and abstinence which were based on dominant public health ideology. But that stance changed. In 2000, the RCP published a report on *Nicotine Addiction in Britain* (see Berridge, 2007). This change was not a story of 'discovery', but rather a realization that strategies needed to be modified and underpinned by science. The smoking field moved towards harm reduction, although not without controversy, because of the realization that lower-class (often female) smokers were resistant to giving up. What could explain such resistance? There were policy implications too. The concept of addiction was linked to the Labour government's anti-poverty strategies in which nicotine replacement therapy (NRT) was free to those on low incomes. These ideas were seen as emanating from US scientific networks which adopted nicotine research through the realm of psychopharmacology. Work by Goldstein and others at Stanford in the 1990s brought work on morphine, heroin and methadone together with that on nicotine and caffeine. Psychiatry was therefore largely absent from the picture, even though many of the harm reduction ideas for tobacco through nicotine replacement had been articulated from a British psychiatric setting in the 1970s and 1980s.

Psychopharmacology was a new arena of expertise which had the power to bring together the three substances. Alan Leshner and Norah Volkow, successive heads of the American drug research agency the National Institute on Drug Abuse, famously announced that addiction is a chronic relapsing brain disease. Psychopharmacology brought the substances together, not least through its powerful visual representations of the addicted brain. The brain of the compulsive cocaine user did not look that different to the brain of individuals addicted to nicotine. In Britain, such scientific interests have been powerful in policy advisory positions in the early twenty-first century. The government's Foresight initiative on the future of psychoactive substances was led by David Nutt and others, and Nutt went on to chair the ACMD. The new chair, Leslie Iversen, is also from the same background. Nutt's agenda around horse riding and ecstasy was covered by the media,[1] but more significant was the psychopharmacological agenda to bring the substances covered in this chapter together, and to encompass legal drugs as well. The 'rational' classification of intoxicating substances fronted an agenda where those current buzz words 'well-being' and 'happiness' could now be based on behavioural modification through drugs of whatever sort, perhaps also through economic motivation and financial incentives, the focus of 'behavioural economics'. So new alliances are in the process of formation, incorporating new forms of economics and psychology, the disciplines which have also had a powerful role to play in the post-war public health scientific enterprise.

Conclusion

The expertise story told by this chapter is a complex one. It has argued against the more traditional model which sees expertise as grappling with problems and bringing relevant ideas and approaches to bear. The idea of a gradual unfolding of understanding has echoes of Whig history. Such a rational or progressive model does not bear scrutiny. Individuals and their professional and scientific associations and networks have helped to form and change the dominant ideological and conceptual ways in which the use of these intoxicants has been perceived. Concepts became significant because of those who supported them and how that meshed with professional, policy and practice objectives. In the chapter, I have outlined the emergence of a psychiatric model of expertise for drugs and alcohol by comparison with a new public health one for smoking. The boundaries between these models are blurred and from the 1970s, public health and psychiatric strategies and concepts moved closer together. Alcohol and drugs drew on population ideas and epidemiology, while the tobacco field incorporated the concept of addiction. All the substances have been affected recently by brain science theories and by the universalizing ideas of psychopharmacology.

---

1 Nutt was dismissed by the Home Secretary after he had compared the risks of taking ecstasy with those of horse riding.

These arenas of expertise do not operate in isolation. Increasingly, they have become part of international networks and flows of expertise or dominant ideas from one country to another. The flow of influence from the USA to the UK has been most apparent in recent times, although other tendencies, such as the development of international scientific networks with a global reach, have been particularly apparent for smoking. Expertise has long been allied with policy activism in the public health model through the role of health pressure groups. This has been less the case for drugs and for alcohol, where the psychiatric model of expertise preferred to operate on the 'inside track' through expert committees and informal contacts. Here too the fields are moving closer together: the new anti-alcohol alliance in the UK has consciously modelled itself on the smoking field in bringing scientists and doctors into a media-focused role. The role of WHO in establishing dominant concepts of addiction internationally and of the expert committee in providing a 'boundary organization' for the elaboration of expertise within government have been important. The history of these intoxicants provides a powerful example of the complexity of changing patterns of expertise and their influence on concepts and on policy.

Bibliography

Berridge, V (1997) 'Doctors and the State: The Changing Role of Medical Expertise in Policy Making' **11**(4) *Contemporary British History* 66–85

Berridge, V (1999) *Opium and the People. Opiate Use and Drug Control Policy in Nineteenth and Early Twentieth Century England* revised edn (London: Free Association Books)

Berridge, V (2001) 'Disease, Risk, Harm and Safety; Trends in Post War British Alcohol Policy' in I Lowy and J Krige (eds), *Images of Disease: Science, Public Policy and Health in Post War Europe* (Luxembourg: EC)

Berridge, V (2004) 'Punishment or Treatment? Inebriety, Drink and Drugs, 1860–2004' **364** *Lancet* 3–5

Berridge, V (2005) 'The "British System" and its History: Myth and Reality' in J Strang and M Gossop (eds), *Heroin Addiction and the British System* vol. 1 (London: Routledge)

Berridge, V (2007) *Marketing Health. Smoking and the Discourse of Public Health in Britain, 1945–2000* (Oxford: Oxford University Press)

Berridge, V (2011) 'The History of Alcohol Research', presentation for the launch of Alcohol Research UK, September 2011, www.alcoholresearchuk. org

Doll R and A B Hill (1950) 'Smoking and Carcinoma of the Lung' **221**(ii) *BMJ* 739–48

Downes, D (1988) *Contrasts in Tolerance: Post War Penal Policy in the Netherlands and in England and Wales* (Oxford: Clarendon Press)

Greenaway, J (2003) *Drink and British Politics since 1830. A Study in Policy Making* (Basingstoke: Palgrave Macmillan)

Mars, S (2005) 'Peer Pressure and Imposed Consensus: The Making of the 1984 *Guidelines of Good Clinical Practice in the Treatment of Drug Misuse'* in V Berridge (ed.), *Making Health Policy: Networks in Research and Policy after 1945* (Amsterdam: Rodopi)

Ministry of Health (1923), Rolleston Committee papers, National Archives MH 58/275 memorandum by Dr E W Adams

Mold, A (2008) *Heroin Addiction. The Treatment of Addiction in Twentieth Century Britain* (De Kalb: Northern Illinois University Press)

Musto, D (1999) *The American Disease: Origins of Narcotic Control* 3rd edn (New York: Oxford University Press)

Spear, B (2005) 'The Early Years of Britain's Drug Situation in Practice: Up to the 1960s' in J Strang and M Gossop (eds), *Heroin Addiction and the British System* vol. 1 (London: Routledge)

Thom, B (1999) *Dealing with Drink* (London: Free Association Books)

Legislation

Dangerous Drugs Act 1920
Harrison Narcotics Act 1914 (USA)
Misuse of Drugs Act 1971

Section 2
Spatial Politics

5

'The Relations of Inebriety to Insurance': Geographies of Medicine, Insurance and Alcohol in Britain, 1840–1911

James Kneale and Shaun French

Introduction

In August 1835 in Manchester Dr Ralph Barnes Grindrod participated in the 'First Teetotal Discussion', a public debate on temperance with the landlord of a local hotel. Grindrod was reportedly the first British doctor to take the pledge and an early proponent of 'medical temperance'. In many ways he epitomizes the aspects of temperance we are most familiar with, uniting medicine, morality and political activism in an assault on the drink trade, as reformers tested the possibilities of a newly emerging public sphere (MacFie, 1899; Grierson, 2001; Kneale, 2001). But Grindrod had another, less spectacular part to play in the battle against alcohol. By 1840 he had agreed to be a medical referee for the United Kingdom Total Abstinence Life Association, which would require him to assess the health of individuals seeking life insurance from this company. Grindrod's role as a referee reminds us that life insurance was set against problematic drinking from the earliest years of organized temperance in Britain, and that there was a good deal more to drink in the nineteenth and early twentieth century than struggles over its regulation.

This chapter examines the relationship between drinking and life assurance in Britain between 1840 and 1911. We have borrowed the title – 'the relations of inebriety to insurance' – from a paper given by Dr Norman Kerr in 1893 (*Proceedings of the Society for the Study of Inebriety*, 1893, pp. 12–14). Kerr was well placed to discuss this topic. He was the first president of the Society for the Study of Inebriety, the chair of the British Medical Association's Inebriates' Legislation Committee, and one of the most influential medical experts on alcohol in nineteenth-century Britain. He thought that life insurance could play an important role in highlighting the dangers of alcohol as well as in fostering temperance, which he described as 'that radical change of personal habits' (Kerr, 1882, p. 565). It seems likely that changing drinking practices and patterns of everyday living and working might have had something to do with falling levels of alcohol consumption before the First World War. Had life insurance shaped these changing patterns?

If insurance did have this effect, it was through its relation to medical science. Medicine remained a key site for the production of ideas about drink and drinkers, despite what Mariana Valverde (1998) calls the 'incomplete medicalisation' of alcohol. Valverde suggests that alcoholism is a 'hybrid condition', both a physiological problem and a 'disease of the will'; current medical practice often involves an uneasy compromise between medicine and psychiatry, and nineteenth-century conceptions of alcohol also blended scientific and moral arguments, or swung from one to another. As a result, alcohol is a good example of what John Law and Vicky Singleton (2005) describe as a 'messy object'. Researching alcoholic liver disease, they argue that while this condition may be different things to different people in different places, this is not simply an epistemological issue of representation or social construction. Rather the disease is something which is 'enacted into being' through different practices (p. 334).

> It is not possible to point to or at a diseased liver without intervening in, or being embedded in, a network of practice (for instance, in a post mortem, an ultrasound scan or a consultation in a GP's surgery). The object depends on relational work of one kind or another, instrumental and interactive, in the hospital and the GP's surgery. (p. 336)

Similarly alcohol is only 'there' when it has entered into a relationship with practices, objects, or bodies, and we have to work out how alcohol is made visible, produced, through different kinds of performance. We are used to examining a limited number of places in which drink is enacted into being, like police accounts of public drunkenness, or court rulings, but this chapter sets out to consider understandings of drink forged in other contexts. Following the work of Bruno Latour (1993) and others, we see different manifestations of alcohol as co-constructions made by drinkers, abstainers, 'lives', doctors and actuaries. Instead of seeing it as a general threat, it is more useful to see how drink became risk or possibility in *very specific ways* as it entered into different relationships with people and other things, just as Grindrod translated medical and social scientific knowledge about alcohol into calculations of risk for the Total Abstinence Life Association.

While British life assurance dates back to the sixteenth century, it took on its modern form in the late eighteenth century. The Equitable Life Assurance Society was the first company to make systematic use of life or premium tables, which were based upon earlier statistical investigations of mortality. These offered the promise of establishing premiums that were both fair and prudent, based largely upon the age of the applicant. In the nineteenth century these actuarial principles became increasingly codified, particularly after the foundation of the Institute of Actuaries in 1848 (French, 2002).

Just as important as the establishment of an actuarial and scientific basis for writing policies was the construction of a socio-legal framework, two pillars of which were set out in the late eighteenth century. First, four years after the formation of the Equitable Life, the principle of *uberrimae fides*, of the utmost good faith, was recognized as applying to life insurance contracts in a key judgment by Lord Mansfield in the case of *Carter v Boehm* 1766 (Law Commission, 2006a). Later codified in the Marine Insurance Act of 1906, the ruling provided a partial solution to the twin insurantial problems of how to manage information asymmetries and moral hazard by placing a legal obligation on the policyholder to disclose all material facts. Second, following growing concerns over the misuse of life insurance the Life Assurance Act was passed in 1774. The Act was significant because it legitimized the practice of insuring lives by drawing a formal distinction between speculation and gambling, on the one hand, and life insurance, on the other. This distinction was founded on the legal principle of *insurable interest*; that is, that a policyholder must be able to prove a legitimate interest in the person insured, either in terms of a 'natural affection', 'potential financial loss' or other 'statutory interest' (Law Commission, 2006b).

The institutionalization of life insurance in Britain allowed life offices to begin to cater to a lower-middle-class market by the middle of the nineteenth century, and 'industrial' insurance firms like the Prudential began to court working-class customers. As competition intensified, 'class' offices developed, seeking out professionals – lawyers, clerics, medical men, military officers – or denominational offices for clergy and laity. A more aggressive generation of offices arrived in the 1860s, but many collapsed, finding the costs prohibitive. Experiments in business organization throughout the century led to changing relationships between central offices and the spaces from which they recruited, shuffling agents, networks, branch offices and supervisors to meet a number of demands – some of which were in tension with one another. Timothy Alborn notes that:

> Many different walks of life needed to come together to develop a market and deliver life insurance to that market. It would be a mistake to imagine that such a heterogeneous mix of people could work together seamlessly... Directors preached profits,

actuaries preached caution, branch secretaries preached energy, and salesmen preached whatever they thought would convince a prospective customer to buy insurance. (2009, p. 77)

In the second half of the nineteenth century more than half of the world's life insurance policies and companies were British; Alborn estimates that 30 per cent of the British population – and a much higher proportion of households – had life insurance policies of some kind by 1890 (ibid. pp. 20, 51).

Historians have demonstrated that life insurance offices brought together medical and social scientific practices to productive effect. Virginia Berridge notes that:

When the question [of the dangers of opiates] first arose in the 1820s and '30s, it was not stimulated by Indian or Chinese events, but by the question of opium eating and life insurance. (1977, p. 371)

Similarly Alborn's study of life insurance and tuberculosis (TB) shows that actuarial calculations and insurance business practices helped to promote the argument that TB was caused by a bacillus (2001). Ray Jureidini and Kevin White suggest that 'the use of the clinical examination was the outcome of the interests of insurance companies' (2000, p. 191). In these cases the meeting of medicine and insurance was *productive*, shaping not just the meanings but also the effects of opium, TB and clinical practice. Was this also the case for alcohol?

This chapter examines a particular 'office', or firm, the United Kingdom Temperance and General Provident Institution (UKT&GPI), which was originally called the Total Abstinence Life Association – Dr Grindrod's employer. We will also consider the ways in which medical and actuarial knowledges and practices sought to define the risks associated with intemperance in ways which would be productive for the firm and its policyholders. Suggesting that insurance might have played a role in changing drinking habits means assessing life assurance as a form of governmentality (Burchell et al., 1991). However, alcohol remained a highly uncertain risk, meaning that this disciplinary net was probably less effective than it might have been – and spread less evenly across Britain than might have been expected. Throughout the chapter the aim is to show that, while alcohol and medicine came together in life insurance, the exact nature of this relationship was shifting, provisional and open to new developments – as it still is today.

The UKT&GPI

In 1840 Robert Warner applied for a life insurance policy. Warner, a 25-year-old Quaker, was working for the family firm of bellfounders. He went on to manage the company and was 'Father' of the Worshipful Company of Founders at the time of his death in 1896 (*Minutes of the Proceedings of the Institution of Civil Engineers*, 1897; Woolley and Johnson, 1903, p. 380). Warner was also an expert on orchids and a Fellow of the Linnaean Society (Warner and Williams, 1862–1875). Hard-working, successful, a pious man and passionate scientist, Robert Warner was eminently respectable. Despite this he was told that he would have to pay a higher premium for his insurance policy: 'You are a teetotaller; and the directors consider teetotal lives are worse than ordinary lives.' (Temperance and Life Assurance Company of North America, 1884, p. 2) Warner was so incensed that he set up his own insurance company, the United Kingdom Total Abstinence Life Association, with Theodore Compton, who had experience of life assurance, acting as secretary. The office, which would become the UKT&GPI, sold its first policy in January 1841 and nearly 600 more during the next two years. In its first five years the mortality rate of the firm's insured lives was half that of the most prosperous of the older insurance companies (Winskill, 1881; Withers, 1951). Abstinence, it seemed, was good for your health, and that was good for business as far as life assurance was concerned.

An early prospectus for the company stated:

> The object of this Association is to afford to persons who entirely abstain from intoxicating beverages, the benefits of their temperance and industry, more fully than is practicable in societies composed of all classes indiscriminately. (United Kingdom Total Abstinence Life Association, 1840a)

Applicants could choose life assurance policies which would pay the assured sum at the time of the holder's death, or others which paid at a specified time, or earlier in case of death; they could choose yet others which paid out at a set time, effectively acting as saving accounts. Another prospectus from the same year lays out the 'conditions of assurance' in more detail:

> Every person assuring in this Association must be a member of a Total-Abstinence Society...Every member of this Association, who breaks his pledge to abstain from intoxicating beverages, will be required to pay a fine of ten shillings for every £100 assured to him.
>
> Every member persisting in the use of intoxicating beverages, or refusing to renew his pledge, will forfeit all the privileges of membership, and be required to pay an additional premium of ten per cent., or two shillings for every pound of the ordinary rate.
>
> Every person convicted of felony, treason, conspiracy, duelling, drunkenness, or fraud, will be excluded from the Association, and his interest therein forfeited. (United Kingdom Total Abstinence Life Association, 1840b, p. 2)

These fines and forfeits were 'the very reverse of the proposal put to Mr. Warner by the directors of the company he proposed to join' (Winskill, 1891, p. 120).

By 1847 the Association had changed its name and its nature, becoming the UKT&GPI. A General Section was opened 'for the insurance of moderate drinkers' (Woolley and Johnson, 1903, p. 380). The two sections ran in parallel and transfers between them were strictly monitored. This proved to be both successful and influential, with other companies adopting 'Temperance Sections'. Woolley and Johnson list 14 British, US, Canadian and New Zealand companies organized on the Institution's principles or that offered policies for abstainers (pp. 382–384), though few lasted past 1900 (Alborn, 2009, p. 40). Other companies allowed abstainers a 5 per cent or even 10 per cent reduction in premiums instead (Bingham, 1922), or offered teetotallers higher bonuses (Kerr, 1882).

In many ways the Association was much like other insurance companies of the time, a specialist 'class' office, but it was also a temperance organization. It shared its premises at 39 Moorgate Street with the offices of the New British and Foreign Temperance Society, the most important 'moral suasion' temperance organization in the south of England (the society became the National Temperance Society (NTS) and later the New Temperance League). A list of patrons and directors from 1840 demonstrates that Warner and his friends were well connected in the temperance movement (Harrison, 1973). They included James Silk Buckingham, who had chaired the House of Commons Select Committee on Drunkenness in 1834, and would become the first president of the London Temperance League in 1851; Samuel Bowly, an important abolitionist; Richard Tapper Cadbury, father of John Cadbury; and John Dunlop, author of the *Philosophy of Artificial and Compulsory Drinking Usages in Great Britain* (1839). The company's physician was Robert Dundas Thomson, who became the medical officer of health for Marylebone in 1856, first president of the Metropolitan Association of Medical Officers of Health, Fellow of the Royal Society and president of the British Meteorological Society.

The others are all important figures in the early teetotal movement: activists drawn from the ranks of manufacturers and traders, doctors, magistrates and social-working clergymen. Seven of these men, including Warner, were members of the NTS's executive committee from 1844; Theodore Compton acted as secretary to both the NTS and the Association (*National Temperance Chronicle*, 1844, p. 249). Together the officers of the Association represented many different aspects of mid-century temperance and it is clear that this venture was a successful combination of business and political cultures. While it is hard to gauge the effectiveness of the UKT&GPI in promoting temperance and abstinence, it was clearly highly profitable. In 1849 the office's total funds amounted to just over £31,000; by 1854 this sum was more than £114,000; in 1868 over £1.1m; and by 1900 about £7m (*Journal of the Institute of Actuaries*, 1848–1851, p. 260; *Trewman's Exeter Flying Post*, 1857, p. 8; *Birmingham Daily Post*, 1869, p. 5; *Wings*, 1900, p. iv). In 1890 the Institution was the eighth largest life office in Britain, in terms of premium income (Alborn, 2009, p. 27).

By 1904 Thomas Palmer Whittaker, the Institution's managing director, was able to consider 60 years of mortality data. Whittaker, a Liberal MP and the son of a famous temperance activist, concluded that 'during the strenuous years of manhood, from twenty-five to sixty years of age, the annual mortality rates among Abstainers were, on the average, 40 per cent. lower than among the Non-Abstainers' (1903–1904, p. 12). Whittaker was closely involved with the prohibitionists of the United Kingdom Alliance (Fahey, 1971), who dominated British temperance in the second half of the nineteenth century, and who made good use of these figures. As well as proving that drinkers tended to live shorter lives, these figures gave a *positive* dimension to abstinence, self-denial and withdrawal from popular custom.

Governmentality, risk and uncertainty in an era of classic liberalism

Insurance represents one of the key practices for transforming uncertainties into risk through calculating future possibilities. In doing so, these futures become something we must take responsibility for, making insurance a form of governmentality (French and Kneale, 2009). The sociologist Pat O'Malley suggests 'neither risk and uncertainty, nor liberalism, are reducible to the other, but much can be learned from examining their nexus' (2004, p. 32). He divides his account of risk and governmentality into three periods: classical liberalism, welfare liberalism and neo-liberalism. Classical liberalism, which was most influential in the decades covered by this chapter, suggested that:

> subjects were to be exposed to uncertainties. Accordingly, freedom was shaped by attitudes and practices – especially foresight and prudence – that were deemed essential to survive independently in this environment. (ibid. p. 30)

O'Malley describes the ways in which foresight became a technique of the self. Bentham argued that there was a need to create 'the disposition to look forward', and to 'accustom men to submit to the yoke of foresight' (Bentham, 1962, cited by O'Malley, 2004, pp. 31, 32). Thrift and prudence were to become essential attitudes and practices, and these new liberal subjects and regimes were highly 'risk averse'. It is worth pointing out that where later neo-liberals would see uncertainty as liberating (Foucault, 2008), classic liberalism emphasized its hazards. Entrepreneurs were to be a small and select band, 'given special licence and protection', as O'Malley puts it (2004, p. 34).

Life insurance exemplifies this form of prudence. James McKenna, 'Father Mathew's right-hand man' (Harrison, 1973, p. 83) and special agent of the NTS, declared that:

> it is also gratifying to be able to report that the blessing of life assurance is becoming universally appreciated by the temperance people. What a happy period in our history, when *men* of all ranks, aye, and *women* too, shall know not the taste of strong drink, when a provision for all shall have been secured in the '*Temperance Provident Institution*'. Then the widow and the orphan shall have the blessings of plenty in their own home, and old age find security in competence and independence. (1844, p. 259, emphases in original)

Alborn (2009) notes that life insurance offices offered their services as substitute breadwinners, stepping in to care for widows and children; they offered security, in its everyday sense of future domestic prosperity. In this way firms drew upon contrasting geographical imaginations of home and workhouse to encourage prudence.

But if insurance provided a key place in which particular kinds of risks could be identified and their costs calculated, this meant that actuaries had to have a good sense of the health of the applicant. Life assurance risks tended to be health issues, and companies had to decide how to cope with bad risks. They could turn down applicants, as Warner had been turned down for his teetotalism, or they could make them pay by demanding higher premiums, or by 'rating up' – treating the applicant as older than their actual age and charging them accordingly. Many of the health issues that most concerned actuaries were inherited or difficult for the applicant to control, as we will see in a moment. But others reflected the lifestyle and habits of the applicant, and these came under great scrutiny. The Institution transferred policyholders who could not prove that they had kept to their pledge to the General Section, which would result in higher premiums or lower final sums; this might well have acted as additional encouragement for the wavering teetotaller.

It also made good business sense. Companies could guard against bad risks when assessing an applicant (through interviews, a proposal form, references from friends or medical attendants, or a medical examination) or after death (by refusing to pay out where there were suspicions about the reason for mortality). It seems likely that the Association turned to medical referees earlier than other firms because its business depended on an accurate assessment of drinking habits:

> A life insurance office could increase its profits (or the bonus it paid its customers) by extending surveillance over its customers beyond the point of sale. This was in fact the business model for the many late Victorian firms that set up abstinence sections, which penalized customers who fell off the wagon by denying their claims, raising their premiums, or (most commonly) shifting them into a risk pool that paid lower premiums. (Alborn, 2009, p. 223)

It is tempting to see this mix of encouragement and threats as a form of discipline. While McKenna emphasized the possibility of future freedom and independence, others saw thrift and prudence as an obligation. Robert Dundas Thomson, the Institution's medical adviser, presented a striking example of this in 1841:

> It is not to be supposed, that the majority of labouring men can appreciate without instruction the bearing of such a proposition [life assurance]...I propose that servants should be advised to forego the purchase of beer with their daily beer money, and to invest it in a Policy of Insurance, or in a deferred annuity. For example a pint of porter daily will cost about *one shilling* and *one penny* per week. If a man were to commence paying this sum at the age of twenty in weekly payments, he would be entitled at the age of 50 to receive £100. (1841, p. 26, original emphasis)

And in *Thrift* Samuel Smiles insisted that *not* saving was 'heartless and cruel':

> to bring a family into the world, give them refined tastes, and accustom them to comforts, the loss of which is misery, and then to leave the family to the workhouse, the prison, or the street...is nothing short of a crime done against society, as well as against the unfortunate individuals who are the immediate sufferers. (1875, p. 112)

Smiles suggested that insurance was the perfect way to calculate and provide for these hazards, though he recognized that it was essentially a middle and upper-class practice. Working-class friendly societies and co-operatives did not involve calculations of risk on actuarial principles, meaning that they did not reward thrift or identify bad habits in the same way. While this moralizing recalls a long history of concern over drinking and the 'reformation of manners', insurance companies like the Institution represented something slightly different to the Sabbatarian or rational recreation movements.

From the actuarial perspective, the 'laws' of mortality stood beyond morality; the Institution's records showed that teetotallers lived longer, and that meant that they would make more from their life assurance.

Having considered how insurance might have worked to produce independent, responsible selves determined to work on their spending and drinking, we now need to examine the role medicine played in these practices – in assessing applicants and the risks they presented.

Assessing intemperance

Throughout the nineteenth century, alcohol was widely used as medical cure, stimulant and anaesthetic; there was little support for the idea that drunkenness was a disease rather than a moral choice (Berridge, 1990; Woiak, 1994). Partly as a result of this, the relationship between medicine and temperance was strained until the 1870s. Brian Harrison reminds us that some of the mutual suspicion between teetotallers and doctors reflected their rather different class and denominational backgrounds: teetotallers 'were the dissenters of the medical world, threatening its established church – the College of Physicians' (1971, p. 161). As we will see in a moment, many insurers were slow to penalize applicants who drank, an attitude personified in insurance agents like S Dolbey of Leicester, who was both an ale and porter merchant *and* the agent for the Royal Exchange Fire and Life, the Accidental Insurance and the Plate Glass Insurance Companies in the 1870s (Wright, 1884). This goes some of the way towards explaining why Warner was unable to find a company that would insure his teetotal life at a normal premium. His company's principles flew in the face of established wisdom, as Winskill noted (1881, p. 249): 'the medical profession almost to a man was against them, and who were they to set themselves up against such learned authorities?'

Despite its unusual medical beliefs, the UKT&GPI employed medicine much as other life offices did, paying doctors to check the health of applicants for life assurance. In the 1840s prospective policyholders would either travel to a life assurance company's offices in London or Edinburgh, or get their doctor to send in a report. Local doctors began to refuse to do this without payment in the 1850s and, although relations between companies and doctors shifted over the century, both sides benefited from their relationship in establishing the health of prospective applicants. The 14 Scottish Assurance Offices paid for nearly 9000 examinations in 1854, for example, and rejected around 1200 applicants; this cost about £6000 (*Edinburgh Medical Journal*, 1855, pp. 553–4).

Examinations were carried out largely by 'eye, hand and ear – assisted only, in the last case, by the stethoscope' (Alborn 2009, p. 258). Doctors considered physiognomy, looking for signs of intemperance like bloated bodies and blotchy faces, and listened to heart and lungs. Handbooks for medical examiners and advisers began to appear, like the *Treatise on the Medical Estimate of Life for Life Assurance* (*Journal of the Institute of Actuaries*, 1858–1860). This described the process of transforming an applicant into a set of risks:

> The principal circumstances affecting the value of individual lives have reference to sex, age, personal peculiarities, habits, occupation, residence, family history, previous ailments, and present health. These are brought before the medical referee, in the printed forms of examination and inquiry adopted by Life Assurance Societies, in a series of questions calculated to elicit the information required. (p. 248)

Some of these questions were designed to test the honesty of applicants. Discussing intemperance, the *Treatise* had warned that: 'At times, the history, previous ailments, or aspect of the party speak openly as to the existence of such habit; at others, it will require all the tact and powers of observation of the medical referee to detect it.' (p. 252) It advised cautious interrogation of the applicant and his friends. These cross-examinations sought to avoid 'adverse selection' (where people are *more* likely to buy life insurance if they think they might be ill), by underwriting (seeking information that evaluates risk).

However, Alborn notes that tensions began to appear between chief medical advisers, based in the firms' main offices, and local doctors (like Grindrod) paid to examine applicants. Differences of opinion or professional ability, combined with the dangers of personal doctors acting in their patients' interests, led to a degree of standardization in examination procedures, codified in the increasingly elaborate forms designed at the centre and sent out to examiners; 'by instructing or reminding doctors what to look for, medical examiners' forms also *routinized* the exam' (2009, p. 244, original emphasis). Medical advisers at head offices sought certainty through measurements of height, weight, chest capacity and pulse, adding blood pressure and urine tests by the end of the century.

> Although they added these new features at the head office as well, a central motivation for introducing them was to compensate for the problem of transmitting incommunicable knowledge at a distance. (ibid. p. 261)

Apart from the last two tests the examination was easy to carry out and unlikely to offend applicants.

The formation of the Life Assurance Medical Officers' Association in 1893 also allowed the development of a consensus over the examination, especially through its *Transactions* journal. Returning to the head office, this information could be considered against mortality and other risk factors. Many companies were concerned enough about drinking to include questions about it on their forms in the middle of the century (Alborn, 2009, p. 225).

This kind of work suggests both objectivity and accuracy, and the close connections between the Institute of Actuaries, Statistical Society of London and the London Epidemiological Society, based on their shared interest in vital statistics and quantitative analysis, promised both a good deal of useful data and the development of methods by which risks could be identified (Lilienfeld and Lilienfeld, 1980). But did the collection of comparative data on drinkers and abstainers represent the 'most comprehensive and exact source of information' available, as the American writer Eugene Lyman Fisk suggested (1917, p. 9)? Many actuaries and medical professionals were more cautious.

Rating and defining intemperance

There were three key problems associated with the information that companies did receive: problems with producing, presenting and using data; questions of calculation (how to rate 'impaired' lives, like those of the intemperate); and disagreements over definitions.

Firstly, actuarial data had to be in a form that doctors could use, and medical information had to be translated for actuaries. A review of the 45th annual report of the Trustees of the Mutual Life Insurance Company of New York concluded:

> It is very much to be regretted that so little use is made of the valuable information which life offices accumulate, especially as to relative mortality of trades and professions. The medical reports, if drawn up on a good plan, and containing statistics compiled on a uniform system, would be very valuable; unfortunately, the medical report before us is so insufficiently compiled as to be absolutely worthless. (*British Medical Journal*, 1888, p. 823)

Medical advisers and professional bodies, like the Institute of Actuaries and its Scottish equivalent the Faculty of Actuaries, were actively engaged in this translation work, through the *Journal of the Institute of Actuaries* and allied publications like *The Transactions of the Life Assurance Medical Officers Association*.

Secondly, how should impaired lives be rated, and could it ever be accurate enough? Some companies were willing to take the risk, but an anonymous review concluded:

> Still the data on which they may found their rates are very defective; and we fear it will be a long time before the experience of

such Offices, in itself, will be sufficiently extensive to enable a fair premium to be paid for every life. (*Journal of the Institute of Actuaries*, 1853–4, pp. 76–8)

Despite this, George Humphreys, actuary to the Eagle Company, investigated the practice of 'assuring unsound lives at an increased rate of premium' (Humphreys, 1875, p. 178). He found that financially the strategy worked, but that 'a great many of the lives had died from causes quite irrespective of the disease for which the addition was originally made' (p. 188). Of the 37 lives who had originally been rated up for intemperance, for example, 11 died of respiratory diseases, seven from liver disease, five from diseases of the nervous system, and so on. None of the 37 died of intemperance as such (p. 187). The Scottish actuary James MacFadyen suggested that, while discussion of this issue 'might not lead to scientific accuracy of treatment, [it] would at least help to bring out clearly the true difficulties of the matter, and perhaps in time might lead to *less diversity of practice*' (Humphreys, 1875, p. 190, emphasis added). This diversity was also visible in a survey of 66 US life offices in the 1890s, which identified at least *nine* different strategies for rejecting, rating up or otherwise disciplining applicants who drank (Woolley and Johnson, 1903, p. 386).

This leads to the third problem with this data – questions of definition. Humphreys was not alone in being unable to define problem drinking, and Kerr called for 'the general acceptance of a workable definition of intemperance, the practice of insurance medical examiners presenting striking contrasts' (*Proceedings of the Society for the Suppression of Intemperance*, 1893, p. 14). H W Porter's review of mortality data from two companies in 1853–1854 made it clear that they did not agree on their definitions of causes of death. Intemperance was returned as both 'delirium tremens' and 'drunkenness', though 'deaths under these heads are mostly from the same cause', reflecting ongoing debates about the nature of alcoholism and drink-related illness (1853–1854, pp. 257, 258). There were other problems: Kerr pointed out that many death certificates did not mention drinking, as medical attendants preferred to avoid any scandal (1882, p. 566).

George Humphreys' discussion of impaired lives also explored this issue, drawing up seven broad headings, one for each major 'cause of addition': 'gout; hernia; affections of the organs of circulation; affections of the organs of respiration; obesity; intemperate habits' and 'family history, or general want of robustness' (Humphreys, 1875, p. 179). However, Humphreys then had to add 'miscellaneous afflictions' to the list, which became by far the biggest category, accounting for a third of all 'impaired lives' considered. 'Intemperate habits' accounted for less than 5 per cent of the total (pp. 179, 181).

For many actuaries and doctors, assessing intemperance was a difficult business; Alborn notes that the difficulty of assessing applicants' habits made it one of the key reasons for legal disputes over claims (2009, p. 236). This undermines the argument that life assurance represented a carefully calculating form of discipline. Constructions of alcohol produced between medicine and insurance seem to work best for populations – the total number of lives assured – rather than for individual policyholders. In this sense it is important to consider insurance as a form of security and to think about its geographies.

Geographies of the Temperance and General Provident

If we shift our attention away from the individual policyholder we begin to see a rather different picture. The life office was more interested in managing a *population of insured lives*. While the two sections of the Institution's life table seem to enforce a disciplinary division of 'healthy' and 'sick', because actuaries drew upon mortality figures for much larger national populations, they approached mortality as a series of graphed distributions, or what Foucault referred to as 'different curves of normality'. If the Institution sought to use insurance to counter intemperance then it was through comparison of the curves for moderate drinkers and abstainers that could be plotted from mortality statistics. Much like the state that supports market forces, the Institution was interested in 'finding support in the reality of the phenomenon' – in this case, drinking – 'and instead of trying to prevent it, making other elements of reality function in such a way that the phenomenon is cancelled out' (Foucault, 2007, p. 59). So while the Institution's figures were very useful to the UK Alliance, they suggested a much less direct approach to intemperance than the prohibitionists' 'juridico-disciplinary' form of regulation. However, Foucault's outline of this form of bio-power is closely connected to the state and to territory, because it is the sovereign who manages its population in a discrete space, examining and working upon particular distributions and circulations of people and things; there are 'differential risks' that show 'zones' of higher and lower risk, which 'means that one can thus identify what is dangerous' (p. 61).

Unlike the sovereign, though, the Institution had no particular interest in territory. In fact actuaries were, on the whole, uninterested in the location of those who applied for life assurance (with the exception of those who would be travelling abroad). It was vitally important for the Institute that the lives in the abstainers' and general sections were identical in every way, because this meant that only alcohol could explain the different mortality rates. This extended to residential location, as Thomas Whittaker pointed out: 'they live in the same towns, often in the same streets, and have similar incomes'

(1903–1904, p. 19). The availability and authority of mortality statistics, from John Graunt's 1662 'Natural and Political Observations Made upon the Bills of Mortality' through to the establishment of the General Register Office, meant that zones of risk were related to the applicant's age first of all, and then to their habits and health as discussed above.

The search for 'universal laws' of mortality in the middle of the nineteenth century sought to transcend questions of location. However, the search for these universals had to start somewhere, with local mortality data, and actuarial principles were initially calculated from London's mortality statistics. Concerns that the capital was demographically unusual led to a search for healthier towns that might stand in for Britain as a whole. The Carlisle and Northampton tables were meant to represent the norm, even while their names drew attention to their geographical specificity. While tables based on the shared evidence of 17 offices were published in 1843, it was still thought necessary to divide lives into 'Town', 'Country' and 'Irish' (Evans, 1997, p. 32).

In this respect there was little explicit interest in territory, even though life offices acted as centres of calculation and considered the lives they insured much as sovereigns approached their populations. However, today geography, usually in the form of postcodes, is increasingly explicitly used as one of many devices for the calculation of more individualized premiums, in keeping with a shift toward a model of 'privatized' rather than 'socialized' actuarialism (French and Kneale, 2012). This seems to be a fairly recent innovation in life assurance, unlike other forms of fire, contents, or buildings insurance, which have long used location as a proxy for risk. Location became even less important in the era of welfare (or national) insurance, because all citizens were in effect insured by the state. Alborn notes 'a defining paradox of insurance when it is provided by the private sector: an equalitarian state will likely exercise less, not more, surveillance than a smaller enclave within the state that seeks to maximize returns for its members' (2009, p. 248).

Yet these populations *did* occupy specific spaces and company life tables reflected the insured population and the distribution of offices, branches and salesmen. In the second half of the nineteenth century, life offices looked to the provinces for new policies, seeking to tap into markets spatially and socially distant from the main centres of London and Edinburgh. The Association's 1840 prospectus shows that sales representatives and medical referees were anything but evenly spread (see Map 1).

Comparing this map to the 1841 Census we can see that 45 of the 79 largest cities in England, Scotland and Wales were not covered by the Association. Birmingham was the largest city without an agent, but Plymouth, Sheffield, Nottingham and Preston were also cut off (respectively the fourth, seventh, eighth, 11th and 13th largest settlements in England; Census of Great

Map 1   Total abstinence life association agents and referees, 1840, drawn from United Kingdom Total Abstinence Life Association (1840b)

Britain 1841/1843, p. 10). The distribution by county is also highly uneven. Lincolnshire was blessed with 13.6 per cent of the Association's agents but contained only 2.1 per cent of the population of England. The West of England (Cornwall, Devon, Somerset and Dorset) contained 18.8 per cent of the agents but only 10 per cent of the English population; Yorkshire, which had a population of a similar size, had only 5.8 per cent of the Association's agents (Census of Great Britain 1841/1843, p. 8).

This pattern could reflect temperance strengths or weaknesses. If agents were placed where there were many abstainers, and therefore many potential policyholders, then this map reflects the core areas of temperance support. But this seems doubtful; Harrison's study of leading teetotallers indicates that about a quarter were born in Lancashire and Yorkshire, for example (1971, p. 148). Lancashire was under-represented in terms of Association agents (7.2 per cent but 11.12 per cent of the population) but was home to 28 per cent of the British and Foreign Temperance Society's (B&FTS) membership in 1834 – which seems odd, given the close link between the B&FTS and the Association (1971, p. 109). It seems more likely that, while some areas were already temperance centres – the West Country, for example – others represented targets for proselytizing and sales, with these agents acting as pioneers in rural areas considered 'backwards' by the movement. Harrison notes that 'by 1834 the teetotal message had not yet reached Wales, Northumberland and Lincolnshire; these areas later featured more prominently in the movement' (1971, p. 109; and see Vieira Paisana, 2002). Later on 'the expanding frontier [of temperance] lay in the town' and it does seem as if the UKT&GPI shifted its emphasis to urban populations, partly as a result of the development of district offices in major cities like Leeds and Manchester (Harrison, 1971, p. 149). The population that might be recruited by these agents had a very definite geography, then, belying attempts to produce a universal set of risks.

Studying trade directories shows that this network of agents developed very unevenly. While some of the agents intended for Lincolnshire towns do not seem to have taken root, there were agents in Horncastle, Lincoln and Louth at some point between 1850 and 1900. More importantly there were also agents in towns not listed in the 1840 prospectus: Boston, Bourn, Dogdyke, Epworth, Grantham, Grimsby, Holbeach, Long Sutton and Market Rasen. Some of these market towns were tiny – Dogdyke's population was 248 in 1871 – but temperance insurance seems to have been more popular in Lincolnshire than in Buckinghamshire or Kent. Bath had a succession of three agents from 1842 until the 1870s, while many other cities, like Norwich, did not have an agent until the main office appointed a district superintendent there in the 1860s.

These geographies were uneven for many different reasons, and further research will be needed before we can find explanations for these patterns.

The Association's population of insured lives was a population of abstainers, at least in 1840, and therefore rather different to the rest of the country. Its concentration in particular towns and cities reflected the strengths and the weaknesses of local temperance support, though the rural character of large parts of this network might have been a deliberate strategy to find abstainers and moderate drinkers in the firm's first years. After 1840 some areas seem to have become more popular, while many others ceased to have any connections to the company. While the lives insured in the temperance section must have always represented a good risk, those in the General Section were a much more mixed bunch.

Conclusions

In conclusion, the relationship between medicinal and insurantial knowledges and practices seems to have been highly productive in terms of nineteenth and early twentieth-century encounters with alcohol. Alcohol was enacted into being by actuaries, doctors and policyholders, and companies like the Institution provided both proof of the dangers of alcohol and a way of inculcating better health and a prudent outlook. The difficulty of assessing intemperance led to more extensive examinations and questioning at the point of sale, driven by the fears of those at the head office. Despite these efforts, actuaries worried that accurately rating or dealing with intemperance was hard to do – though some firms believed that they were at least still making money out of it, probably because they were extraordinarily conservative in their calculations. Life assurance might also have worked as more than a simple disciplinary technology; in its production of a population of insured lives and calculation of different curves of normality it resembles apparatuses of security.

This material allows us to consider a different set of spaces in which alcohol became known as a risk, where different kinds of drinkers were considered and created by actors other than the police and judiciary. The insurance business had its own geographies, which shaped the production of these knowledges. Though the lives insured by the Institution would always be different to the wider population because so many of them were abstainers, geography became even more important because of the uneven distribution of agents and lives. Mortality statistics and calculations took shape *between* these points and the central office in London, but these tensions must have co-existed with the ordinary day-to-day medical practice of doctors going about their business of assessing applicants.

Crucially, though, this kind of medical engagement with alcohol was an ordinary affair (cf. Mcfall, 2009). In 1872 Dr Dickinson, of St George's Hospital, published his investigation of the effects of heavy drinking in the

BMJ. Dickinson's study was based on post-mortems of nearly 300 subjects, half of whom had been employed in the liquor trade while the other half had not, and suggested that there little difference between the two groups in terms of kidney disease and effects on other organs (Dickinson, 1872). An anonymous response suggested that:

> the best field for observing the morbid effects of alcohol is neither the *post mortem* theatre nor the hospital ward, but the daily round of private practice, where, the reticence of the patient being supplemented by the candour of his friends, habits of intemperance can rarely be concealed from the medical attendant. (*British Medical Journal*, 1872, p. 584)

Dickinson's response, and the rather bad-tempered debate that followed, concentrated on questions of research method and calculation, particularly the difficulty of making intemperance visible.

This reminds us of the need to investigate the unsensational ways in which medicine and alcohol came together; to remember Dr Grindrod's work for the Total Abstinence Association as well as his temperance lectures. We would like to suggest that, while this work was not spectacular, it was still important in the way that it fed into debates about alcohol and medicine, and, in its own way, remained quite controversial into the early twentieth century.

Acknowledgments

Shaun French would like to acknowledge the assistance of the British Academy (grant number SG090467) in the preparation of this chapter. Our thanks to Catherine D'Alton and Miles Irving of University College London Geography Drawing Office for producing the map, to David Raymont, librarian at the library of the Institute and Faculty of Actuaries in London, for indispensable assistance in the archives, and to the participants – particularly Phil Withington and the other organizers – of the Cambridge Socio-Legal Group meeting on Intoxicants held in March 2011.

Bibliography

Alborn, T (2001) 'Insurance Against Germ Theory: Commerce and Conservatism in Late-Victorian Medicine' 75 *Bulletin of the History of Medicine* 406–45

Alborn, T (2009) *Regulated Lives: Life Assurance and British Society, 1800–1914* (Toronto: University of Toronto Press)

Bentham, J (1962) *The Works of Jeremy Bentham* vol. 1, J Bowring (ed.) (New York: Russell & Russell)

Berridge, V (1977) 'Opium Eating and Life Insurance' **72** *British Journal of Addiction* 371–7

Berridge, V (1990) 'The Society for the Study of Addiction 1884–1988' **85** *British Journal of Addiction* 983–1087

Bingham, W J P (1922) *Alcohol and Life Assurance* (London: United Kingdom Alliance)

Birmingham Daily Post (1869) 'Commercial and Monetary. From our City Correspondent', 26 May, p. 5

British Medical Journal (1872) 'The Morbid Effects of Alcohol' **2** *BMJ* 583–4

British Medical Journal (1888) 'Notes on Books' **2** *BMJ* 823

Burchell, G, C Gordon and P Miller (eds) (1991) *The Foucault Effect: Studies in Governmentality* (Hemel Hempstead: Harvester Wheatsheaf)

Census of Great Britain (1841), *Abstract of The Answers and Returns Made Pursuant to Acts 3 & 4 Vic. c.99 and 4 Vic. c.7 Intituled Respectively "An Act for Taking an Account of the Population of Great Britain," and "An Act to Amend the Acts of the Last Session for Taking an Account of the Population."* Enumeration Abstract. BPP 1843 XXII (496)

Dickinson, W H (1872) 'Alcohol as a Cause of Renal Disease' 2(621) *BMJ* 573–5

Dunlop, J (1839) *The Philosophy of Artificial and Compulsory Drinking Usages in Great Britain* (London: Houlston & Stoneman)

Edinburgh Medical Journal (1855) 'Statistics. Medical Examinations in Scotland for Life Assurance Companies' **1** *Edinburgh Medical Journal* 553–4

Evans, J (1997) 'Mortality, Behold and Fear' in D Renn (ed.), *Life, Death and Money* (Oxford: Blackwell)

Fahey, D M (1971) 'Temperance and the Liberal Party – Lord Peel's Report, 1899' **10** *The Journal of British Studies* 132–59

Fisk, E L (1917) *Alcohol: Its Relation to Human Efficiency and Longevity* (New York: Funk & Wagnalls)

Foucault, M (2007) *Security, Territory, Population: Lectures at the Collège de France 1977–1978* (Basingstoke: Palgrave Macmillan)

Foucault, M (2008) *The Birth of Biopolitics: Lectures at the Collège de France 1978–1979* (Basingstoke: Palgrave Macmillan)

French, S (2002) 'Gamekeepers and Gamekeeping: Assuring Bristol's Place Within Life Underwriting' **34** *Environment & Planning A* 513–41

French, S and J Kneale (2009) 'Excessive Financialisation: Insuring Lifestyles, Enlivening Subjects, and Everyday Spaces of Biosocial Excess' **27** *Environment & Planning D: Society & Space* 1030–53

French, S and J Kneale (2012) 'Speculating on Careless Lives: Annuitising the Biofinancial Subject' **5** *Journal of Cultural Economy*

Graunt, J (1662) 'Natural and Political Observations Made upon the Bills of Mortality', reprinted by the Institute of Actuaries (1964) **90** *Journal of the Institute of Actuaries* 1–61

Grierson, J (2001) *Temperance, Therapy and Trilobites: Dr Ralph Grindrod, Victorian Pioneer* (Malvern: Cora Weaver)

Harrison, B (1971) *Drink and the Victorians* (London: Faber)

Harrison, B (1973) *Dictionary of British Temperance Biography* (Sheffield: Society for the Study of Labour History)

Humphreys, G (1875) 'On the Practice of the Eagle Company with Regard to the Assurance of Lives Classed As Unsound, and on the Rates of Mortality Prevailing Amongst the Lives Classed, Assured During the Sixty-Three Years Ending 30 June 1871' **18** *Journal of the Institute of Actuaries* 178–95

Journal Of The Institute Of Actuaries (1848–1851) 'Reports Of Assurance Companies' **1** *Journal Of The Institute Of Actuaries* 245–62

Journal of the Institute of Actuaries (1853–1854) 'Review of *An Investigation of the Deaths in the Standard Assurance Company* by Dr Robert Christison and *Medical Statistics of Life Assurance – Observations on the Causes of Death among the Assured of the Scottish Widows' Fund and Life Assurance Society, from 1846 to 1852* by Dr James Begbie' **4** *Journal of the Institute of Actuaries* 76–8

Journal of the Institute of Actuaries (1858–60) 'Treatise on the Medical Estimate of Life for Life Assurance' **8** *Journal of the Institute of Actuaries* 248–63

Jureidini, R and K White (2000) 'Life Insurance, the Medical Examination and Cultural Values' **13** *Journal of Historical Sociology* 190–214

Kerr, N (1882) 'The Public Medicine Aspects of the Alcohol Question' **2**(1134) *BMJ* 565

Kneale, J (2001) 'The Place of Drink: Temperance and the Public' **2** *Social & Cultural Geography* 43–59

Latour, B (1993) *We Have Never Been Modern*, C Porter (trans.) (Cambridge MA: Harvard University Press)

Law Commission (2006a) *Insurance Contract Law: A Joint Scoping Paper* available at www.lawcom.gov.uk/insurance_contract.htm

Law Commission (2006b) *Insurance Contract Law Issues Paper 1: Misrepresentation and Non-Disclosure*, available at www.justice.gov.uk/lawcommission/docs /ICL1_Misrepresentation_and_Non-disclosure.pdf

Law, J and V Singleton (2005) 'Object Lessons' **12** *Organization* 331–55

Lilienfeld, A M and D Lilienfeld (1980) 'The 1979 Heath Clark Lectures: The Epidemiologic Fabric II: The London Bridge – It Never Fell' **9** *International Journal of Epidemiology* 299–304

MacFie, C (1899) 'On The Duty of the Profession with Regard To Alcohol' *BMJ* 194–200, 22 July

McKenna, J (1844) 'Agents' Reports. James McKenna – Lancashire. Special Agent', *National Temperance Chronicle*, 16 October, p. 259

Mcfall, L (2009) 'The Agencement of Industrial Branch Life Assurance' **2** *Journal of Cultural Economy* 49 – 65

Minutes of the Proceedings of the Institution of Civil Engineers (1897) 'Obituary of Robert Warner', 128, pp. 363–4

National Temperance Chronicle (1844) 'Executive Committee', 16 October, p. 249

O'Malley, P (2004) *Risk, Uncertainty and Government* (London: Glasshouse Press)

Porter, H W (1853–1854) 'Medical Statistics of Life Assurance Companies: To the Editor of the Assurance Magazine' 4 *Journal of the Institute of Actuaries* 256–61

Proceedings of the Society for the Suppression of Intemperance (1893) 'Inebriety and Insurance', 12–14 February, p. 35

Smiles, S (1875) *Thrift* (London: John Murray)

Temperance and Life Assurance Company of North America (1884) 'Temperance, Longevity, Insurance. A Tract For The Times', pamphlet published at the office of the *Canada Citizen*, Toronto

Thomson, R D (1841) *Digestion: The Influence of Alcoholic Fluids on that Function, and on the Value of Health and Life. With a Scheme for Rendering the Working Classes Independent of Parish Relief* (London: John Snow)

Trewman's Exeter Flying Post (1857), advertisement for United Kingdom Temperance and General Provident Institution, 29 October, p. 8

United Kingdom Total Abstinence Life Association (1840a) 'Prospectus of the United Kingdom Total Abstinence Life Association' (London: volume of prospectuses of Assurance Societies sent by the Clerical, Medical and General Life Assurance Society R826-G)

United Kingdom Total Abstinence Life Association (1840b) 'The United Kingdom Total Abstinence Life Association' (London: volume of prospectuses of Assurance Societies sent by the Clerical, Medical and General Life Assurance Society R826-G)

Valverde, M (1998) *Diseases of the Will: Alcohol and the Dilemmas of Freedom* (Cambridge: Cambridge University Press)

Vieira Paisana, J M (2002) *Tipplers, Drunkards and Backsliders: The Temperance Movement in England 1830–72, Including a Case Study of Lincoln*, unpublished PhD thesis, Universidade do Minho, Braga

Warner, R and B Williams (1862–1875) *Select Orchidaceous Plants, with Notes on Their Culture by Benjamin S Williams*, 2 vols (London: Lovell Reeve)

Whittaker, T P (1903–1904) 'Alcoholic Beverages and Longevity', collected in *Institute of Actuaries Life Assurance Tracts* XIII

Wings (1900), advertisement for United Kingdom Temperance and General Provident Institution, 1 August, 8, p. iv

Winskill, P T (1881) *The Comprehensive History of the Rise and Progress of the Temperance Reformation from the Earliest Period to September 1881* (Warrington: P T Winskill)

Winskill, P T (1891) *The Temperance Movement and its Workers: A Record of Social, Moral, Religious, and Political Progress, with an Introduction by F R Lees* vol. 2 (London: Blackie)

Withers, H (1951) *Pioneers of British Life Assurance*, C Nicholas (ed.) (London and New York: Staples Press)

Woiak, J (1994) '"A Medical Cromwell to Depose King Alcohol": Medical Scientists, Temperance Reformers, and the Alcohol Problem in Britain' **54** *Social History* 337–65

Woolley, J G and W E Johnson (1903) *Temperance Progress in the Century* (London and Philadelphia: Linscott)

Wright, C N (1884), advertisement for United Kingdom Temperance and General Provident Institution, *Commercial and General Directory of Leicester and Fifteen Miles Round, including the Towns of Loughborough, Hinckley, Melton, and Market Harborough*, 1883–84 (Leicester: C N Wright)

Legislation

Life Assurance Act 1774
Marine Insurance Act 1906

6
Alehouse Licensing and State Formation in Early Modern England

James Brown

Introduction

Unlike other commodities intoxicants are 'almost universally subject to rules and regulations', and a blizzard of lawmaking surrounded the inns, taverns and alehouses of early modern England (Wilson, 2005, p. 6). The processes by which Tudor and Stuart polities attempted to legislatively come to grips with drinking houses via stacks of centrally issued Acts, statutes, proclamations and other national directives has a long historiographical pedigree. Initiated by the Webbs in their 1903 opus *The History of Liquor Licensing in England*, the narrative has subsequently been placed on a sounder empirical footing by Peter Clark for alehouses and, more recently, painstakingly reconstructed by Judith Hunter for all types of public drinking place (Webb and Webb, 1903; Roberts, 1980; Clark, 1983; Hunter, 1994; 2002; Brandwood et al., 2004, pp. 6–8). We now have a generally agreed picture of legislative refinement with the 1552 Licensing Act; a renewed flurry of activity under the early Stuarts (with four Acts passed in the first decade of the 1600s alone); consolidation during the 1620s and 1630s; few legislative innovations during the civil wars; and a renewed phase of legislation during the 1650s. Yet, while the contours and motivations of national policy and the steady march of centrally articulated laws and powers are now clear for the English case, we know far less about the nuts and bolts of regulatory regimes locally, especially below the level of the county. Indeed, historians of drinking have generally narrowed their spatial and conceptual horizons to the view from Whitehall, and have accordingly tended to prioritize the role of central agencies in the formulation and implementation of drink-related policy projects; a 'high politics' of alcohol, in James Nicholls' phrase (Nicholls, 2009, p. 2). With the important exception of a seminal early article by Keith Wrightson

(Wrightson, 1981) – a rural case study which opened up a vital perspective that has not been applied rigorously to other contexts by later work – where historians have linked these projects to broader processes of state formation, it has usually been within classical, Eltonian paradigms: the elaboration of standardized national licensing programmes, directed from the centre, is seen as an attribute of the linear evolution of a centripetal territorial state (for example, von Stürler, 1975; Kümin, 2007, pp. 74–5).

By means of a case study of the regulation of one type of drinking house (alehouses) in one type of community (the port town of Southampton), and building on Wrightson's earlier contribution, this article seeks to demonstrate that the extremely close and important relationship between drink and state formation can only be properly appreciated if we extend our perspective beyond Westminster and look as well to the administrative micro-sociologies through which drinking policy was filtered on the ground. The importance of local agents and instruments to early modern governance has been a frequent refrain in recent characterizations of sixteenth- and seventeenth-century English polity. The work of Mike Braddick and Steve Hindle in particular has shown how the authority to govern in early modern England was widely distributed both geographically and socially, penetrating horizontally across space and vertically through the social order (Braddick, 1991; 2000; Hindle, 2000). According to Hindle:

> [t]he institutions and individuals through which authority was mediated... were dispersed in the sense of both physical distance and social status. In practice, this meant that those individual officers who exercised authority in parish and township, many of them living in communities over which they exercised authority, were representatives of the state. (Hindle, 2000, p. 20)

In turn, state formation is not something which unfolded centrally, but rather was both the medium and the outcome of complex processes of dialogue between dispersed social and political communities, processes which were particularly intense at the community level. As Hindle describes it, building on Braddick's earlier insight:

> parliamentary legislation, conciliar order, or royal proclamation were not the end of the law-making process but merely its beginning... The structures of authority were elastic, multi-lateral and had both geographical extent and social depth, and the negotiation of authority at highly localised levels was therefore inherent in the process of state formation. From this perspective, state formation is less a matter of centralisation than of the social dynamics consequent upon the localisation of state power. (Hindle, 2000, p. 20; Braddick, 1991)

It is this definition of state formation and these dynamics as they criss-crossed around alehouses with which this chapter is concerned. I will argue, in particular, that the regulation and specifically licensing of alehouses was a vital (in Southampton, the foremost) *topoi* or pretext around which central–local and local–local identities and relationships were expressed and reshaped in this important period of transition and restructuring.

Firstly, some caveats. The article looks only at a single urban community (an incorporated port characterized by some extremely distinctive topographical and political arrangements), and says nothing about other varieties of town or the experiences of villages and the countryside. However, there remains a need to 'make the space in question precise' (Foucault, 1980, p. 68), and the intention is to emphasize the emplaced and localized character of the regulation of drink in this period as well as to make claims about typicality. It also looks exclusively at alehouses, specifically their licensing; other regulative priorities and strategies are not discussed, nor is the licensing of taverns and inns, which was dominated to a far greater extent by the central state, and involved a very different set of motivations, personnel and relationships. The argument unfolds in four parts. Section one sketches some important geographical, institutional and administrative contexts. Section two looks at licensing regimes in action, paying particular attention to a *cause célèbre* surrounding alehouses which captured Southampton imaginations at the turn of the seventeenth century. Section three looks in more detail at the strategies and motivations of the protagonists in the dispute. The article concludes by suggesting that, if we understand state formation as consisting largely of the working out of distributed sets of relations within the early modern English polity, then alehouses had a much more significant role as a motor of these processes than has been previously acknowledged.

Geographical, institutional and administrative contexts

Our setting is the port town and incorporated borough on the English south coast. Southampton seems an unlikely case study for the drink historian. It had relatively few permanent inhabitants (its resident population in 1596 is placed by an adjusted census at just 4200, half that of a major provincial centre such as York) (Taylor, 1980, pp. 196–7), and for most of the early modern period it would seem confined to the parallelogram described by its medieval walls. However, this is an optical illusion. As a busy continental port, Southampton experienced a constant flow of mariners, soldiers and merchants. This mobile population encouraged a flourishing infrastructure of commercial hospitality – alehouses, taverns and inns – that belied its intimate spatial and demographic dimensions. As early as 1531, the governing corporation complained that 'every other house is a brewer or tapper [retailer]'

(Merson, 1952, p. 44), while by the turn of the seventeenth century there was one public house for every 11 household heads (Brown, 2008, p. 28). Good survival across various categories of sources for the period around 1620 has enabled a partial cartographic recovery of this distinctive landscape of drink (Map 1): there three licensed wine taverns and eight fully privileged inns are show in cross-matched black and 42 alehouses (of around 60 in total that were trading at this point) are depicted in grey. All three kinds of drinking establishment were made targets of central government regulation at various stages of their early modern careers. Taverns had formally to be licensed from a freestanding Act of 1553 (a centrally handled but inefficient enterprise overseen by a succession of avaricious royal favourites), while even innkeepers were briefly compelled to obtain licences under the provisions of an ill-fated and deeply unpopular scheme devised by the monopolist Sir Giles Mompesson and implemented between 1617 and 1621, when it was declared illegal and repealed by Parliament (Hunter, 2002, pp. 70–3). However, of all drinking establishments it was alehouses which were viewed with most trepidation by Westminster and, unlike the other two varieties of drinking place, were systematically targeted by central legislation throughout the early modern period.

Alehouses, also known as tippling houses, represented the broad base of early modern England's victualing pyramid (Clark, 1983). They were operated from ordinary dwelling houses, offered a basic range of consumption options and overnight accommodation and were run 'by the poor for the poor'. They also aroused intense political anxieties in national governors. While a core of legitimate hospitality functions were always acknowledged, they were increasingly regarded as places 'where petty crime was planned, stolen goods were received, prostitution was organised, idle political talk went unchecked, riot might be contemplated; a place where violence, which so easily accompanied the effects of drink, was common' (Fletcher, 1996, p. 230. See also Clark, 1978; Wrightson, 1981). Underpinning this was a wider religious attack on public drunkenness and idleness, increasingly condemned from both pulpit and in print with the spread of the Reformation, which fixed on the growing number of alehouses as both primary cause of and synecdoche for the problem (Nicholls, 2009, pp. 5–20).

This growing sense of the alehouse as a threat to public order and morality informed a profound desire to regulate, and alehouse licensing, a complex and enduring project initiated by the Licensing Act of 1552, formed the cornerstone of this ambitious effort (1552, 5/6 Edward VI c. 25). Although partially predicated on economic impulses, the Act was first and foremost a carefully engineered piece of social discipline designed to reduce the 'intolerable hurts and troubles...through such abuses and disorders as are had and used in common alehouses and tippling houses'. Stipulating the licensing of

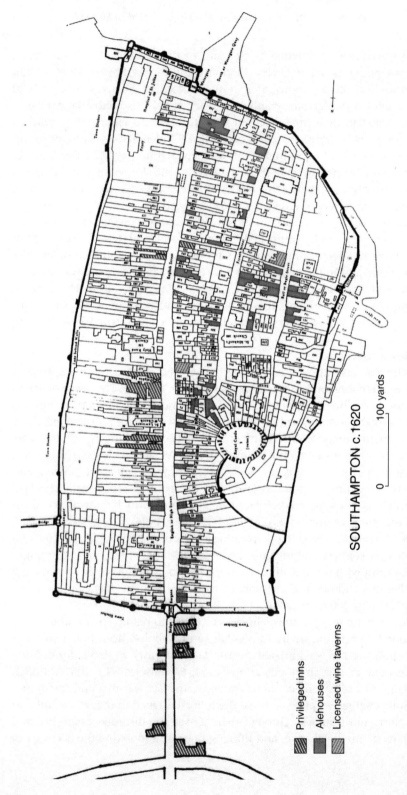

SOUTHAMPTON c.1620

0   100 yards

Privileged inns

Alehouses

Licensed wine taverns

Map 1: Southampton c. 1620 showing the positions of taverns, inns and alehouses

individuals rather than premises (who would be 'bound by recognizance'), it was designed to arrest the microbe-like proliferation of alehouses within local communities; to ensure that only suitable individuals might be authorized to trade; that sureties could be taken to guarantee effective governance over a wide range of criteria; and to enable the revoking of retail privileges and the suppression of disorderly houses (powers which had been in place since 1494). The Act was refined and expanded by several additional proclamations, privy council orders and locally generated bye-laws in the later decades of the sixteenth century, while there was another burst of statutory rigour in the Jacobean period, which saw the passing of four new Acts – in 1603, 1606 and 1609 – and the release of an exhaustively detailed proclamation on 19 January 1619, which clarified several issues and represented an important codification of law and practice (1603, 1 James I c. 9; 1606, 4 James I c. 4; 1606, 4 James I c. 5; 1609, 7 James I c. 10). In characteristic fashion, the authority to license alehouses was delegated from the first Act to local agents in the form of county Justices of the Peace (JPs); licences could only be granted at quarter sessions or by two magistrates acting together out of sessions, while JPs were only to grant as many licences as they thought 'convenient' for their locality. This effectively locked local elites 'into a national system of control…reinforcing politically unifying points of contact between central and local government while identifying an internal threat to national stability' (Nicholls, 2009, p. 11).

In Southampton, the unique arrangement and concentration of offices arising from borough status gave the common council – an oligarchic, self-perpetuating group of 12, drawn exclusively from the mercantile elite – almost complete authority over the regulation of alehouses within the urban domain and its rural hinterland. In their capacity as JPs, they presided over the town's own quarter sessions, held in the Guildhall over the Bargate, which was technically the main judicial instrument for the dissemination of newly minted alehouse legislation to parish officers; the taking of recognizances and issuing of licences; and the prosecution of alehouse-keepers who retailed without licence or who suffered other disorders in their houses. However, in Southampton, the sessions was divested of many of its usual functions, and seems 'regularly to have exercised only that of taking the recognizances of alehouse-keepers'. Instead, the close relationship between the quarter sessions and the common council 'contributed to a pattern of administration in the assembly that largely superseded other channels' (Connor, 1978, pp. 10–15). The assembly, weekly meetings of the aldermanic common council which took place in a specially constructed Audit House built into the High Street, consolidated a wide variety of administrative and judicial business on a summary or petty sessional basis. Alehouses often fell within its more flexible remit: it enforced assize orders; prosecuted drunkenness; conferred and withdrew alehouse licences on a rolling *ad hoc* basis; and served as the fore-most mechanism for the recording and oral transmission of central legislation relating to alehouses. On 21 March 1607, for example, three days after they arrived by messenger, the assembly read out both of James I's statutes of the previous year to the constables so they could 'warn the tipplers' and pasted 'a copy of the king's...letter to the mayor and justices of this town' into the relevant Assembly Book (Horrocks, 1917, pp. 55–60).

As elsewhere, participation in the processes of government was not the preserve of Southampton's social elites, and magistrates operating through the quarter sessions and the assembly were supported in their activities by the court leet, the borough's only judicial body not composed exclusively of council members (Withington, 2005). The court leet, an ancient mano-rial jurisdiction originally designed to detect agricultural defects, func-tioned through the presentments of 12 sworn jurors, drawn squarely from the middling sort, heard at an annual 'law day' held on the fourth Tuesday after Easter in a wooded clearing to the north of the town (Hearnshaw and Hearnshaw, 1908; Bailey, 2002, pp. 178–92; French, 2007). These local tribu-nals, staffed by prosperous urban yeomen and craftsmen and modest prop-erty-holders, are typically seen as having been eclipsed by higher jurisdic-tions, especially quarter sessions and the church courts, by the later decades of the sixteenth century (for example, Braddick, 2000, pp. 137–8). However, a growing body of work is emphasizing that in many areas they continued to offer 'local, inexpensive, and neighbourly justice' to early modern people well into the 1600s (King, 1980a; 1980b; 1982; McIntosh, 1984; King, 1990; Shoemaker, 1991, pp. 21–2; McIntosh, 1998; Hindle, 1999, pp. 837–8). Southampton was one such case. Its leet jurors presented on a wide range of civil and non-felonious 'nuisance' misdemeanours, supervising ditches, highways and bridges, minor bloodsheds and affrays, and recommending bye-laws relating to these issues.

They also exhibited an especially keen eye for alehouses, both as part of their remit – regulating the quality of food and drink, and especially weights and measures, within the community – and through the supplementary issues on which they voluntarily presented, in particular by offering up opin-ions on the 'fitness' of individual alehouse-keepers, and reporting disorderly or unlicensed institutions (Webb and Webb, 1908, p. 96; McIntosh, 1998, p. 39). However, for the collection of the amercement (the small cash fine usually issued by the court) or, more seriously, for a referral to the assembly or quarter sessions, the leet jurors remained 'entirely reliant on the goodwill of the senior burgesses' to which they presented; a frequent source of tension, as we will see below (Connor, 1978, p. 13; McIntosh, 1984, p. 76). All three judicial instruments (quarter sessions, assembly and court leet) depended for their successful functioning on the information provided by what has been termed an 'unacknowledged republic' of parish officers – beadles, constables and nightwatchmen – who were the 'workhorses' of seventeenth-century local administration and who were officially charged with the grass-roots monitoring of alehouses across the town's five wards (Wrightson, 1980, p. 22; Kent, 1986; Goldie, 2000).

Licensing regimes

In theory, this was a well-oiled bureaucratic machine: connected to Westminster by printed order books, regular articles of inquiry, and an administrative chain of being which linked the humblest parish constable to the monarch, alehouses were subject to surveillance and scrutiny at various levels. First and foremost, the careful recording of the names and occupations of licensees and their sureties in assembly books, sessions rolls and (from the 1650s) dedicated recognizance files (Figure 1) was part of a wider and intensifying project of state-sponsored information-gathering (Voekel, 1998; Higgs, 2004, pp. 28–63; Groebner, 2007, pp. 65–95). The 1619 proclamation was particularly programmatic on issues of administrative detail, and served as a vade mecum for the documentation of alehouse-keeper identities; boilerplate text for all licences was provided for the first time, while town clerks were exhorted to 'engross the recognizance and original in parchment' (sending a copy to the alehouse-keeper) and to 'write out and bring with them to every sessions of the peace...a register book containing the true names, surnames and places where every alehouse-keeper licensed doth dwell' (Larkin and Hughes, 1973, pp. 410–11; Caplan and Torpey, 2001). The resulting documents of record, lodged in a 'great chest and deal box' in the Audit House parlour, were not only symbolically freighted 'treasured and guarded possessions' (Withington, 2004, p. 206). They also placed up-to-date knowledge about alehouse-keepers at the fingertips of local governors, serving as 'active archives' to be consulted for everyday decisions of policy (Griffiths, 2008, pp. 400–2; 2004). Time and again we see records in circulation, even beyond the confines of sessions; in

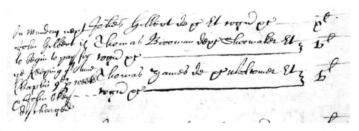

Figure 1:   Names of licensees in the Southampton recognizance files

1655, for example, the leet jurors prosecuted 24 retailers 'not being of the company of the tipplers licensed delivered unto us by the town recorder' (Southampton Record Office (SRO), SC6/1/58, fo. 38). The Audit House scriveners responsible for keeping this information legible and up to date took special care with the records of licensing, and took pains to ensure that their successors had the necessary information to hand. In 1659, for example, at the top of a list of 'books and writings' conveyed to the incoming town clerk was the 'rolls of alehouse-keepers licensed' (SRO, SC2/1/8, fo. 159r). Easily detectable within the town by the signboards which they were commercially compelled to display, alehouses were also subjected to the scopic operations of constables, beadles and watchmen and, at times, that of the mayoralty. For example, in 1639 mayor Robert Wroth, a zealous future commissioner for securing the peace of the Commonwealth, who had a particular disdain for alehouses, recorded £1 2s in his accounts 'for several misdemeanours in…unlicensed alehouses in my several nightly walks' (SRO, SC5/3/23, fo. 4r; on Wroth's subsequent career see Durston, 2001, p. 62).

Despite this sophisticated governmental apparatus, the priorities of local governors were not always in line with those of their Westminster superiors. Mayor Wroth in particular seems to have been in the minority: as a rule of thumb the port's magistracy does not seem to have been wholehearted about the alehouse licensing project, and responded haphazardly and unpredictably to central directives about alehouses throughout the Elizabethan and early Jacobean periods. As in other places, the immediate impact of the 1552 Act was 'not exactly dramatic' (Clark, 1983, p. 169; Fletcher, 1996, p. 241). It was not entered into the relevant Book of Remembrance (which recorded the minutes of the sixteenth-century assembly), while the Book of Fines reveals only sporadic payments for ale and beer licences between 1552 and 1586, and at wildly varying rates (SRO, SC5/3/1, fos 116r, 118r-v, 124r, 149v, 153r, 154r, 161v, 175r, 184v, 186v). In 1586 Mayor Andrew Studley recorded a large single payment of £8 5s. for 30 licences (with fees varying between 3s 4d and 8s), although these seem to have been open-ended rather than renewed on an annual basis (SRO SC5/3/1, fo. 201v). In 1607, in response to the statutes of the previous year, the assembly ordered that 'upon Wednesday next all the tipplers as well licensed as not licensed shall be warned by the several sergeants in their wards to come to the House to be ordered as the law requires' (Connor, 1978, pp. 108–9), but it was not until 1613 that another systematic list of 24 licensees appears in the Assembly Books (Horrocks, 1924, pp. 77–8), while quarter sessions (for which order books survive from 1609) do not carry regular annual recognizances of alehouse-keepers until 1619, when the proclamation cited above clarified several details of the scheme and attempted to introduce a greater degree of standardization in paperwork across the realm (SRO, SC9/2/1, fos 38r–39v). This does seem to have had the desired effect; from this date the port's registration practices seem to have been systematic, with individuals and those providing their sureties named in full, and the recurrence of the same names in subsequent years suggesting that a system of annual permits was now in place (SRO, SC9/2/1, fos 55r–56v, 80v–82v, 95r–96v, 104v–106v). From at least the 1660s, licensees' recognizances were recorded in designated books for ease of access and consultation (SRO, SC9/2/11).

Instead, from their first presentment of 1552 – when they presented 'all tipplers which sell beer and ale without sureties contrary to the commandment given them ... in the article' while the ink was still drying on the Act – it was the middling leet jurors who threw themselves most wholeheartedly into the grass roots implementation of central licensing initiatives (Hearnshaw and Hearnshaw, 1905, p. 24). They could not take recognizances or issue licences, but routinely 'backed up JPs' by presenting lists of unlicensed or disorderly establishments, despite the fact that the identification of illegal alehouses was also technically outside of their jurisdiction (McIntosh, 1984, p. 82). As in other contexts where they remained active, these subordinate officers of the crown exceeded their remit and, armed with licensing documents, their own local knowledge, and the information transmitted to them orally by constables, beadles and nightwatchmen, doggedly matched up the paper trail to street-corner geographies. As early as 1552 some tipplers in Bag Row (the poorest street in the town) and nine more from other parishes were presented for their want of 'sureties', with further clusters of presentments in 1571, 1574 and 1580, with the correct statutory fine of 20*s* recommended in all cases (Hearnshaw and Hearnshaw, 1905, 1906, 1907, pp. 30–1, 43, 65, 72, 103, 121, 200, 214). Even after quarter sessions became more consistent in their pursuit of rogue sellers in the early seventeenth century, leet jurors continued to present the names of those not 'being of the company of the tipplers licensed delivered unto us by the town clerk' as well as those, in line with the provisions of the 1606 statute, of the brewers who had supplied them with beer (Hearnshaw and Hearnshaw, 1908, pp. 447, 508–9; SRO, SC6/1/31, fos 24v–25r; SC6/1/47, fo. 14r; SC6/1/51, fo. 22r). Their scrupulous cross-referencing of 'the town clerk's notes' with the pattern on the ground became more sustained from 1655 when 15 unlicensed individuals were to be 'strongly enquired after and the law swiftly put into execution'; from this point a list of 'tipplers unlicensed' became a formulaic annual fixture of their presentment portfolio.

Indeed, as the exasperated preambles of many of their presentments suggest ('we present as many times we have done before', 'which heretofore hath been often presented and not as yet redressed'), the leet jurors expressed constant frustration at the failure of their magisterial superiors to act on their centrally inspired recommendations for the suppression of illegal alehouses (for similar concerns in another context, see Morrill, 1976, p. 33). These faultlines were exposed at various points in the sixteenth and seventeenth centuries, but are revealed with particular clarity at the turn of the 1600s when the number of borough alehouses had increased sharply and alarmingly in response to the harvest crisis and economic dislocations of the 1590s (as elsewhere, the town's poor took up ale-selling on a temporary basis during dearth periods to ward off destitution). Southampton's unique run of stall and art rolls allows us to reconstruct this upturn with particular confidence and clarity. Prepared annually by the court leet jurors on the basis of first-hand information supplied to them by ward beadles, the stall and art rolls are comprehensive rosters of all non-burgesses who retailed commodities within the borough, organized by ward, in which all sellers of ale and beer were flagged with a 'tip' (denoting 'tippler') in the margin of the leet book regardless of whether or not they were officially licensed (Figure 2). This is a neat piece of *de facto* logic and administrative 'function creep' that allows us to get to the 'dark figure' of unlicensed establishments and to recover something approaching real totals for the years in which records survive (Figure 3) (Clarke, 1991). Put simply, in the nine years between 1595 and 1604, the rolls suggest that the number of alehouses leapt dramatically, nearly doubling across all of the port's wards, from 39 to 69; an alehouse to inhabitant ratio of 1:61, or 1:13 if only male household heads are included.

The leet books from 1597 to 1600 do not survive, but 1601's book, with jurors horrified by their own figures and the multiplication of new signboards that must have confronted them as they went about their daily business, opens with a strongly worded complaint about 'the inordinate and unnecessary number of alehouse-keepers within every ward of this town as well allowed as not allowed'. They rehearsed conventional complaints with unusual vividness (alehouses were 'receptacles of all lewd persons and authors of them in their vices and wickedness') and urged 'your worships to have such due consideration as in justice appertains and that some of

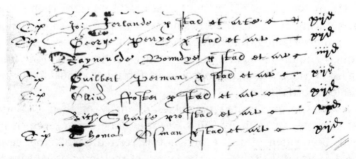

Figure 2:   Leet book showing sellers of ale and beer flagged with 'tip' in margin

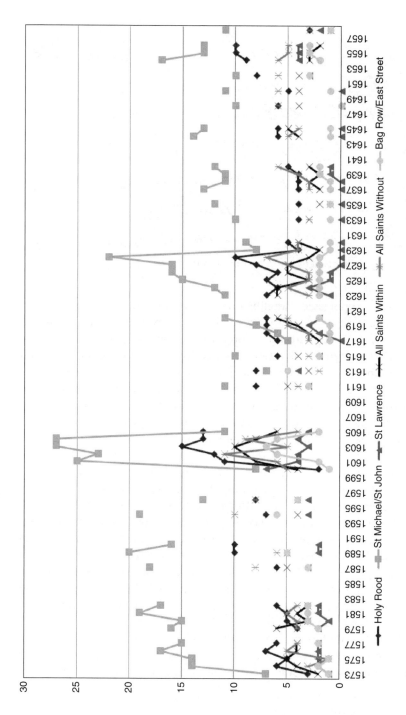

Figure 3: Number of tipplers by year in Southampton's wards

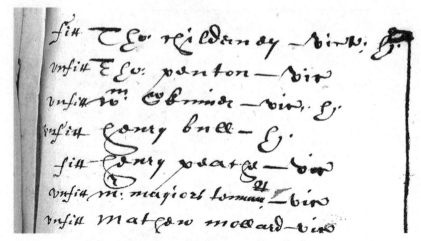

Figure 4:   Tipplers sorted by jurors as 'fitt' or 'unfitt'

them may be suppressed', singling out Peter Hendrick's turbulent establish-ment on the West Quay for immediate removal (Hearnshaw and Hearnshaw, 1906, p. 34). In 1602, with no action forthcoming, exasperation was creep-ing in. They presented 'as oftentimes heretofore we have done the intol-erable number of tipsters...and though some of them were indicted at the last quarter sessions notwithstanding there is no redress, desiring that it may better be looked unto, they being very evil members within the town'. They urged the mayor and justices to call those who are not licensed 'and to put down at least half a hundred, there be too, too many' (SRO, SC6/1/26, fo. 22r).

In 1603, with no action forthcoming and the number of borough alehouses at an all time high, they tried a new shock tactic, and took the unusual step of appending to their presentment a tabular ward-by-ward breakdown of the town's entire alehouse-keeping population (an 'amassing' in their words), based on verified information supplied to them by ward beadles (Figure 4). They ventured an additional layer of 'social sorting'; to assist the desired purge, 'such of them as we think fitt to be allowed we have totted them...with this word (fitt), and such as we think not fitt we have likewise totted them with this word (unfitt)' (SRO, SC6/1/28, fo. 19r; the concept of social sorting is from Lyon, 2003). By 1604, when even this unprecedent-edly detailed moral biopsy had failed to provoke a magisterial response, the patience of the leet jury was exhausted, and they all but stated that it was not only unlicensed alehouse-keepers who were brushing aside the law:

> We present the unnecessary numbers of tipplers...and table keep-
> ers within this town where...as the town clerk informs us, there

is not any one allowed in form of law these two years...but that they and all the others have forfeited their recognizances by their nuisances and disorderly behaviour...the last year we made a large presentment with the names of such as were thought fit and unfit to be allowed but find nothing reformed we desire you that speedy redress may be had of this palpable abuse.

By 1605, according to the stall and art rolls, the number of alehouses had been substantially reduced. However, this had far more to do with the 1604 plague outbreak, a 'watershed' in Southampton's demographic history, than a sudden outburst of persecutory rigour on the part of the magistrates; perhaps an epidemiological variant of Dorchester's famous 'fire from heaven' (on this fascinating 1613 episode, when a conflagration was widely interpreted in providential terms, see Taylor, 1980; and Underdown, 1992).

Strategies and motivations of the protagonists

Why, with access to state-of-the-art management information and a cadre of such diligent informers, did several successive magistracies fail to enforce central measures and take concerted action against the town's spiralling number of alehouses, something that seems especially surprising given the well-documented Puritan sympathies of the Southampton bench (Merson, 1961, p. 67; Collinson, 1982, pp. 160, 173–4)? At one level, problems may have been practical; despite the regular issuing of articles of inquiry and printed editions of statutes, it was famously difficult for early modern magistracies to keep fully abreast of the Acts generated by Westminster, while the kind of spectacular suppression campaign required in this case would have been extremely challenging to mount. However, it seems more likely that magisterial inactivity in this case was a deliberate decision not to implement drinking policies perceived as harmful to the local community and economy, intimately related to the broader culture of pragmatic paternalism which the Southampton bench seems to have operated. In short, magistrates would have been fully aware of the ways in which the bumper crop of alehouses, licensed or otherwise, was easing pressure on both the town's indigent and the civic budget during a period of unprecedented economic dislocation and distress (not to mention the general advantages of an extensive hospitality infrastructure to a marine economy). Cheap, nutritive small ale was always in demand during a harvest crisis, while conferring licences on out-of-work labourers, or turning a blind eye to an unlicensed retailer if they happened to be in poverty, was effectively a form of out relief that saved artisans from destitution and prevented them from becoming dependant (or 'chargeable') on parish rates (Hindle, 2004, pp. 59–60). Rather than the reflexive enactment of a central policy of suppression, the magistracy developed discretionary licensing solutions, tailor-made to the local scenario, aimed at supporting individuals in their alehouse-keeping in ways designed to ease both local suffering and the town's purse. Unlicensed retailers were 'tolerated' if they happened to be poor, for example, while some more distinctive schemes and solutions, apparently unique to Southampton, have their genesis in this period; licensed alehouse-keepers were frequently compelled to devote a percentage of their operating profits to the poor, for example (such an arrangement is described in the margin of the recognizance depicted in Figure 1), while they might be required to take in orphans or the offspring of town paupers (on these measures see Brown, 2008, pp. 161–73).

Here, then, is an example of the agenda of local government being set in accordance with local, rather than national, priorities, and a manifestation not of bureaucratic sloth but of a particular kind of active magistracy. The Southampton bench had the judicial confidence to decide how, when and where central licensing policy should be discharged, quietly spiking aspects of legislation which would not have been helpful, and redefining and/or extending others before implementation (with the novel extension of licensing conditions into arenas of social welfare representing the best example). These attempts of the magistracy to bring central licensing policy more into line with local welfare and fiscal priorities through innovation and experiment became more strident in the course of the seventeenth century, peaking in 1659 when, as in Dorchester and Salisbury some years previously, the common council attempted to integrate alehouse licensing into a brewery scheme (Slack, 1972, pp. 182–3). With regard to the 'daily an increase of poor people within this town and county and therefore a further increase of maintenance for their relief', the assembly decreed that alehouses should thereafter take their beer only from 'one or more' licensed brewers, with the 'benefit and profit' generated by the licensees to be 'dispensed and converted to the relief of the poor'. Three days later a single candidate had been nominated, alderman Richard Walker, and the terms of the arrangement slightly altered. Rather than donating his inflated profits, Walker would pay for a three-year monopoly at the rate of £80 annually in quarterly instalments: £50 of this was allocated the workhouse, with the remaining £30 to be distributed 'to other poor people according to the discretion of the mayor and justices of this corporation'. A new brewhouse was constructed for Walker Above Bar, and two months later all alehouse-keepers were instructed 'from this day forward' to 'take and buy their beer and ale only of Mr Richard Walker', an injunction that was built into their recognizances. However, the scheme proved controversial, and in early 1660 the assembly books contain a tantalizing reference to a 'debate of the difference between Mr Walker and Mr Knight concerning the brewhouse', the latter no doubt leading brewer William Knight. The disagreement was evidently resolved in

Knight's favour, as the same day it was 'judged convenient' that JPs should license alehouses 'according to the usual course, and former order made to the contrary...notwithstanding'. Indeed, the margin next to the original entry contains a rueful note that the 'order [was] suspended' (SRO, SC2/1/8, fos 151v, 152r, 159v, 161r).

The responses of the leet jury to the turn of century alehouse spike (specifically, the perceived lackadaisical responses of the magistracy to it) are equally bewildering at first inspection. Local benches generally enjoyed the compliance of subordinate officers when they modified or selectively enforced national policies that would have been detrimental to community interests had they been adopted *in toto* and, as leading ratepayers, the middling householders who comprised the leet jury certainly had a powerful vested interest to reduce the local welfare burden through legislative innovation (Fletcher, 1996, pp. 117, 142). Instead, these humble servants of the state seemed to have found in their highlighting of the alehouse problem a particularly attractive means of social and vocational self-expression. This consisted of two interrelated but discrete components. The first, and most extensively rehearsed, is largely socio-economic. As is almost axiomatic from the work of Wrightson and others, the economic developments of the sixteenth century engendered increasing social polarization within local communities that dramatically amplified the cultural differentiation between wealthy inhabitants (especially a consolidating 'middling sort') and the poor (the 'meaner', 'worser', or 'vulgar' sorts) (Wrightson, 2003, pp. 182–3; Wrightson, 1986, pp. 177–202). Against the backdrop of these structural processes, we can readily see in the jurors' alehouse campaign a public attempt on the part of a consolidating middle to both distance itself from and reform the traditional drinking habits and survival strategies of their poorer neighbours. Tellingly, the fact that many leet jurors were themselves inn-holders and taverners suggests that this conventional distaste might have been inflected by a degree of economic self-interest and protectionism; and middling households were also those most likely to have been alienated by the public disorders and breaches of the peace often associated with alehouse culture.

However, as well as these abstract processes of stratification, we can also discern in the jurors' alehouse offensive this conventional reform of manners being superimposed by the creation and performance of another kind of identity, tied to political and administrative developments as well as social and economic transformations. We know that as a result of their extensive participation in parish government, local office-holders were increasingly likely to both internalize and identify with the values of the central state (a process accelerated after the creation of the civil parish between 1598 and 1601), and to seek to demonstrate their administrative competence and trustworthiness at every opportunity (Hindle, 2000, pp. 204–30). It is this framework, rather than that of the reformation of manners or social polarization *per se*, that offers the most convincing paradigm for approaching the jurors' alehouse crusade, especially given the general increase in confidence on the part of surviving urban leet juries at the turn of the century (King, 1980a; 1980b; McIntosh, 1984; King, 1990). That is to say, they seem to have regarded the tenacious pursuit of alehouse-keeping offences as an opportunity to reify their judicial authority and to demonstrate the extent of their legalism, bureaucratic knowhow and close familiarity with central directives. On several occasions they referenced specific items of statutory guidance when cajoling the magistracy; and their use of 'fitness' to structure the census of 1603 was drawn straight from the conceptual vocabulary of the statute of that year (1603, 1 James I c. 9). Such calculated appeals to central provisions had always been part of their rhetorical strategy when faced with institutional inertia on the part of the bench. In 1596, for example, before the statistical exercises of the early 1600s, they claimed that Edward Stanton 'a tippler Above the Bar' was married to 'a very lewd woman' and is therefore 'not worthy to be admitted nor permitted neither by law nor by orders lately conceived by Her Majesty's Privy Council' (Hearnshaw and Hearnshaw, 1906, p. 315: the Act in question was probably 1585 5 Elizabeth I c. 5). This is not to suggest that the leet jurors were the dogged emulators of central policy. Indeed, no less than the magistrates, they were also capable of legislative innovation and administrative creativity; they recommended several bye-laws relating to alehouses and saw them through to implementation (not discussed in this article), while both their customization of the stall and art rolls to track alehouse-keepers (Figure 2) and their annotated tabular enumeration of 1603 (Figure 4) are striking pieces of bureaucratic representation.

The role of alehouses in state formation

National directives were not the end of the story of alehouse regulation, but merely its beginning (Hindle, 2000). With the important exception of Wrightson's early rural community study (Wrightson, 1981), existing work has been too preoccupied with the warp and weft of central policy at the expense of the multilateral mosaic of local apparatuses through which it was reproduced, especially within the urban scene – attendant upon the 'localisation of alcohol regulation' represented by the 1552 Act and its refinements (Nicholls, 2009, p. 18) – which could introduce priorities and power struggles unforeseen by Westminster. Indeed, if we understand early modern state formation as consisting largely of the process by which relationships between different agencies along the circuits of authority were operationally defined and redefined, then alehouses, specifically their regulation by licensing, emerge as one of the foremost pretexts for and facilitators of these developments in early modern England. Why was this the case? These institutions raised a peculiarly pressing set of economic, social and moral questions; as Anthony Fletcher describes it, '[t]here was no social institution that caused more heart-searching and dispute...than the alehouse' (Fletcher, 1996, p. 229). Their licensing was a live issue not just in the corridors of power but also within communities, where a whole range of tangible effects on urban populations and topographies encouraged local agencies to engage with and in many cases to share and help formulate central priorities. However, this engagement was complicated by the fundamental ambiguity of the alehouses – specifically, their fiscal advantageousness on the one hand, versus their role in encouraging public disorder on the other – leading local constituencies to respond differently to central licensing provisions depending on the precise nature of their governing responsibilities (Kümin, 1999). The licensing of alehouses was particularly likely to manifest tensions between groups without direct responsibility for civic budgets (national legislators, subordinate officers), and those charged with balancing the books (urban magistracies), tensions which in turn provided opportunities for these entities to stake certain kinds of claims about their judicial purpose and identity. The regularity of new legislation relating to alehouse licensing emanating from the centre, not to mention the supplementary bye-laws developed and promulgated locally, kept these themes on the agenda throughout the early modern period, guaranteeing that local administrative and legal relations would be continually rearticulated around them.

Finally, while not fully developed in this article, the fluid notion of 'spatial politics' provides us with a flexible and coherent vocabulary for exploring these problems (Kümin, 2009). While used at various points throughout the discussion, the neat analytical dichotomy of 'national' and 'local' (or 'centre' and 'periphery') distorts the distribution of authority within the early modern state. England's system of government was neither national nor local but a continuum of co-ordinates that was 'more or less long and more or less connected' (Latour, 1993, p. 122). As such, the national/local double-bind risks hermetically sealing these arenas, implicitly conferring a false homogeneity and stability upon each; 'central' policy on licensing fiercely debated in Parliament (often in dialogue with community interests) before finding definitive expression in Act and statute book, for example, while 'local' alehouse priorities were far from unified or coherent. Space, specifically the concept of spatial politics, allows us to move beyond these limiting interpretative binaries and to render the complexity of the situation more faithfully. At one level, it is appropriate terminology for describing the perennial renegotiation of interests around a concrete place (the alehouse). Moving outwards, it conveys a powerful sense of the overlapping administrative geographies, tied to particular sites and scales, through and across which this renegotiation took place: parishes and wards; the corporate town and borough, and its liberties; the county of Hampshire; the realm. Finally, deployed metaphorically, it helps us conceive of the judicial and legal spaces self-consciously inhabited by our protagonists (leet jury; common council; Parliament, privy council and monarch); the different conceptual spaces inhabited by the alehouse; the simultaneity of these different conceptualizations; and the fact that they were always *in process*.

Bibliography

Bailey, M (2002) *The English Manor c. 1200–c. 1500* (Manchester and New York: Manchester University Press)

Braddick, M (1991) 'State Formation in Early Modern England: A Problem Stated and Approaches Suggested' **16** *Social History* 1–17

Braddick, M (2000) *State Formation in Early Modern England, c. 1550–1700* (Cambridge: Cambridge University Press)

Brandwood, G, A Davison and M Slaughter (2004), *Licensed to Sell: The History and Heritage of the Public House* (Swindon: English Heritage)

Brown, J R (2008) 'The Landscape of Drink: Inns, Taverns, and Alehouses in Early Modern Southampton' (PhD Thesis, University of Warwick)

Caplan, J and J Torpey (2001) 'Introduction', in J Caplan and J Torpey (eds), *Documenting Individual Identity: The Development of State Practices in the Modern World* (Princeton and Oxford: Princeton University Press)

Clark, P (1978) 'The Alehouse and the Alternative Society' in D Pennington and K Thomas (eds), *Puritans and Revolutionaries: Essays in Seventeenth-Century History presented to Christopher Hill* (Oxford: Oxford University Press), pp. 47–72

Clark, P (1983) *The English Alehouse: A Social History 1200–1830* (London: Longman)

Clarke, R A (1991) 'The Tax File Number Scheme: A Case Study of Political Assurances and Function Creep' **7** *Policy*

Collinson, P (1982) *The Religion of Protestants: The Church in English Society 1559–1625* (Oxford: Clarendon Press)

Connor, W J (1978) 'Introduction' in W J Connor (ed.), *The Southampton Mayor's Book of 1606–08*, Southampton Records Series 21 (Southampton: University of Southampton)

Durston, C (2001), *Cromwell's Major Generals: Godly Government During the English Revolution* (Manchester and New York: Manchester University Press)

Fletcher, A (1996) *Reform in the Provinces: The Government of Stuart England* (New Haven and London: Yale University Press)

Foucault, M (1980) 'Questions on Geography' in C Gordon (ed.), *Power/ Knowledge: Selected Interviews and Other Writings 1972–1977* (New York and London: Pantheon)

French, H R (2007) *The Middle Sort of People in Provincial England, 1600–1750* (Oxford: Oxford University Press)

Goldie, M (2001) 'The Unacknowledged Republic: Office-Holding in Early Modern England' in T Harris (ed.), *The Politics of the Excluded c. 1550–1640* (Basingstoke: Palgrave Macmillan), pp. 153–94

Griffiths, P (2004) 'Bodies and Souls in Norwich: Punishing Petty Crime, 1540–1700' in S Devereaux and P Griffiths (eds), *Penal Practice and Culture, 1500–1900: Punishing the English* (London and New York: Palgrave Macmillan)

Griffiths, P (2008) *Lost Londons: Change, Crime, and Control in the Capital City, 1550–1660* (Cambridge: Cambridge University Press)

Groebner, V (2007) *Who Are You? Identification, Deception and Surveillance in Early Modern Europe* (trans.) (New York: Zone Books)

Hearnshaw, F J C and D M Hearnshaw (eds) (1905) *Southampton Court Leet Records: vol. I 1550–77* Southampton Records Society 1 (Southampton)

Hearnshaw, F J C and D M Hearnshaw (eds) (1906) *Southampton Court Leet Records: vol. II 1578–1602* Southampton Records Society 2 (Southampton)

Hearnshaw, F J C and D M Hearnshaw (eds) (1907) *Southampton Court Leet Records: vol. III 1603–24* Southampton Records Society 4 (Southampton)

Hearnshaw, F J C and D M Hearnshaw (eds) (1908) *Leet Jurisdiction in England, Especially as Illustrated by the Records of the Leet Court of Southampton* (Southampton)

Higgs, E (2004) *The Information State in England: The Central Collection of Information on Citizens Since 1500* (Basingstoke and New York: Palgrave Macmillan)

Hindle, S (1999) 'Hierarchy and Community in the Elizabethan Parish: The Swallowfield Articles of 1596' **42** *The Historical Journal* 835–51

Hindle, S (2000) *The State and Social Change in Early Modern England c. 1550–1640* (Basingstoke: Palgrave Macmillan)

Hindle, S (2004) *On the Parish? The Micropolitics of Poor Relief in Rural England, 1550–1750* (Oxford: Clarendon Press)

Horrocks, J W (ed.) (1917) *Assembly Books of Southampton: vol. I, 1602–1608* Southampton Record Society 19 (Southampton)

Horrocks, J W (ed.) (1920) *Assembly Books of Southampton: vol. II, 1609–1610* Southampton Record Society 21 (Southampton)

Horrocks, J W (ed.) (1924) *Assembly Books of Southampton: vol. III, 1611–1614* Southampton Record Society 24 (Southampton)

Horrocks, J W (ed.) (1925) *Assembly Books of Southampton: vol. IV, 1615–1616* Southampton Record Society 25 (Southampton)

Hunter, J (1994) 'Legislation, Royal Proclamations and other National Directives Affecting Inns, Taverns, Alehouses, Brandy Shops and Punch Houses 1552–1757' (PhD Thesis, University of Reading)

Hunter, J (2002) 'English Inns, Taverns, Brandy Shops and Punch Houses: The Legislative Framework, 1495–1797' in B Kümin and B A Tlusty (eds), *The World of the Tavern: Public Houses in Early Modern Europe* (Aldershot: Ashgate), pp. 65–82

Kent, J (1986) *The English Village Constable 1580–1642: A Social and Administrative Study* (Oxford: Oxford University Press)

King, W J (1980a) 'Leet Jurors and the Search for Law and Order in Seventeenth-Century England: "Galling Persecution" or Reasonable Justice?' **13** *Histoire Sociale/Social History* 305–23

King, W J (1980b) 'Regulation of Alehouses in Stuart Lancashire: An Example of Discretionary Administration of the Law' **129** *Historical Society of Lancashire and Cheshire* 31–461

King, W J (1982) 'Untapped Resources for Social Historians: Court Leet Records' **15** *Journal of Social History* 699–705

King, W J (1990) 'Early Stuart Courts Leet: Still Needful and Useful' **23** *Histoire Social/Social History* 271–99

Kümin, B (1999) 'Useful to Have but Difficult to Govern: Inns and Taverns in Early Modern Bern and Vaud' **3** *Journal of Early Modern History* 153–75

Kümin, B (2007) *Drinking Matters: Public Houses and Social Exchange in Early Modern Central Europe* (Basingstoke: Palgrave Macmillan)

Kümin, B (2009) *Political Space in Pre-industrial Europe* (Aldershot: Ashgate)

Latour, B (1993) *We Have Never Been Modern* (Brighton: Harvester Wheatsheaf)

Larkin, J F and P L Hughes (eds) (1973) *Stuart Royal Proclamations* (Oxford: Oxford University Press)

Lyon, D (2003) 'Surveillance as Social Sorting: Computer Codes and Mobile Bodies' in D Lyon (ed.), *Surveillance as Social Sorting: Privacy, Risk, and Digital Discrimination* (London), pp. 13–20

McIntosh, M K (1984) 'Social Change and Tudor Manorial Leets' in J A Guy and H G Beale (eds), *Law and Social Change in British History* (London: Royal Historical Society), pp. 73–85

McIntosh, M K (1998) *Controlling Misbehavior in England, 1370–1600* (Cambridge: Cambridge Univesity Press)

Merson, A L (ed.) (1952) *The Third Book of Remembrance of Southampton 1514–1602: vol. I 1514–40* Southampton Records Series 2 (Southampton)

Merson, A L (1961) 'Elizabethan Southampton', in J B Morgan and P Peberdy (eds), *Collected Essays on Southampton* (Southampton: County Borough of Southampton)

Morrill, J S (1976) *The Cheshire Grand Jury 1625–1659: A Social and Administrative Study* (Leicester: Leicester University Press)

Nicholls, J (2009) *The Politics of Alcohol: A History of the Drink Question in England* (Manchester and New York: Manchester University Press)

Roberts, S K (1980) 'Alehouses, Brewing and Government under the Early Stuarts' 2 *Southern History* 45–71

Shoemaker, R (1991) *Prosecution and Punishment: Petty Crime and the Law in London and Rural Middlesex c. 1600–1725* (Cambridge MA: Harvard University Press)

Slack, P A (1972) 'Poverty and Politics in Salisbury 1597–1666' in P Clark and P Slack (eds), *Crisis and Order in English Towns 1500–1700: Essays in Urban History* (London), pp. 117–63

Stürler, M von (1975) 'Die Konzessionierten Wirtschaften im Kanton Bern' 37 *Berner Zeitschrift für Geschichte und Heimatkunde* 19–27

Taylor, J R (1980) 'Population, Disease and Family Structure in Early Modern Hampshire, with Special Reference to Towns' (PhD thesis, University of Southampton)

Underdown, D (1992) *Fire From Heaven: Life in an English Town in the Seventeenth Century* (New Haven: Yale University Press)

Voekel, S (1998) '"Upon the Suddaine View": State, Civil Society and Surveillance in Early Modern England' *Early Modern Literary Studies* 1–27

Webb, S and B Webb (1903) *The History of Liquor Licensing in England* (London: Longmans Green)

Webb, S and B Webb (1908) *English Local Government from the Revolution to the Municipal Corporations Act: The Manor and the Borough* (London: Longmans Green)

Wilson, T M (2005) 'Introduction' in T M Wilson (ed.), *Drinking Cultures: Alcohol and Identity* (Oxford and New York: Berg)

Withington, P (2004) 'Agency, Custom and the English Corporate System' in H French and J Barry (eds), *Identity and Agency in English Society, 1500–1800* (Basingstoke: Palgrave Macmillan)

Withington, P (2005) *The Politics of Commonwealth: Citizens and Freemen in Early Modern England* (Cambridge: Cambridge University Press)

Wrightson, K (1980) 'Two Concepts of Order: Justices, Constables and Jurymen in Seventeenth-Century England' in J Brewer and J Styles (eds), *An Ungovernable People: The English and their Law in the Seventeenth and Eighteenth Centuries* (London: Hutchinson)

Wrightson, K (1981) 'Alehouses, Order and Reformation in Rural England 1590–1660' in S Yeo and E Yeo (eds), *Popular Culture and Class Conflict 1590–1914: Explorations in the History of Labour and Leisure* (Brighton: Harvester), pp. 1–27

Wrightson, K (1986) 'The Social Order of Early Modern England: Three Approaches' in L Bonfield, R M Smith and K Wrightson (eds), *The World We Have Gained: Histories of Population and Social Structure* (Oxford: Blackwell), pp. 177–202

Wrightson, K (2003) *English Society, 1580–1680* 2nd edn (London: Routledge)

Legislation

1552 5/6 Edward VI c. 25 (Licensing Act of 1552)
1585 5 Elizabeth I c. 5
1603 1 James I c. 9
1606 4 James I c. 4
1606 4 James I c. 5
1609 7 James I c. 10

Section 3
Culture and Practice

7
Renaissance Drinking Cultures and Popular Print

Phil Withington

Basil Fawlty may well have regarded the argument of this chapter an exercise in the 'bleeding obvious'. Intoxicants are, after all, ubiquitous in modern British society. They play a central role in the lives of many different sorts of people, be it as the defining substances of choreographed rituals and rites of passage; as the lubricants of everyday interaction; as sources of social identity and signifiers of taste, distinction, age, class, gender and ethnicity; as markers of social inclusion and exclusion. Intoxicants are prominent in all manner of 'artistic' achievement and activity, from literary and visual culture to music and the moving image – they, and the manner of their consumption, serve as subject-matter, plot device, the perceived source of artistic creation and inspiration. Modern governments are obsessed with intoxicants – with their regulation and policing, with assessing and calibrating their impact on biological and social bodies, with balancing the social and medical costs of intoxicants against the huge revenues they generate. The modern media is equally fixated, engendering 'moral panics' about this substance, that addiction, or yet another mode of illicit and dangerous imbibing. And it is not just governments (or journalists) who profit from intoxication – from legitimate producers to illicit traffickers to local growers and retailers to the regiments of scientists and organizations dedicated to their study (and, in certain instances, eradication), intoxicants are a living.

The argument of this chapter is that not only are intoxicants central to most aspects of contemporary life, they were equally prominent during what historians often call the 'early modern' era – the historical epoch to which many of the defining features of modern societies, Britain included, can be traced. So far so 'bleeding obvious'. Sir Keith Thomas long ago observed that 'Drink, for example, was built into the fabric of social life' of England during the sixteenth and seventeenth centuries – that 'it played a part in nearly every public and private ceremony, every commercial bargain, every craft ritual, every private occasion of mourning or rejoicing' (Thomas 1971, p. 21).

Another leading historian of early modern England, Keith Wrightson, like-wise notes that 'drink was an essential and ubiquitous social lubricant' and that the 'alehouse gained a growing centrality in popular leisure and recreation' (Wrightson 1981, pp. 6, 10). Work on European drinking cultures tends to similar conclusions: although the type of beverage and the rituals of their consumption varied from one region to the next, drink was integral to most kinds of social behaviour (Tlusty, 2001). There is, in short, something of an historical consensus regarding the significance of drink in this period (Porter, 1985). It is, then, hardly surprising that such deeply ingrained habits perpetuated into the modern world. Indeed, it would be much more unexpected if our intoxicated present had comparatively sober historical antecedents.

What follows is not meant to challenge the orthodoxy that intoxicants in general – and alcohol in particular – were the props and stirrups of early modern sociality. Rather it seeks to query some of the interpretative inferences upon which, in English historiography at least, this orthodoxy has been built, and to show how these inferences underestimate the full role of intoxicants – and extent of intoxication – in early modern England. The first is that early modern drunkenness became the especial preserve of 'popular culture' and the poorer, less educated members of society over the course of the sixteenth and seventeenth centuries. The second is that excessive drinking was a source of solace which became fundamentally at odds with 'elite' conceptions of appropriate behaviour and consumption. The third is that excessive drinking came to be regarded as a remnant of traditional life and that, accordingly, it was on the basis of *modern* cultural developments that England's social and intellectual elites looked to escape the customs of their forbearers and reform the habits of their inferiors. This chapter suggests, in contrast, that English social and intellectual elites embraced and consumed intoxicants throughout the early modern era; that elite drunkenness was often implicitly and sometimes explicitly taken to be normative; and that it was precisely 'early modern' cultural developments – in particular the attitudes and practices associated with the English Renaissance – which provided affluent and educated Englishmen with modern templates for consuming intoxicants. Just as levels of consumption increased, so the rules of intoxication changed.

In addition to these substantive historical points, the chapter makes two further observations. The first is that intoxication, like all social behaviour, must be learnt from generation to generation: it involves skills and recognized modes of deportment which become specific to the context and milieu in which consumption takes place, and which are inherited and perhaps altered inter-generationally. In this respect, Renaissance intoxication offers a nice example of how requisite social skills were learnt and adapted over the course of the later sixteenth and seventeenth centuries. The second point is that the historical neglect of intoxication among early modern elites parallels in many respects contemporary debates about intoxicants. By promoting pricing as a tool of policing, for example, modern governors and their medical advisors imply a meaningful relationship between chronic consumption and low incomes. In so doing, they ignore the drinking habits of more affluent groups at the expense of the less affluent, effectively penalizing the latter. This is despite the very strong correlation between levels of public drinking and standards of living which, since the eighteenth century, have fallen and risen proportionally to each other (Chartres, 1990, pp. 198, 324).

The argument divides into three sections. The first outlines the historical orthodoxy surrounding early modern intoxication and the sociological narratives which have informed it. The second introduces more recent work by literary and cultural historians which has emphasized the drinking habits of affluent and educated groups as well as some of the educational and technological developments which informed the way drinking was aestheticized and valorized. The final section considers the interplay between literary drinking tropes and drinking practices 'on the ground', with especial attention paid to the relationship between England's burgeoning drinking and legal cultures.

There are a number of reasons why early modern historians have tended to equate drunkenness with the lower orders. Early modern drinking began to be taken seriously as a historical subject with the advent of the 'new social history' in the 1970s. Reflective of the more general 'sociological turn' then sweeping the humanities, social historians aimed to 'recover the experience of the mass of the English people' for the first time; to utilize largely untouched archives – in particular local legal records – in order to do so; and to draw on the tools of social science in order to interpret this virgin material (Wrightson, 1982, p. 12; Hobsbawm, 1971). The results were in many respects spectacular. However, the methodological assumptions underpinning this agenda clearly influenced the kind of story that was told. By concentrating on 'the masses' – whoever they might be – 'the elites' were ignored. By focusing on local archives and legal records, other kinds of evidence – such as printed works – were implicitly or explicitly disparaged. And reliance on methodologies then current in the social sciences meant that popular 'experience' was interpreted through the prisms of cultural Marxism, functional anthropology and the grand narratives of German sociology.

The treatment of drinking by Thomas and Wrightson, two of the most influential practitioners of the new social history, encapsulate the prevailing tenor of this kind of approach. We have already seen that Thomas, as a pioneer of English historical anthropology, was well aware of the social ubiquity of early modern intoxicants. However, he interpreted this ubiquity in awkwardly functionalist and socially partial terms. Alcohol was, Thomas suggests, 'an essential narcotic which anaesthetized men against the strains of contemporary life. Drunkenness broke down social distinctions, and brought a temporary mood of optimism to the desperate.' In particular, 'the poor took to drink to blot out some of the horror of their lives' (Thomas 1971, pp. 22–3). For Thomas, the grim utility of impoverished stupefaction was in contrast to the collective inclinations of more affluent social groups who became eager protagonists of what Norbert Elias termed the *civilizing process* (Elias, 1983). This was the development by which, as Thomas puts it, the 'revival' of 'classical doctrine' facilitated a 'movement to develop new standards of bodily control and social decorum' that 'covered a wide range of behaviour'. This 'cult of decorum led to a profound divergence between the streams of polite humour and folk humour'; by the end of the seventeenth century, for example, 'it was only the vulgar who could go on laughing without constraint'. The same was true, of course, for drinking (Thomas 1977, pp. 79, 81; Burke, 2000, p. 39).

Wrightson likewise focused on the fortunes of the most elusive and humble of drinking institutions – the rural alehouse – in order to recover the experiences associated with it. As he explained, 'Not only did the alehouse-keepers serve the poor; they were frequently poor themselves.' (Wrightson 1981, p. 2; Clark 1978, pp. 48, 52–7) He accordingly discovered a vibrant 'plebeian' drinking culture which, over the course of the seventeenth century, came into increasing conflict not simply with moralists and legislators but also the 'better sort' of village householder who became unwilling to countenance the 'evil' and 'idle' habits perceived to take place there. This conflict was reflected in campaigns to enforce a national system of licensing through the institutions of voluntary local governance: indeed 'at the level of the local community, the struggle over the alehouses was one of the most significant social dramas of the age' (Wrightson, 1982, p. 167; Clark, 1983). There was much more than drinking at stake. On the one hand, alehouses stood at the heart of parish neighbourhoods – they were 'the centres *par excellence* of the social lives of the common people'. On the other hand, by 'attacking the major centres of popular sociability', other neighbours – in particular those with 'Puritan' inclinations – 'were dissociating themselves from the customary behaviour of their neighbourhoods and aligning themselves with a definition of good order and social discipline derived from their social superiors' (Wrightson 1982, pp. 168–9). Wrightson draws a clear genealogy between this repressed tradition of popular rural sociability and the working-class public houses of the Victorian industrial city (Wrightson 1981, p. 1). He also aligns the forces of 'Reformation' – of order, discipline, and sobriety – with that powerful early modern configuration of 'new learning', godly evangelism and social superiority.

These conclusions have subsequently been endorsed by more extensive accounts of modern intoxication. David Courtwright explains the initial allure and success of 'psychoactive substances' in early modern Europe as 'dire utility' – they helped 'peasants and workers cope with lives lived on the verge of the unliveable'. He suggests that it is 'no coincidence that the rapid growth of European distilling, and the explosive growth of tobacco imports, took place during "the general crisis of the seventeenth century"': for a whole host of reasons 'these were people who could use a smoke and a drink'. Moreover, just as ordinary people took drugs primarily 'to cope', so their betters and governors initially tried to prevent them doing it; as Courtwright explains, the 'nonmedical use of novel drugs provoked much disgust and repression during the first half of the 1600s, the great formative century of the psycho-active revolution'. These 'official' scruples were overcome, however, by the realization that huge fiscal gains could be made out of intoxicants. They were further eased by the introduction of other, non-hallucinogenic substances in the later seventeenth century – chocolate, milder tobacco, coffee and tea – which were 'more compatible with the emergent capitalist order' and appealed to the kind of civil tastes and habits associated with the 'civilizing process' (Courtwright, 2001, pp. 59, 152).

This is not how it seemed to contemporaries. The formation of the Societies for the Reformation of Manners in the 1690s might well suggest the mobiliza-tion of sober, civil and respectable opinion against the unreformed habits of the labouring poor. That astute social observer, Daniel Defoe, thought differ-ently. Although an early proponent of the movement, Defoe nevertheless pamphleteered against the London Society in 1700 and quit the Edinburgh branch in 1709. He argued that while the targets of reforming campaigns were invariably 'the Plebs', the main culprits of drunkenness were 'the Gentry', who 'caressed this Beastly vice at such rate, that no companion, no servant was thought proper, unless he could bear Quantity of Wine' (Defoe, 1700, p. 16). Leading reformers were also aware of the problem, Josiah Woodward railing against the more recent 'Sons of Wine' and 'Libertines' who were 'indefatigable in raking out of all the Heathen Authors, and our Modern plays, all expressions that may seem to favour his Licentiousness' (Woodward, 1699, pp. 154–5). Both authors traced England's chronic drunkenness to the Restoration. However, not only did these habits have much longer and more complex antecedents. They emanated, in large part, from the same Renaissance culture that encouraged the call for civility in the first place.

This has become apparent thanks largely to developments in literary history, which over the past decade or so has seen the intoxicating habits of both literary authors and audiences become an important area of study (Raylor, 1994; Smyth (ed.), 2004; O'Callaghan, 2007). Contra the new social history, this literary historiography is as concerned with elite – or at least educated – culture as 'the masses'. Its focus is printed genres rather than series of archives. And since the apparent demise of the New Historicism – the vogue for theoretically informed criticism which dominated the discipline during the 1980s – the main interpretative priority has been to recover the meanings with which contemporaries imbued phenomena like drinking *at the time*. In addition to this 'literary turn', a new generation of social historians has begun asking important questions about the popular dissemination, appeal and consumption of ostensibly 'elite' ideas and perspectives through various media. Such media include genres of cheap print, such as ballads; the visual imagery which accompanied the texts (though England remained visually illiterate throughout most of the early modern period); and also the increasing array of material artefacts and objects – drinking glasses, tobacco pipes, punch-bowls – which not only facilitated consumption but also helped define and lend meaning to particular instances of 'company' or sociability (McShane, 2004a; Shepard, 2005; Withington, 2007; Brown, 2008; Hancock, 2009; Hailwood, 2010; McShane, 2010).

The larger context for these new approaches to intoxication is a number of well-known cultural changes associated with 'early modernity'. Perhaps the most important of these is what Lawrence Stone somewhat unfortunately termed the 'educational revolution' (Stone, 1964). In a sample of ten counties, there were 34 schools open to the laity in 1480; by 1606, 410 new schools had been endowed or founded: this made for one school for every 4400 people and every 12 miles. Stone suggested that when the proliferation of 'private schools' is also taken into account then the rise in the provision of humanist teaching – i.e. schooling based on a curriculum of classical rhetoric, grammar, history and logic – was 'perhaps twice as great...as the increase of places at endowed grammar schools would suggest' (Stone 1964, pp. 46–7). The infrastructures of further education also increased. Six of Cambridge's 14 pre-nineteenth-century colleges were founded in the sixteenth century as were nine of 21 colleges in Oxford. The populations of both universities, as well as the Inns of Court and Chancery in London (regarded as a third university at the time), expanded accordingly (see Chart 1). According to Stone, there can 'be little doubt that in the peak decade of the 1630s not less than 1,240 young men were entering higher education every year' in England. This represented about 2.48 per cent of the annual male age-group (i.e. all men between the ages of 16 and 20) – a percentage not again achieved until 1931, when 2.3 per cent of the age-group entered further education. As he puts it, 'In quantitative terms, English higher education did not get back to the level of the 1630s until after the first World War; did not surpass it until after the second.' (Stone 1964, pp. 56, 69)

The 'educational revolution' neither began nor ended with the expansion of the grammar schools, universities and Inns of Court. Although it is notoriously difficult to measure, it seems clear that rates of illiteracy declined significantly during the sixteenth and seventeenth centuries. In the only attempt at

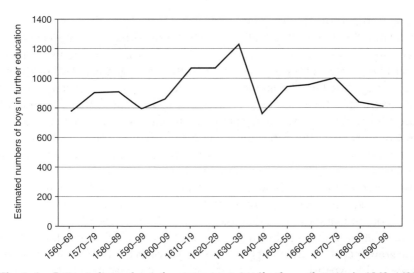

Chart 1: Estimated number of young men in 'further education', 1560–1699 (decennial averages) (from Stone, 1964, p. 54). Figures include Inns of Court and Chancery, the universities, private academies (after 1660) and study abroad

Table 1:   Levels of illiteracy in early modern England (Cressy, 1980)

Date	Men	Women
1485–1507	90%	99%
1558	80%	95%
1642–1645	70%	90%
1714	55%	75%

a systematic survey, David Cressy took the capacity to sign one's name as an indicator of literacy and used legal depositions as his main type of evidence – people who used a fully formed signature were taken to be 'literate' and those who made a sign or mark illiterate. It was on this basis that Cressy concluded that 'By the end of the Stuart period the English had achieved a level of literacy unknown in the past and unmatched elsewhere in early modern Europe.' (Cressy, 1980, 176)

The rate of transition was different according to social group, the acquisition of literacy reflecting the changing dynamics of the social and patriarchal order as well as urban/rural differences. There was, for example, a clear and sharp distinction between the number of yeomen who could not sign their name (which halved from 50 per cent to 25 per cent between the late sixteenth and late seventeenth centuries) and the number of husbandmen and labourers (which remained close to 80 per cent, with a dip in the early seventeenth century). A serious problem with Cressy's findings is that he conflates the quite distinct skills of reading and writing – which were taught separately and at different times in a child's life – as 'literacy'. He also assumes that both sets of skills can be ascertained through signatures. Although this method may well serve as an index of writing ability, it is clear that it seriously underestimates the capacity to read, which was taught at home or through the ministrations of local clergy before a child attended petty school. To take just one example: the Yorkshire labourer John Stephenson signed his name with a mark in 1686. The same year it was nevertheless reported by William Holderness that 'John Stephenson had a book in his hand and he told him that it was a book of Arithmetic which he had taken out of Roger Rayes house and desired this examinant not to tell Rayes it for he designed to learn something out of it and carry it home again.' (BI CPII 3692, 1686)

Another indicator of the widening social distribution of reading skills is the growth of the market in print. Chart 2 provides a very crude index of the scale of this expansion by showing the number of vernacular printed editions catalogued on the English Short Title Catalogue (ESTC). Chart 3 represents this as the proportion of vernacular printed editions *per capita* between 1550 and 1750. The data does not in any way reflect the full amount of printed material in circulation: single editions generated print-runs ranging from the hundreds to the thousands depending on genre, and much of the cheapest and most popular material simply does not survive. The basic upward trend in consumption is nevertheless clear enough.

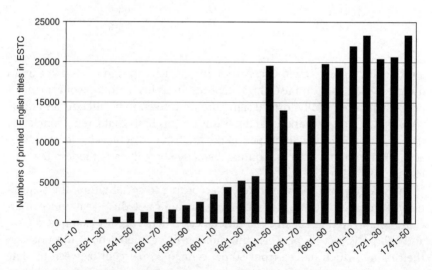

Chart 2: Number of English printed titles in English Short Title Catalogue (ESTC) per decade (ESTC on 6 February 2011)

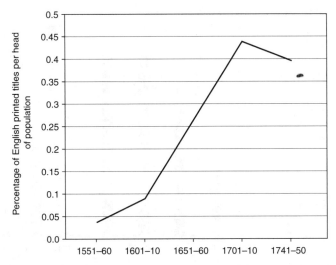

Chart 3:   English printed titles per capita, 1551–1751 (Wrigley and Schofield, 1981, p. 528)

In only three generations this 'educational revolution' contributed to an expanding social elite which was classically educated, culturally homogenous and deeply committed to the printed word. It also helped create a wider popu-lace that was receptive to the range of printed genres so produced. Clearly, the immense religious fermentation and controversy of the Reformation was encouraged by these developments: it has been estimated that some 42 per cent of surviving printed works in the mid-seventeenth century were reli-gious or moralistic in nature. The implications for legislation and governance were also considerable. Wrightson notes that whereas

> in 1584 only 48% of the Members of Parliament had experi-enced education at the universities or Inns, by 1640–2 some 70% of members had undergone higher education. In 1584, some 54% of the active justices of Somerset and 50% of those of Northamptonshire had attended a university or Inn or both, but by 1636 the respective proportions were 86 and 82%. (Wrightson 1982, pp. 192–3)

This was, indeed, a remarkably fecund period for the Inns, which in addition to benefiting from the astonishing increase in civil litigation (see Chart 4 and Table 2) also served as centres of literary and theatrical activity (Winston, 2010).

The early modern expansion in education, literacy and print had obvi-ous ramifications for religious, governmental and legal life. However, the implications for English drinking habits were also significant. Alex Shepard

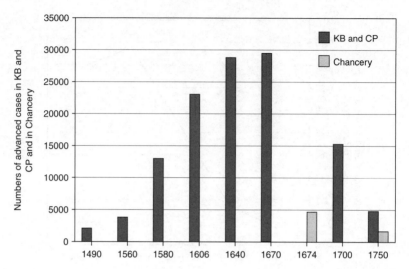

Chart 4: King's Bench (KB) and Common Pleas (CP) plus Chancery 1490–1750 (Brooks, 1989, pp. 361–4)

Table 2: Legal causes in Westminster courts per 100,000 of total population (from Brooks, 1986, p. 78)

Date	Legal causes
1560	479
1606	1351
1823–1827	653
1975	560

has shown that the semi-sanctioned drunkenness of the Elizabethan and early Stuart universities was integral to male bonding, camaraderie and rites of passage (Shepard 2003, pp. 103–13). Students learnt not merely to study but to drink. The Inns are another case in point. Michelle O'Callaghan has argued that from as early as the 1590s, London's legal neighbourhood witnessed the formation of new modes of sociability, with their locus in the surrounding taverns and inns, which supplemented the rich culture of *communitas* that had long characterized the life of the Inns themselves. She suggests that this emergent sociability 'had well-defined rituals based on cultures of revelling at the universities and the Inns of Court and the humanist revival of classical convivial traditions' (O'Callaghan, 2007, p. 5). Typical was the 'Sireniacs' frequented by Ben Jonson, who 'looked back to the Greek *symposium* and Roman *convivium*, as well as placing themselves in the company of the drinking societies of contemporary Europe'. What was already 'a highly diversified and sophisticated culture' of 'convivial socie-ties' at the turn of the century accelerated 'in volume and tempo' in the 1620s (Raylor, 1994, pp. 160–1). As Timothy Raylor has shown, a new spate of fraternities had their antecedents not merely in the humanist nexus of grammar school, university and Inns but also the 'military companies' which had performed so lamentably in the Thirty Years War (Raylor, 1994, p. 162). Known by names like the 'Order of the Bugle' and the 'Order of the Blue', they emulated the ancient Greek *hetaireia* and *komos* – modes of 'ritualized degenerate behaviour' – rather than the *symposium* and *conviv-ium* (Raylor, 1994, p. 71). And they brought a new level of 'riotous speech and behaviour' to an already 'complex *habitus* in which young men could learn and practise ways of speaking, dressing and modes of behaviour that distinguished them within a wider society of gentlemen' (O'Callaghan, 2007, p. 13).

Viewed in these terms, the cultural homogeneity of England's gentry, lawyers, physicians and clerics – not to mention playwrights and poets – takes on a slightly different hue. Social historians are familiar with early modern gentlemen processing the 'stacks of statutes' emanating from Westminster or learning their magisterial duties from John Dalton's *The Country Justice*. They have been less quick to consider the readership for a witty dialogue like *Wine, Beer, Ale and Tobacco, Contending for Superiority* (probably written by the playwright James Shirley) which was initially sold by the bookseller of legal texts, John Grove, from his shop in Furnivall Inn Gate in 1629, and was reprinted twice thereafter. This dramatized a dialogue between 'Wine, A Gentleman', 'Sugar, His Page', 'Beer, A Citizen', 'Nutmeg, His Prentice', 'Ale, A Country-man', 'Toast, One of his rural Servants', 'Water, A Parson' and 'Tobacco, A Swaggering Gentleman'. Personified as social types, these drinks and their accoutrements move in and out of each other's 'society' and 'company' – as they term it – discuss-ing their relative social standing and superiority over each other. Nor have historians explained the apparently inexhaustible demand for popular 'miscellanies' like John Cotgrave's *Wits Interpreter*, first published in 1655. Miscellanies were anthologies of ancient and modern quotes, epigrams, jests and trivia designed to be learnt and recited in company: certain titles, such as *Politeuphia, Wit's Commonwealth* (1598), were published tens of times throughout the seventeenth century. Among other things *Wits Interpreter* promised to teach 'the Art of Drinking, by a most learned Method' (Cotgrave, 1655, pp. 329–38; Smyth, 2004, p. 205). Other types of performative genre – i.e. texts intended to be performed, or to enhance performance, in what one 1659 'lover of mirth' described as 'true-hearted society' – were also among the best-sellers of the age. Staples included jest-books and ballads; and drinking was often either their subject-matter or the anticipated context for their consumption (Anon, 1659; McShane, 2004a; Hadfield, 2010; Hailwood, 2010).

The performative nature of these 'drinking genres' points to an important feature of early modern drinking: it was valorized and aestheticized primarily as a mode of sociability. It can also be seen that of the thousands of young men who benefited from the 'educational revolution' in the later sixteenth and seventeenth centuries, many would have partaken in 'true-hearted society' as students and innsmen. More to the point, they would have continued to experience it thereafter, either directly through practice or vicariously in print. Others found work in the print trade, authoring or co-authoring the texts in which various kinds of drinking ritual, ethos, convention and patois – not to mention the witty aphorisms and interjections requisite of 'society', 'fellowship' and 'company' – were invoked, rehearsed, celebrated and satirized. It should be emphasized that they did this not merely for their social peers but also the popular market. As Angela McShane has shown, even the most humble one-penny ballads could boast classical antecedents and referents; prominent 'poetical wits' like Ben Jonson and Thomas Shadwell wrote ballads; and, although his background is obscure, Matthew Parker, the 'king of the seventeenth-century balladeers', placed himself in a vernacular literary tradition that encompassed Chaucer, Spencer and the Earl of Surry (McShane, 2004b, p. 72; Raymond, ODNB). Humanist writers like Spencer and Rabelais regarded bawdiness, corporeality and drunkenness as legitimate poetic registers: the sharp distinction extrapolated by critics like Michael Bakhtin between the 'carnivalesque' popular and rarefied elite would have made little sense to them (Bakhtin, 1968; Bowen, 1998; Hadfield, 2010, pp. 1–19). Likewise the very nature of miscellanies, which anthologized extant materials for popular consumption, brought the work of ancient and modern authors into wider circulation.

The argument so far may well seem like the 'bleeding obvious'. Drinking was not the preserve of the lower orders in early modern England. On the contrary, it was culturally reinvigorated – and in some quarters actively celebrated – by that cultural process we can conveniently call the Renaissance. This was true in terms of modern styles of sociability adopted in London and the universities. It is also true in terms of the swathes of performative printed literature which conveyed (positively or negatively) the conventions and 'wit' required of drinking to a wider audience. One line of enquiry that follows is the myths of intoxication which accumulated around so many of the literary talents of the age – the 'university wits' of the 1590s were known as copious drinkers; so too were the 'Sons of Ben' who clubbed with Ben Jonson, the Royalist poets of the civil war years, the Restoration 'wits' thereafter. As Michelle O'Callaghan's work on 'wit', Angela McShane's study of toasting and Mark Hailwood's recent account of 'good fellowship' show, equally significant are the language and tropes through which drinking – including excessive drinking – was valorized (O'Callaghan, 2007; Hailwood, 2010; McShane, 2010). In all three instances it was the sociability of drinking, rather than its more dubious physiological consequences, which writers eulogized. Of course, identifying the tropes in contemporary literature is one thing; showing that those tropes informed social practices another. The final part of the discussion therefore describes three incidents in which men with connections to the law can be found drinking in ways resonant with literary prescription.

The first of these involved a Yorkshire cleric, Mr Reginald Hopwood, meeting his attorney, Mr John Robinson, in Widow Webster's alehouse in Market Weighton (in the East Riding) in 1673 to discuss 'some suites' (Withington, 2007). Robinson described how:

> and so being sat together one Thomas Squire [another lawyer] came into the same room and sat down in company with them where after a while they began to be merry and the said Thomas Squire began to speak Latin to the said Mr Hopwood and did convince or at least urge that the said Hopwood did then speak *falso Latin* and gave him then very reflecting words and did as this examinant remembering press several cups upon him…which Ale and the passion he the said Mr Hopwood then was urged to did somewhat intoxicate the said Mr Hopwood, and as this deponent now remembers the said Mr Hopwood's prick was then to be seen by the company there but did not hang out of his breeches [as had been alleged by Squire] and this examinant he now remembers was the first that see the same and being merry…told Mr Squire thereof who put his pipe to it under the table. (BIHR D/C CP 1673/5)

Here we have, then, two Yorkshire lawyers and a cleric at first 'making merry' in the ways prescribed by miscellanies and other manuals of wit (the men have a Latin competition, engage in one-upmanship) before their merriness leads to outright intoxication. Such 'witty' company must have met all the time: this one only survives because Hopwood was reported for bringing his office into disrepute.

If the drinking of Hopwood, Robinson and Squire was inflected with 'wit' then that of another minister, John Warter, nicely illustrates how the culture of 'loyal' toasting which had flourished during the civil wars had infiltrated the very heart of Restoration civic governance. Warter's travails were anticipated by the bequest of the wine merchant Marmaduke Rawdon to the city of York in 1669. Rawdon left 'one drinking cup of pure gold' (worth £100) with 'the city arms and my arms graven upon it' together with a £10 silver chamber pot, 'both which are to go from Lord Mayor to Lord Mayor' (he added that 'if these two be converted to any other use the value thereof to return to my executor') (Davies, 1863, p. xxxiii). Warter's fate was sealed by the decision of the corporation in 1677 to celebrate the 'happy nuptials' of Princess Mary and William of Orange – a procession of citizens and invited guests would drink the health of the royal couple before adjourning to dinner in the Guildhall (Withington, 2005, pp. 133–4). Warter subsequently admitted to the church courts that he 'hath unseasonably frequented Taverns and alehouses and hath been addicted to the drinking of strong beer and wine and ale'. However, he also stressed that on the day in question, when he was reported to be 'so overtaken with strong drink that the streets would scarce hold you', he was:

> neither in Alehouse nor tavern neither did he spend one penny that day but confesses he dined with the Lord Mayor of the city of York and went after dinner with other company...to the Guildhall...and there did amongst other company drink several sorts of wine insomuch that when [he] came from the said hall he found that the wine had got into his head and he believes that by reason thereof he did stagger in the streets. (BI CPH 3314, 1677)

It was, in effect, civic toasting of the royal nuptials rather than any alehouse tippling which left Warter reeling in the streets.

The final incident occurred 50 years earlier, also in York. It involved Anthony Carthorne, a minor official in the Council of the North, who (luckily for us) had the misfortune to be called as witness in a defamation case involving a kinswoman in 1629. As a result his character as a reliable witness was questioned by the other party. It transpired that he was 'much addicted to drunkenness and to haunt and frequent alehouses very disorderly'; that he was 'noted and defamed for a common drunkard within the city of York'. Indeed one witness explained that Carthorne

> was and is such a person as is termed a good fellow, and such as one will keep company and spend his money with his friends, the which he endeavours to refrain as much as he can but that he is drawn away some time by his friends and wits and is such as one as used to go to alehouses and drink hard sometimes, in so much that...he hath sometimes been so overtaken with drink, as that he was not fit to keep company any longer.

It was recalled that on one occasion Carthorne 'drinking in the house of Mr Whalley within the parish of St Sampson's with some company at which time a wager was laid, about the striking the top of the house or chamber where they were with their feet'. Carthorne succeeded and

> demanded the wager, whereupon some quarrel cross betwixt him and some of the said company which was with him, and being moved onto the street they began to fight, whereupon the constable of that parish...came and set both him and the rest of the company in the stocks in the Thursday Market (BI CPH 1823, 1629).

The identification of Carthorne as a good-fellow, wit and hard drinker – as a man somewhat removed from the civil niceties of ordinary respectability on account of his company – nicely resonates with the trope of 'good fellow' circulating in print at that time (Hailwood, 2010). The contemporaneous ballad *Roaring Dick of Dover* began 'Here's a Health to all Good-Fellows/that intend with me to join/At the tavern or the Alehouse/and will freely spend their coin./But for such as hate strong liquor/are not for my company/O it makes my wits the quicker/when I taste it thoroughly' (Anon, 1632). *The Mad Merry Pranks of Robin Good-Fellow*, attributed to that quintessential good fellow Ben Jonson, painted a slightly different character – his was a spirit from 'Fairy Land' who visited earth to inflict 'revel rout', 'merry be' and 'good sport' on unsuspecting mortals (Jonson, 1625). Allegorical rather than descriptive, the conceit of a supernatural mischief-maker nevertheless invoked qualities to which early modern drinkers could aspire.

The experiences of Carthorne, Warter and Hopwood suggest the social entrenchment of at least three styles of Renaissance 'company' over the course of the seventeenth century – of good-fellows, toasts and wits. They suggest that lawyers, clerics and officials – men at the heart of the legal, religious and civic establishments – were extremely active in this entrenchment, and that their habits were at one with the surge in printed literature venerating drink and sociability. As such it is appropriate to finish with *The Delights of the Bottle*, a 1670s ballad attributed to the Restoration dramatist Thomas Shadwell. As the son of a Norfolk lawyer, student at first Gonville and Caius College in Cambridge and then Lincoln's Inn, passionate admirer of Ben Jonson, eminently clubbable (he was a member of the Green Ribbon Club) and the author of comedies like *The Libertine*, Shadwell is emblematic of the 'Heathen Authors or our Modern Plays' bewailed by Woodward. *Delights of the Bottle* began: 'Love, and wine, are the bonds that fasten us all/The world but for this to confusion would fall;/Were it not for the pleasures of love and good wine,/Man-kind for each trifle their lives would resign'. It was, Shadwell proclaimed, a life 'none would refuse, but a Beggar or Cit/Who to [carry on] the humour, wants money or wit' (Shadwell, 1675). If the ballad's philosophy was simple – 'bleeding obvious', even – then it also reflected over a century of cultural change.

Bibliography

Archival references
Borthwick Institute of Historical Research, University of York (BI)
Printed works
Anon (1659) *Mirth in Abundance* (London)
Anon (1632) *Roaring Dick of Dover* (London)
Bakhtin, M (1968) *Rabelais and his World*, Helene Iswolsky (trans.) (Cambridge MA: MIT Press)
Bowen, B C (1998) *Enter Rabelais, Laughing* (Nashville: Vanderbilt University Press)
Brooks, C W (1986) *Pettyfoggers and Vipers of the Commonwealth* (Cambridge: Cambridge University Press)
Brooks, C W (1989) 'Interpersonal Conflict and Social Tension' in A L Beier et al. (eds), *The First Modern Society* (Cambridge: Cambridge University Press)
Brown, J (2008) 'The Landscape of Drink: Inns, Taverns and Alehouses in Early Modern Southampton' (PhD thesis, University of Warwick)
Burke, P (2000) 'A Civil Tongue. Language and Politeness in Early Modern Europe' in P Burke, P Harrison and P Slack (eds), *Civil Histories* (Oxford: Oxford University Press)
Chartres, J (1990) 'No English Calvados? English Distillers and the Cider Industry in the Seventeenth and Eighteenth Centuries' in J Chartres and D Hey (eds), *English Rural Society, 1500–1800* (Cambridge: Cambridge University Press)
Clark, P (1978) 'The Alehouse and Alternative Society' in D Pennington and K Thomas (eds), *Puritans and Revolutionaries: Essays in Seventeenth-Century History Presented to Christopher Hill* (Oxford: Oxford University Press)
Clark, P (1983) *The English Alehouse: A Social History 1200–1830* (London: Longman)
Cotgrave, J (1655) *Wit's Interpreter* (London)
Courtwright, D (2001) *Forces Of Habit. Drugs and the Making of the Modern World* (Cambridge MA: Harvard University Press)
Cressy, D (1980) *Literacy and the Social Order* (Cambridge: Cambridge University Press)
Davies, R (ed.) (1863) *The Life of Marmaduke Rawdon: Now Printed from the Original MS. in the Possession of Robert Cook*, XLII (London: Camden Society)
Defoe, D (1700) *The Poor Man's Plea* (London)
Elias, N (1983) *The Civilizing Process*, Edmund Jephcott (trans.) *I. The History of Manners* (Oxford: Blackwell)
Hadfield, A (2010) 'Spenser and Jokes' **25** *Spenser Studies: A Renaissance Poetry Annual*

Hailwood, M (2010) 'Alehouses and Sociability in Seventeenth-Century England' (PhD Thesis, University of Warwick)

Hancock, D (2009) *Oceans of Wine. Madeira and the Emergence of American Trade and Taste* (New Haven: Yale University Press)

Hobsbawm, E J (1971) 'From Social History to the History of Society' **100**(1) *Daedalus* 20–45

Jonson, B (1625) *The Mad Merry Pranks of Robin Good-Fellow* (London)

McShane, A (2004a) 'Roaring Royalists and Ranters' in Smyth (ed.), *The Pleasinge Sinne*

McShane, A (2004b) "Rime and Reason": The Political World of the English Broadside Ballad, 1640–1689' (PhD thesis, University of Warwick)

McShane, A (2010) 'The Extraordinary Case of the Flesh Eating and Blood Drinking Cavaliers' in A McShane and G Walker (eds), *The Extraordinary and the Everyday in Early Modern England* (Basingstoke: Palgrave Macmillan)

O'Callaghan, M (2007) *The English Wits. Literature and Sociability in Early Modern England* (Cambridge: Cambridge University Press)

Politeuphia, Wit's Commonwealth (1598)

Porter, R (1985) 'The Drinking Man's Disease: The Pre-History of Alcoholism in Georgian Britain' *British Journal of Addiction* 80

Raylor, T (1994) *Cavaliers, Clubs and Literary Culture: Sir John Mennes, James Smith and the Order of the Fancy* (Newark DE: University of Delaware Press)

Raymond, J, 'Matthew Parker', Oxford Dictionary of National Biography (ODNB)

Shadwell, T (1675) *The Delights of the Bottle* (London)

Shepard, A (2003) *Meanings of Manhood in Early Modern England* (Oxford: Oxford University Press)

Shepard, A (2005) "Swil-Bolls and Tos-Pots": Drink Culture and Male Bonding in England, 1560–1640' in L Gowing, M Hunter and M Rubin (eds), *Love, Friendship and Faith in Europe, 1300–1800* (Basingstoke: Palgrave Macmillan)

Shirley, J(?) (1629) *Wine, Beere, and Ale, Together by the Eares. A Dialogue, Written First in Dutch by Gallobelgicus, and Faithfully Translated Out of the Originall Copie, by Mercurius Britannicus, for the Benefite of His Nation* (London)

Smyth, A (ed.) (2004) *A Pleasinge Sinne: Drink and Conviviality in Seventeenth-Century England* (Woodbridge: Boydell & Brewer)

Smyth, A (2004) '"It Were Far Better Be a Toad, or a Serpant, Then a Drunkard": Writing about Drunkenness' in Smyth (ed.), *Pleasinge Sinne*

Stone, L (1964) 'The Educational Revolution in England, 1560–1640' **28** *Past and Present* 1

Thomas, K (1971) *Religion and the Decline of Magic* (Harmondsworth: Penguin)

Thomas, K (1977) 'The Place of Laughter in Tudor and Stuart England', *Times Literary Supplement*, 2 January

Tlusty, B A (2001) *Bacchus and the Civic Order: The Culture of Drink in Early Modern Germany* (Charlottesville VA: University of Virginia Press)

Winston, J (2010) 'The Literary Associations of the Middle Temple' in R Havery (ed.), *Middle Temple History* (Oxford: Hart Publishing)

Withington, P (2005) *The Politics of Commonwealth* (Cambridge: Cambridge University Press)

Withington, P (2007) 'Company and Sociability in Early Modern England' **32** *Social History* 3

Woodward, J (1699) *An Account of the Societies for Reformation of Manners in London and Westminster, and Other Parts of the Kingdom* (London)

Wrightson, K (1981) 'Alehouses, Order and Reformation in Rural England, 1590–1660' in E Yeo and S Yeo (eds), *Popular Culture and Class Conflict 1590–1914: Explorations in the History of Labour and Leisure* (Brighton: Harvester)

Wrightson, K (1982) *English Society 1580–1680* (London: Hutchinson)

Wrigley, E A and R S Schofield (1981) *The Population History of England: A Reconstruction* (London: Edward Arnold)

8
On the Cultural Domestication of Intoxicants

Craig Reinarman

Introduction

We fret so much about the iniquity of addiction in modern societies it is easy to lose sight of the ubiquity of intoxication in human history. Prehistoric cave dwellers drew hallucinogenic mushrooms on their walls. Drunken celebrations dotted the calendars of ancient Greece and Rome. Breugel painted a sixteenth-century Flemish village in full, intoxicated revelry. The indigenous people of the Americas ingested psychoactive plants for pleasure, wisdom and healing.

The fact that these modes of intoxication did not inevitably lead to the evils so often linked to drug use suggests the *possibility* that intoxicants can be culturally domesticated. By this I do not mean that drugs can be rendered risk-free or harmless, but rather that the use practices of most users might be tamed such that associated harms are substantially reduced and the drugs become part of a culture's quotidian repertoire of intoxication.

In the case of currently illicit drugs, this process entails individual learning and cultural development that encourages less harmful use practices among users and a consequent reduction in fear and stigmatization of them by others. Less fear and stigma in turn reduces the likelihood that a drug and its users will be marginalized, which increases the likelihood that use practices can be tamed and harms reduced, and so on in a virtuous circle. Currently, licit drugs are partly domesticated already, so the process would look somewhat different, but there is certainly potential for further domestication if use practices take account of risk.

The concept of cultural domestication seems utopian, unless it is compared to the punitive prohibition paradigm that has governed global drug policy for roughly the past century. The core premise of drug prohibition is that formal social control (criminal law) can change behaviour and eliminate or at least radically reduce the use of certain intoxicants. Even if this could ever succeed, the process of excluding these intoxicants from society entails ostracizing users, which tends to marginalize them in deviant subcultures where the moderating influence of conventional users and norms is reduced.

Cultural domestication has the potential to invert this prohibitionist logic by keeping drugs and their users within the fold of society. This was a core premise that underlay the Dutch approach to cannabis decriminalization (Englesman, 1989). The process of cultural domestication relies as well on the informal social controls that users themselves build into their use practices to reduce the risk that intoxication will harm them or disrupt their social functioning.

Cultural domestication is of course contingent on various conditions. There are many ways that this process can be blocked or, once begun, run off the rails. Certainly, cultural domestication will vary by drug and mode of ingestion. Cultures will vary in their capacity for and style of domestication over time. The degree of cultural domestication can also be expected to vary according to the degree of social integration of users. There are other contingencies, known and unknown. In this chapter, I explore the conditions of possibility for the cultural domestication of intoxicants.

Tracing a lineage

In thinking about intoxicants and culture in this way I stand on the shoulders of several scholars who have been important influences. In US scholarship, Alfred Lindesmith's (1947) close-up study of opiate addiction was seminal. He complicated the biological theories of opiate addiction that held sway in the early twentieth century by showing that physiological dependence and withdrawal symptoms are necessary but not sufficient. He found a cultural-cognitive component in the process of becoming an addict. Users had to learn, usually from other addicts, that an additional dose will alleviate withdrawal symptoms. Then they had to decide to obtain and ingest that dose and to recognize that this makes them physically dependent. (Weinberg's chapter in this volume deepens and complicates this approach by outlining a sociology of 'the loss of control').

In the 1950s, sociologist Howard S Becker took a lead from Lindesmith and used in-depth interviews and analytic induction to identify a three-step process by which people become marijuana users: learning proper smoking technique so that the drug will produce real effects; learning to recognize these effects as stemming from the drug; and learning to interpret the resulting sensations as enjoyable. Each step is learned in interaction with experienced users, in the course of which the new user develops a 'motivation to use marihuana which was not and could not have been present when he began use' (1963, p. 58).

Implicit in this analysis was a culture of users in which experienced marijuana smokers teach neophytes. Becker developed this approach more explicitly in a subsequent article on LSD, where he outlined a broader 'natural history of the assimilation of an intoxicating drug by a society' (1967, p. 171). He noticed that as LSD use became more common in the 1960s, the incidence of 'psychotic episodes' or 'bad trips' declined. He hypothesized that such 'psychotic episodes' were not so much caused by the drug's operation on the brain as by the underdevelopment of what he called 'user culture'. People coming to an intoxicant for the first time, he wrote,

> do not have a sufficient amount of experience with the drug to form a stable conception of it as an object....No drug-using culture exists, and there is thus no authoritative alternative with which to counter the possible definition, when and if it comes to mind, of the drug experience as madness. 'Psychotic episodes' occur frequently.
>
> [But over time] individuals accumulate experience with the drug and communicate their experiences to one another. Consensus develops about the drug's subjective effects, their duration, proper dosages, predictable dangers and how they may be avoided; all these points become matters of common knowledge, validated by their acceptance in a world of users. A culture exists.... 'Psychotic episodes' occur less frequently in proportion to the growth of the culture to cover the range of possible effects and its spread to a greater proportion of users.
>
> The incidence of 'psychoses,' then, is a function of the stage of development of a drug-using culture. (1967, p. 171; see Maloff et al., 1982)

Using a comparative anthropological approach, MacAndrew and Edgerton made a similar argument in *Drunken Comportment* (1969). They found, contrary to conventional wisdom, that behaviour while drunk varied widely across cultures. Drunkenness caused consciousness alteration and disinhibition everywhere, but the *forms* this took were culture-specific. In certain cultures (e.g. the USA and UK), drunkenness was associated with both violence and sexual aggression. In other cultures, drunkenness was associated with violence but not sexual aggression. In still others, drunkenness was related to sexual aggression but not violence. And in a few cultures, alcohol was associated with neither. MacAndrew and Edgerton concluded that, despite the fact that the pharmacological properties of ethanol and the physiological processes by which humans metabolize it were the same across all cultures, no uniform set of behavioural consequences followed from intoxication. Behaviour while intoxicated, then, is not so much 'caused' by pharmacology and physiology as 'taught' by cultures to their members (see Heath, 1987, on how culture affects drinking practices and problems).

Zinberg and Harding (1982) advanced this line of thinking further, prompted in part by the problem of heroin use by American soldiers during the Vietnam War. Up to this point, experts and addicts alike believed that 'once a junkie, always a junkie'. But longitudinal research showed that despite a high prevalence of heroin addiction in Vietnam, the vast majority of soldier-addicts did not continue to use heroin after returning home, i.e. once outside the horrors of that war (Robbins et al., 1974). That social setting of use, and the extreme psychological sets characteristic of that setting, provided a more cogent explanation of opiate addiction in this population than the conventional clinical complex of pharmacological and physiological variables thought to cause opiate addiction.

In *Drug, Set, and Setting*, Zinberg (1984) argued that even intoxicants thought to be inherently addicting *could* be used in a controlled fashion. He showed that the pharmacological properties of the drug are not all-determining but rather interact with the psychological sets users bring to the situation of use and the characteristics of the settings of use. Like Becker, he developed a theory of controlled use of intoxicants based upon informal sanctions and protective practices that users themselves develop to regulate their use and reduce risk. In his introduction, Zinberg credited a visit to the UK, where heroin addicts looked different than those he had seen in the USA. During the 40 years of the Rolleston era (c. 1926–1968), opiate addiction in England was primarily treated as a private matter between patient and physician. In this period, most heroin addicts who did not succeed in treatment were prescribed the doses they needed and so did not resemble the iconic street junkie but, rather, managed jobs and families like everyone else (Trebach, 1982, pp. 85–117; Zinberg, 1984, p. ix).

Parker et al. (1998, pp. 150–8) offer an insightful related thesis about the 'normalization' of drug use among young people. They describe 'how a "deviant," often subcultural population or their deviant behavior is…accommodated in a larger grouping or society', or how illicit drug use has moved out of subcultures into culture. This thesis emerged from their longitudinal survey of British youth, which showed that recreational drug use had become 'deeply entrenched' in youth culture over the 1980s and 1990s. They do not claim that all or even most young people ingest illicit drugs, but rather that a sizeable minority does so without shocking the rest. They offer an array of evidence on this point: widespread availability of illicit drugs; high prevalence of current use; an open-ended intention toward future use; and the fact that both users and abstainers are 'drug-wise', which indicates the 'moral accommodation' of drug use. Their respondents blur the line between licit and illicit and fit drug use into leisure alongside sports, shopping and social events.

Despite the claims common to drug war discourse that drug use leads to school failure, addiction and crime, Parker et al. note that drug use is common among otherwise 'well-behaved, middle-class students' who go on to higher education, career success and normal family lives. The same basic patterns have been found across other European societies among socially integrated young people (Eisenbach-Stangl et al., 2009). While prevalence rates vary, the normalization of drug use has occurred among youth in virtually all modern Western societies.

Parker and colleagues are careful to note that this 'growing "matter of factness" about drug use' does not mean drug use is necessarily safe. They argue that the 'process of normalisation demands regulation and *management*' (1998, p. 152). They also note that such regulation and management are not feasible in the policy context of a 'war on drugs' in which it cannot be publicly admitted that normalization has occurred. Their survey data do show, however, that despite formal laws against them, forms of drug use long believed to be inherently pathogenic have been normalized and that drug users have 'routinized' risk management by their own informal means. Such normalization and the routinization of risk management are aspects of cultural domestication.

The process of cultural domestication can also be seen in its absence. Alexander (2008), for example, argues that certain features of modern industrial societies encourage drug misuse. His thesis is that neoliberal globalization has led to economic dislocation, undermined 'psychosocial integration' and generated a cultural malaise that facilitates addictive behaviours. His theory of the conditions likely to produce problematic intoxicant use also helps us imagine the conditions likely to facilitate cultural domestication.

Comparing cases

In this section I explore the notion of cultural domestication empirically through paired case summaries. I selected them to contrast different forms and uses of similar drugs in different cultures under different circumstances,

Table 1   Paired case summaries

More culturally domesticated	Less culturally domesticated
Wine in the Mediterranean	Gin in eighteenth-century England
Coca chewing in the Andes	Crack cocaine in inner cities
Cannabis in the Netherlands	Marijuana in the USA

one showing greater cultural domestication, the other less. Each pair illumi-
nates a different form or aspect of domestication.

Wine in the Mediterranean

Wine drinking and drunkenness were common in ancient Greece and Rome.
Greeks, Etruscans and Romans all made wine central to their cultures and
spread their benevolent view of the vine to new regions. They tended to
consider wine a sign of civilization and to regard societies that did not have
wine as uncivilized (I rely here on Levine, 2006). Greeks afforded a special
place to Dionysus, the wine god sometimes called 'the liberator'. Several
public festivals at the heart of democratic culture in Athens were in honour of
Dionysus. Wine was also conspicuously consumed at private symposia (literally 'drinking together'). Plato wrote of wine as 'the gift of Dionysus'. Paul
Veyne and other historians of antiquity have observed that the Roman empire
also loved Bacchus, 'the god of sociability and pleasure'. 'Bacchic imagery
was ubiquitous, and its meaning was obvious...No other image was as widely
disseminated.' Veyne notes that Bacchus was depicted as 'a benevolent, civi-
lising god who soothed the mind' (1987, pp. 192–3). Although there were
a few notable exceptions, wine consumption in the ancient Mediterranean
world was omnipresent, highly valued and generally unproblematic.

Writing of the sixteenth-century Mediterranean world, Braudel found 'lands
of wine and vineyards' (1972, p. 236), where wine was intrinsic to the ritual
of family meals and was understood more as food than intoxicant. He notes
that wine has long been an essential 'provision', stored in cellars along with
grains and firewood for winter. 'Throughout the Mediterranean the grape
harvest was an occasion for merrymaking and license, a time of madness', he
writes. This entailed 'various abuses' and some authorities tried stern measures to suppress these 'pagan customs', but Braudel found no evidence that
these succeeded. 'Is there any way of fighting the combination of summer
and new wine, of preventing collective revelry?' (1972, pp. 256–9)

Wine is still central to the cultures of the northern, European side of the
Mediterranean. In the present day, Italy and France have higher per capita
rates of alcohol consumption than many other parts of Europe and yet lower
rates of most alcohol-related problems (aside from cirrhosis) and of alcoholism treatment (Lolli et al., 1958; Takala et al., 1992, pp. 292–9). Again,
because wine tends to be consumed within the orbit of family meals, there
is less drinking-to-drunkenness and fewer alcohol-related public order problems than in many other European cultures. Part of the explanation for
this is substance-specific – wine is far less potent than vodka or scotch. But
another key part is the taming influences that stem from the long history and
manifold embeddedness of wine drinking in the European cultures along the
Mediterranean.

Gin in eighteenth-century England

The 'gin epidemic' or 'craze' in England that ran from roughly 1720 to 1750, provides a sharply contrasting case and a different angle of vision on cultural domestication. Gin was the term then used for new, mass-produced, distilled spirits. By all accounts these potent new beverages wreaked havoc in London. Distilled spirits had been available before, but were expensive and thus used largely by elites or for medicinal purposes. In the 1720s, however, the large landowners who dominated Parliament found themselves with surplus grain and falling prices. After the invention of an inexpensive distillation device, little capital was required to become a distiller, so the number of domestic distillers grew sharply, happy to help the landowners solve their surplus grain problem. Parliament passed protectionist legislation that insulated British distillers from foreign competition and eased licensing requirements for manufacturing and marketing gin (Warner, 2002, pp. 29–36). Production and sales increased, making gin both cheap and widely available (which had the added virtue of raising revenues desperately needed by the Crown).

These new forms of drink sped up the process of intoxication for they contained far higher proportions of alcohol than traditional, organic alcoholic beverages like beer, hard cider and mead. In this sense the spread of distilled spirits constituted an "acceleration" of intoxication that paralleled other intensifications during early industrialization (Schivelbusch, 1993).

It was not merely the exceptional potency of gin, however, that made it a social catastrophe. Gin was introduced on a mass scale to a growing population of rural refugees forced off the land when enclosures and other structural economic shifts rendered traditional subsistence livelihoods more difficult. They migrated into cities in search of work (Thompson, 1966, pp. 214–19). As shown in Hogarth's famous prints from that period (particularly *Gin Lane*), these new urban poor lived under horrid conditions – high unemployment, low wages, long hours, overcrowded housing, poor nutrition, no sanitation, rampant disease. As Warner summarized it:

> Gin was the original urban drug. Cheap, potent, and readily available, it met the needs of an urban population, numbing countless thousands to the fatigue, hunger and cold that was the lot of London's working poor. (2002, pp. ix–x)

Beyond the shock of urban impoverishment and a powerful new drug, the geographic displacement of these former agrarian peasants also had uprooted them from the ways of life they had known, from the cultural traditions, rhythms and rituals of their villages (Williams, 1973). Beer had long been enculturated, but when gin was first introduced, there were no norms surrounding its use that might have mitigated excessive consumption. In such a context, gin had the same disastrous consequences among England's urban poor as whiskey had on North American Indians (Schivelbusch, 1993, p. 156).

Modern-day Londoners who live near nightclubs might beg to differ, but the 'gin epidemic' did eventually come to an end. A series of Gin Acts passed between 1729 and 1751 sharply raised taxes on gin and restricted retail sales. Combined with falling wages and rising food prices, this made gin unaffordable to the poor. At this point, Warner concludes: 'Gin began its slow climb out of the gutter and into the liquor cabinets of polite society.' (2002, p. 224) – in which context, I would add, gin-drinking practices were gradually but to some significant degree tamed.[1]

Coca in the Andes

Coca leaf chewing, or *acullico*, has been a cultural tradition in the Andes region of northwestern South America for millennia. The Aymara and Quechua cultures made coca leaf chewing sacred hundreds of years before the Inca conquest in the fifteenth century and it continued to be a valued ritual even while the Spanish Conquistadors and their priests tried mightily to stamp it out as a "vulgar superstition" (Mortimer, 1974).

In 1993, the World Health Organization (WHO) joined with the United Nations Inter-regional Crime and Justice Research Institute (UNICRI) to organize a study of cocaine use in 22 countries. The researchers reviewed various literatures and interviewed a wide array of experts in each site. They found three dominant patterns: coca chewing in the Andes; cocaine hydrochloride sniffing among the Western, urban middle classes; and cocaine injection and crack smoking among the urban poor. The authors found that cocaine injection and crack smoking entailed high risks; that recreational cocaine sniffing entailed some risks to health but had not been destructive for most users; and that coca chewing 'appears to have no negative health effects and has positive therapeutic, sacred, and social functions for indigenous Andean populations' (WHO/UNICRI, 1995, p. 2).[2]

In addition to its use as a mild stimulant to ward off fatigue, hunger and cold during arduous work often at high altitudes, coca has served as a currency, a medicine, a gift to loyal subjects and a symbol in rituals and community ceremonies. Coca is part of sacred rites that make offerings to the gods and 'spiritualize the earth'. As the report summary notes, coca helps create 'social cohesion and cooperation between community members' and

---

1 Murdock (1998) makes a related argument that the rise of women's drinking in the USA helped domesticate the inebriety and violence that characterized male drinking spheres like the saloon by means of gender-integrated drinking rituals like home-based cocktail parties.

2 This report was suppressed at the insistence of the US delegate because these findings so sharply contradicted official US policy positions. A press summary, cited above, was issued, but even this is now unavailable.

to generally enhance 'sociability' (WHO/UNICRI, 1995, pp. 1–4). Coca chewing has remained 'very stable' and unproblematic...indigenous peasants chew large quantities of coca leaves for decades yet manifest no ill effects from extended use...and [this] has not been reported to lead to any noticeable mental or physical health damage' (1995, pp. 5–6).

The authors note that: 'Consumption of coca leaf is fully integrated into the Andean cultural tradition and worldview.' As with the comparison of wine in the Mediterranean vs gin in industrializing England, cultural domestication is certainly easier with the mild, organic form of the intoxicant than with highly processed and concentrated forms. But the more potent alkaloid forms of coca (cocaine hydrochloride or powder and cocaine base or crack) are produced for export in jungle 'labs' across the region, and yet their low-cost availability has not led to an epidemic of use among the indigenous population. This suggests that the deep, long-standing integration of coca into Andean cultures and the norms surrounding its myriad uses help to insulate people from the most risk-laden use practices.

Crack in American inner cities

In 1985 a potent new form of cocaine use emerged in the USA: crack. When the crack scare began, politicians and the media outdid each other with horror stories of individuals, families and whole communities being destroyed by it. They spoke as if crack was a completely different drug from cocaine, but it is simply cocaine hydrochloride powder that has been processed into its base form, which users heat to a vapour and inhale. This mode of ingestion delivers more cocaine to the brain much faster, producing a fleeting but far more intense high. Also new was the way it was marketed – renamed 'crack' and sold in small, inexpensive units on ghetto street-corners. Congress quickly passed laws that sharply increased prison sentences for possession and sale of crack (Reinarman and Levine, 1997).

Many claimed that crack was 'the most addictive substance ever known'. This had been said of other drugs in earlier drug scares, beginning with the temperance crusade against alcohol. Still, addiction treatment experts and former crack users agreed that crack cocaine produces a powerful rush and is easy to abuse; many users have binged compulsively on it and done themselves serious harm. Most people who try crack, however, do not continue to use it for very long. For 25 years the US government's National Survey on Drug Use and Health has found that about 80 per cent of those who had ever tried crack had not used it in the past year.

Drug control authorities and politicians claimed that crack was 'spreading to all parts of society'. This turned out to be false. Whatever its allures, crack never spread far into suburban high schools, college campuses, or the broad working and middle classes. Crack's extreme high is widely thought to be exceptionally difficult to manage and perhaps for this reason few people are drawn to it. Crack use remains concentrated in a small slice of the most vulnerable part of the population, the marginalized, inner-city poor. The fact that crack use did not spread across the general population and that most people who did use it stopped may be indicators of how difficult it is to domesticate.

Yet the setting was an intrinsic part of the danger. Politicians and the media repeatedly cited crack as a major cause of violent crime. It is true that many crack abusers committed crimes. At first, everyone assumed that this stemmed from the addict's craving, but subsequent research showed that was generally not the case. A key study of New York Police records, for example, showed that most 'crack-related homicides' stemmed from the tinderbox context in which crack was *sold*: high unemployment, desperate poverty, huge profits to be made in illicit drug markets, no access to legal means of dispute resolution, and easy access to firearms (Bourgois, 1995; Goldstein et al., 1997; Reinarman and Levine, 1997). That is, most 'crack-related homicides' had to do with the exigencies of the illicit market – dealers fighting over lucrative sales turf, forcibly collecting debts, etc. While crack use has persisted at nearly the levels of 25 years ago, crack *markets* have stabilized or moved indoors and rates of violent crime have declined dramatically since the mid-1990s.

Although the harsh new crack laws did not stop use, they did drive a ten-fold increase in the number of drug offenders in US prisons, from about 50,000 in 1981 to more than 500,000 in 2010. This helped triple the prison population and gave the US the highest incarceration rate in the world. As both the US Supreme Court and Congress have recently admitted, the punitive policy response to crack in the 1980s exacerbated the problems of the poor by severely disrupting inner-city families and communities.

So, yes, crack did have devastating effects on many urban neighbourhoods, but this did not stem solely from its pharmacological properties or high potential for misuse. As with gin in eighteenth-century London, a powerful new form of drug use was introduced into a population already faced with severe, multi-generational economic dislocation, high unemployment, grinding poverty, declining public services, and pre-existing crime problems, all of which were deepened by the largest and most racially skewed imprisonment wave in US history. In addition to the powerful punch of the crack high, this constellation of conditions was a recipe for extreme use practices, not for culturally integrated use and moderating norms.

Comparison with coca chewing among Andean peasants suggests, however, that more than poverty was at work in the crack era devastation. The potency of crack and the directness of the mode of ingestion matter, but the degree of social dislocation and the lack of cultural integration also contributed to the difference in consequences. The fact that most people who tried crack did not continue to use it and that it did not spread far outside the context of extreme hardship suggests that stable communities, life chances and the norms characteristic of conventional life helped insulate people from crack's allure.

Cannabis in the Netherlands vs marijuana in the USA

Since the 1980s, the Netherlands has been the only country that allows the legal sale of cannabis. Several hundred 'coffee shops' are licensed for retail sales of small amounts to adults. In 2005, 22.6 per cent of Dutch people aged 12 and over reported having ever used cannabis, while 5.4 per cent reported having used it in the past year (Trimbos Institute, 2007, p. 26).

In the US, cannabis (marijuana) remains criminalized, with 858,408 Americans arrested for marijuana offences in 2009, 758,593 (88.4 per cent) for possession alone (FBI, 2010). Yet 41 per cent of Americans aged 12 and over reported having ever used marijuana in 2008, while 10.3 per cent reported having used it in the past year, nearly double the Dutch prevalence rates (SAMHSA, 2009).

Availability is not destiny. Despite widespread lawful sales of cannabis, Dutch prevalence rates have remained in the middle of the pack in Europe – higher than Scandinavian countries, but lower than Spain, France, Germany, Italy, Denmark, Ireland and England (EMCDDA, 2009). Dutch rates of other illicit drug use similarly trail those of the US and numerous other European societies.

Despite such striking differences in law and prevalence, our study comparing representative samples of experienced cannabis users in Amsterdam and San Francisco found that they shared many informal social controls. Strong majorities in both cities reported that they had informal rules they used to regulate their use, and these rules showed similar patterns of selectivity about the circumstances under which they use cannabis. There were situations in which they would use cannabis (at home, at parties) and situations in which they would not (around children or people who might be offended, at work or school). Respondents in both cities also reported rules about the types of people with whom they would use cannabis (spouses, friends) and those with whom they would not (parents, bosses). In both cities, respondents generally used cannabis in the evenings and on weekends, but rarely during weekdays. These self-imposed rules kept their use within certain bounds and seemed to be based on two guiding principles: use cannabis in such a way that it remains pleasant and useful; and avoid using in ways that might disrupt their lives or social functioning (Reinarman et al., 2004; Reinarman and Cohen, 2007; cf. Maloff et al., 1982).

While these regulatory rules suggest that cannabis has been culturally domesticated to a significant degree in both societies, we did find one telling difference. Respondents were asked what potency of cannabis they preferred – mild, moderate, strong, or very strong. Nearly all expressed a clear preference, but 65 per cent of Amsterdam respondents preferred mild or moderate strains of cannabis, compared to 43 per cent of San Francisco respondents. Conversely, 57 per cent of San Francisco respondents reported a preference for strong or very strong cannabis, compared to 35 per cent of Amsterdam respondents (Reinarman, 2009).

Many factors could conceivably account for this, including differing drug use norms and cultural repertoires of intoxication (MacAndrew and Edgerton, 1969; Alasutari, 1992). My hypothesis is that policy may impact user expectations about supply. A core objective of drug prohibition is to eliminate or at least reduce supply, but this can have unintended paradoxical consequences, including increasing potency (Westermeyer, 1976). During US alcohol Prohibition (1920–1933), for example, when manufacture and sale of alcoholic beverages were criminalized and supplies became uncertain, consumption of higher alcohol-content distilled liquor increased while consumption of milder alcoholic beverages like beer and wine decreased (Warburton, 1932; Morgan, 1991; Levine and Reinarman, 2006). Some of this may have been due to the black market's economic incentives toward production of less bulky, easier-to-smuggle distilled spirits. But Prohibition also pushed drinking underground into settings like 'speakeasies' where hard-drinking norms held sway. After Repeal, however, when drinkers could again choose from the full range of potencies, consumption of beer and wine increased while that of distilled liquor decreased (Miron and Zweibel, 1991).

The same dynamic may be at work among cannabis users, with drug law enforcement in San Francisco pushing users toward a preference for greater potency. When supplies are not always reliable in quality or quantity, as in San Francisco, more users are likely to feel they cannot always be certain of adequate potency or dependable supplies and thus opt for stronger strains. In the Dutch policy context, where a stable market affords users steady supplies and a wide choice of cannabis potencies, a strong majority preferred milder strains.

Although we found signs of cultural domestication of cannabis in both cities, the sharp difference in potency preferences suggests greater cultural domestication in the Dutch context. Long before their *de facto* decriminalization of cannabis, there were two features of Dutch history and culture that supported cultural domestication. First, before there was a nation called the Netherlands, the people living there had to deal with the omnipresent threat of flooding, a problem little deterred by punishment. So the Dutch became ingenious about regulating the flow of water by accommodating it, channelling it in safe directions. Regulatory accommodation remains their instinctive approach to social problems, as if inscribed on their cultural DNA. Second, early Dutch success in international trade brought commodities from around the world, including spices, teas, coffees, food delicacies, wines, spirits, opium and hashish, all of which the Dutch group together as *genotmiddelen* – substances that give pleasure to the senses.

With regulatory accommodation as their default solution to problems and their long experience with *genotmiddelen*, the Dutch have rendered intoxicants more *mundane* than have other cultures. They are less prone to anti-drug hysteria and punitive laws and more inclined toward pragmatic policies based on the concept of *gedogen* (to tolerate, to allow what is not allowed), which keep drug users within the taming fold of society rather than casting them out.

Provisional propositions

Historical, ethnographic, and survey research show that users develop self-regulating rules, rituals and protective practices that work against use patterns that overly disrupt daily functioning. Because users themselves develop these informal social controls for their own purposes, they tend to be more readily adhered to than the formal social controls imposed on them by the state. Many of the policies that came to be called 'harm reduction' explicitly built upon such aspects of user culture as a strategy for enticing street addicts toward less risky practices and more contact with service agencies. (These policies helped reduce the spread of HIV/AIDS and have been adopted in 70 countries in the past 25 years.)

Before pushing the notion of cultural domestication further, however, I must note that moderating user cultures are contingent outcomes; they do not always develop. Some user cultures favour extreme use. Russia is a case in point. Both the Tsar and the Bolsheviks tried prohibitionist policies, but these were no match for Russians' love of vodka and norms that encourage drinking-to-drunkenness. This genre of intoxication is not unique to deviant subcultures and is widely regarded as a serious public health problem and a factor in declining life expectancy in Russia.

To the extent that informal social controls and moderating user cultures do develop, the cultural domestication thesis would predict a rise over time in the ratio of ceremonial and connoisseurial use practices to more extreme, escape-to-oblivion use practices (see Collins, 2011). In general, the greater the level of cultural domestication of a drug, the more likely rates of problematic use and problems related to it will stabilize and gradually decline, albeit never to zero. Cultural domestication does not mean there is no abuse or risk; it means only that the normative architecture within which drug use occurs helps the *majority* of users integrate their drug use into the rhythm of their lives in ways that avoid *most* problems *most* of the time.

As cultural domestication proceeds, we would expect to see a reduction of anxiety about and fear of a drug, and a corresponding reduction in demonizing discourse that stigmatizes users. For example, I once asked an official in the Dutch Ministry of Justice why Dutch politicians never seem to use the scare-mongering rhetoric about illicit drugs that American politicians so commonly deploy. He looked at me quizzically and said, 'Who would believe them?' If my argument above holds, the Dutch find such rhetoric less resonant and persuasive than other people because they have gone further toward cultural domestication of intoxicants.

We would also expect cultural domestication to affect law and policy. Durkheim (1901) predicted that as the division of labour in modern industrial societies grew more differentiated, crime would be less often seen as an offence against the *conscience collective* and that punishment would therefore gradually shift away from retribution toward restitution. There are notable exceptions such as the USA, but restitution has become more common while corporal punishments and the death penalty have become less common. Similarly, as a drug becomes culturally domesticated, we would expect to see a gradual shift away from punishment-based, prohibitive policies toward health-based, regulative policies. The trend toward traffic-ticket-type fines for marijuana possession in Australia and parts of the USA as well as the passage of medical marijuana laws in 17 US states and Washington DC support this point. As cannabis has become normalized, Switzerland, Portugal, Spain and other modern democracies have moved toward Dutch-style decriminalization. While injection drug use has not become normalized, dozens of countries have embraced syringe exchanges as a pragmatic public health strategy.

Certain conditions seem conducive to cultural domestication. As Becker argued, the *longer* an intoxicant has been in use in a culture, the more likely a user culture and cultural recipes have developed. With venerable drugs like wine and coca, it is difficult to disentangle whether the drug has been used for a long time because it has been domesticated or has been domesticated because it has been used for a long time. But it seems more likely that cultural domestication develops from various conjunctures than from a specific set of factors in a certain causal sequence.

The cases compared above suggest that the more *culturally embedded* a form of drug use is in popular practices and rituals, the greater the influence of the moderating norms of conventional society, and the less likely it is that users will employ extreme use practices. Cultural embeddedness can, however, cut both ways; extreme use practices can also become embedded. As Withington's chapter on Renaissance drinking cultures shows, for example, heavy drinking and drunkenness were part of masculine camaraderie not just among the poor but also among educated English elites of the early modern era. Their heavy drinking was 'valorized' as a style of sociability and the 'skills and recognized modes of deportment' characteristic of it were learned and passed on. Present day Britain has seen the rise of a binge and brawl drinking culture, due in significant part to the promotion of a 'night-time economy' in which liberal-ized licensing, liquor promotions, and the design of clubs led to 'factories of drunkenness'. This reminds us that the relationship between cultural embed-dedness and cultural domestication is indeterminate, contingent not least upon the presence of moderating drug use norms in conventional society.

Drinking wine in the context of family meals in Italy or chewing coca in the context of community celebrations in Peru suggest that, when intoxica-tion takes the form of a ritualized release, the risk of harm may be reduced. This can also hold for even extreme states of intoxication (Maloff et al., 1982; Walton, 2001). For example, Scandinavian drinking patterns are marked by high rates of drinking-to-drunkenness but relatively low rates of overall alco-hol consumption. While Scandinavians certainly get intoxicated, this is far more often *episodic* than chronic and generally takes place within normative bounds.

The possibilities for cultural domestication also depend upon how the pharmacological properties of an intoxicant interact with human physiology. As the Regan and Ersche chapters illustrate, recent research in neuroscience has shown how repetitive, extreme use of some intoxicants can fundamen-tally alter pathways in the brain. All else being equal, it is easier to domesti-cate wine and beer than more potent, higher alcohol-content drinks; easier to domesticate coca chewing than crack smoking. This suggests that the closer an intoxicant is to its organic state, and the less it is processed to heighten potency, the less dramatic its impact on the brain and the easier it will be to domesticate. A similar point can be made about mode of ingestion: the more natural and gradual the ingestion (by mouth vs injection), the less physi-ological risk and the easier the intoxicant is to domesticate.

But potency and mode of ingestion are choices made by users in concrete cultural contexts. Perhaps the most central if obvious point here is how much the social context of drug use matters. As Warner notes, the gin craze did consti-tute 'a public health crisis, but its root cause was poverty and not gin' (2002, p. 17). And just as crack use remains concentrated in the most impoverished communities, the hardships endured by most Russians go some way toward explaining their heavy drinking norms. Greater poverty and inequality tend to mean more social dislocation and less cultural domestication. The more marginalized the user population, the more extreme their use practices are likely to be and the more destructive the consequences. This in turn fuels the reciprocal demonization of an intoxicant and its users, which makes it easier to pass punitive laws that further marginalize them, and so on in a vicious circle.

Many additional contingencies and confounding influences can affect the possibilities for cultural domestication. Even under conducive conditions,

there can be cultural lag in which the pharmaceutical technology of intoxication, licit and illicit, outstrips culture's capacity to modulate it. Moreover,
the forces of globalization are altering and in many cases undermining
cultures at a rapid pace. In contrast to the ancient, seemingly timeless
Mediterranean and Andean cultures, the acceleration of trade, the collapse
of the former Soviet Union, and the integration of the European Union have
erased borders and led to multiple migrations, cascading diasporas and the
hybridization of cultures. Under these circumstances, it seems likely there
will be more dislocation and normative disorientation obstructing the
cultural domestication of intoxicants. Even within a given society, there
is the problem of new generations. Prohibitionist drug policies typically
inhibit the inter-generational transmission of user lore, protective practices
and other informal social controls, so young people must often learn the
lessons of preceding generations *de novo*, sometimes the hard way.

About 2500 years ago, Euripedes wrote a prescient play called *The Bacchae*
in which he suggested that the suppression of intoxication is both futile
and likely to lead to more destructive excess (Levine, 2006). Formal social
controls that prohibit use of certain drugs make it difficult for user cultures
to develop. A reasonable person might look at the current situation and
conclude that the cultural domestication of intoxicants in the modern world
is increasingly difficult. And yet, despite all the obstacles drug laws put in
the path of informal social controls, drug users do seem continuously to
invent them – *if only because they wish to continue to experience episodic intoxication without disrupting their lives*. The more such informal controls can be
developed in a self-conscious and explicit manner, the greater the degree of
cultural domestication and the greater the potential for reducing harm.

By comparison, drug laws and other formal state controls are weak weap-
ons. What keeps most people from going overboard with intoxicants is not so
much law as cultural recipes – the norms, rituals and rules that guide intoxication practices. Pharmacological properties of drugs and the physiological
characteristics of users are important but not determinative because drug use
is always embedded in a constellation of conditions that shape use practices,
patterns, meanings and outcomes. Efforts to develop a transcultural, univer-
salistic science of addiction and to stamp out drug abuse tend to neglect the
natural experiments in the control of intoxicants that are going on in user
cultures. Those territories invite further exploration.

Acknowledgments

Thanks to Alex Stevens, Geoffrey Hunt, Harry G Levine, Marsha Rosenbaum,
Darin Weinberg and the Cambridge 'Intoxication' conference participants for
insightful comments.

Bibliography

Alasutari, P (1992) *Desire and Craving: A Cultural Theory of Alcoholism* (Albany NY: State University of New York Press)

Alexander, B K (2008) *The Globalisation of Addiction: A Study in Poverty of the Spirit* (New York: Oxford University Press)

Becker, H S (1963) *Outsiders: Studies in the Sociology of Deviance* (New York: Free Press)

Becker, H S (1967) 'History, Culture, and Subjective Experience: An Exploration of the Social Bases of Drug-Induced Experiences' **8** *Journal of Health and Social Behavior* 162–76

Bourgois, P (1995) *In Search of Horatio Alger: Selling Crack in El Barrio* (New York: Cambridge University Press)

Braudel, F (1972) *The Mediterranean and the Mediterranean World in the Age of Philip II* vol. 1 (New York: Harper and Row)

Collins, R (2011) 'Drug Consumption: A Social Ritual? The Examples of Tobacco and Cocaine' in G Hunt, M Milhet and H Bergeron (eds), *Drugs and Culture* (Aldershot: Ashgate)

Durkheim, E (1901) 'Deux lois de l'evolution penale' **4** *L'Année Sociologique* 65–95

Eisenbach-Stangl, I, J Moskalewicz and B Thom (eds) (2009) *Two Worlds of Drug Consumption in Modern Societies* (Aldershot: Ashgate)

Engelsman, E L (1989) 'Dutch Policy on the Management of Drug-related Problems' **84** *British Journal of Addiction* 211–18

EMCDDA (European Monitoring Centre on Drugs and Drug Abuse) (2009) *Drug Situation in Europe* (Lisbon: EMCDDA) www.emcdda.europa.eu/situation/cannabis/3

FBI (Federal Bureau of Investigation) (2010) *Crime in the United States 2009* (Washington DC: US Department of Justice), Table 29

Goldstein, P et al. (1997) 'Crack and Homicide in New York City' in C Reinarman and H G Levine (eds), *Crack in America* (Berkeley CA: University of California Press)

Heath, D (1987) 'Anthropology and Alcohol Studies' **16** *Annual Review of Anthropology* 99–120

Levine, H G (2006) 'Drunkenness and Civilization: A History of Intoxication in Western Cultures' in S Scheerer et al. (eds), *Kriminalitats–Geschichten, Hamburger Studien zur Kriminologie und Kriminalpolitik*, Band 41 (Hamburg, Germany).

Levine, H G and C Reinarman (2006) 'Alcohol Prohibition and Drug Prohibition' in J Fish (ed.), *Drugs and Society* (New York: Rowman Littlefield)

Lindesmith, A R (1947) *Opiate Addiction* (Evanston IL: Principia Press)

Lolli, G, E Serriani, G Golder and P Luzzatto-Fegiz (1958) *Alcohol in Italian Culture* (Glencoe IL: Free Press)

MacAndrew, C and R Edgerton (1969) *Drunken Comportment* (Chicago IL: Aldine)

Maloff, D, H S Becker, A Fonaroff and J Rodin (1982) 'Informal Social Controls and their Influence on Substance Use' in N E Zinberg and W Harding (eds), *Control Over Intoxicant Use* (New York: Human Sciences Press)

Miron, J and J Zweibel (1991) 'Alcohol Consumption During Prohibition' **81** *American Economic Review* 242–47

Morgan, J P (1991) 'Prohibition is Perverse Policy' in M B Kraus and E P Lazeare (eds), *Searching For Alternatives: Drug Control Policy in the US* (Stanford CA: Hoover Institution Press)

Mortimer, W G (1974 [1901]) *History of Coca: 'The Divine Plant' of the Incas* (San Francisco CA: And/Or Press)

Murdock, C G (1998) *Domesticating Drink: Women, Men, and Alcohol in America, 1870–1940* (Baltimore MD: Johns Hopkins University Press)

Parker, H, J Aldridge and F Measham (1998) *Illegal Leisure: The Normalization of Adolescent Recreational Drug Use* (London: Routledge)

Reinarman, C (2009) 'Cannabis Policies and User Practices' **20** *International Journal of Drug Policy* 28–37

Reinarman, C and H G Levine (1997) *Crack in America: Demon Drugs and Social Justice* (Berkeley CA: University of California Press)

Reinarman, C, P Cohen and H Kaal (2004) 'The Limited Relevance of Drug Policy: Cannabis in Amsterdam and San Francisco' **94** *American Journal of Public Health* 836–42

Reinarman, C and P Cohen (2007) 'Law, Culture, and Cannabis' in M Earleywine (ed.), *Pot Politics: Marijuana and the Costs of Prohibition* (New York: Oxford University Press)

Robbins, L, D Davis and D Nurco (1974) 'How Permanent was Vietnam Drug Addiction?' **64** (suppl.) *American Journal of Public Health* 38–43

Schivelbusch, W (1993) *Tastes of Paradise: A Social History of Spices, Stimulants, and Intoxicants* (New York: Vintage)

SAMHSA (Substance Abuse and Mental Health Services Administration) (2009) *Results from the 2008 National Survey on Drug Use and Health: National Findings* (Rockville MD: Office of Applied Statistics, SAMHSA, US Department of Health and Human Services), Tables 2.1A, 2.1B

Takala, J-P, H Klingemann and G Hunt (1992) 'Afterword: Common Directions and Remaining Divergences' in H Klingemann et al. (eds), *Cure, Care, or Control: Alcoholism Treatment in Sixteen Countries* (Albany NY: State University of New York Press)

Thompson, E P (1966) *The Making of the English Working Class* (New York: Vintage)

Trebach, A (1982) *The Heroin Solution* (New Haven CT: Yale University Press)

Trimbos Institute (2007) *Drug Situation 2006: The Netherlands: Report to the EMCDDA* (Utrecht: Trimbos-Instuut), Table 2.1

Veyne, P (1987) 'The Roman Empire' in P Veyne (ed.), *History of Private Life: From Pagan Rome to Byzantium* (Cambridge MA: Harvard University Press)

Walton, S (2001) *Out of It: A Cultural History of Intoxication* (New York: Three Rivers Press)

Warburton, C (1932) *The Economic Results of Prohibition* (New York: Columbia University Press)

Warner, J (2002) *Craze: Gin and Debauchery in an Age of Reason* (New York: Random House)

Westermeyer, J (1976) 'The Pro-Heroin Effects of Anti-Opium Laws in Asia' **33** *Archives of General Psychiatry* 135–9

Williams, R (1973) *The Country and the City* (Oxford: Oxford University Press)

WHO/UNICRI (1995) *WHO/UNICRI Cocaine Project: Press Release WHO/20: Publication of the Largest Global Study on Cocaine Use Ever Undertaken* (Geneva: WHO), 14 March

Zinberg, N E (1984) *Drug, Set, and Setting: The Basis for Controlled Intoxicant Use* (New Haven CT: Yale University Press)

Zinberg, N E and W M Harding (eds) (1982) *Control and Intoxicant Use* (New York: Human Sciences Press)

9
Nudge Policy, Embodiment and Intoxication Problems

Angus Bancroft

Embodiment and liberal subjectivity

Intoxication represents a threat to individual autonomy, the self-willing, self-activating, self-making personhood at the heart of liberal philosophy. In the dominant Anglo-Saxon culture of countries like the UK, USA, Canada and Australia it is walled off from day-to-day life, surrounded by strict moral regulations and conceived of as a space of abandonment, where necessary repressions are briefly suspended. Recent developments in psychopharmacology and neuroscience have challenged the basis for thinking of individual behaviour and choice-making as inherently free and unfettered and they create interesting disruptions of this liberal subjectivity. In this chapter I want to examine these developments and their implications for the construction of intoxication as a public problem with regards to the expanding sphere of 'nudge' public policy and in the memory work involved in addiction recovery.

Social scientists have worked with two competing models of the subject in a democratic society. One is the citizen, a deliberative individual who engages with ideological projects and selects between competing ideas of good governance. The other neo-liberal model, which has governed welfare reform in Britain since the 1980s, is of an individualized consumer who sees decisions in terms of maximizing their own interests. Nudge politics calls both these models into question. It cuts beneath the justification for both and brings out the limits of this kind of choice, selection and autonomy. The challenge is that we are still working explicitly with these two competing models just as the basis for them is being undercut.

There is an expanding politics and practice targeted on the brain, termed neuroculture (Frazzetto and Anker, 2009). Neuroculture is the combination of scientific knowledge of connections between the brain and experience, the regulatory, surveillance and policing functions that are making use of it, public discourses about the neuronal drivers of behaviour, and the growing economy which encompasses psychopharmacology and neuromarketing (Wilson et al., 2008; Williams et al., 2011). The collection of public policies that goes by the name of 'nudge' draws on neuroculture to adjust what is called the choice architecture of everyday life, the way in which choices are structured and presented, to match the limitations and naturalized inclinations of the brain revealed by neuroscience. Nudge is the set of policy proposals and principles that take advantage of that rather than working against it (Thaler and Sunstein, 2008).

Behaviour is embodied. Everything we do is mediated by the physical body, its senses and ingrained habits, organic pathways, abilities and limits. In states of intoxication the body melds with culture, and it is the interface between the body and culture that exercises policy makers. Public policy on intoxication has implicitly been concerned with embodied behaviour. Intoxication is characterized by a sequence of damaged bodies, bodies in decline, chaotic, diseased, dependent and infectious bodies. Now policy debate in the UK is becoming more explicitly led by a particular understanding of embodiment in which it is the normal state of appetites and desires that needs to be managed.

Sin taxes and sumptuary laws have existed to manage behaviour and discourage people from making socially damaging choices. Taxes on alcohol and cigarettes have been used to raise the cost of 'sin' and to encourage people to choose better habits, to become self-acting, sober subjects. The novelty with nudge politics is that there is no longer an ideal subject to become. It dethrones both the deliberative citizen *and* the rational consumer. There are still good and bad choices, but there are no longer good and bad ways of making choices.

These developments are changing the nature of 'the subject', meaning the kind of individual and their capacities that are taken as normal by scientists, social scientists, doctors, social workers, civil servants and the panoply of devices and institutions intended to intervene between desire and action. The classic liberal subject is defined as an autonomous, rational individual capable of making choices. The liberal subject was for a long time the basis for conceiving behaviour in economic thinking. Any person not behaving according to that notion of subjectivity was deviant, and the study of them could be safely relegated to sociology. Alternatively, the subject could be defined as limited, inadequate, fundamentally irrational and in need of further work, in need of governing. In this conception, the previously deviant subject becomes central to our thinking about normal life.

The role of intoxication in this is twofold. Psychoactive substances are used to alter the relationship between self and the world. The public policy concern is with a lasting alteration from autonomy to dependency, a temporary, pathological desire or vulnerability, and more recently, normalized suboptimal behaviour, which has come under the auspices of nudge policy. The last generalizes beyond intoxication to many other areas of human activity. Examples of public health campaigns around autonomy and excess are: the Home Office's *Know your Limits* (2009) campaign to highlight the danger of binge drinking; and the National Health Service's *Unhooked* campaign on smoking and addiction (National Health Service, 2007). The message is that, to restore one's autonomy, one must be separated from nicotine, or from excessive drinking. The threat to autonomy in these campaigns is external to the body, consisting of the cultural validation of heaving drinking, or exposure to addictive chemicals. The approach appears to be the classically liberal one of restoring rational, sober autonomy. Within the *Unhooked* campaign there is also the possibility that the threat to autonomy is internal or internalized in the addicted, nicotine dependent body. For public policy the addicted body can be a threat as the brain may be changed in ways that encourage damaging behaviour.

Neuronal public policy

The public-citizen and neo-liberal models of subjectivity both put choice at the heart of decision-making. However, we mostly do not choose to make choices. Choice is usually forced, often paralysing (Schwartz, 2005) and rarely free in a strict sense. In structuring and managing choice, policy planners have long relied on what psychologists call the reflective system, the deliberative, choice-making ego at the heart of the autonomous liberal subject. Nudge social policies have emerged from the field of behavioural economics. They attempt to explain resistance to the tools used for producing optimal choice, such as sin taxes, health education and drug prohibition and also produce desirable outcomes without nagging and coercion. Nudge theorists trace these problems to the automatic system, a grouping of systems and functions which is pre-reflective and is a powerful governor of decision-making (Thaler and Sunstein, 2008).

Nudge principles seek to recognize the limits of rationality. Mostly people take the path of least resistance in making choices. It follows that in constructing the choice architecture the default option should be the optimal one. Errors should be anticipated and designed out. Individuals should be fed instantaneous responsive feedback so that they cannot be anything but aware of what they are doing. Choices should be mapped, so if I choose *a* I know I will end up with *c* but *d* is now less likely happen. Choice filtering should ensure beneficial choices are not neglected. Perverse incentives should be removed and real costs highlighted (Thaler et al., 2010). Policies might include changing the size of alcohol measures to encourage lower alcohol consumption, defaulting to individual payments for drinks rather than rounds or tabs to reduce binge drinking, or raising the per-unit cost of alcohol. A Behavioural Insights Team has been set up in the Cabinet Office, trailed in the media as the 'nudge unit' (Behavioural Insights Team, 2010). Nudge has the merits to its proponents of being more cost effective and subtle than the prevailing combination of oversight, education and coercion recently favoured in particular by the previous Labour government of the UK and the current Scottish National Party government in Scotland. It appeals to politicians as it has the appearance of being a high impact, low cost set of policies (Reuter and Stevens, 2007; Stevens, 2007).

Nudge challenges the division between public and private. There has been a long-standing debate on the extent of public health intervention that has been in part about the extent of the sphere of public interest, and to what degree personal choices are private ones. Bans on smoking in private spaces such as pubs and nightclubs are driven by the claim that a particular private action has detrimental effects on other members of the public. Opponents claim to defend the private sphere of free will and personal authority. Neuropolitics undercuts this debate about the legitimate boundary between public and private and where unconstrained free will may be exercised by challenging the concept of free will in its entirety. Some debates on coercion and surveillance in addiction treatment already do this by claiming that the dependent smoker, heroin user or other abject addict has their free will compromised. To turn this around, the architecture of public policy is adapted to an erroneous concept of free will that does not exist.

How is intoxication embodied?

To tease apart the nudge approach a little I want to separate behaviour as embodied and also embedded – in users, environments and objects – and point out how public policy contributes to the construction of the latter two. Intoxication is embedded in environments and contexts. Users' bodies and minds become drug-savvy in a process that includes the development of tastes for various forms of intoxication, what is called 'body work' (Shilling, 2011). This is Norman Zinberg's well-known formulation of 'drug, set and setting' (1984). It is frequently assumed that 'setting' is the only socially constructed element of the formula, the other two largely being given, preformed. In fact, substance and set are as contingent and constructed as setting. The three are inseparable from each other, making up intoxication networks of actors and objects such as drugs, paraphernalia, drug-use settings. Public policy can intervene at each point.

In Anglo-Saxon societies we uphold free will as a valued cultural norm, its restoration an aim of addiction treatment, while uncovering more and more examples of the limits of free will. It can help our understanding if we acknowledge both that embodiment is implicit in many policy and practice approaches *and* that we understand its limits. Cognition is grounded in the body and environment while not being limited to them (Wilson, 2002). A caveat is that it is just as important that we understand how cognition is not limited in this way, for example, by our use of automatic or cybernetic systems to extend cognitive capacities, and the creation of cognitive or responsive environments and abstraction systems. Intoxication can function to extend cognition and channel it, and it is that which is culturally valued about the experience. For example, alcohol induced myopia enhances the shared experience of group drinking.

The drug, the substance, is not just a chemical concoction; it is an object of intoxication culture that both literally and metaphorically becomes a different drug in a different form or context. It includes the mode of drug delivery. This is a technology, such as the pill (capsule), the intravenous needle, the pipe, or the cigarette, which shapes the intoxication experience of drug consumption and its meanings. There is its potency, the proportion of the active agents, and the combination of these, against the inert chemicals. Potency has been a live political issue recently in the UK. Cannabis was prohibited in 1928 in the UK, and was classified as a Class B restricted substance in 1971. It was downgraded to the less restrictive Class C in 2002. The British government in 2009 reclassified cannabis from C to Class B. The government in part justified its *volte face* with its claim that new strains of cannabis often called 'skunk' had a much higher tetrahydracannabinol (THC) content than in past decades, though the evidence shows nothing like the hyperbolic claims made for it (Advisory Council on the Misuse of Drugs, 2005; Hardwick and King, 2008). There is a feedback effect here as this development is also driven by user preferences for a more hallucinogenic or dissociative high (Anon., 2011), and the 'mephedrone effect' whereby hyped-up media reports of danger are taken by users as evidence of quality (Measham et al., 2010).

Potency is an individual, social and political quality, as well as a chemical attribute. The nature of chemical potency is also in part subjective. Higher pharmacological strength does not necessarily mean a 'better' or 'stronger' effect for the user. Street heroin is often cut with substances to enhance the psychoactive experience, so a less chemically pure dose may be experienced as much more effective, potent or desirable. This is the case with some street heroin users who are prescribed medicinal heroin, which they find less preferable, as it is not the same drug (Bergschmidt, 2004). There are various physical features and attached attributes of the substance (name, brand, colour, texture, taste, viscosity, status, side effects, smell, smoke), which may or may not have an effect on the user's experience. The experience of pleasure and addiction are embedded. Supposedly objective, separable physical qualities such as potency and quality blur into each other. The chemical consistency and the drug's other physical qualities are modified by various factors, in some cases clinical need, in others marketing, taxation, regulation and so on, all of which are hidden nudges in the architecture of choice.

Set is frequently summed up as a preformed array of dispositions, consisting of the user's personality and attitudes that they bring to the substance. However, set is an active disposition, enacted in the act of consumption, and produced through experience. Smoking technique might be part of set, but this is something learned and developed by the user. It is also demonstrative. For instance, smoking styles signal masculinity or femininity. Hence 'set' is reflected in others, and adjusted to the user's assumptions and guesses about their reactions. The self is constructed by set. For instance, the Home Office's injunction to 'know your limits' encapsulates a mind/body dualism, that puts the sober, self-knowing individual in charge as the guardian of their body, against sexually transmitted infections, violence, and in the case of women, against sexual assault. Risk and blame are measured and assigned, and these discourses then form part of the user's set. Set can involve 'priming' the body by exposure (Gervais et al., 2006). Many cultural proclivities such as learned intoxication styles become part of the set (MacAndrew and Edgerton, 1969).

Setting consists of the social circumstances and physical environment of substance use. The limits and salient constituents of setting are often left undefined in the formula. People are part of the setting, and the user themselves is part of the setting that is consumed by them and others. The user therefore is always constitutive of the setting, at the same time as it constitutes his or her experiences. Sensual elements of the setting – sound, smell texture, surfaces, space – may be deliberately constructed to create a desired intoxicant experience, and manage or limit it as can be seen in the social space of a rave, a traditional pub or a superpub. The setting may be constructed to support surveillance of the user. It may limit some interactions and encourage others, or renarrate pleasure as risk. These elements require the user to adapt their 'set' to the setting. Hence there is a link between environment and cognition. The experience of intoxication is locally specific, and the setting is an active part of this experience.

Polydrug use and the associations that develop between one drug and another form another part of set and setting. For example, a strong link exists between the use of alcohol and cigarettes, which was broken and reshaped by the smoking ban. Another connection common in 1980s raves was between ecstasy and Lucozade, and many ravers looked with disdain on those who mixed ecstasy and alcohol. These associations are made out of the combination of drug effects, which enhances the experience, and the norms and potential of that particular setting. The conduit between them is embodiment. The sensations of addiction, sweetness, potency, tipsiness and so on are embodied. The user must adapt their body to become drugwise, just as all substances in common use have been adapted to the human body.

In the discourse of the drug war the user's body becomes a subject of the drug, a 'selfish brain', but they are mutually constitutive. Elements of setting are sensed through the body, and the user must learn to discern those that are desirable from those that are not. For instance, it takes time to experience the deep, vibrating sonic volume and intense heat of some nightclubs as pleasurable physical sensations rather than uncomfortable. In embodiment is found a relationship to the intoxicant that allows it to be construed as all powerful, as a commanding, persuasive object, or as mundane, an everyday object of leisure. For instance, the potential and experience of addiction is incorporated into smokers' experiences (Gillies and Willig, 1997). Nicotine becomes an 'agent', a subject, supposedly the driver of addiction though it does not fulfil some of the dependence criteria common to other drugs (Hughes, 2006). Hence the hidden nudges of policy and public health discourses, which now seem less benign, define the user as a limited subject, vulnerable at a cellular level.

Embodied drug use

There are identifiable brain substrates implicated in addiction. Dependent behaviour is disrupted when insula is damaged (Naqvi et al., 2007). Vulnerability can be inherited (Legrand et al., 2005). Risk and contagion spreads from watching films with smoking (Tickle et al., 2001), and from watching parents smoke. There is an embodied memory, with smoking vulnerability lasting three years after a single cigarette (Fidler et al., 2006). Increasingly we can describe public problems in genetic terms (Pickersgill, 2009; Campbell, 2010; Kushner, 2010). Added to this sense that the intoxicated enters a cognitive swamp is the extension of cognitive faculties using drugs (Sahakian and Morein-Zamir, 2011).

The process of recognition is crucial to intoxication. There are various elements to intoxication experiences: pleasure, satiation, craving, side effects, perceptual distortion, dependence. Not all are recognized by the user until reflected on and labelled as such (Becker, 1953). There is a directive as well as automatic process. Users may choose to be situated in particular ways. They shape the embodied context of intoxication. Intoxication settings and drug consumption rituals are inseparable parts of the experience. Techniques involve distancing – the intoxicated self is different from the real self, or the intoxicated self is the more genuine one, a more real self than the sober self. The self is entangled with the drug (Gibson et al., 2004).

Modernity means living with constant ambivalence. Pleasure is risk. Leisure is hard work. Treatment creates addiction. Drugs of all sorts can represent this ambivalence and also be a way of helping us live with it. Cocktails of psycho-active medications are taken, analogous to the psychoactive repertoires of illicit drug users (Hunt, 2001; Martin 2006; Measham and Moore, 2009). Two important developments are: medications to cope with some of those stresses and strains that seem to be products of modern society; and the application of modernity – the modern principle of perfectibility – to the mind and body – that is, selves are objects to be. The conclusion from this section is that the set of embodied processes behind nudge are not necessarily fixed and we consciously seek to alter the unconscious aspects of our behaviour, encapsulated in Bourdieu's habitus (Bourdieu, 1977).

Key problem processes

There has been lengthy debate about definitional dynamics versus objective approaches to defining public problems, which boils down to the question of the extent to which socially salient harms are an aspect of society or a mirror for it (Spector and Kitsuse, 1972). In this section I want to disentangle the various processes through which a particular issue coheres as a public problem.

There are structural contexts in which harm is brought into being (Acker 2010). For example, the structural inequality of power, resources and cultural capital divides crack-cocaine use and users into two groups (Reinarman and Levine, 2004). Poor crack-cocaine users are criminalized. Their crack use is treated in the context of the criminal activity they engage in to obtain crack. For wealthy users their crack use is defined as a problem of dependence. One set of users exists with limited social trouble but serious personal difficulties. The other set of users is exposed to severe risks of violence, imprisonment, robbery and, for women, sexual violence (Bourgois, 1989). These structurally patterned risks are shaped by gender, age, locality and ethnicity, as well as class position (Maher 1997; Bourgois and Schonberg, 2009; Brown 2010). Infrastructures ground public problems, such as the treatment system, enforcement, the welfare state and institutions like family. Enforcement may have paradoxical effects and increased use by driving attempts at creating brand/dealer loyalty and increasing the trade's profitability (Skott and Thorlund Jepsen, 2002). The 'male' character of many twentieth-century British pubs was a creation of licensing law, which excluded children under 14 from licensed premises, along with their mothers (Moss, 2009).

An array of technologies and techniques are deployed around public problems; at an individual level, there are diagnostic instruments and treatment pathways. At a wider level, social surveys collect data on populations. These contribute to scoping and defining the problem, and often these days putting a number on it – the cost of binge drinking, the cost of smoking, the cost of addiction (Allender et al., 2009). Definitions, subcultural, social, scientific and legal mediate the experience of users and the interpretation of their behaviour by others (Decorte, 2001). Drug experiences also facilitate transitions and mediate interactions (Mayet et al., 2010). Cigarette smoking can mediate the transition to cannabis use and vice versa. The user becomes prepared, but also has to unlearn some behaviours. Public problems have their rhetoric. Users perform addiction (Bourgois, 2000) and themselves are required to account for treatment failure so as not to be seen as cheating the system (Throsby, 2009).

Public problems are represented. The media reporting on mephedrone tracked its sales closely. A spike in 'buy mephedrone' queries on Google search corresponded with reports on the tragic death of 14-year-old Gabrielle Price who died following a heart attack at a party in Sussex, where she had allegedly taken mephedrone. The widespread reporting of her death was an ideal advertisement for the advantages of mephedrone. In a *Daily Mail* headline, mephedrone was 'The deadly drug that's cheap, as easy to order as pizza...and totally legal' (27 November 2009). The death of Gabrielle Price was read purely as confirmation of the drug's potency. Online retailers reported a significant spike in sales following reporting of her death which was eventually attributed to natural causes in the pathologist's report, the findings of which were rather less well publicized. Information shapes outcomes, for instance by generating stereotype threat (Looby and Earleywine, 2010). Male cannabis users exposed to a summary of research claiming that cannabis affected cognitive functioning performed worse on cognitive tests than controls. Females in the same group performed better.

Problem processes construct problem objects. For example, the debate about cannabis potency referenced above defines cannabis as a single, homogenous drug that becomes more or less dangerous over time. Users and those working in the field know there are many strains of that one drug, and many ways to consume it, which make for a very different 'drug' in each instance. Underlying much of the approach to public problems is the pathologization of non-reflexive behaviour, meaning the way that distinction between intoxications that are or are not problems is not articulated through what you do or possess but how you possess it. Intoxication that is not reflexive is pathologized in high culture (Scruton, 2007).

Problem processes and objects mesh to form supporting infrastructures. A drug use culture has many supporting infrastructures, such as the criminal justice system, social and medical research programmes and pharmaceutical companies. The Misuse of Drugs Act 1971 restricts competition from less harmful competitors, by judging ecstasy, LSD and magic mushrooms, crack and heroin to be of equal risk, and by removing much of the cost base required for normal businesses. The public problem infrastructure creates new market opportunities: Users turned to so-called 'legal highs' such as mephedrone because they could legally buy them online and they will not be arrested for possession, not necessarily because they are safer, better known, better supported by a drug use culture. Researchers shape scientific knowledge but often we forget these contexts – as if the problems of illicit drugs appeared out of the blue. The key to public problems is the act of assembling the above, putting together data, organizations and policies.

Public problems sometimes appear as if they are ever expanding and so it is important to be aware of the use of limiting techniques, statements defining how far the problem goes and where it ends. Limiting techniques can be seen in the strategy paper on alcohol pricing by the UK government, which is careful to define the problem in terms of a minority of uncontrolled heavy drinkers, in contrast to the Scottish government which embeds the problem squarely in Scottish culture (Scottish Government, 2009; *Daily Telegraph*, 2012; Secretary of State for the Home Department, 2012). Limits can be placed by volume of consumption, time, place, purpose and context. There are also natural limits imposed by drama fatigue, saturation of public attention, and exhaustion of institutional carrying capacity (Hilgartner and Bosk, 1988).

Recovery and plasticity

A contrast with nudge and neuropolitics that conceive of the brain and self as rather rigid is the conception of the self in addiction treatment and theory which takes it as having qualities of both homeostasis and plasticity. The brain is homeostatic, meaning it likes to be in a stable state. Hence drug-induced highs do not last and damaging habits become intransigent. Neuronal adaptation is the brain reforming itself to cope with excessive stimulation. The brain is also plastic. Reward pathways are created so that we can learn new, adaptive behaviours. This synaptic plasticity means strong associations develop between drug-related habits, environments, actions and drug-use behaviour.

Problem processes can impede or support recovery from problem drug use. Structural contexts, infrastuctures, rhetorics, all shape recovery from dependence. Definitions of recovery are powerful with real world effects on who is defined as recovered and who is not (White, 2007). There can also be harmful shoving, more than nudging. Harmful outcomes can be generated by drug enforcement (Marx, 1981; Duncan, 1994; Cooper et al., 2005; Cooper et al., 2009; International Centre for Science in Drug Policy, 2010;). There is a lexicon of recovery, neo-liberal, transforming self, autonomy (Nettleton et al., 2010). A structure of drug courts, counselling, media discourse and medicine exists around this (Reinarman, 2005). These recovery infrastructures are not just transforming the self but the whole set of embodied practice.

Recovering an authentic self and reinventing past experiences is a way of attaining an identity as a recovering or recovered addict. Creating the non-addict self can involve creating recovery narratives (Hanninen and Koski-Jannes, 1999). The narrative is often defined in terms set by treatment professionals (McIntosh and McKeganey, 2000) but is also a feature of natural recovery. Accounts can become self-fulfilling – researchers, professionals and addicts in recovery share the same terminology and concepts of how their recovery progresses. For example, to Alcoholics Anonymous (AA), the body is always alcoholic. In the AA story, recovery is always contingent. Recovery can involve making the body addiction resistant. The use of antagonists and partial agonists such as buprenorphine and methadone, which require regular re-dosing, are well established and intended to render heroin use undesirable. Ibogaine has been used successfully as a one-time treatment for opiate addiction. Recreational drug vaccines such as those in development against nicotine and cocaine use will change the body's 'memory', directing future choices and doubtless generating the usual raft of unintended consequences (Hasman and Holm, 2004).

Recovery narratives often centre around re-labelling – reinterpreting drug effects as addictive and also working on generating a drug/alcohol-free, non-dependent future. Pleasure moves from being the main justification for drug use to a mere temporary moment. Effects that may have been desire, like enhanced alertness, are then redefined as false. The true self must be recovered from the false, hateful self of the addict, for instance, by re-creating formative and key transitional experiences. This can be contrasted with the outsider pride many current opiate addicts show in their activities. Reconstructing retrospective narratives is also part of looking forward and constructing pathways for recovery and lifestyle change, structural assistance and vocational rehabilitation (Grönbladh and Gunne, 1989).

Recovery is the work of memory and recognition. The process can be assisted by a pharmaceutical reshaping of body and memory. Pharmaceuticals can be used to manage memory (Glannon, 2006). Narrative identity can be changed by altering the salience of specific memories, such as the use of the beta-adrenergic antagonist propranolol in preventing post-traumatic stress disorder following trauma by inhibiting memory consolidation (Bell, 2008). Ethical and political concerns form around the question of whether this is a new innovation or the extension of what we do every day, which is to manage our memories and experiences to create a self-satisfying personal narrative. Drinking alcohol to make a family occasion easier to bear or taking paracetamol to cope with the resulting hangover is in some way messing with the authenticity of the situation but is for many people considered a legitimate act. The risk with drugs that work on memory in various ways is one of producing unexpected and irrecoverable alterations in one's sense of self. Use of memory management drugs or other technologies also makes us less certain as to what the 'true self' is, or if such a thing could in fact exist. Cocktails of psychoactive medicines can be incorporated into everyday lives (Martin, 2006), making them part of a being a fully realized self in some situations. Policy can intervene in recovery in unintended ways. Substitution with cannabis is a common reported technique for recovery or harm reduction but this is made more difficult as a result of criminalization (Reiman, 2009). Similarly, the use of LSD, psilocybin, salvia and ibogaine to develop a sober, non-addicted self becomes difficult when those substances are criminalized.

Surveillance is embodied, constructing a record external to the user, an 'automatic embodied memory'. The embodied memory is the trace or metabolite of the drug left in the system, in a lock of hair or urine. This embodied memory is thoroughly alienated from the user. Drug testing, in prison, work or the home, lets the body tell tales. The body becomes alien, betraying the user. The body's memory tells. The public problem process encodes bias. We do not develop tests for substances that are not problematic. Those who are vulnerable to scrutiny are scrutinized, whether teenagers, convicts, military personnel, schoolchildren and other institutionalized persons. People in rehab sometimes voluntarily submit to external bio-surveillance, much as Coleridge employed a man to physically keep him out of the apothecaries that supplied him with laudanum. Coercion is desired because of what addicts experience as the overwhelming power of addiction – so addiction justifies some measure of voluntary submission to coercion. Home drug tests are marketed to middle-class families (Moore and Haggerty, 2001). Parents engage in automatic supervision of children and substitute carers. The discourse of the National Institute on Drug Abuse, Parents – The Anti-Drug and other campaigns recruit parents as allies in the drug war. The *quid pro quo* is that this gives the parents a tool to establish trust in the child, while of course showing that he/she *cannot* be trusted. Rather than spend every minute quizzing them and monitoring them, a simple test will ensure that they are not up to no good.

Recovery work and the more widespread forms of embodied surveillance can also involve restructuring the subject and work with a subjectivity very different from the choice-making. Recovery constructs a future sober self. Problem processes embody mistrust. As with nudge, we are encouraged to think of ourselves in this way, as limited subjects with the capacity for creating and embodying our 'better' selves, using techniques of the self and prosthetic pharmaceuticals.

Practices of intoxication

Objects have a rhetoric. They are persuasive. They can define, though not dictate, the terms of their use. Intoxicants mediate such issues as class, in the case of wine, gender, in the case of sugar, and *savoir faire*, in the case of absinthe. Each quality is constructed in relationship to others in the rhetoric of intoxication, so the sweetness of sugar only exists in relation to the bitterness, acidity, saltiness, sourness and umami of other substances. The robust masculine refinement of a Primitivo wine contrasts with the untutored femininity of a Merlot. The bohemian suave of absinthe defines itself against the clodhopping indelicacy of pasteurized lager. Material culture reproduces and affirms these social relationships. Social relationships become in part relationships between objects. The complex back-and-forth constantly regenerates the materiality of intoxication within a sensual culture. Objects are socially constituted and mediated; and themselves are constituting and mediating (Dant, 1999). The autonomous self and attempts to establish it are part of this rhetoric.

There is a cultural residue in the intoxication environment. The material culture of intoxication is created within global flows, technology and the residue of past efforts. There is no natural, herbal high here. Opium, cannabis and coca are all cultivars, plants bred to enhance their intoxicant qualities. Agriculture and industries have been built on the intensification and distribution of intoxication, in fermentation, distillation and the development of modern chemistry. The development of society's productive capacities has been driven by commodification. In Marxist theory, commodities are fetishized, imbued with power and value which has the appearance of being innate, so disguising the conditions of their production. Intoxicants could be seen to challenge the theory of commodity fetishism – after all, their value as intoxicants seems to *really* be innate in the substance – or they could be seen as a perfect manifestation of it, with the social relationships that make heroin risky, crack evil, sugar sweet and so on being recreated in the relationship between drug, set and setting.

Modernity places supreme faith in the autonomous individual, while creating multiple threats to that autonomy, apparent in the language of addiction and risk (Reith, 2004). The DSM-IV (*Diagnostic and Statistical Manual of Mental Disorders*) definition of dependence is framed in the terms of loss of autonomy, being unable to stop using, excessive intoxication interfering with work or personal life. It is proposed that DSM-V adds behavioural dependencies as a new category (DSM-5 Task Force, 2011). The languages of addiction and risk combine to create a narrative of pathological consumption, emptying out intoxication of other meanings. This narrative embeds risk and addiction in the drug as object and in the body of the drug user, which becomes risky, addiction-prone and vulnerable. The discourse around smoking exemplifies this. The smoker becomes at risk through their nicotine-sensitized body, and becomes risky to others, through passive smoking, or the danger of 'priming' other people's bodies for addiction. Smoking and passive smoking primes the body by exposing it to nicotine, which generates a neurochemical lattice of dependence (Fagerström and Sawe, 1996; Groman and Fagerström, 2003). In recent years there has been a reassertion of the biochemical model of addiction, both in scientific rhetoric and public discourse, firmly enclosing addiction in the body of the user. This is supported by the development of addiction medications and vaccines, which further emphasize that addiction is a physiological process (Hall and Carter, 2004; Hasman and Holm, 2004; Hayry, 2004; Maurer et al., 2005). One proposal is to vaccinate children presumed to be at risk of addiction in later life. Discourse and technology merge in the user's body.

Conclusion

Nudge policy as it has been implemented in the UK defines individuals in terms of action and consumption, rather than deliberation and citizenship. Politics has become less about what we can do and more about what we should not. It is argued that public problem policies are incorporating an approach that relies on embodied cognition and conceptualizes the subject as limited. Social policy has always remade subjects. UK welfare policy since 1945 has cohered around needy subjects: the disabled, the pensioner and the unemployed. Treatment merges with social and criminal policy to configure certain types of person as an addict, or mentally ill, and also defines some who have a drug problem as not belonging to this type, as in high-status heavy drinkers. The nudge phenomenon is part of the process whereby policy has grown outwards from these needy or deviant subjects to embrace the normal, body-as-consumer. It conceives of the subject as fundamentally lacking in autonomy and rationality. This means that addiction is normalized – there ceases to be anything deviant about it. Given everyone is in some way limited in their subjectivity, there may be no justification for picking on one group of dependents at all.

There are other ways of conceiving neuropolitics than the prevailing claim of limited subjectivity. Timothy Leary proposed the resistant and culturally constructive use of psychedelics. He claimed that psilocybe would produce a 'peak experience', an ecstatic, transcendent moment, which would wash away years of socialization. In contrast to the claim that humans are neurologically rigid, according to Leary, humans were made rigid by society and their natural plasticity could be freed by judicious use of psychedelics (Leary et al., 1965). As it is currently formulated, neuropolitics does a good job of highlighting the constructed nature of the choice architecture but can miss the structured nature of that architecture and the processes of power, group interest and redefinition of problems that go on with it.

Bibliography

Acker, C J (2010) 'How Crack Found a Niche in the American Ghetto: The Historical Epidemiology of Drug-related Harm' 5 *BioSocieties* 70–88

Advisory Council on the Misuse of Drugs (2005) *Further Consideration of the Classification of Cannabis under the Misuse of Drugs Act 1971* (London: Home Office)

Allender, S et al., (2009) 'The Burden of Smoking-related Ill Health in the UK' 18(4) *Tobacco Control* 262–7

Anon. (2011) 'Increasing THC Content in Your Outdoors Weed', *How to Grow Weed Outdoors*, available at www.howtogrowweedoutdoors.com /Increasing_THC_Content.html

Becker, H (1953) 'Becoming a Marihuana User' 59(3) *American Journal of Sociology* 235–42

Behavioural Insights Team (2010) *Applying Behavioural Insight to Health* (London: Cabinet Office), available at www.cabinetoffice.gov.uk/resource-library/applying-behavioural-insight-health

Bell, J (2008) 'Propranolol, Post-traumatic Stress Disorder and Narrative Identity' 34(11) *Journal of Medical Ethics* e23

Bergschmidt, V B (2004) 'Pleasure, Power and Dangerous Substances: Applying Foucault to the Study of "Heroin Dependence" in Germany' 11(1) *Anthropology and Medicine* 59–73

Bourdieu, P (1977) *Outline of a Theory of Practice* (Cambridge: Cambridge University Press)

Bourgois, P (1989) 'Crack in Spanish Harlem: Culture and Economy in the Inner City' 5(4) *Anthropology Today* 6–11

Bourgois, P (2000) 'Disciplining Addictions: The Bio-Politics of Methadone and Heroin in the United States' 24 *Culture, Medicine and Psychiatry* 165–95

Bourgois, P and J Schonberg (2009) *Righteous Dopefiend* (Berkeley: University of California Press)

Brown, R A (2010) 'Crystal Methamphetamine Use Among American Indian and White Youth in Appalachia: Social Context, Masculinity, and Desistance' 18(3) *Addiction Research and Theory* 250–69

Campbell, N D (2010) 'Toward a Critical Neuroscience of "Addiction"' 5 *BioSocieties* 89–104

Cooper, H L F et al. (2009) 'Geographic Approaches to Quantifying the Risk Environment: Drug-Related Law Enforcement and Access to Syringe Exchange Programmes' 20(3) *International Journal of Drug Policy* 217–26

Cooper, H L F, N Krieger and D Wypij (2005) 'Police Drug Crackdowns and Hospitalisation Rates for Illicit-Injection-Related Infections In New York City' *International Journal of Drug Policy*

Daily Telegraph (2010) 'Nicola Sturgeon Proposes 45p Minimum Alcohol Price' *Telegraph.co.uk*, available at www.telegraph.co.uk/news/newstopics /politics/scotland/7977352/Nicola-Sturgeon-proposes-45p-minimum-alcohol-price.html

Dant, T (1999) *Material Culture in the Social World* (Buckingham: Open University Press)

Decorte, T (2001) 'Drug Users' Perceptions of "Controlled" and "Uncontrolled" Use' **12**(4) *International Journal of Drug Policy* 297–320

DSM-5 Task Force (2011) 'Substance-Related Disorders | APA DSM-5', *DSM-5: The Future of Psychiatric Diagnosis*, available at www.dsm5.org /ProposedRevisions/Pages/Substance-RelatedDisorders.aspx

Duncan, D F (1994) 'Drug Law Enforcement Expenditures and Drug-Induced Deaths' **75**(1) *Psychological Reports* 57–8

Fagerström, K and U Sawe (1996) 'The Pathophysiology of Nicotine Dependence: Treatment Options and the Cardiovascular Safety of Nicotine' **6**(3) *Cardiovasc Risk Fact* 135–43

Fidler, J A et al. (2006) 'Vulnerability to Smoking After Trying a Single Cigarette Can Lie Dormant for Three Years or More' **15** *Tobacco Control* 205–9

Frazzetto, G and S Anker (2009) 'Neuroculture' **10**(11) *Nature Review Neuroscience* 815–21

Gervais, A et al. (2006) 'Milestones in the Natural Course of Onset of Cigarette Use Among Adolescents' **175**(3) *CMAJ* 255–61

Gibson, B, S Acquah and P G Robinson (2004) 'Entangled Identities and Psychotropic Substance Use' **26**(5) *Sociology of Health and Illness* 597–616

Gillies, V and C Willig (1997) '"You Get the Nicotine and That in Your Blood": Constructions of Addiction and Control in Women's Accounts of Cigarette Smoking' **7**(4) *Journal of Community and Applied Social Psychology* 285–301

Glannon, W (2006) 'Psychopharmacology and Memory' **32**(2) *Journal of Medical Ethics* 74–8

Groman, E and K Fagerström (2003) 'Nicotine Dependence: Development, Mechanisms, Individual Differences and Links to Possible Neurophy-siological Correlates' **115**(5–6) *Wien Klin Wochenschr Wien Klin Wochenschr* 155–60

Grönbladh, L and L Gunne (1989) 'Methadone-assisted Rehabilitation of Swedish Heroin Addicts' **24**(1) *Drug and Alcohol Dependence* 31–7

Hall, W and L Carter (2004) 'Ethical Issues in Using a Cocaine Vaccine to Treat and Prevent Cocaine Abuse and Dependence' **30**(4) *Journal of Medical Ethics* 337–40

Hanninen, V and A Koski-Jannes (1999) 'Narratives of Recovery from Addictive Behaviours' **94**(12) *Addiction* 1837–48

Hardwick, S and L King (2008) *Home Office Cannabis Potency Study 2008* (St Albans: Home Office Scientific Development Branch Sandridge)

Hasman, A and S Holm (2004) 'Nicotine Conjugate Vaccine: Is There a Right to a Smoking Future?' **30**(4) *Journal of Medical Ethics* 344–5

Hayry, M (2004) 'Prescribing Cannabis: Freedom, Autonomy, and Values' **30**(4) *Journal of Medical Ethics* 333–6

Hilgartner, S and C L Bosk (1988) 'The Rise and Fall of Social Problems: A Public Arenas Model' **94**(1) *The American Journal of Sociology* 53–78

Home Office (2009) *Home Office: Street Dares (Know Your Limits)*, available at www.youtube.com/watch?v=Uym6fcrSda8&feature=youtube_gdata_player

Hughes, J R (2006) 'Should Criteria for Drug Dependence Differ Across Drugs?' **101** *Addiction* 134–41

Hunt, N (2001) 'Reasoning and Restricted Choices within Recreational Repertoires' **12** *International Journal of Drug Policy* 425–8

International Centre for Science in Drug Policy (2010) *Effect of Drug Law Enforcement on Drug-Related Violence: Evidence from a Scientific Review* (Vancouver: International Centre for Science in Drug Policy)

Kushner, H I (2010) 'Toward a Cultural Biology of Addiction' **5** *BioSocieties* 8–24

Leary, T, R Metzner, M Presnell, G Weil, R Schwitzgebel and S Kinne (1965) 'A New Behavior Change Program Using Psilocybin' **2**(2) *Psychotherapy* 61–72

Legrand, L, W Iacono and M McGue (2005) 'Predicting Addiction' **93**(2) *American Scientist* 140

Looby, A and M Earleywine (2010) 'Gender Moderates the Impact of Stereotype Threat on Cognitive Function in Cannabis Users' **35**(9) *Addictive Behaviors* 834–9

MacAndrew, C and R B Edgerton (1969) *Drunken Comportment* (London: Nelson)

Maher, L (1997) *Sexed Work: Gender, Race, and Resistance in a Brooklyn Drug Market* (Oxford: Oxford University Press)

Martin, E (2006) 'The Pharmaceutical Person' **1**(03) *BioSocieties* 273–87

Marx, G T (1981) 'Ironies of Social Control: Authorities as Contributors to Deviance through Escalation, Nonenforcement and Covert Facilitation' **28**(3) *Social Problems* 221–46

Maurer, P et al. (2005) 'A Therapeutic Vaccine for Nicotine Dependence: Preclinical Efficacy, and Phase I Safety and Immunogenicity' **35**(7) *European Journal of Immunology* 2031–40

Mayet, A et al. (2010) 'The Mediation Role of Licit Drugs in the Influence of Socializing on Cannabis Use Among Adolescents: A Quantitative Approach' **35**(10) *Addictive Behaviors* 890–5

McIntosh, J and N McKeganey (2000) 'Addicts' Narratives of Recovery from Drug Use: Constructing a Non-Addict Identity' **50**(10) *Social Science and Medicine* 1501–10

Measham, F and K Moore (2009) 'Repertoires of Distinction: Exploring Patterns of Weekend Polydrug Use Within Local Leisure Scenes Across the English Night Time Economy' **9**(4) *Journal of Criminology and Criminal Justice* 437–64

Measham, F et al. (2010) 'Tweaking, Bombing, Dabbing and Stockpiling: the Emergence of Mephedrone and the Perversity of Prohibition' **10**(1) *Drugs and Alcohol Today* 14–21

Moore, D and K D Haggerty (2001) 'Bring it on Home: Home Drug Testing and the Relocation of the War on Drugs' **10**(3) *Social and Legal Studies* 377–95

Moss, S (2009) '"A Grave Question" The Children Act and Public House Regulation, c. 1908–1939' **3**(2) *Crimes and Misdemeanours* 98–117

Naqvi, N H et al., (2007) 'Damage to the Insula Disrupts Addiction to Cigarette Smoking' **315**(5811) *Science* 531–4

National Health Service (2007) *NHS – Hooked*, Miles Calraft Briginshaw Duffy, available at www.youtube.com/watch?v=anFK9SA5kKw&feature=youtube_gdata_player

Nettleton, S, J Neale and L Pickering (2010) ' "I Don't Think There's Much of a Rational Mind in a Drug Addict When They Are in the Thick of It': Towards an Embodied Analysis of Recovering Heroin Users' **33**(3) *Sociology of Health and Illness* 341–55, available at: http://onlinelibrary.wiley.com.ezproxy.webfeat.lib.ed.ac.uk/doi/10.1111/j.1467–9566.2010.01278.x/abstract

Pickersgill, M (2009) 'Between Soma and Society: Neuroscience and the Ontology of Psychopathy' **4**(1) *BioSocieties* 45–60

Reiman, A (2009) 'Cannabis as a Substitute for Alcohol and Other Drugs' **6**(35) *Harm Reduction Journal*

Reinarman, C (2005) 'Addiction as Accomplishment: The Discursive Construction of Disease' **13**(4) *Addiction Research and Theory* 307–20

Reinarman, C and H G Levine (2004) 'Crack in the Rear-view Mirror: Deconsruching Drug War Mythology' **31**(1–2) *Social Justice* 182–99

Reith, G (2004) 'Consumption and its Discontents: Addiction, Identity and the Problems of Freedom' **55**(2) *British Journal of Sociology* 283–300

Reuter, P and Stevens, A (2007) *An Analysis of UK Drug Policy* (London: UK Drug Policy Commission), available at www.ukdpc.org.uk/docs/UKDPC%20drug%20policy%20review%20exec%20summary.pdf

Sahakian, B J and S Morein-Zamir (2011) 'Neuroethical Issues in Cognitive Enhancement' **25**(2) *Journal of Psychopharmacology* 197–204

Schwartz, B (2005) *The Paradox of Choice: Why More is Less* (London: Harper Collins)

Scottish Government (2009) *Changing Scotland's Relationship with Alcohol: A Framework for Action* (Edinburgh: Scottish Government)

Scruton, R (2007) 'The Philosophy of Wine' in *Questions of Taste: The Philosophy of Wine* (Oxford: Signal Books)

Secretary of State for the Home Department (2012) *The Government's Alcohol Policy* (London: TSO/Crown Copyright)

Shilling, C (2011) 'Afterword: Body Work and the Sociological Tradition' **33**(2) *Sociology of Health and Illness* 336–40

Skott, P and G Thorlund Jepsen (2002) 'Paradoxical Effects of Drug Policy in a Model with Imperfect Competition and Switching Costs' **48**(4) *Journal of Economic Behavior and Organization* 335–54

Spector, M and J I Kitsuse (1972) *Constructing Social Problems* (Menlo Park CA: Cummings Publishing Company)

Stevens, A (2007) 'Survival of the Ideas that Fit: An Evolutionary Analogy for the Use of Evidence in Policy' **6**(01) *Social Policy and Society* 25–35

Thaler, R H and C R Sunstein (2008) *Nudge: Improving Decisions About Health, Wealth, and Happiness* (New Haven CT: Yale University Press)

Thaler, R H, C R Sunstein and J P Balz (2010) *Choice Architecture*, SSRN eLibrary, available at http://papers.ssrn.com/sol3/papers.cfm?abstract_id=1583509

Throsby, K (2009) 'The War on Obesity as a Moral Project: Weight Loss Drugs, Obesity Surgery and Negotiating Failure' **18**(2) *Science as Culture* 201

Tickle, J J et al. (2001) 'Favourite Movie Stars, their Tobacco Use in Contemporary Movies, and Its Association with Adolescent Smoking' **10**(1) *Tobacco Contro* 16–22

White, W L (2007) 'Addiction Recovery: Its Definition and Conceptual Boundaries' **33**(3) *Journal of Substance Abuse Treatment* 229–42

Williams, S J, P Higgs and S Katz (2011) 'Neuroculture, Active Ageing and the "Older Brain": Problems, Promises and Prospects' *Sociology of Health and Illness*, online first, available at: http://onlinelibrary.wiley.com /doi/10.1111/j.1467–9566.2011.01364.x/abstract

Wilson, M (2002) 'Six Views of Embodied Cognition' **9**(4) *Psychonomic Bulletin and Review* 625–36

Wilson, R, J Gaines and R P Hill (2008) 'Neuromarketing and Consumer Free Will' **42**(3) *Journal of Consumer Affairs* 389–410

Zinberg, N E (1984) *Drug, Set and Setting: The Basis for Controlled Intoxicant Use* (New Haven CT: Yale University Press)

Section 4
Intoxication and the Self

10
Beastly Metamorphoses: Losing Control in Early Modern Literary Culture

Cathy Shrank

> For if the states that on the earth the roome of God supply
> Declyne from virtue untoo vice and live disorderly,
> Too Eagles, Tygres, Bulles and Beares, and other figures straunge
> Both too theyr people and themselves most hurtfull doo they chaunge.
> And when the people give themselves to filthie life and synne,
> What other kinde of shape thereby than filthie can they winne?
> (Golding 1567, sig. A2r)

Ovid's *Metamorphoses* was a foundational text in the sixteenth and seventeenth centuries. Studied at school, imitated by an array of poets, and alluded to in the public theatres (for example, in William Shakespeare's *Cymbeline* and *Titus Andronicus*), Ovid's 15-book poem was part of the early modern cultural psyche. Arthur Golding's 1567 translation (cited above) was the first English version of the full text to be drawn directly from the Latin and, as such, was an important conduit for the dissemination of the work into the English literary tradition and imagination (Lyne, 2001, pp. 27–79). Golding's preliminary verses lend a moral gloss to the tales of gluttony, rape and illicit desire that follow by emphasising how succumbing to so-called 'bestial' instincts leads directly to their mutation into animal form, with characters like 'Elpenor and his mates' (Odysseus' sailors) 'transformed intoo swine | For following theyr filthie lust in women and in wyne' (sig. A2r). As such, they serve as fables, cautioning the reader against indulging in similarly 'brutish' behaviour, a warning that would resonate all the more strongly for erudite readers, who could remember their classics, since Elpenor survived his time as a pig only to die as a result of falling off a roof whilst sleepy and 'sodden with wine' (Homer, 1996, 10.612).

Within Golding's prefatory verses, however, Elpenor's ignominious fate – a tragic and all-too-realistic accident – is skirted over; Golding instead chooses to associate Elpenor's drunkenness not with his ultimate demise but his earlier transformation into a beast, when he was bewitched by the sorceress Circe (a figure who, as we will see, features repeatedly in the early modern discourse surrounding drunkenness). By envisaging the metamorphosis of humans into beasts as a result of their appetites, Golding depicts sinful living as a process of degeneration, a term which invokes more than a sense of moral decline. Derived from the Latin verb *dēgenerāre*, it means 'to depart from [one's] race or kind' (Oxford English Dictionary (OED), 2011) and is a concept which haunts early modern writings about the self and about the external and internal forces that assault it.

Golding's anatomy of selfhood in his preface focuses on a division between the body and the soul: 'this lumpe of flesh and bones, this bodie, is not wée; | Wee are a thing which earthly eycs denyed are to sée. | Our soule is wée, endewd by God with reason from above' (sig. A2r). These verses consequently highlight the vulnerability of the human soul (that which makes us 'we') when it is inevitably and continually in contact with our own corporeality. Whilst the former is divine ('common to us all, with God of heaven himself'), the latter is 'common with the beastes, a vyle and stinking pelf' (sig. A2r). Maintaining one's status as fully human therefore depends on exerting self-control, with the higher, rational part of the self bridling what is seen as our baser, more animalistic urges, for 'if wée suffer fleshly lustes as lawless lordes too reigne, | Than are we beastes; wée are no men, wée have our name in vaine' (sig. A2v).

In Golding's words, 'our bodie is but as our house' (sig. A2r); continual vigilance and household management is thus necessary to keep it clean and unpolluted. That sense of a self constantly exposed to and under pressure from external forces is also inherent to early modern understandings of physical and mental health. Pre-modern medicine inherited from Greek and Latin medical texts the theory of the four humours or complexions. Every body comprised four principal fluids ('humours'): black bile, yellow bile (also known as choler), blood and phlegm (Porter, 1999, pp. 57–8). Each individual was seen as predisposed to have one dominant humour which made them prone to certain diseases and – importantly in a discussion of self – which determined their temperament: a tendency for an excess of yellow bile made one 'choleric'; an excess of blood ('sanguis', in Latin), 'sanguine'; an excess of phlegm, 'phlegmatic'; an excess of black bile, 'melancholic'. Moreover, since each of these fluids was by nature either cold and wet (phlegm), cold and dry (black bile), hot and dry (choler), or hot and wet (blood), you could alter your internal balance – and thus both your bodily health and personality – by manipulating external factors: you could warm yourself up by consuming hot foods like pepper, or rhenish wine; or you could dampen yourself down (rarely advisable) by moving to a marsh and eating food categorized as cold and damp, like pigeon's lungs or cucumbers (Elyot, 1539; Boorde, 1547). According to pre-modern medical theory, that is, the 'self' was not a stable entity, but in continual flux, subject – like Golding's soul – to outside forces.

The experience of travel is probably when early modern commentators found these humoral shifts most marked, resulting in striking changes in behaviour and taste, as in William Thomas's observation that although 'before time [he] could in maner brooke no fruite, and yet after [he] had been a while in Italie, [he] fell so in love withall that as longe as [he] was there, [he] desyred no meate [foodstuff] more' (Thomas, 1549, sig. A2v). Certainly, in the metamorphic discourse surrounding the effects of alcohol that we are about to explore, two countries in particular recur: Italy (known in English polemic as a seat of lechery, violence and the Church of Rome) and the Low Countries (renowned for excessive consumption of beer and, by the early seventeenth century, as a breeding ground for religious sects). We will return to the theme of religious difference towards the end of this paper. For now, though, I want to take images of beastly metamorphoses as a starting point for investigating early modern attitudes to drunkenness as a state which makes one less than human; the subsequent section of the essay will then map how characteristics of drunkenness became applied to other apparent moral failings (particularly tyranny and religious error) as a sign of opprobrium.

Three key faculties divided humans from beasts in the early modern understanding of the world: reason, speech and a conscience, which allows them to recognize God and identify moral lapses (Thomas, 1984, pp. 31–2; Fudge, 2006, pp. 7–38). It is easy to see how an excess of drink robs humans of all three, as in Joshua Sylvester's poem, 'Of a drunken man':

> His head growes giddie, and his foote indents,
> A mightie fume his troubled braine torments,
> His idle prattle from their purpose quite,
> Is abrupt, fluttering, all confused, and light. (Albott et al., 1600,
> p. 352, ll. 1–4)

The drunkard's reason is shown to be befogged (obscured by a 'mightie fume'), his language reduced to a 'prattle' – a verb indicating 'childish' speech ('prattle, *v.*', OED, 2011) – which here fails to communicate adequately with others, being 'from their purpose quite'. The result is that the drunkard is transformed, appearing 'more like a foule swine than sober man' (l. 8), a poetic line which draws on the commonplace association of drunkards and pigs: 'as drunk as a swine' was proverbial (Dent, 1981, S1042; cf. Golding, 1567, sig. A2r).

The correlation between drunkards and certain specific animals, including pigs, can be traced to a biblical legend which seems to have become established by the mid-fourteenth century (Janson, 1952, pp. 240–8).

This tale attributes the transformative effects of alcohol to the time of Noah, who fertilised the first post-diluvial vineyard with the blood of four creatures: a lion, an ape, a pig and – depending on the version – either a sheep or a goat. The wine consequently took on the supposed characteristics of the various creatures, so that in their cups, men (depending on their humoral disposition) would become angry like a lion (the choleric); foolish like an ape (the sanguine); overly loving, like a sheep, or lecherous like a goat (the phlegmatic); or wallow in their own filth, like a pig (the melancholic).[1] Of course, as Keith Thomas observes, 'there was little objective justification for the way in which the beasts were perceived...Men attributed to animals the natural impulses they most feared in themselves – ferocity, gluttony, sexuality.' (Thomas, 1984, pp. 40–1)

Early modern writers continued to play, often inventively, on this theme. Thomas Heywood's *Philocothonista, or the Drunkard, Opened, Dissected and Anatomized* (1635), for instance, features on its frontispiece a tableau of different man–beast hybrids – animal heads fused onto human bodies – variously carousing, brawling, smoking, guzzling and vomiting, whilst being served immense tankards by a (fully human) barmaid. Its opening pages then proliferate, and modify, the animalistic classifications of the Noah legend, likening drunkards – their senses 'stupifie[d]' by 'Cyrcean Cups' – to various animalistic types. The subsequent roll-call of drunks highlights a key aspect of early modern discourses of intoxication: namely, the lack of differentiation between what we would now term 'alcoholics' or 'problem drinkers', and people who drink and become drunk. In Heywood's list, only the porcine drunks resemble habitual drinkers, who

> by spending whole dayes, and consuming night after night in Tavernes, and Tipling-houses, returne from thence, either led or carried, who oft times stumbling, lie wallowing in the kennells, and so appeare no other then Hoggs and swine, newly come durty and dawbed out of the puddles (p. 6).

For the other types, it is merely that drink exposes certain innate traits which are usually restrained by reason and civility, so that the 'asinine' drunks become 'rude, ignorant...and unmanerly' (p. 2); the canine drunks, belligerent, for 'when their braines are heated in the blood of the Grape, they will fasten on thee like Mastiffes' (p. 3). The ovine drunks, meanwhile, become tearful, 'weep[ing] in a kind of superstitious piety' (p. 4), and the vituline (calf-like) drunks 'like Calves or Apes...when they begin to bee Cup-shot...leap

---

1 The association of different animals with different dispositions is not entirely stable; sometimes the melancholic is linked with lambs, the phlegmatic with pigs. See Janson, 1952, p. 248.

and daunce, and caper, toy, laugh, sing, and prattle' (pp. 4–5). The 'vulpine' type, moreover, does not even seem intoxicated, but poses another danger for the unwary drinker and hence a further reason to avoid that sort of company and occasion. As Heywood explains:

> Others are said to bee drunke as Foxes, and those are they who Insidiate men in their Cups, and urge others, quaffing and health-ing for no other purpose then to intrap them in their speeches, and bring them into trouble, or to catch some advantage at their words, thereby to supplant them in their estates, and such may bee call'd Pollitick Drunkards; of whom Cicero speakes. (ibid. p. 6)

This type of drinker is a stereotypically Machiavellian character: 'politic' was a word which came to be shorthand for the Machiavellian schemer, whilst the fox alludes to Chapter 18 of Niccolò Machiavelli's *The Prince*, composed in 1513, in which rulers are advised that they should imitate both the fox (for cunning) and the lion (for strength), but that 'those best able to imitate the fox have succeeded best' (Machiavelli, 1988, p. 62). The fox-like tippler might be a beast, in other words, but he is far from losing control. He might drink as a fox, but he hardly qualifies as 'drunk'.

Heywood's pamphlet indicates the mixed traditions – of classical myth, biblical commentary, political discourse and medical writing – on which moralists like him were drawing. Writers might choose to analyse the effects of drunkenness in mainly medical terms, as in the explication of why drunkenness impairs the faculty of speech in *The Problemes of Aristotle* (1595), which employs humoral theory to explain 'why drun[k]ards have not a perfect kind of speech', arguing that the tongue, being 'full of pores, and spungie... receiveth great moysture'; becoming, as a result, 'full of naughtie humors' it 'is made thicke and grosse' (Anon., 1595, sig. F4v). More often, however, they deployed the authority inherent in a range of otherwise potentially incompatible discourses. Thomas Adams exemplifies the inter-knotting of these traditions, drawing on a heady combination of animal-lore, religious polemic and classical mythology (in particular, the legend of the Homeric enchantress, Circe, who changed Odysseus' men into swine):

> Of all creatures voyde of reason, it is observed of [pigs], that they will swill till they swel, drinke till they burst. If Circe's Cup (or if you wil, the Vintners, the Victuallers) hath transformed man into a drunken hogge, this is a moist place that Satan affects. If the head be well tippled, he gets in; and makes the eyes wanton, the tongue blasphemous, the hands ready to stabbe, the throate an open Sepulcher to devoure. (Adams, 1615a, p. 31)

The bestial transformation of the drunkard described by Adams is also given a pseudo-medical basis; alluding to humoral theory, Adams recounts how Satan

> finds no rest in dry places. Perhaps the Devill loves the low Countries, and wet ground. In a moderate, temperate, dry braine, he findes no footing: but in the soule of the swilling drunkard, as a foggy and fenny ground, hee obtaines some residence. Abstemious moderation, and temperate satisfaction of nature is too dry a place, for so hot a spirit as hell fire hath made him, to quench his malicious thirst. (ibid. p. 351)

Alcohol, then, is seen as having a transformative effect on mind and body.

The dehumanising consequences of excessive drink – with particular attention to its cerebral impact – are likewise noted in the encyclopaedia *Batman uppon Bartholome* (1582), which cites the first-century Arab physician Isaac, who 'sayth in this manner: if wine be oft taken, anone by dronkenesse it quencheth the sight of reason, and comforteth beastly madnesse' (Batman, 1572, p. 330). With reason extinguished, the body is left without a proper guide and is 'as it were a ship in the sea with out sterne, and without loades man [pilot]'; as a direct consequence, 'the drunken man favoreth the thing that should not be favoured, and graunteth that should not be graunted'. Under the influence of drink, 'wise men' become 'fooles', and 'of good men and well willed, dronkenesse maketh evill men and wicked'.

The association of madmen, drunkards and fools recurs throughout early modern writing. 'Doubtlesse you perswade your selfe that all, who should read your booke, would be madde, or drunke, or senseless', hectors George Abbot in his riposte to Dr Thomas Edmund Hill, making all three states synonymous (1604, p. 21); in contrast, those who agree with Abbot's own outlook are commended for their '*sober* understanding' (p. 232, emphasis added). A direct equation is consequently drawn between drunkenness and insanity. Thomas Adams' *Mysticall Bedlam* (1615) even describes drunkenness as 'a voluntary madnesse, and makes a man so like a beast, that whereas a beast hath no reason, hee hath the use of no reason: and the power or faculty of reason suspended, gives way to madnes' (Adams, 1615b, p. 61).

As we saw in the Golding extract earlier, human behaviour is thus seen as the outcome of a constant tussle within the human soul between reason and will, with the baser urges ('will') perpetually trying to wrest control from the superior, rational faculty. This struggle is mapped by the humanist, statesmen and occasional medical writer, Thomas Elyot, in the early 1530s:

> men beinge in the state of Innocency have than the figure of man, the soule having the hole pre-eminence over the body. But after if it happen that the appetites and desires of the body so moch do

> increase, that they have the hole possession of the body and that the affections of the soule, that is to say vertues, be suppressed or putte to silence, than the lyfe becommeth beastely: than loke in what beastes the sayde appetites be mooste vehemente: he, in whome is the semblable appetite, may be sayde hathe his soule in that best inclosed... A cruel man or Tyraunt in to a tigre or lion, a glotton or a drunkard in to a wolfe or a swine, and so further of other. (Elyot, 1533, sigs D8v-E1r)

A state of inebriation dulls reason, giving the passions full rein, hence the well-documented propensity when drunk to indulge in anger or lust. Alexander the Great – who murdered his friend Clitus when in his cups – is frequently used as a warning example here (Bullein, 1562, fol. 73r; Heywood, 1635, pp. 11–13), behaviour which the ancient Greek historian Plutarch, for one, attributes to Alexander's humoral make-up, noting that 'this natural heate that Alexander had, made him (as it appeareth), to be given to drunke & to be hasty' (Plutarch, 1579, p. 724).

The unbridled passions of a drunkard thus allow an easy slippage, whereby drunkenness becomes applied figuratively to other states of mental disorder: E G's *Naturall and Morall Historie of the East and West Indies* (Alcosta, 1604), for example, includes an episode where a Spaniard, hearing Italian lapidaries valuing his emerald of 'excellent lustre and form', becomes 'drunke with this discourse' (p. 249). Similarly, in early modern parlance, you could be 'drunk' 'with...passions' (Aggas, 1588, p. 18) and, above all, 'with love' (Achilles, 1638, p. 10). That love should be seen as disorientating and destabilising (like strong drink) is perhaps unsurprising; the metamorphic powers of love are expressed eloquently by the Elizabethan physician William Bullein, who describes – in a lengthy section on the 'perturbacions of the Mynde' – how love

> doth degenerate many, in a maner out of kind, making them more effeminate than womon: changing Mars into Venus. It altereth complexions [humoral makeups], maners & conditions, and maketh of free men slaves, of wyse men fooles... Somtyme it doth depryve the wittes and senses reasonable, and maketh Men more madder than Dogges, crueller then Wolfes, more shameless than Apes, renting their clothes, waking [staying awake all night] in their beds, fasting at their bordes [tables]. (Bullein, 1562, fol. 74v)

The extract from Bullein recapitulates the ideas of degeneration and the overpowering of one's rational senses found in Golding's preface. The reference to apes – one of the four animals to which drunkards are likened in the Noah legend – further strengthens the connection between lovers and drunkards.

The link between apes and drunkards is partly due to the perceived fool-ishness of both, apes being regarded as creatures that imitate rather than think and act for themselves (see Janson, 1952, pp. 199–237); but the verbal characteristic – of 'chattering' – granted apes in this period also invokes the perceived oral inadequacies of drunkards. As the OED defines it, 'chatter' is:

> To talk rapidly, incessantly, and with more sound than sense. Esp[ecially] said of children; but often applied vituperatively to speech which one does not like. Also said of apes and other animals whose voice suggests human chattering. (OED, 2011, 'chatter, *v.*', sense 2)

As such, this verb serves a similar function to 'prattle' in Sylvester's poem 'Of a drunken man' encountered earlier (Albott et al., 1600, p. 352). To chatter and to prattle: both imply childish or redundant talk, that is, talk without import or reason.

That love and drunkenness are seen to share characteristics is, as I have noted, probably unsurprising. Perhaps less predictable is the recurrent asso-ciation between drunkenness and tyranny, and drunkenness and religious error. Tyranny is tied to drunkenness in two basic ways: first, tyrants, like drunkards, have a well-recorded tendency towards anger. As the physician Bullein explains (deploying the terminology of physical or military struggle which makes the self a battleground in the incessant contest between body and soul, passions and reason), 'Providence and pacience, make men strong, and cause them to get the victory of themselves: and to be able to wythstand anger, which is a common passion of cruell Beastes, Tyrauntes, & Fooles', a quotation in which we once again see an alliance between beasts and those humans who have abandoned themselves to irrational behaviour (Bullein, 1562, fol. 73r).

Secondly, tyrants habitually lead lives of debauchery, further evidence of their subjection to their own passions, and this tendency towards self-indul-gence is frequently epitomised by the excessive consumption of alcohol. Take, for example, the emperor Aulus Vitellius Germanicus, whose appearance as 'drunke Vitellius' alongside 'bloudy Nero, cruell Commodus, | Luxurious Tarquine…| Tarpeia false, [and] Semiramis unchaste' indicates his status as an archetypal drunkard, since he features in a roll-call of notables epitomising various moral failings (Andrewe, 1604, sig. F1r). As Suetonius records, 'being given most of all to excessive bellie cheere and crueltie; [Vitellius] devided repast into three meales every day at the least, and sometime into foure, to wit, Breakfast, Dinner, Supper and rere-bankets' (Holland, 1606, p. 235), a 'rere-banquet' or 'rere-supper' being a sumptuous late-night feast, often for men only, during which they would drink excessively (OED, 2011; cf, Huloet, 1572, sig. D1v: 'a rere banquet or drynking').

The state of drunkenness can, however, also take on a more figurative aspect. That it does so is in part due to the pervasive use in early modern discourse of the metaphor of the 'body politic', which imagines the polity in terms of the human body. Just as the human body is affected by liquor, so too the state of a nation can become inebriated by what it consumes. As John Dee writes, translating one of the Socratic dialogues from Plato's *Republic*, tyranny comes about when 'a Cittie doth thirst too much after libertie, and lighteth on badde rulers, which give her a deeper draught thereof then is expedient, shee is drunke therewith' (1598, sig. X1v). The metamorphosis of a tryant – from 'Protectour of the people' into 'a wolfe' which 'glutteth himselfe with … unjust deaths … sucking with his tongue and unpure mouth, the blood of his neere kindred' (sig. X2ᵛ) – is further likened to the effects of drunkenness, not simply by the images of insatiable gorging just cited, but in the accompanying explanation of how a man can allow such corrosive passions to overcome his better nature. Socrates observes that 'there is in every one some vehement, rude and unlawful kind of desires, yet even in those who seem to be very moderate, which appeareth in sleeping' (sig. X4ᵛ); these 'unlawful' desires are ones which

> move themselves in our sleepe, when the reasonable part of our soule, which is quiete and beareth rule therein, is at rest: and the brutish and rude part being drunken and glutted with meat, doth stirre, [and] … seekes to enjoy her accustomed pleasures (sig. X4ʳ).

In sum, just as in the drunkard reason loses control over will, so too with the tyrant, and as the dialogue proceeds, tyrant and drunkard begin to fuse, one into the other. 'Hath not the drunkard a Tyrannicall mind?' demands Socrates: 'Moreover, the man that is furious and out of his right mind, doth he not take upon him to command not men only, but the gods also, and hopes to compasse his desire?' The overweening confidence expressed here, the selfish blindness to all but your own urges: these are attitudes ascribable to tyrant and drunkard alike.

The association between tyranny and drunkenness is to some extent circumstantial (tyrants are often drunkards, and both are soon angered). On one level at least the connection between drunkenness and religious error is similarly behavioural, since the drunkard's lifestyle renders him more likely to 'prefer an ale-house before the house of God', as the vicar Robert Abbot puts it in a sermon preached at the burial of William Rogers, a 'prodigall and bibing' apothecary (1639, fol. 7r, sig. A3r). Further to that, since the Bible tells how humans are made in God's likeness (Genesis 1:27), to pollute one's body with drink is, logically, to defile God's work; in Abbot's words, such sin 'woundeth the Conscience, defaceth the Image of GOD' (1639, sig. D4ʳ). Yet religious delusion – like tyranny – is also figured through metaphors of drunkenness and metamorphosis, and it is notable that the quotation about the 'madde, or drunke, or senseless' cited earlier (Abbot, 1604, p. 21) comes not from a diatribe about drunkenness but papistry. Roger Ascham's *Scholemaster* (1570) thus imagines once-decent Englishmen returning 'out of Italie worse transformed, than ever was any in Circes Court' (sig. H4v). As a staunch Protestant writing about the potential pollution of an English body by Catholic Italy, the influences Ascham fears are as much political and religious as relating to habits of unwarranted consumption. The monstrously hybrid 'Englese Italianato' he denounces has 'the belie of a Swyne, the head of an Asse, the brayne of a Foxe, the wombe of a wolfe'. As we have seen, where the pig is associated with drunkenness, greed and filthy living, the ass is also connected to drunkenness, as well as being proverbially stupid; the fox, meanwhile, symbolises Machiavellianism, and the wolf the alleged rapaciousness of the Church of Rome, preying on Christ's flock; compare, for example, the figuring of Catholic priests as wolves in the 'May' and 'September' eclogues in Edmund Spenser's *Shepheardes Calendar* (1579) or polemical texts such as John Phillips' *Frendly Larum*: 'So doth this Romish Wolfe, not spare to take his praie: | And where he may, no Sheep nor Lambe, his teeth can scape awaie' (Phillips, 1570, sig. B1r).

At the root of the connection between the religiously blind and the drunkard is the sense in which their reason has, in some way, become clouded, and it is interesting to note that the verb 'intoxicate', from the Latin *toxicāre*, 'to smear with poison' (OED, 2011) was used of the corrupting effects of religious heterodoxy well before its now commonplace association with drugs and alcohol; the earliest quotation cited in the OED is from John Skelton's *Colyn Clout* (composed c. 1529), where it means 'To "poison"; to corrupt morally or spiritually' (OED, 2011, 3a), and is used of the damaging effect of religious heterodoxy:

> Suche maner of skystmatykes
> And half heretykes
> That wolde intoxicate ...
> The Churchs high estates. (Skelton, 1545, sig. C1v)

In this way, false doctrine is like strong liquor, making – in Thomas Adams' words – 'The Brain-sicke ... drunke with Opinion; and that so strange, that sleepe which helps other drunkards, doth them no good.' (1616, p. 5) Indeed, for Adams, the effects of this intoxicating opinion on the brain-sick mirror other side effects of drink: their affliction is compared to 'an Head-ach called the Migram' (p. 3), and because

> their ambitious singularity is often so violent, that it if be not
> restrained, it growes to a kind of frenzy, and so the Migram turns

into the Staggers [and]…they reele into the lowe-Countries [a location associated with religious sects]. (p. 5)

As the brain-sick 'reel' and 'stagger', they acquire symptoms associated with drunkenness, as detailed in Sylvester's verse 'Of a drunken man' (cited earlier) – 'His trembling tent all topsi-turvie wheeles' (Albott et al., 1600, p. 356, l. 6) – or found in the biblical simile of Psalm 107:27–8, which uses the analogy of a ship in a stormy sea to depict the travails of human life, and also their solution: 'They are tossed to and fro, and stagger like a drunken man, and all their cunning is gone. Then they crye unto the Lord in their trouble, and he bringeth them out of their distress.'

The impact of the Bible on both moralising drunkenness and the metaphors which attach to it should not be underestimated: it was, after all, a text that was heard on a weekly, if not a daily basis. The Bible is full of instances in which excessive drinking leads directly to regrettable moral lapses or outbreaks of foolishness: Noah falling asleep naked, an incident which provokes him to curse his son Ham (Genesis 9:21–25); the worship of false idols at Balthazzar's feast (Daniel 5:4); Lot having unwitting intercourse with his daughters (Genesis 9:32–35), with the result that – as the gloss to *The Geneva Bible* tells us – 'as [the offspring] were borne in most horrible incest, so were they and their posteritie vile and wicked' (Bible, 2007, fol. 8ᵛ). Moreover, drunkenness also features as a key strategy for expressing opprobrium in the description of the Whore of Babylon in the Book of Revelations: as the Whore rides on the many-headed beast, she bears a drinking cup; 'the inhabitants of the earth are drunken with the wine of her fornication' (17:2); and she herself is 'drunken with the blood of Saintes, & with the blood of the Martyrs of Jesus' (17:6). Conversely, sobriety figures as the state in which one is most receptive to God; as such, the 40-year fast imposed on the Israelites in the wilderness becomes part of God's purpose: 'Ye have eaten no bread, nether dronke wine, nor strong drinke, that he might knowe, how that I am the Lord your God.' (Deuteronomy 29:6), words echoed by Hannah in the Temple of the Lord. 'I am a woman troubled in spirit', she tells the priest Eli: 'I have dronke nether wine nor strong drinke, but have powred out my soule before the Lord.' (1 Samuel 1:15) And as St Paul instructs the Ephesians: 'be not drunke with wine, wherein is excesse: but be fulfilled with the Spirit' (Ephesians 5:18).

Within the Bible drunkenness is recurrently associated with sinfulness and moments in human history when events take a turn for the worse; in contrast, abstinence signals moral worth. However, as indicated earlier, the connotations of drunkenness also assume a metaphorical aspect. Consider, for instance, the drunkard's tendency to lurch and trip. This becomes emblematic of those who fail to recognize God: 'They grope in the darke without light: & he maketh them to stagger like a drunken man.' (Job 12:25)

This comparison between drunkards and the spiritually unenlightened gains further purchase since both activities occur in darkness: 'they that be dronken, are drunken in the night', St Paul states (1 Thessalonians 5:7), an opinion duly noted by Abbot in the funeral sermon cited earlier (Abbot, 1639, fol. 42ᵛ). Since the Bible constantly quotes and requotes itself, the resonances of one passage help shape the interpretation of others. Job 12:25 is thus informed by Proverbs 4:19 ('The wicked are in darkness & they stumble'), a verse appropriately chosen by Abbot as the text for his 1639 sermon on the deceased apothecary. As such, when reading the Bible – and particularly when selecting and juxtaposing quotations from it to bolster an argument or structure a sermon – the moralising effect is cumulative and cyclical, building disapprobation, as drunkenness is associated with a failure to recognize one's God, and such errors of faith are in turn associated with the shameful state of inebriation, a condition which reveals one's inner weakness and utter degeneration. As Thomas Adams writes, translating a Latin epigram by the Protestant theologian Theodore Beza, 'hee that's drunken, is no man' (1615b, p. 62).

This essay has so far drawn on an array of genres, including moral poetry and prose (Golding, Sylvester, Andrewe, Heywood), history (Holland, Plutarch), an educational tract (Ascham), a sermon (R Abbot), political treatise and dialogue (Dee, Elyot), an early encyclopaedia (Batman), religious polemic (G Abbot), and a medical handbook (Bullein). All share similar attitudes to the bestial effects of immoderate drinking and – since the human self is perceived as a battleground in a continual struggle between reason and will – all have in common the explicit aim of teaching their readers self-control, of encouraging and equipping them to rein in their baser urges. When Robert Abbot concludes his sermon with 1 Corinthians 10.11 – 'All these things happened unto them for ensamples: and they are written for our admonition upon whom the ends of the world are come.' (1639, fol. 101ᵛ) – his meaning is no different from Golding's argument about the didactic purpose of literature, which declares that 'when thou read'st of God or man in stone, in beast, or trée, | It is a myrrour for thy self thyne owne estate to sée' (1567, sig. A2r).

It is also striking that these different genres draw on a shared pool of ideas about drunkenness and a common set of strategies for representing it, not least among them the notion that the 'Circean Cup' (Heywood, 1635, frontispiece) effects some kind of metamorphosis, unleashing the beast within. The final section of this essay turns to depictions of drunkenness in early modern drama in order to map what happens to these varied discourses – generally used to lambast drunkenness – when it came to performing intoxication on stage.

A drunken episode plays a crucial role in William Shakespeare's *Othello* (1604), allowing Iago (the villain of the piece) to discredit his rival Cassio and setting in motion a plot that will see the stage heaped with corpses in the final act. Although created some 30 years before *Philocthonista*, Shakespeare's Iago resembles one of Heywood's 'vulpine' drinkers 'who Insidiate men in their Cups, and urge others, quaffing and healthing for no other purpose then to intrap them in their speeches, and bring them into trouble' (1635, p. 6). Knowing Cassio's weakness for wine – that he has no head for it, and that, easily intoxicated, he is also easily riled – Iago tempts him to 'a stope [stoup] of wine' (Shakespeare 2005a, 2.3.30) by pressing toasts (Heywood's 'healthing[s]') upon him.

If Iago pre-empts Heywood's fox-like, 'Pollitick' drinker, then Cassio embodies the 'canine': the courteous (possibly even fawning) 'spanell' who turns pugnacious mastiff once his brain is 'heated in the blood of the Grape' (Heywood, 1635, p. 3). In his cups, Cassio epitomises the belligerent drunk, fighting and taking offence where none is meant. Sobering up, however, he rehearses the moralists' arguments, anatomizing the well-charted effects of drunkenness, such as speaking nonsense. 'Drunk? and speak parrot? and squabble? swagger? swear? and discourse fustian [bombastically] with one's own shadow?' he wonders (2.3.279–81). Like a vast swathe of sixteenth- and seventeenth-century writers, he thus comments on the way in which alcohol deprives humans of reason and turns them into beasts: 'O [God], that men should put an enemy in their mouths to steal away their brains! that we should, with joy, pleasance, revel, and applause, transform ourselves into beasts!' (2.3.289–92) Cassio's speech here captures the double-edged position that drinking holds in many cultures: that – even as it holds the potential to unleash incivility ('barbarous brawl[ing]', as Othello puts it, 2.3.172) – it is often a substance around which civility and companionability are structured (cf. Smyth, 2004). Further to that, the scene is also revealing because it highlights the lack of differentiation between the 'occasional' and 'habitual' drunkard. Drunkenness is judged by behaviour. As such, it is easy for Iago to paint Cassio as a habitual drunkard: "Tis evermore [the] prologue to his sleep', Iago tells Montano: 'He'll watch the horologe [clock] a double set | If drink rock not his cradle.' (2.3.129–31) The label is, moreover, one which (a more sober) Cassio himself accepts: 'he shall tell me I am a drunkard! Had I as many mouths as Hydra, such an answer would stop them all.' (2.3.303–5) But Cassio is also perplexed by the effects of wine. As Thomas Adams would, some ten years later (1615a), Cassio labels alcohol as diabolic: 'Every inordinate cup is unblessed, and the ingredient is a devil', he cries (2.3.300–1; cf. Adams 1615a). He does so, though, not merely as a moraliser – lambasting or counselling against indulgence – but because he is struggling to explain the physical effects of alcohol and can find no other way to articulate the sense of becoming other than, or less than one's self: he addresses the 'invisible spirit of wine' not as 'devil' because he believes it to be such, but because 'thou has no name to be known by' (2.3.281–2).

Early modern drama does not strive for realism; it is a self-consciously artificial form, which constantly meditates upon its representational status. Nonetheless, there is something very credible about Cassio's temptation and the speed with which he succumbs to the pressure to drink. Even if the alacrity with which Cassio becomes intoxicated (and then sobers up) is less convincing, the depiction of this process on stage nevertheless seems grounded in observed experience. The final example studied in this essay – Shakespeare's *Tempest* (c. 1610–1611) – does not, as *Othello* does, so much rehearse discourses about drinking as deconstruct them.

Shakespearean comedy is noticeably less didactic than many of the other texts cited here, but the treatment of the two shipwrecked drunkards, Stefano (butler to the king of Naples) and Trinculo (the court jester), along with Caliban, the islander whom they enthral with alcohol, reflects – but also modulates – the key theme explored hitherto: namely, the transformative effects of drink, which changes men into beasts, so that they lose sight of reason and can be lured into false worship. The scenes between Stefano, Trinculo and Caliban are thick with metamorphic imagery, from the image of Trinculo who can 'swim like a duck' but is 'made like a goose' (Shakespeare, 2005b, 2.2.130–31) to the punishments that Caliban imagines in store for them at the hands of the magician Prospero ('We shall lose our time, | And all be turn'd to barnacles, or to apes | With foreheads villainous low', 4.1.247–9), or Ariel's description of the trio 'red-hot with drinking' reacting like 'unback'd colts' and following his tabor 'calf-like' (4.1.171, 176, 179). However, Shakespeare also plays on the usual dynamic. It is not so much that the alcohol consumed turns these men into beasts; rather, it warps their vision and understanding so that they wrongly perceive Caliban as animal. In their first encounter, the then-sober (and consequently non-bestial) Caliban is misidentified as, successively, a 'fish' (2.2.25), a 'moon-calf' (a deformed creature) (2.2.135–6), and 'a puppy-headed monster' (2.2.154–5): enough beasts to fill a menagerie.

A similar distortion of reason initially motivates Trinculo and Stefano's attempt to overthrow the island's ruler, Prospero, as they labour under the misconception that a mere butler could ever be king (a serious disruption of the social order for any self-respecting political theorist in the early modern period). It is subsequently that same befuddlement of their rational faculties that brings about the defeat of their enterprise, as they are distracted by false baubles – 'the glistering apparel' laid out by Ariel (4.1.193 SD) – just as Caliban, after drinking from Stefano's bottle, was induced to worship him: 'I prithee be my god.' (2.2.149) Like the baser instincts struggling to gain control over the self in the continual battle between reason and will, this drunken rabble attempts to usurp the body politic; but here it is not the soul – the rational part – which is incapacitated by alcohol, but the baser elements: Trinculo and Stefano. There is also an added irony in that it is the character whom they categorize as only half-human – Caliban, their 'man-monster' (3.2.12) – who is the most clear-sighted. Even under the influence of alcohol, he recognizes the 'glistering apparel' for what it is: 'trash' (4.1.224). Moreover, unlike his inebriated companions, who speak in the prose generally granted in Shakespearean drama to the lower sorts and comic characters (fools), Caliban never wavers from verse: he remains articulate, even in drink. It is also Caliban who shows the greatest self-awareness and ability to reflect on the events just past:

> ...I'll be wise hereafter,
> And seek for grace. What a thrice-double ass
> Was I to take this drunkard for a god,
> And worship this dull fool! (5.1.295–6)

Shakespeare's comedy thus plays with some of the early modern truisms about drunkenness. Nevertheless, when it comes to the forces of correction, he is singing from the same hymn-sheet as moralists such as Ascham and Abbot the vicar. Caliban reforms because of his terror of chastisement, and that is precisely the prophylactic that Ascham and Adam recommend: 'let Gods feare be the bridle' Ascham instructs us (1570, p. 26); 'Looke upon your examples and fear and tremble' intones Adams (Abbot, 1639, fol. 101r). Ultimately, it seems, it is a passion – fear – that most effectively regulates human behaviour and ensures that reason prevails over will in the battle for the self. Reason alone is not sufficient: it needs an animal instinct to sharpen its resolve.

Bibliography

Abbot, G (1604) *The Reasons Which Dr Hill Hath Brought for the Upholding of Papistry ... Unmasked* (Oxford: Joseph Barnes)

Abbot, R (1639) *The Young-Mans Warning-peece: Or, A Sermon Preached at the Burial of William Rogers Apothecary* (London: R Badger)

Achilles, T (1638) *The Loves of Clitophon and Leucippe* (London: William Turner)

Adams, T (1615a) *The Blacke Devil* (London: William Jaggard)

Adams, T (1615b) *Mysticall Bedlam* (London: George Purslowe)

Adams, T (1616) *Diseases of the Soule* (London: George Purslowe)

Aggas, E (trans.) (1588) *A Caveat for France* (London: John Wolfe)

Albott, R et al. (1600) *Englands Parnassus* (London: for N L[ing] et al.)

Alcosta, J (1604) *The Naturall and Morall Historie of the East and West Indies*, E G (trans.) (London: Val Sims)

Andrewe, T (1604) *The Unmasking of a Feminine Machiavelli* (London: Simon Stafford)

Anon. (1595) *The Problemes of Aristotle with other Philosophers and Phisitions* (Edinburgh: Robert Waldgrave).

Ascham, R (1570) *The Scholemaster* (London: John Day)

Batman, S (1572) *Batman uppon Bartholome his Booke De Proprietatibus Rerum* (London: Thomas East)

Bible (2007) *The Geneva Bible: Facsimile of the 1560 Edition* (Peabody MA: Hendrickson Publishers)

Boorde, A (1547) *A Compendyous Regyment or a Dyetary of Helth* (London: William Powell)

Bullein, W (1562) *Bulleins Bulwark* (London: John Kingston)

Dee, J (trans.) (1598) *Aristotles Politiques, or Discourses of Government. Translated out of Greeke into French, with Expositions Taken Out of the Best Authours, Specially Out of Aristotle Himselfe, and Out Of Plato* (London: Adam Islip)

Dent, R W (1981) *Shakespeare's Proverbial Language: An Index* (Berkeley: University of California Press)

Elyot, T (1533) *Of the Knowledg which Maketh a Wise Man* (London: Thomas Berthelet)

Elyot, T (1539) *The Castel of Helth* (London: Thomas Berthelet)

Fudge, E (2006) *Brutal Reasoning: Animals, Rationality and Humanity in Early Modern England* (Ithaca NY: Cornell University Press)

Golding, A (1567) *The .xv. Bookes of P Ovidius Naso, Entytuled Metamorphosis* (London: William Seres)

Heywood, T (1635), *Philocothonista, or the Drunkard, Opened, Dissected and Anatomized* (London: Robert Raworth)

Holland, P (trans.) (1606) *The Historie of Twelve Caesars* (London: for Matthew Lownes)

Homer (1996) *Odyssey*, R Fagles (trans.) (New York: Viking Penguin)

Huloet, R (1572) *Huloets Dictionarie* (London: Thomas Marsh)

Janson, H W (1952) *Apes and Ape Lore in the Middle Ages and Renaissance* (London: Warburg Institute)

Lyne, R (2001) *Ovid's Changing Worlds: English Metamorphoses, 1567–1632* (Oxford: Oxford University Press)

Machiavelli, N (1988) *The Prince*, R Price (trans.), Q Skinner and R Price (eds) (Cambridge: Cambridge University Press)

OED (2011) www.oed.com

Phillips, J (1570) *A Frendly Larum* (London: William How for Richard Jones)

Plutarch (1579) *The Lives of the Noble Romanes and Grecians*, T North (trans.) (London: Thomas Vautrollier and Edward Wright)

Porter, R (1999) *The Greatest Benefit to Mankind: A Medical History of Humanity from Antiquity to the Present*, paperback edn (London: Fontana Press)

Shakespeare, W (2005a) *Othello* in G Blakemore Evans et al. (eds), *The Riverside Shakespeare* 2nd edn (Boston: Houghton Mifflin)

Shakespeare, W (2005b) *The Tempest* in G Blakemore Evans et al. (eds), *The Riverside Shakespeare* 2nd edn (Boston: Houghton Mifflin)

Skelton, J (1545) *A Litel Boke called Colyn Cloute* (London: Robert Copland for Robert Wyer)

Smyth, A (2004) 'Introduction' in A Smyth (ed.), *A Pleasing Sinne: Drink and Conviviality in 17th-Century England* (Cambridge: D S Brewer), pp. xiii–xxv

Spenser, E (1579) *Shepheardes Calendar* (London: Hugh Singleton)

Thomas, K (1984) *Man and the Natural World: Changing Attitudes in England, 1500–1800* (Harmondsworth: Penguin)

Thomas, W (1549) *The Historie of Italie* (London: Thomas Berthelet)

11

Intoxicants and Compulsive Behaviour: A Neuroscientific Perspective

Karen D Ersche

Introduction

Psychologically, the term 'compulsion' refers to an inappropriate repetition or perseveration of responding. In the context of drug addiction, compulsivity has been defined as persistence or perseverance of behaviour in the absence of reward or despite punishment (American Psychiatric Association, 1994). Thus, compulsivity reflects the persistence with which drug-dependent individuals act to obtain and consume drugs, despite the risk of job loss, family break-up or imprisonment precipitated by further drug use. However, not everybody who takes drugs develops addictive behaviour. The transition from recreational drug use to addiction is often described as a process in which natural rewards are gradually replaced by drug rewards; an initially hedonic motivation to consume drugs is replaced over time by a less pleasurable, more habitual pattern of drug consumption (Everitt and Robbins, 2005).

This chapter aims to give an introduction to the neuroscientific basis of drug abuse and the development of addiction. This will provide a foundation for a better understanding of the addictive potential of most drugs and the neural network subserving the mechanisms leading to the compulsive consumption of drugs. This knowledge will fuel the discussion as to whether there is a genetic vulnerability, potentially increasing the risk for developing addiction in some individuals but not in others. As much as drug use is widespread in society, there are a variety of terms that are being used to describe the various forms of drug use. To begin with, the common terminology used to describe drug-taking will be introduced.

Recreational drug use describes the consumption of psychoactive substances for social and relaxing purposes rather than for medical or spiritual reasons.

People who use drugs recreationally neither experience a compulsive drive to take drugs nor suffer from negative consequences caused by drug abuse. For the use of alcohol this would mean, having an occasional drink in a social situation without taking it to excess, which would include any form of harmful drinking, or legal and social problems associated with it (World Health Organization (WHO), 1994). Recreational drug use may also reflect a certain life-style, for example, occasional use of 'club drugs' or cannabis is part and parcel of some subcultures (United Nations Office on Drugs and Crime, 2000). While the term *use* has been considered a neutral term reflecting the general consumption of substances, the term *substance misuse* is more frequently employed as a non-judgmental term to take into account the problems related to consumption. Substance misuse refers to the use of alcohol or other substances in a way that is inconsistent with medical practice. It covers the intake of alcohol above the recommended levels as well as the ingestion of prescribed drugs without prescription (Royal College of Psychiatrists and Royal College of Physicians, 2000).

The term *problem drug use* focuses merely on problems involved for society, relating to the pattern of the substance used. It is defined as 'intravenous drug use or long duration/regular use of opiates, cocaine or amphetamines', not including substances such as ecstasy, cannabis or hallucinogens. The term is mainly employed to compare national estimates, trends in prevalence and incidence, and rates of substance misuse between different countries. It represents a key piece of information in the development and monitoring of political strategies. While problem drug use refers to the negative consequences of heavy drug use for society, *substance abuse* refers to the negative effects that prolonged drug consumption has for the individual. The *Diagnostic and Statistical Manual of Mental Disorders* (DSM-IV-TR) (American Psychiatric Association, 2000) defines substance abuse as problematic use which does not involve compulsion, significant tolerance, or symptoms of withdrawal, but which causes significant cognitive, social, interpersonal and legal problems. However, the term *abuse* is controversial since it implies a judgment of 'wrongdoing'; thereby placing the responsibility for the condition on the individual, leaving environmental, genetic and pharmacological factors aside. In view of this ambiguity, WHO substitutes the term *abuse* with *harmful use* in the *International Classification of Diseases* (ICD-10) (WHO, 1992). The Royal College of Psychiatrists and the British Medical Association have further recommended avoiding the term abuse in medical practice altogether because of its judgmental implications (Royal College of Psychiatrists, 2001).

Addiction, as defined by WHO, is the

> repeated use of psychoactive substances, to the extent that the user is periodically or chronically intoxicated, shows a compulsion

to take the preferred substance, has great difficulty in voluntarily ceasing or modifying substance use, and exhibits determination to obtain psychoactive substances by almost any means (WHO, 1994).

As early as the 1960s, WHO recommended abandoning the term addiction in favour of substance dependence because 'the term addiction also conveys the sense that such substance use has a detrimental effect on society, as well as on the individual', thereby feeding the social stigma that is attached to people who are dependent on drugs (WHO, 1994). Consequently, the term addiction disappeared from the international diagnostical manuals for psychiatric disorders such as the DSM and the American Psychiatric Association stopped using the term addiction and addict in its publications. The diagnostic term *substance dependence* corresponds roughly with the characteristics of addiction. As Table 1 shows, DSM-IV-TR defines substance dependence as

Table 1: DSM-IV-TR criteria for the diagnosis of substance dependence (Reprinted with permission from the Diagnostic and Statistical Manual of Mental Disorders, Fourth Edition, Text Revision, (Copyright © 2000). American Psychiatric Association.)

A maladaptive pattern of substance use, leading to clinically significant impairment or distress, as manifested by three (or more) of the following, occurring at any time in the same 12-month period:

1. Tolerance, as defined by either of the following:
  (a) A need for markedly increased amounts of the substance to achieve intoxication or desired effect.
  (b) Markedly diminished effect with continued use of the same amount of the substance.

2. Withdrawal, as manifested by either of the following:
  (a) The characteristic withdrawal syndrome for the substance.
  (b) The same (or a closely related) substance is taken to relieve or avoid withdrawal symptoms.

3. The substance is often taken in larger amounts or over a longer period than was intended.
4. There is a persistent desire or unsuccessful efforts to cut down or control substance use.
5. A great deal of time is spent in activities necessary to obtain the substance (e.g. visiting multiple doctors or driving long distances), use the substance (e.g. chain-smoking), or recover from its effects.
6. Important social, occupational, or recreational activities are given up or reduced because of substance use.
7. The substance use is continued despite knowledge of having a persistent or recurrent physical or psychological problem that is likely to have been caused or exacerbated by the substance (e.g. current cocaine use despite recognition of cocaine-induced depression, or continued drinking despite recognition that ulcer was made worse by alcohol consumption).

a syndrome involving compulsive use, with or without tolerance and withdrawal, and which is associated with a cluster of behavioural, cognitive and social problems.

Nevertheless, the choice of the term *dependence* as a replacement for addiction also has its critics. One major argument is that dependence is widely associated with *physical dependence*, which is characterized by tolerance and symptoms of withdrawal. However, substance dependence, as described in the diagnostical manuals such as DSM-IV-TR, confusingly includes both physiological dependence and *psychological dependence* characterized by intensive craving, compulsive drug-seeking, and loss of control over drug intake. As can be seen in Table 1, for a diagnosis of substance dependence, either form of dependence may be met (American Psychiatric Association, 2000). However, patients who receive opiates over longer periods for relief of chronic pain develop physical dependence without experiencing symptoms of psychological dependence. These patients would be regarded as substance dependent but not as drug addicted.

It is also of note that substance dependence in psychiatric diagnostic manuals is categorized as a *disorder*, not a *disease*, although in more recent years the disease model of drug addiction (Jellinek, 1960; Leshner, 1997) has become popular. Considering drug addiction as a disease may remove the negative moral connotation, but critics argue, for example, that there is no laboratory test to undoubtedly determine whether an individual suffers from drug addiction or not. Since substance dependence is diagnosed on the basis of mental and behavioural symptoms, as other mental disorders, the rationale for classifying drug addiction as a disease, but not schizophrenia or depression that also have neurobiological underpinnings, is also arguable.

Despite these conflicts, in conceptual terms *drug addiction* is currently regarded as:

> a complex neuroadaptive process through which drugs of abuse alter cellular and molecular aspects of neural function in such a way as to render the brain circuits mediating various behavioural effects of these drugs...guiding behaviour in maladaptive directions (White, 2002).

Accordingly, in this chapter the term *drug addiction* will be employed when referring to theoretical models of addictive circles, whereas the term *substance dependence* will be used when referring to the clinical population. The discussion surrounding the terminology may exemplify the stigma that is closely linked with drug use. The US Department of Health and Human Services is drafting guidelines for more appropriate and less stigmatizing use of language in relation to substance use disorders. Therefore, in accordance with the terminology recommended in these guidelines, in this chapter individuals who are meeting the criteria for substance dependence will not be referred to as *abusers* or *addicts* but with the less stigmatizing term of *chronic drug users*.

The complex relationship between reward and drugs of abuse

The subjective experience of pleasure and well-being obtained from psychoactive substances is often described as *rewarding* and reinforcing. It is generally held that the pleasurable feelings induced by psychoactive substances positively reinforce drug self-administration, and thereby establish a more frequent or regular pattern of drug use. Negative reinforcement, i.e. escaping from aversive states such as withdrawal or stress through drug intake, is also considered to play an important role in the maintenance of chronic drug-taking behaviour (Kreek and Koob, 1998). More recently it has been suggested that negative reinforcement may also account for initial drug-taking in some situations (Baker et al., 2004). For example, unpleasant emotions such as stress or emotional pain may be reduced by the intake of drugs.

The powerful reinforcing effects of psychoactive drugs are, for many people, the motivation to take drugs in the first place. Drug reinforcement also plays a central role in the development of addiction. Almost all drugs of abuse, as well as natural reinforcers stimulate the brain reward centre by releasing the brain chemical dopamine. The phenomenon of chronic drug use may be best understood by elucidating the different functions of reward. At present rewards are considered to serve the three basic functions (Dickinson, 1980; Schultz, 2000): pleasure, motivation and learning. In the following, the relationship of these three different reward functions are explained in relation to drug abuse.

Reward and pleasure

The hedonic aspect of reward is the pleasure (*liking*) felt when a rewarding stimulus such as food, drink, sex or psychoactive drugs is taken. Intracranial self-stimulation (ICSS) is a method to measure such pleasurable effects and to explore the brain circuitries involved in reward processing (Olds and Fobes, 1981, for review). Generally, electrodes have been placed into selected areas of an animal's brain and the animal is then trained to press a lever to obtain electrical stimulation in these brain areas. Olds and Milner (1954) observed, using this method, that animals will even self-administer electrical shocks until exhaustion and at the expense of food and drink when electrodes have been placed into dopamine rich areas in the midbrain. In other words, the reinforcement from electrical stimulation in these brain areas seemed more potent than other rewards such as food. The observation that prior administration of dopaminergic antagonists that blocked the reinforcing effects of electric shocks and food rewards (e.g. Bailey et al., 1986) led to the assumption that pleasure was mediated by increased levels of dopamine. Wise et al. (1978) formulated the *anhedonia hypothesis* suggesting that a reduction in dopamine neurotransmission results in a loss of pleasure. Although the hypothesis has been very popular, it has also been criticized as being too simplistic and incomplete. In particular, the accumulating evidence that administration of a dopamine antagonist or dopamine depletion in the nucleus accumbens (NAcc) does not eradicate simple responses to food or the motivation to eat food rewards called the anhedonia hypothesis into question (Salamone et al., 2003). Furthermore, increased levels of dopamine in the midbrain have been found in aversive as well as in appetitive conditions (Blackburn et al., 1992). Berridge and Robinson (1998) have suggested that dopamine may contribute to pleasurable experiences but that it is not sufficient to elicit pleasure. More recent research showed that opioid neuropeptides are critically involved in the liking of food rewards (Kelley et al., 2002). However, there is some evidence for dopamine playing a certain role in the pleasurable effects of rewards. Thus, different lines of investigation have revealed that the magnitude and suddenness of the increase in midbrain dopamine mediates the intensity of a pleasurable experience but not the pleasure per se (Drevets et al., 2001). For example, the euphoric feeling of a 'rush' induced by a psychostimulant drug is related to a sharp increase in dopamine levels but not to high levels of dopamine per se (Volkow et al., 1999b).

Reward and motivation

Since rewards are not only 'liked' but also 'wanted', the second function of reward focuses on its motivational aspects. Associations between features of the reward (e.g. the smell, colour or a cue paired with the reward) and the reinforcing effects of the reward, increase the salience of the reward, and thereby elicit the motivation to seek it out (Robinson and Berridge, 2001). In other words, wanting is a motivational conditioned response aimed at achieving the reward. Dopamine antagonists or dopamine depletion in the NAcc in animals reduce their motivation to show the instrumental behaviour to obtain the food rewards (e.g. pressing a lever or climbing over a barrier) but do not change the animal's willingness to eat the food (see Salamone and Correa, 2002, for review). Support for the role of dopamine in the motivational aspect of reward was provided by Chang et al. (1996) who found that in rats self-administering cocaine, neural activation was highest in the anticipatory phase prior to pressing the lever. Berridge (2004) labelled this motivational aspect of reward *wanting* but similar concepts are *incentive salience, appetite* and *craving*, all mediating reinforcement behaviour. According to Berridge (2003), wanting is clearly dissociated from the affective value of rewards, i.e. the liking, pleasure or rush, both regulated by different neural mechanisms. Thus, repeated drug use does not intensify the pleasurable effect of the drug (i.e. the rush) but increases the craving (i.e. wanting) for the drug. Di Chiara and North (1992) proposed a similar division of reward: a consummatory, pleasurable aspect of reward associated with the opioid system and an incentive aspect regulated by the dopamine system.

It has also been suggested that the rewards not only lead to approach and consummatory behaviour (i.e. appetitive motivation) but also to avoidant behaviour (i.e. aversive motivation) (Bozarth, 1994). Thus, the dopamine increase following punishment or stress, as measured by microdialysis in animal experiments, may reflect the incentive to seek safety in face of environmental cues of danger (Ikemoto and Panksepp, 1999). The release of dopamine (and endogenous opioid peptides) during negative states may also explain why some people seek stressful and painful situations or engage in risky behaviours such as bungee jumping or dangerous driving (Matthews et al., 2004). Most people avoid risky situations, but it seems that, in sensation-seekers, cognitive processes do not label stressors as threatening, thereby enabling pleasure from engaging in risky behaviours (Bozarth, 1994).

Reward and learning

Rewards also entail a cognitive aspect and play an important role during learning (Schultz et al., 1997). There are two forms of dopamine signalling implicated in reward processing: a fast phasic dopamine response, spatially limited to the relevant synapse; and a slower tonic response, which is spatially more diffuse. Unpredicted rewards produce a sharp increase in phasic firing of dopamine neurons, which diminishes over the course of learning until the reward becomes predictable (Schultz, 2000). Non-delivery of an expected reward leads to a depression of phasic dopamine (Schultz et al., 1997, for review). Changes in tonic dopamine responses, in contrast, may be relevant for preparing the organism to respond appropriately to the previously rewarded environmental cues (Floresco et al., 2003). Such 'reward-driven learning' reflects an anticipated error in the expectation of the reward (Schultz and Dickinson, 2000). According to Schultz (1998), midbrain dopamine neurons are needed for the processing of rewards and the learning of approach behaviour by predicting both the occurrence as well as the timing of the reward. Hence, the prediction error, as reflected in a change in phasic dopamine transmission, serves as a 'teaching signal' for learning or maintaining approach behaviour (Shultz, 2004, for review). This view of the function of the prediction error, however, is not shared by Redgrave et al.

(1999), who suggested that the prediction error serves as a signal to switch the behavioural responses rather than to learn or maintain a response.

The brain reward centre

On the basis of the findings with electrical ICSS in experimental rats, the medial forebrain bundle, a diffuse system of fibres that connects structures in the limbic region with various areas of the brain stem, has been suggested as the 'reward centre' of the brain (Olds and Milner, 1954). Stimulation in most sites of the medial forebrain bundle produced strong and immediate rewarding effects, which, however, were short-lived, as they lasted no longer than the stimulus itself. The sites in which ICSS can produce such pleasurable responses were labelled as the 'brain reward system' or the 'pleasure centre' (Wise, 1980). However, it is still under debate as to whether these sites form a single system or are involved in multiple pathways working in parallel (Bozarth, 1994). Electrophysiological and neurochemical studies showed that the rewarding stimulation by ICSS was caused by activation of a descending pathway of the medial forebrain bundle to the ventral tegmental area (VTA), followed by activation of the ascending mesolimbic dopamine pathway (Wise and Bozarth, 1984).

At present, the dopaminergic VTA in the midbrain has been suggested as the centre of the reward-processing pathway (Wise and Bozarth, 1984), which projects to the NAcc in the ventral striatum and to other surrounding areas such as the amygdala, the bed of the nucleus stria terminals, lateral septal area and lateral hypothalamus. The VTA plays an important part in mediating reward via the mesolimbic pathway, projecting to NAcc, olfactory tubercle, amygdala and the orbitofrontal cortex. In contrast, the substantia nigra in the midbrain mainly projects to the dorsal striatum and the dorsolateral part of the prefrontal cortex and is considered to mediate motor activity and habits as well as higher cognitive function.

The wider neural circuitry of reward processing

Single neuron recordings in monkeys have challenged the view on dopamine functions that derived from findings with ICSS, suggesting that just dopamine efflux in the VTA is associated with reward (Wise, 1980). Recording of dopamine neurons in different areas within dopamine pathways, however, showed that brain areas, even beyond the medial forebrain bundle, are implicated in reward processing (Schultz, 2000). Reward sensitive dopamine neurons have been found in the striatum, dorsolateral and orbitofrontal prefrontal cortex, anterior cingulate cortex, amygdala and hypothalamus (see Schultz, 2000, for review). Furthermore, the processing of reward-related information has shown to be highly specialized. For example, both the occurrence of a salient stimulus and information about the reward's intensity are signalled by dopamine neurons in the amygdala (Pratt and Mizumori, 1998), whereas striatal dopamine neurons particularly respond to stimuli with behavioural and motivational significance such as types of rewards, sensory object properties or the spatial movements (Schultz et al., 2003). Schultz (2000) hypothesized that striatal neurons are not only involved in reward detection but also in goal representation. Evidence for this is that dopamine neurons in the orbitofrontal cortex showed a specialization in the processing of motivational aspects of rewards (Tremblay and Schultz, 1999) and their relevance to the organism (Rolls et al., 1989). Orbitofrontal neurons are also able to distinguish rewards from punishers (Thorpe et al., 1983). Neurons in the dorsolateral prefrontal cortex, in contrast, respond when reward delivery is delayed, probably to maintain information about the reward available for the planning and execution of behaviour (Watanabe, 1996). Thus, findings from single cell recordings clearly demonstrated that activation of dopamine neurons is not exclusively related to pleasurable incentives but also to novel, aversive and motivationally relevant stimuli.

With technological advances in functional neuroimaging techniques, reward pathways in humans have been increasingly investigated. In brief, neuroimaging research in humans has revealed two key findings. First, the neural network involved in reward processing in humans and animals is over-lapping (McClure et al., 2004; O'Doherty, 2004, both for review). Important areas implicated with reward processing are the striatum, in particular the NAcc in the ventral striatum, orbitofrontal cortex and amygdala. Second, rewarding stimuli are processed in the same way, regardless of the type of reward. Thus, primary reinforcers such as food, drink or sexual stimulation involve the same processing pathways as social reinforcers such as beauti-ful or smiling faces, humour, pleasant music, social co-operation, roman-tic love or maternal attachment. Furthermore, conditioned rewards such as money, positive feedback or conditioned abstract cues also recruit the same brain areas. Although the components of reward processing have been iden-tified, research is now aiming to increase our understanding of the specific roles different brain areas play within the reward-processing pathway, and more importantly, how they interact during reward-directed behaviours and decision-making. At present, functional roles of different brain areas within reward processing such as the amygdala, orbitofrontal cortex and ventral striatum are largely in keeping with findings from animal research. Thus, the ventral striatum has shown to respond with respect to the predictability of rewards in humans (Berns et al., 2001), which is in line with the findings from electrophysiological recordings in monkeys suggesting that dopamine neurons in the striatum are signalling prediction error (Schultz et al., 1997). As suggested by Schultz (2000), neuroimaging research has also demonstrated that the amygdala and the striatum both encode the salience of reinforcing stimuli, while the relative reward value and its relevance for choice selection is processed in the orbitofrontal cortex.

Psychoactive substances and reward processing

Reward from psychoactive drugs involves activation of the same areas that were activated by ICSS, namely the mesolimbic dopamine system (Kornetsky, 1985). Most strikingly, all drugs of abuse, regardless of their pharmacological characteristics, seem to make ICSS more rewarding by decreasing the threshold required by the animal to achieve the same level of reward (Kornetsky, 1985). This ability corresponds to the drug's tendency to produce addiction, which is termed *addiction liability* (Fraser et al., 1961).

Drugs of abuse stimulate the reward pathway by increasing dopamine levels, primarily in the NAcc (Di Chiara and Imperato, 1986). However, the mechanisms that increase dopamine levels differ greatly between different substances. The stimulant drugs, amphetamine and cocaine, both increase extracellular dopamine directly by binding to the dopamine transporter, either promoting dopamine release or blocking dopamine reuptake (Seiden et al., 1993). In light of this direct influence on the dopamine concentration, amphetamine and cocaine have been regarded as the prototype drugs of reward (Adinoff, 2004). All the other drugs affect the dopamine system indirectly (see Wise, 1998, for review). Opiates, for example, increase dopamine by removing the GABAergic inhibitory influence on dopamine modulation (Van Ree et al., 1999), cannabinoides interacting with opioid peptides also influence dopamine levels in the midbrain (Gardner and Vorel, 1998). Hallucinogens like phencyclidine increase dopamine via the glutamate transmission on GABAergic cells, which modulate dopamine firing. While alcohol increases extracellular dopamine by stimulating the firing rate of dopaminergic cells in the VTA via GABA receptors (Mereu and Gessa, 1985), nicotine depolarizes the dopamine neurons by binding on cholinergic receptors (Rice and Cragg, 2004). While the acute intake of psychoactive substances increases levels of dopamine in the midbrain dopamine system, drug abstinence following repeated administration leads to a decrease in dopamine in this brain system, which may induce drug craving and withdrawal (Bozarth, 1994).

Neuroimaging studies have provided evidence for the involvement of mesolimbic dopamine during drug-induced reinforcement. For example, chronic drug users who had been administered cocaine or heroin during scanning, reported feeling 'high' while activation in the ventral striatum significantly increased (Breiter et al., 1997). Similar results were found in healthy volunteers who had been administered amphetamine (Drevets et al., 2001). The dopamine release induced by amphetamine in the ventral striatum, as assessed by decreased D2-receptor radiotracer binding, significantly correlated with the self-reported 'high'. The observation that healthy volunteers who reported pleasurable effects of psychostimulant administration displayed lower levels of dopamine D2 receptor binding compared to healthy volunteers who found drug administration unpleasant (Volkow et al., 1999) may suggest that individual differences may exist in striatal dopamine neurotransmission, which predispose drug-taking behaviour.

The common currency of all drugs of abuse is the ability to powerfully enhance activation of brain reward mechanisms, which is subjectively experienced as a 'rush' or 'high'. Natural rewards, such as food, sex or social appraisal also stimulate dopamine neurons in the NAcc, but unlike psychoactive drugs, natural rewards undergo short-term habituation, i.e. a process that attenuates the effect with repeated stimulation (Di Chiara, 2002). In other words, psychoactive drugs have a powerful ability to initiate dopamine release in a more sustained manner than natural rewards, independently from previous drug exposure or drug availability. Furthermore, psychoactive drugs are far more potent than natural rewards, since the magnitude of the drug-induced dopamine increase is by far greater than that by natural rewards. For example, while dopamine levels in the NAcc increase by 45 per cent following a food reward, administration of amphetamines leads to an increase in extracellular dopamine of about 500 per cent (Hernandez and Hoebel, 1988). In view of such powerful reinforcing properties of psychoactive substances, natural rewards increasingly lose attraction, which devalues their ability to motivate behaviour. While natural rewards are perceived as less rewarding and sensitization to the drug's effects develop, psychoactive drugs increasingly exert control over the individual's behaviour (Bozarth, 1994; Cardinal and Everitt, 2004).

Neuropathology of drug addiction

The transition from repeated drug use to drug addiction entails drug-induced changes in brain areas implicated in the processing of rewards, the learning of associations and in the control of behaviour. It is thought that these neuroadaptive changes underlie addictive behaviours described in DSM-IV-TR (American Psychiatric Association, 2000).

Steps in the development of drug addiction

The mesolimbic dopamine system is not only involved in reward processing but is also implicated in learning and motivation for conditioned behaviours (see Robbins and Everitt,1996, for review). Elevation in dopamine in the NAcc signals the occurrence of a novel and important stimulus that requires an appropriate behavioural response (Schultz, 2000). Therefore, the dopamine signal is passed on to a wider neural network to develop an adequate behavioural response strategy. In other words, dopamine is the key element in initiating and establishing adaptive changes within these cortical networks (Kalivas, 2002). Consequently, repeated administrations of psychoactive substances do not just interfere with reward processing, but also result in dysregulation in learning and motivation (Robbins and Everitt, 1999). In the following section, three important processes in the transition from regular drug use to drug addiction are highlighted: sensitization, associative learning and compulsive drive, which may represent underpinnings for cognitive impairment and maladaptive behaviours.

Sensitization to the effects of the drug

The prolonged and repeated drug-induced increase in extracellular dopamine in the VTA initiates synaptic processes that produce a phenomenon called *behavioural sensitization,* which refers to an enhanced behavioural response to a drug or to drug-related stimuli after repeated use (Robinson and Berridge, 1993). While sensitization increases the response to the drug, the phenomenon of tolerance refers to the decreasing effectiveness of the drug following repeated use. In other words, more of the substance is needed to achieve the desired effect on mood or concentration (Koob and LeMoal, 1997). Both phenomena involve different neuroadaptive changes and therefore may coexist (Hyman and Malenka, 2001).

The phenomenon of sensitization is not limited to the drug itself but may also include learned responses to specific cues or contexts, which has been labelled *context-dependent sensitization.* In other words, like the psychoactive drug itself, a specific context or a cue associated with the drug may become able to excite dopamine neurons in the VTA and increase dopamine levels in the NAcc (Berke and Hyman, 2000, for review). In addition, there are also internal states such as stress that can increase the strength at excitatory synapses on midbrain dopamine neurons, which has been termed *context-independent sensitization.* Sensitization is closely linked with the process of associative learning.

Associative learning

Natural rewards as well as psychoactive drugs increase dopamine transmission in the NAcc, but unlike natural rewards, the reinforcing effects of drugs exceed those of natural rewards by several-fold and are not subject to habituation (Di Chiara and Imperato, 1988). If drugs are used repeatedly, their powerful reinforcing properties strengthen associations between the pleasurable effects of the drugs and stimuli that are associated with or predictive of the drug such as music or certain people (Robbins and Everitt, 1996). In other words, regular drug use stimulates the mesolimbic dopamine system repetitively and profoundly, which affects learning in three different ways: firstly, it strengthens these '*stimulus – outcome* associations', such that, for example, a certain song evokes memories of drugs; secondly, it also strengthens associations between *actions* that lead to drug use and *the effects of the drug*. In other words, the pleasurable effects of drugs facilitate the learning of where to get the good quality drugs or how to best prepare or mix them to obtain the desired effects. And, thirdly, the drug-induced stimulations of the dopamine system also facilitate habit-learning. This means that these actions leading to drug use are directly reinforced as well, creating powerful '*stimulus-response habits*'. For example, hearing a certain piece of music directly activates the habit of ringing the dealer's number to score some drugs, and the subsequent habitual patterns of preparing and using the drugs (Everitt and Robbins, 2005).

One method to investigate associative learning under laboratory conditions is with the conditioned place preference paradigm. Rats repeatedly receive drug and saline injections each in a different chamber. When they are given free access to the two chambers, they show a preference for the chamber in which they had previously received drug injections. In addition, if the rats had previously been trained to press a lever in order to receive the injection, the rats will show this conditioned response as soon as they enter the chamber (Stolerman, 1992). Lesions to the basolateral amygdala impair the acquisition of place preference as well as the learning of behaviour patterns to obtain the drug, indicating a prominent role of the amygdala in the establishment of such drug-stimulus-associations (Everitt et al., 1999). Evidence from neuroimaging studies shows that the amygdala is also implicated in drug-related associations in humans as well. For example, when, during the scanning session drug users are presented with drug-related cues, e.g. a spoon, they show activation in the amygdala (Grant et al., 1996). Once established, drug-stimulus associations are long-lasting, and exposure to people, places and things that are related to drug use may trigger drug craving (Childress et al., 1986).

Neuroimaging studies using cue-reactivity paradigms have, however, shown that presentations of drug cues not only activate the amygdala but also a wider neural network including the orbitofrontal cortex, the dorsolateral prefrontal cortex and the anterior cingulate cortex. Prefrontal activation in response to drug-related cues is not surprising because striato-thalamo-cortical loops connect the brain reward system with brain areas that are involved in the regulation of motivational drive. In other words, interactions between the NAcc, amygdala and hippocampus are implicated in the formation of associations between the pleasant drug effects and contextual stimuli. These associations may induce cravings, so that executive control from the prefrontal cortex over the NAcc would be needed to guide subsequent behaviour, i.e. helping drug users to act according to their plans and goals. In chronic drug users, exposure to drug-related cues can lead to uncontrolled and irresponsible behaviour because the drug-induced changes in dopamine transmission result in impulsive actions that get out of control as the 'rational brake' in the prefrontal cortex fails to regulate behaviour appropriately (Jentsch and Taylor, 1999).

Drug-taking habits and compulsive drive

The persistence with which individuals act to obtain and consume drugs despite the aversive consequences precipitated by further drug use, is a hallmark of addiction. Dopamine neurotransmission is believed to play an important part in this process as it drives conditioned learning and facilitates the formation of habits. Habits are behaviour patterns that occur independently from a goal, i.e. they are not motivated by the rewarding outcome (Balleine and Dickinson, 1998). In the context of addiction, this means that individuals with a drug-taking habit are no longer motivated by the pleasurable effects of the drug. Habitual drug-taking is termed compulsive when the drug user is not deterred from drug-taking by the aversive effects the drugs has on his/her life (Everitt et al., 2008).

At a neurological level, the formation of habits has been explained by a shift in the control of behaviour from the prefrontal cortex towards the striatum, and within the striatum from the NAcc (ventral part) to the caudate nucleus (dorsal part) (Everitt and Robbins, 2005). The dorsal striatum is a key area in the formation of habits by establishing stable '*stimulus–response* associations' (Packard and Knowlton, 2002). This is a normal process of learning, and it has been shown in experimental animals that repeated exposure to psychostimulant drugs facilitate the development of habitual responses (Nelson and Killcross, 2006). It has thus been suggested that regular cocaine use may accelerate habit formation, and indeed, research in primates has shown that with prolonged use of cocaine more dorsal parts of the striatum are activated by the drug (Letchworth et al., 2001).

Volkow and Fowler (2000) have also suggested that the compulsive use seen in human drug users is due to dysfunction of the dopaminergic striato-thalamo-orbitofrontal circuitry, connecting reward processing areas in the midbrain with the inhibitory areas in the frontal lobe. They suggest that a lack of inhibition is the key element of drug addiction, including the suppression of emotional, cognitive and behavioural responses (Goldstein and Volkow, 2002). According to Goldstein and Volkow (2002), chronic drug users, experiencing the strong rewarding effects of psychoactive substances and the withdrawal symptoms involved, consequently overvalue drug-related reinforcers and undervalue alternative rewards. Dysfunction of the anterior cingulate cortex and the orbitofrontal cortex, brain areas implicated in salience attribution and response inhibition respectively, biases drug users' behaviour towards increased drug use, leading to compulsive drug-seeking.

Vulnerability markers for addiction

As explained above, addictive drugs affect brain circuitries implicated in a variety of cognitive functions including attention, learning of associations, and executive control over behaviour and thoughts. However, not everyone who uses drugs develops addictive behaviours. Survey data suggests that less than 20 per cent of people who try cocaine will become dependent on it within 10 years of their first use (Wagner and Anthony, 2002), but the likelihood of developing dependence is further increased for people who have a family history of drug or alcohol abuse (Merikangas et al., 1998). In other words, there seems to be a genetic risk but we currently know very little about how the risks for drug dependence are inherited. Cognitive dysfunction or impulsive personality traits might be markers for addiction vulnerability (Verdejo-Garcia et al, 2008), possibly reflecting malfunction in neural networks that are implicated in dependence and therefore rendering individuals vulnerable. On the other hand, it is well known that cognitive function and a person's personality change over the course of drug dependence, suggesting that these are the result of long-term exposure to potentially neurotoxic drugs of abuse. Moreover, chronic drug abuse has been associated with significant impairments, particularly in executive functions and impulsive behaviour patterns. Addressing this question of causality is important because doing so would help to clarify the health risks associated with drug abuse, to identify individuals with a significant risk of developing drug dependence, and to ensure a more rational development of therapeutic or preventative interventions in future.

The question of causality can be directly addressed by experiments in which animals are administered drugs and cognitive function and behaviour is measured before, during and after chronic drug exposure, but this type of experiment would be inconceivable in humans. The concept of endophenotypes therefore offers a useful strategy for elucidating underlying factors that may render humans vulnerable for drug dependence. *Endophenotypes* have been described as the neurobiological correlates of a disorder, which are genetically determined and relatively stable over time (Gottesman and Gould, 2003). As inherited traits, endophenotypes are over-represented in non-affected family members as compared to the general population. Individuals at risk for drug dependence typically have deficits in self-control which possibly reflects a diminished ability to recruit prefrontal networks for regulating behaviour. Recently, Ersche and colleagues (2010; 2012) showed that not only drug-dependent individuals lack self-control but also their brothers and sisters who do not abuse drugs. Impaired regulatory abilities in those siblings without a history of chronic drug abuse might indicate a developmental dysfunction of prefrontal control. Indeed, the sib-pairs' poor performance on a behavioural test of self-control was associated with weakened inferior prefrontal cortical connectivity (Ersche et al., 2012), further supporting the idea of an underlying neurocognitive endophenotype for drug addiction.

Bibliography

Adinoff, B (2004) 'Neurobiologic Processes in Drug Reward and Addiction' **12**(6) *Harvard Review of Psychiatry* 305–20

American Psychiatric Association (2000) *Diagnostic and Statistical Manual of Mental Disorders* 4th edn Text Revision (Washington DC: American Psychiatric Association)

Bailey, C S, S Hsiao and J E King (1986) 'Hedonic Reactivity to Sucrose in Rats – Modification by Pimozide' **38**(4) *Physiology and Behavior* 447–52

Baker, T B, M E Piper, D E McCarthy, M R Majeskie and M C Fiore (2004) 'Addiction Motivation Reformulated: An Affective Processing Model of Negative Reinforcement' **111**(1) *Psychological Review* 33–51

Balleine, B W and A Dickinson (1998) 'Goal-Directed Instrumental Action: Contingency and Incentive Learning and their Cortical Substrates' **37**(4–5) *Neuropharmacology* 407–19

Berke, J D and S E Hyman (2000) 'Addiction, Dopamine, and the Molecular Mechanisms of Memory' **25**(3) *Neuron* 515–32

Berns, G S, S M McClure, G Pagnoni and P R Montague (2001) 'Predictability Modulates Human Brain Response to Reward' **21**(8) *Journal of Neuroscience* 2793–8

Berridge, K C (2003) 'Pleasures of the Brain' **52**(1) *Brain and Cognition* 106–28

Berridge, K C (2004) 'Motivation Concepts in Behavioral Neuroscience' **81**(2) *Physiology and Behavior* 179–209

Berridge, K C and T E Robinson (1998) 'What is the Role of Dopamine in Reward: Hedonic Impact, Reward Learning, or Incentive Salience?' **28**(3) *Brain Research Reviews* 309–69

Blackburn, J R, J G Pfaus and A G Phillips (1992) 'Dopamine Functions in Appetitive and Defensive Behaviors' **39**(3) *Progress in Neurobiology* 247–79

Bozarth, M A (1994) 'Pleasure Systems in the Brain' in D Warburton (ed.), *Pleasure: The Politics and the Reality* (New York: John Wiley & Sons)

Breiter, H C, R L Gollub, R M Weisskoff, D N Kennedy, N Makris, J D Berke, J M Goodman, H L Kantor, D R Gastfriend, J P Riorden, R T Mathew, B R Rosen, and S E Hyman (1997) 'Acute Effects of Cocaine on Human Brain Activity and Emotion' **19**(3) *Neuron* 591–611

Cardinal, R N and B J Everitt (2004) 'Neural and Psychological Mechanisms Underlying Appetitive Learning: Links to Drug Addiction' **14**(2) *Current Opinion in Neurobiology* 156–62

Chang, J Y, J M Paris, S F Sawyer, A B Kirillov and D J Woodward (1996) 'Neuronal Spike Activity in Rat Nucleus Accumbens During Cocaine Self-Administration under Different Fixed-Ratio Schedules' **74**(2) *Neuroscience* 483–97

Childress, A R, A T McLellan and C P O'Brien (1986) 'Abstinent Opiate Abusers Exhibit Conditioned Craving, Conditioned Withdrawal and Reductions in Both Through Extinction' **81**(5) *British Journal of Addiction* 655–60

Di Chiara, G (2002) 'Nucleus Accumbens Shell and Core Dopamine: Differential Role in Behavior and Addiction' **137**(1–2) *Behavioural Brain Research* 75–114

Di Chiara, G and A Imperato (1986) 'Preferential Stimulation of Dopamine Release in the Nucleus Accumbens by Opiates, Alcohol, and Barbiturates: Studies with Transcerebral Dialysis in Freely Moving Rats' **473** *Annals of the New York Academy of Sciences* 367–81

Di Chiara, G and A Imperato (1988) 'Drugs Abused by Humans Preferentially Increase Synaptic Dopamine Concentrations in the Mesolimbic System of Freely Moving Rats' **85**(14) *Proceedings of the National Academy of Sciences of the United States of America* 5274–8

Di Chiara, G and R A North (1992) 'Neurobiology of Opiate Abuse' **13**(5) *Trends in Pharmacological Sciences* 185–93

Dickinson, A (1980) *Contemporary Animal Learning Theory* (Cambridge: Cambridge University Press)

Drevets, W C, C Gautier, J C Price, D J Kupfer, P E Kinahan, A A Grace, J L Price and C A Mathis (2001) 'Amphetamine-Induced Dopamine Release in Human Ventral Striatum Correlates with Euphoria' **49**(2) *Biological Psychiatry* 81–96

Ersche, K D, P S Jones, G B Williams, A J Turton, T W Robbins and E T Bullmore (2012 forthcoming) 'Abnormal Brain Structure Implicated in Stimulant Drug Addiction' *Science*

Ersche, K D, A J Turton, S Pradhan, E T Bullmore and T W Robbins (2010) 'Drug Addiction Endophenotypes: Impulsive Versus Sensation-Seeking Personality Traits' **68** *Biological Psychiatry* 770–3

Everitt, B J, D Belin, D Economidou, Y Pelloux, J W Dalley and T W Robbins (2008) 'Neural Mechanisms Underlying the Vulnerability to Develop Compulsive Drug-Seeking Habits and Addiction' **363** *Philosophical Transactions of the Royal Society B-Biological Sciences* 3125–35

Everitt, B J, J A Parkinson, M C Olmstead, M E R C Arroyo, P A T R Robledo and T W Robbins (1999) 'Associative Processes in Addiction and Reward The Role of Amygdala-Ventral Striatal Subsystems' **877**(1) *Annals of the New York Academy of Sciences* 412–38

Everitt, B J and Robbins, T W (2005) 'Neural Systems of Reinforcement for Drug Addiction: From Actions to Habits to Compulsion' **8**(11) *Nature Neuroscience* 1481–9

Floresco, S B, A R West, B Ash, H Moore and A A Grace (2003) 'Afferent Modulation of Dopamine Neuron Firing Differentially Regulates Tonic and Phasic Dopamine Transmission' **6**(9) *Nature Neuroscience* 968–73

Fraser, H F, G D Van Horn, W R Martin, A B Wolbach and H Isabell (1961) 'Methods for Evaluating Addiction Liability. (a) "Attitude" of Opiate Addicts Toward Opiate-Like Drugs. (B) a Short-Term "Direct" Addiction Test' **133** *Journal of Pharmacology and Experimental Therapeutics* 371–87

Gardner, E L and S R Vorel (1998) 'Cannabinoid Transmission and Reward-Related Events' **5**(6) *Neurobiology of Disease* 502–33

Goldstein, R Z and N D Volkow (2002) 'Drug Addiction and its Underlying Neurobiological Basis: Neuroimaging Evidence for the Involvement of the Frontal Cortex' **159**(10) *American Journal of Psychiatry* 1642–52

Gottesman, I I and T D Gould (2003) 'The Endophenotype Concept in Psychiatry: Etymology and Strategic Intentions' **160**(4) *American Journal of Psychiatry* 636–45

Grant, S, E D London, D B Newlin, V L Villemagne, X Liu, C Contoreggi, R L Phillips, A S Kimes and A Margolin (1996) 'Activation of Memory Circuits During Cue-Elicited Cocaine Craving' **93**(21) *Proceedings of the National Academy of Sciences of the United States of America* 12040–5

Hernandez, L and B G Hoebel (1988) 'Food Reward and Cocaine Increase Extracellular Dopamine in the Nucleus Accumbens as Measured by Microdialysis' **42**(18) *Life Sciences* 1705–12

Hyman, S E and R C Malenka (2001) 'Addiction and the Brain: the Neurobiology of Compulsion and its Persistence' **2**(10) *Nature Reviews Neuroscience* 695–703

Ikemoto, S and J Panksepp (1999) 'The Role of Nucleus Accumbens Dopamine in Motivated Behavior: A Unifying Interpretation with Special Reference to Reward-Seeking' **31**(1) *Brain Research Reviews* 6–41

Jellinek, E M (1960) *The Disease Concept of Alcoholism* (New Haven: Hillhouse Press)

Jentsch, J D and J R Taylor (1999) 'Impulsivity Resulting from Frontostriatal Dysfunction in Drug Abuse: Implications for the Control of Behavior by Reward-Related Stimuli' **146**(4) *Psychopharmacology* 373–90

Kalivas, P W (2002) 'Neurocircuitry of Addiction' in K Davis et al. (eds), *Neuropsychopharmacology: The 5th Generation of Progress* (Philadelphia: Lippincott Williams & Wilkins)

Kelley, A E, V P Bakshi, S N Haber, T L Steininger, M J Will and M Zhang (2002) 'Opioid Modulation of Taste Hedonics Within the Ventral Striatum' **76**(3) *Physiology and Behavior* 365–77

Koob, G F and M LeMoal (1997) **278** 'Drug Abuse: Hedonic Homeostatic Dysregulation' *Science* 52–8

Kornetsky, C (1985) 'Brain Stimulation Reward: a Model for the Neuronal Bases for Drug-Induced Euphoria' in R M Brown, D P Friedman and Y Nimit (eds), *Neuroscience Methods in Drug Research* (Rockville, Maryland: NIDA Research Monograph)

Kreek, M J and G B Koob (1998) 'Drug Dependence: Stress and Dysregulation of Brain Reward Pathways' **51**(2) *Drug and Alcohol Dependence* 23–47

Leshner, A I (1997) 'Addiction is a Brain Disease, and it Matters' **278** *Science* 45–7

Letchworth, S R, M A Nader, H R Smith, D P Friedman and L J Porrino (2001) 'Progression of Changes in Dopamine Transporter Binding Site Density as a Result of Cocaine Self-Administration in Rhesus Monkeys' **21**(8) *Journal of Neuroscience* 2799–807

Matthews, S C, A N Simmons, S D Lane and M P Paulus (2004) 'Selective Activation of the Nucleus Accumbens During Risk-Taking Decision Making' **15**(13) *Neuroreport* 2123–7

McClure, S M, M K York and P R Montague (2004) 'The Neural Substrates of Reward Processing in Humans: The Modern Role of fMRI' **10**(3) *The Neuroscientist* 260–8

Mereu, G and G L Gessa (1985) 'Low-Doses of Ethanol Inhibit the Firing of Neurons in the Substantia-Nigra, Pars Reticulata – a Gabaergic Effect' **360**(1) *Brain Research* 325–30

Merikangas, K R, M Stolar, D E Stevens, J Goulet, M A Preisig, B Fenton, H P Zhang, S S O'Malley and B J Rounsaville (1998) 'Familial Transmission of Substance Use Disorders' **55**(11) *Archives of General Psychiatry* 973–9

Nelson, A and S Killcross (2006) 'Amphetamine Exposure Enhances Habit Formation' **26**(14) *Journal of Neuroscience* 3805–12

O'Doherty, J P (2004) 'Reward Representations and Reward-Related Learning in the Human Brain: Insights from Neuroimaging' **14**(6) *Current Opinion in Neurobiology* 769–76

Olds, J and P Milner (1954) 'Positive Reinforcement Produced by Electrical Stimulation of Septal Area and Other Regions of Rat Brain' **47** *Journal of Comparative and Physiological Psychology* 419–27

Olds, M E and J L Fobes (1981) 'The Central Basis of Motivation: Intracranial Self-Stimulation Studies' **32**(1) *Annual Review of Psychology* 523–74

Packard, M G and B J Knowlton (2002) 'Learning and Memory Functions of the Basal Ganglia' **25**(1) *Annual Review of Neuroscience* 563–593

Pratt, W E and S J Y Mizumori (1998) 'Characteristics of Basolateral Amygdala Neuronal Firing on a Spatial Memory Task Involving Differential Reward' **112**(3) *Behavioral Neuroscience* 554–70

Redgrave, P, T J Prescott and K Gurney (1999) 'Is the Short-Latency Dopamine Response Too Short to Signal Reward Error?' **22**(4) *Trends in Neurosciences* 146–51

Rice, M E and S J Cragg (2004) 'Nicotine Amplifies Reward-Related Dopamine Signals in Striatum' **7**(6) *Nature Neuroscience* 583–4

Robbins, T W and B J Everitt (1996) 'Neurobehavioural Mechanisms of Reward and Motivation' **6**(2) *Current Opinion in Neurobiology* 228–36

Robbins, T W and B J Everitt (1999) 'Interaction of the Dopaminergic System with Mechanisms of Associative Learning and Cognition: Implications for Drug Abuse' **10**(3) *Psychological Science* 199–202

Robinson, T E and K C Berridge (1993), 'The Neural Basis of Drug Craving – An Incentive-Sensitization Theory of Addiction' **18**(3) *Brain Research Reviews* 247–91

Robinson, T E and K C Berridge (2001) 'Incentive-Sensitization and Addiction' **96**(1) *Addiction* 103–14

Rolls, E T, Z J Sienkiewicz and S Yaxley (1989) 'Hunger Modulates the Responses to Gustatory Stimuli of Single Neurons in the Caudolateral Orbitofrontal Cortex of the Macaque Monkey' **1**(1) *European Journal of Neuroscience* 53–60

Royal College of Psychiatrists and Royal College of Physicians (2000) *Drugs: Dilemmas and Choices* (London: Gaskell Press)

Royal College of Psychiatrists, (2001) *Mental Illness: Stigmatisation and Discrimination Within the Medical Profession* (Glasgow: Bell & Bain Ltd)

Salamone, J D and M Correa (2002) 'Motivational Views of Reinforcement: Implications for Understanding the Behavioral Functions of Nucleus Accumbens Dopamine' **137**(1), *Behavioural Brain Research* 3–25

Salamone, J D, M Correa, S Mingote and S M Weber (2003) 'Nucleus Accumbens Dopamine and the Regulation of Effort in Food-Seeking Behavior: Implications for Studies of Natural Motivation, Psychiatry, and Drug Abuse' **305**(1) *Journal of Pharmacology and Experimental Therapeutics* 1–8

Schultz, W (1998) 'Predictive Reward Signal of Dopamine Neurons' **80**(1) *Journal of Neurophysiology* 1–27

Schultz, W (2000) 'Multiple Reward Signals in the Brain' **1**(3) *Nature Reviews Neuroscience* 199–207

Schultz, W, P Dayan and P R Montague (1997) 'A Neural Substrate of Prediction and Reward' **275** *Science* 1593–9

Schultz, W and A Dickinson (2000) 'Neuronal Coding of Prediction Errors' **23** *Annual Review of Neuroscience* 473–500

Schultz, W (2004) 'Neural Coding of Basic Reward Terms of Animal Learning Theory, Game Theory, Microeconomics and Behavioural Ecology' **14**(2) *Current Opinion in Neurobiology* 139–47

Schultz, W, L Tremblay and J R Hollerman (2003) 'Changes in Behavior-Related Neuronal Activity in the Striatum During Learning' **26**(6) *Trends in Neurosciences* 321–8

Seiden, L S, K E Sabol and G A Ricaurte (1993) 'Amphetamine: Effects on Catecholamine Systems and Behavior' **33**(1) *Annual Review of Pharmacology and Toxicology* 639–76

Stolerman, I (1992) 'Drugs of Abuse – Behavioral Principles, Methods and Terms' **13**(5) *Trends in Pharmacological Sciences* 170–6

Thorpe, S J, E T Rolls and S Maddison (1983) 'The Orbitofrontal Cortex – Neuronal-Activity in the Behaving Monkey' **49**(1) *Experimental Brain Research* 93–115

Tremblay, L and W Schultz (1999) 'Relative Reward Preference in Primate Orbitofrontal Cortex' **398** *Nature* 704–8

United Nations Office on Drugs and Crime (2000) *Demand Reduction – A Glossary of Terms* (New York: United Nations Publication)

Van Ree, J M, M A Gerrits and L J Vanderschuren (1999) 'Opioids, Reward and Addiction: An Encounter of Biology, Psychology, and Medicine' **51**(2) *Pharmacological Reviews* 341–96

Verdejo-Garcia, A, A J Lawrence and L Clark (2008) 'Impulsivity as a Vulnerability Marker for Substance-Use Disorders: Review of Findings from High-Risk Research, Problem Gamblers and Genetic Association Studies' **32**(4) *Neuroscience and Biobehavioral Reviews* 777–810

Volkow, N D and J S Fowler (2000) 'Addiction, A Disease of Compulsion and Drive: Involvement of the Orbitofrontal Cortex' **10**(3) *Cerebral Cortex* 318–25

Volkow, N D, G J Wang, J S Fowler, J Logan, S J Gatley, A Gifford, R Hitzemann, Y S Ding and N Pappas (1999a) 'Prediction of Reinforcing Responses to Psychostimulants in Humans by Brain Dopamine D-2 Receptor Levels' **156**(9) *American Journal of Psychiatry* 1440–3

Volkow, N D, G J Wang, J S Fowler, J Logan, S J Gatley, C Wong, R Hitzemann and N R Pappas (1999b), 'Reinforcing Effects of Psychostimulants in Humans Are Associated with Increases in Brain Dopamine and Occupancy of D-2 Receptors' **291**(1) *Journal of Pharmacology and Experimental Therapeutics* 409–15

Wagner, F A and J C Anthony (2002) 'From First Drug Use to Drug Dependence: Developmental Periods of Risk for Dependence Upon Marijuana, Cocaine, and Alcohol' **26**(4) *Neuropsychopharmacology* 479–88

Watanabe, M (1996) 'Reward Expectancy in Primate Prefrontal Neurons' **382** *Nature* 629–32

White, F J (2002) 'A Behavioral/Systems Approach to the Neuroscience of Drug Addiction' **22**(9) *Journal of Neuroscience* 3303–5

WHO (1992) *The ICD-10 Classification of Mental And Behavioural Disorders: Clinical Descriptions and Diagnostic Guidelines* (Geneva: World Health Organization)

WHO (1994) *Lexicon of Alcohol and Drug Terms* (Geneva: World Health Organization)

Wise, R A (1998) 'Drug-Activation of Brain Reward Pathways' **51**(1) *Drug and Alcohol Dependence* 13–22

Wise, R A and M A Bozarth (1984) 'Brain Reward Circuitry – 4 Circuit Elements Wired in Apparent Series' **12**(2) *Brain Research Bulletin* 203–8

Wise, R A, J Spindler, H de Wit and G J Gerber (1978) 'Neuroleptic-Induced "Anhedonia" in Rats: Pimozide Blocks Reward Quality of Food' **201** *Science* 262–4

Wise, R A (1980) 'The Dopamine Synapse and the Notion of "Pleasure Centers" in the Brain' **3** *Trends in Neurosciences* 91–5

12
Praxis, Interaction and the Loss of Self-Control

Darin Weinberg[1]

Introduction

Our remit in this section of the book is to speak to the relevance of self to our understanding of intoxication and intoxicant use. In her chapter, Cathy Shrank looks at the images and explanations of the loss of self-possession pertaining to intoxicants in sixteenth- and seventeenth-century medical, poetic and political texts. Ciaran Regan, in his chapter, tells of the neurological plasticity of the human brain, our neurological distinctiveness as individuals and the relation of these phenomena to intoxication. For my part, I want to focus on the self as social agent or as active participant in social interaction and how addictions to intoxicants emerge in the course of social interaction as surrogates for that self. My argument is that by so doing, we may begin to address an element of addiction that, while central to the meaning of this concept, has proven equally elusive to both the biomedical and the social sciences of addiction. That is, the identification of instances in which people are empirically observed not only to have engaged in socially disapproved or even dangerous drug use but to have actually succumbed to addiction, or to have lost control of their drug use. Because it is in and through social interaction with one another, rather than esoteric analyses of our minds or bodies, that evidence of addiction is normally gathered, a systematic understanding of what counts as interactional evidence of addiction should be a particularly important scientific priority.

In the first section of the paper I demonstrate that both the ascendant medical and social scientific accounts of addiction curiously leave aside the question of self-control in favour of alternative framings of addiction and addictive behaviour. In the second section I explore the possibility of a sociology of the loss of self-control. Drawing upon ethnographic data collected in

---

1 Some passages in this chapter have been variously adapted from Weinberg, 1997a; 1997b; 2002; 2005.

three treatment programmes, I examine the empirical grounds upon which members of these programmes in practice based their findings that either they or their peers had lost control of their drug use. I then consider how to best explain these indigenous findings sociologically.

Biomedical theories of addiction and their limitations

For most of the twentieth century, mainstream scientific research on addiction was agreed on the importance of distinguishing between hard drugs (defined by the fact that they produce physiological withdrawal symptoms) and soft drugs (defined by the fact that they do not do so). In addition to their capacity to produce physiological withdrawal symptoms, continued usage of hard drugs was also observed to produce a physiological tolerance such that users required ever-increasing quantities to produce the same effect. Along with their capacity to produce intensely rewarding psychological effects, the combination of physiological withdrawal symptoms and tolerance to hard drugs were said to foster development of powerful visceral compulsions that often destructively eclipse people's regard for other aspects of their lives. Hence, it was that these three effects, the development of physiological withdrawal symptoms, tolerance and continued persistence in use despite harmful effects became the hallmark of genuine addictions as opposed to the mere bad habits that one might acquire with respect to soft drugs.

But the era has now passed when people could speak confidently of a distinction between drugs that produce genuine, or *physical*, addictions and drugs that produce only a more nebulous *psychological* addiction. The single most important catalyst to this era's passing was the advent of crack. Crack cocaine is widely recognized as extremely addictive by clinical professionals and non-professionals alike but, oddly enough, it produces no gross physiological withdrawal symptoms (Gawin, 1991). By 'gross physiological withdrawal symptoms' I mean symptoms like vomiting, cramping, delirium tremens, runny nose, itchy eyes and so on which implicate specific physiological effects of withdrawal (this is in contrast to more psychological effects like anxiety or stress headaches which are less clearly linked to specific physiological effects of withdrawal). The same can also be said of nicotine, and all of the so-called behavioural addictions like sex, gambling, eating etc. Furthermore, reliance on the distinction between physical and psychological addiction always suffered another serious analytic problem: relapse. Many consider relapse, or the resumption of a dis-preferred pattern of behaviour despite one's desire not to, as the defining mark of addiction. Theories that trade on the distinction between genuine physical addiction and a much less severe psychological addiction cannot remain consistent in their explanations of relapse. Insofar as relapse occurs after withdrawal symptoms have cleared and have ceased to exert an influence on behaviour, our explanations of relapse must inevitably turn to prospective causal variables above and beyond physiological withdrawal and physiological tolerance.

So exactly how do current biomedical theories account for relapse? They do so neurologically (cf. Koob et al., 1989; Koob, 2006). According to neurologists working in this area, prolonged drug use may induce a compensatory neurological adaptation which, in effect, amounts to the production of not only a physiological tolerance but also an anatomical tolerance to the drug in the nervous systems of heavy drug users. While the development of this type of tolerance may or may not induce gross physiological withdrawal symptoms upon removal of the drug, it does produce what neurologists call anhedonia, or a marked decrease in the capacity of one so afflicted to experience pleasure after drug use has been discontinued. During this period former substance users remain in a comparatively depressed state and thus significantly more vulnerable than they might otherwise be to stimuli that cue them to consider the analgesic effects of drug use.

This approach is instructive in a number of important ways. First and foremost, it has important practical payoffs in that it informs our efforts to generate pharmacological therapeutic interventions. Drugs like Naloxone have proven to be life-saving for people in acute stages of opiate overdose and others like Methadone and various anti-depressant medications have improved the quality of life for former heavy drug users who might otherwise have remained without help.

However, this said, the neurological model does suffer from significant theoretical limitations. Most fundamentally, insofar as they seek to predicate their theories of compulsive drug use on the presumption that the ingestion of certain chemicals *invariably* produces pleasurable experiences (cf. Gardner, 1992), neurologists systematically neglect how cultural learning and social context shape whether and how drug use becomes pleasurable or compelling for people. If our effort is to understand patterns of drug use in people, then blindness to the socially contingent meanings and practical relevances that drug use has for users is a rather serious theoretical handicap. More specifically, if our effort is to understand how people might lose self-control over their drug use, understanding the meaning and practical relevance of drug use and drug-induced experiences is absolutely indispensable.

Let me make the case for this position in a bit more detail. Most neurological research on addiction assumes the existence of a mechanism or mechanisms common to all human nervous systems that causally link the physical events caused by drug ingestion in the brain, on the one hand, and the drug-seeking activities of particular users on the other. This assumption jibes rather poorly with the manifest empirical fact that not all people enjoy drug-induced experiences.[2] It also jibes rather poorly with the fact that particular people may enjoy these experiences under some circumstances and wholly detest them under other circumstances (an example I often give to students is to contrast the experience of being drunk at a party to the experience of being drunk in a final exam). These facts cast considerable doubt on the prospects of ever fully reducing subjective and particular experiences of pleasure, pleasure seeking, pain, or pain avoidance to the generic functions or dysfunctions of generic neurological structures.

Above and beyond the challenges of providing for the social contextual variability of drug effects neurologically (challenges that the work of people like Ciaran Regan is beginning to successfully overcome), it must also be noted that current neurological theories of addiction speak only to the hypothesis that heavy drug use increases the propensity of drug users to pursue further drug use. For those of us interested in addiction per se, it is important to note that this hypothesis remains silent as to the nature of self-control and the capacities of certain drugs or activities to threaten our self-control. If, then, we wish to conduct research into the nature of addiction as such, we cannot rest content with theories that speak only to increases or decreases in our desire for various things or activities. If the loss of self-control is the defining criterion of addiction, as most leaders in the field now readily acknowledge (cf. O'Brien et al., 2006; West, 2006), then it is absolutely indispensable for addiction research to include clear concepts of what the self actually is such that we find it capable of moving into and out of control of human actions in the first place. It is only then that we will learn how things like addictions might come to attenuate the causal relationship between selves and their actions. To date, neurological theories have remained conspicuously silent on the nature of the self, self-control, or the manner in which drugs might undermine them.

Sociological theories of addiction and their limitations

In contrast to neurological research on addiction, sociological research has exhibited a sustained concern with social meaning, the social contextual

---

2 The Harvard philosopher Richard Moran (2002) writes incisively on this matter: 'It is sometimes said that certain drugs "produce" pleasure, but this is true only in the same sense that either string quartets or ripe cheeses "produce" pleasure. In both cases we can provide the cause without producing the effect, because the person exposed to either the drug or the music doesn't like it, doesn't see what there is to enjoy in it. What was the very form of hazy, druggy pleasure for someone else is for this person merely some unpleasant dizziness and disorientation. Even here, when we speak of drugs "doing" this or that, finding pleasure in the experience is a matter of being inclined to take pleasure in what is given. And the fact that such "know-how" may simply come naturally or spontaneously to the person does not make his engagement any the less active, any more than it does for ordinary physical skills or habits of inference.'

variability of drug effects and the relationship between addiction and the self (cf. Lindesmith, 1938; Becker, 1953; 1967; Denzin, 1993). However, it conspicuously fails to speak to two essential questions that arise from listening to addicts describe their problems and from observing them in the conduct of their lives. First, it does not explain how we are to understand addicts' reports that, under certain circumstances, they feel they are truly *overwhelmed*, rather than just *rationally persuaded*, by their desire to use drugs. And, second, it does not account for the repeated *cycle* of abstinence and relapse. We should expect to see all addicts who experience serious and recurrent drug-related problems 'mature out' (Winick, 1962), but unfortunately we don't. What is it about some people's drug involvements that compel continuance even after repeated association of the behaviour with negative experiences and despite their stated desires to abstain?

Marsh Ray (1961) is the sociologist who most explicitly addressed the cycle of abstinence and relapse, and his is probably also the most widely cited theoretical statement of how relapse can be understood from a sociological vantage point. According to Ray's theory, the cycle of abstinence and relapse should be understood as a process during which the former user consciously oscillates between a commitment to his using and non-using self-concepts. Ray concludes his classic essay,

> socially disjunctive experiences bring about a questioning of the value of an abstainer identity and promote reflections in which addict and non-addict identities are compared. The abstainer's realignment of his values with those of the world of addiction results in the redefinition of self as an addict and has as a consequence the actions necessary to relapse. (Ray, 1961, p. 140)

This theory suggests relapse is a process necessarily involving conscious deliberation and comparisons between one's using and non-using identities. As one can see, Ray's is an extremely cognitivist and, indeed, rationalist, construal of the relapse process. The relapser is an individual who rationally evaluates the pros and cons of being an addict versus being an abstainer before deciding to relapse. But does this sound like addiction? If Ray is correct, what sense is there in thinking that addicts require any kind of therapeutic assistance whatsoever? The difficulty is that Ray, like most social scientists, fails to entertain as even the most remote possibility the prospect that human behaviour might not always issue directly from the conscious reflections and deliberate assertions of the self. The recurrent reports made by addicts themselves of feeling overwhelmed, and indeed afflicted, by their addictions are categorically dismissed in favour of an axiomatic theoretical commitment to conceptualizing all human action as the product of a fully conscious cost–benefit analysis wherein the self remains, by definition, unassailably secure as the inevitable and irreplaceable origin of everything people do.

So whereas biomedical theorists lack any concept of self or self-control that might facilitate their explanation of how heavy drug use might attenuate our self-control, extant sociological self-centric theorizing requires that we axiomatically dismiss any possibility of a loss of self-control altogether. If addiction is to be taken seriously as a genuine cause of human suffering and as a problem deserving of therapeutic assistance rather than societal indifference or merely coercive social control, we need a theoretical approach that is supple enough to provide for the manifest variety of ways in which drug use fosters further drug use, the variety of ways in which patterns of drug use cause users to suffer, and, most importantly, that can somehow provide for the causes of that suffering without automatically reducing them to either the neurologists' universal structures and functions/dysfunctions of the human nervous system nor to the sociologists' invariant construal of all human behaviour as inevitably self-governed.

Toward a sociology of the loss of self-control

Quite unlike the depictions of addicted behaviour we find in received sociological accounts, the people I studied did not uniformly depict relapse as a self-governed act but often characterized it as a deeply troubling and mysterious loss of self-control. This can be seen, for example, in the following field-note excerpt from my research with homeless people presumed to suffer from addictions:

> I've promised myself I wouldn't use a thousand times and really meant it. And then I use. I mean it's like there are two sides of me. The rational reasonable person who knows he's gonna die if he keeps on living the way he is and the insane one who just doesn't care. My reasonable side of me can be as sure as it wants to be but when those drugs appear in front of me the insane one takes over and all those reasons I had not to use are just gone. They just disappear. And I use. It's like my mind just goes dead and my addiction takes over. I hate myself right afterwards and I'm completely confused by the fact that I just used. I didn't want to but I did. It's all well and good to say you need to make a commitment but for some of us that's not enough. We need something more than that and it doesn't help for people to be all smug about how we need to make a commitment and it's all that simple.

Well-known writers on addiction like Stanton Peele (1989) and John Davies (1992) have suggested that such accounts are in no way valid descriptions of the reality of addiction but merely socially functional for those who provide and/or believe them. Cultures like our own furnish people with the narrative of addiction which they embrace and apply strategically to fulfil their own self-interests. I dispute neither the claim that these accounts are socially functional nor that they reflect conceptual commitments prevalent in the cultures to which putative addicts belong. What I do dispute is the claim that either of these facts necessarily forecloses on an account being also descriptively valid (Haraway, 1991). Moreover, the radical reduction of such accounts to mere tokens of a priori conceptual commitments and/or the instrumental strategies of those who provide them systematically fails to account for either the phenomenology of addiction as a source of suffering or for the ways in which addictions become empirically observable as consequential causal agents over the course of ongoing social interaction. In what follows I propose one way of overcoming both of these rather serious failings.

Distinguishing selves and addictions in therapeutic practice

In the treatment programmes within which I have conducted ethnographic research, people distinguished human agency, or self-governed action, from the nonhuman agency of people's addictions primarily on the basis of three discretionary considerations: 1. provisional assessments of the distinctive character of people's addictions (or in the terms of the local vernacular, their particular 'patterns'); 2. provisional assessments of people's particular practical circumstances; and 3. provisional assessments of who particular programme participants were as individuals (Weinberg, 2005). Space constraints preclude a thorough discussion of these elements of recovery work but a few examples should suffice to make my case.

Because they believed one of the distinctive characteristics of addiction to be denial, programme members expected one another to exhibit openness to the opinions of other programme members regarding their problems and not display too much commitment to their own sense of their relative vulnerability to relapse. In the following data excerpt, Sean (all programme participants' names are pseudonyms) interprets Tony's failure to acknowledge that addiction is a 'sneaky disease' as a failure to display competent human agency within the practical context of their recovery programme, and, hence, as evidence that Tony was presently under the influence of his addiction. This determination appears to reflect both Sean's understanding of addiction as a particular type of mental affliction and the manner in which Tony should have been undertaking to recover from it. Tony had been opining that he was no longer vulnerable to craving because he was taking a new medication. Sean replied:

> '...be careful, 'cause this disease we got is sneaky. And you know
> a lot of the times when you're the most confident that you got

it licked, that's when it jumps on you 'cause you start subjectin' yourself to risks you don't need...'

Tony said 'Oh man, that's bullshit. I mean I know what you're sayin' and I've heard it before but I don't agree with that shit. Nobody can tell me what I feel...'

After Tony got up Sean looked over to me, shook his head and said 'That boy's in trouble. Did you see how defensive he got when I just said be careful? I mean that is classic, *classic*, addict behavior. If I had to isolate one symptom that was classic addicted thinking, *that'd* be it.'

In stark contrast to the received sociological wisdom, Sean's estimation of the boundaries of Tony's human agency in this episode was not predicated upon a simple one-to-one correspondence between Tony's personal conduct, on the one hand, and his self-government on the other. Rather, it was predicated upon his expectations regarding the distinctive manner in which Tony's putative addiction would, if it did, exercise its nonhuman agency in and through Tony's personal conduct. Sean exhibits his expectation that there were in fact at least *two* potential causal agents that might become manifest in Tony's conduct: 1. Tony's own human agency as a self-governing actor; and 2. the nonhuman agency of Tony's addiction, which might very well overpower Tony's human agency – hence the remark that Tony was 'in trouble'. In the same sense that Sean was interacting with Tony as a fellow human agent in this exchange, he was also interacting with Tony's addiction as a nonhuman agent. Indeed, in noting to me the trouble he felt Tony was in, Sean was responding to the causal influence he seemed to see Tony's addiction exercising in that very encounter ('If I had to isolate one symptom that was classic addicted thinking, that'd be it.'). The social interactions that took place in my research settings suggest the wisdom of regarding human and nonhuman agencies as equally capable of driving personal experience and conduct, rather than viewing one as necessarily epiphenomenal of the other (Weinberg, 1997b; 2005).

In the above data excerpt we see how basic expectations regarding the nature of addiction could colour people's interpretations of one another's behaviour. However, these expectations were not the only sources of such interpretations. Instead, they competed for attention with provisional assessments of people's practical circumstances in governing whether people's actions were seen to exhibit their addictions or sound personal judgments. In the following instance, for example, a client had dropped out of the programme and was accumulating considerable debts using crack cocaine. She was contacted by a counsellor but resisted this counsellor's efforts to place her into an inpatient recovery setting. In the absence of mitigating factors, counsellors usually regarded such resistance to treatment as evidence of the fierce hold individuals' addictions had over them. However, in this case there were mitigating circumstances and, despite the intensity of this client's relapse and continuing drug use, her resistance was treated as evidence of competent human agency rather than addiction,

> She's resisting it because she doesn't want to lose her apartment. You know she moved into that apartment next to her parents' place, and it's kind of a good situation for her. If she goes into inpatient treatment she's afraid she'll lose her place. I can understand how she feels. She's in a tough situation.

In addition to provisional assessments of the nature of one another's addictions and personal circumstances, distinctions between human agency and the nonhuman agency of addiction were also based on programme members' provisional assessments of one another's unique personal characteristics as individuals. Programme members drew upon their knowledge of the details of one another's unique biographical histories to inform assessments of whether, and specifically how, the causal effects of their addictions were or were not evident in their behaviour. In the following data excerpt taken from a group therapy session, Sherry's recent 'willfulness' is read as evidence of her addiction reasserting itself. Paula, a counsellor, had mentioned her surprise when she saw Sherry's name on a list of people recently written up for poor behaviour. Paula said:

> 'Let's start with you Sherry. I was surprised to see your name on this list. What's up?' Sherry said, 'I'm surprised too, I don't know.' Sherry mentioned what she thought she had been written up for – things like not going to meetings and refusing to get to her kitchen assignment on time. Paula said, 'Sounds like a lot of 'em you got behind that willful behavior of yours...'
>
> Sherry nodded, smiled, and said, 'Yep, it does look like that. I think it is my being willful.'
>
> Paula said, 'When you start having good ideas, when you start thinking that you know better than everybody else what's good for you, that's a good time to start getting suspicious and to check yourself. When you start saying "I don't think I need to go to group." or "I don't think I need to get up and do my chore." that's the kind of thing that's gonna get you kicked out of here and you'll be right back out there where you were. *That's your disease talkin' and tryin' to get you to relapse*. It's real important that when you start getting those willful feelings that you find somebody to talk to and check yourself.'
>
> Sherry nodded sheepishly in agreement.

It was only thanks to Sherry's otherwise encouraging performance of late, coupled with a known history of putatively drug-related obstinance, that it became reasonable to attribute her recent and 'willful' misbehaviour to her addiction's nonhuman agency rather than her own human agency. If we view diagnosis as a strictly technical rational enterprise (see Kirk and Kutchins, 1992, pp. 220–3), then clinical judgments like this may be considered aberrations – at best, mistakes, and at worst, deeply disturbing instances of personal oppression carried out under the auspices of clinical medicine (cf. Szasz, 1961). However, if we view such diagnoses as grounded in the moral order of community living, then things cease to appear quite so grave. Seen in this light, Sherry's 'willfulness' resisted being construed as an exhibit of her own human agency because it was inconsistent with the human agent Paula perceived Sherry to have become ('I was surprised to see your name on this list.'). Given its inconsistency with Paula's current impressions of Sherry, Sherry's 'willfulness' became eminently available for reading as an effect of her 'disease' that was 'tryin'' to get [her] to relapse'. While by strictly technical rational lights, 'willfulness' may seem a very odd category of behaviour indeed to attribute to nonhuman causes, the practical circumstances in which Paula and Sherry found themselves allowed for this attribution without a hitch. Most fundamentally, these circumstances involved the sustenance of moral community between them.

In opposition to the dogmatic libertarian commitments of authors like Thomas Szasz, I want to suggest that interventions like that taken by Paula with Sherry above can indeed be understood as empowering rather than repressive. They can be understood as empowering to the extent that we take seriously, as did Paula and Sherry, the notion that particular people actually can periodically lose control of their behaviour, that they actually can be overwhelmed by the nefarious influence of intra-personal nonhuman agents in the form of addictions. By these lights, quelling addictions per se is not an act of repression. It is an act of freeing people from the havoc wreaked upon them by an unwelcome affliction. Of course, different commentators, including putative addicts themselves, may very well debate the characteristics of their addictions and the relative influence that these nonhuman agents have over their personal conduct in any given instance. In fact, such debates formed the bulk of what passed for clinical work in my research settings. But the fact that the characteristics and relative influence of people's addictions on their activities are intrinsically contestable hardly disqualifies them from being taken seriously as nonhuman agents. Indeed, it might be argued that it is precisely in this resistance to unequivocal description and human control that the nonhuman agency of addictions is most robustly in evidence.

Conclusion

In contrast to received sociological accounts, the moral economy of therapeutic practice in the treatment programmes in which I conducted ethnographic fieldwork did more than simply inform how programme participants produced, sustained and amended their linguistic descriptions and/
or cognitive beliefs about the respective addictions from which they were
presumed to suffer. It actually gave empirical form to these addictions as
causally influential things-in-the-world. Addictions were observed to exercise causal influences over people's perceptions and behaviours and, in
so doing, altered not only people's descriptions and beliefs but also the
course of specific interactions and the contours of therapeutic community life itself. Rather than merely observing or describing their addictions,
programme members undertook strident campaigns to subdue the actions
they attributed to them (see also Mol and Law, 2004). This work, in effect,
animated their addictions as nonhuman agents, and engaged programme
participants in interactional struggles with these disorders as collectively
confirmed realities. Hence, the work of recovery amounted to a good
deal more than a process of ideological or cultural conversion. Instead, it
consisted in collective struggles to overcome particular troubles conceived
and, indeed, empirically observed as the effects of addictions as materially
embodied causal agents.

Equally, though, in contrast to biomedical accounts, the nonhuman agents
with which residents struggled were constituted *only* in and through the
moral economy of programme practice. Not only did people's addictions
often take forms bearing no evident relationship to formally codified psychiatric nosologies (e.g. wilfulness), but assessments of both their presence and
absence in people's behaviour were dictated *only* by the locally meaningful
organization of programme affairs and participants' expectations regarding
themselves and one another as collaborators in those affairs. Thus it should
be resolutely noted that genetic, neurological and other forms of biological
evidence that might be used to great advantage in other settings for the treatment of addiction had absolutely no part in it.

This is by no means to argue that the loss of self-control can be scientifically understood only within the context of social praxis and interaction. It
is, rather more modestly, simply to assert that praxis and interaction constitute a fundamental medium within which the loss of self-control emerges as
an empirically observable event and that this medium is not easily explained
by means of the analytic tools provided by the scientific disciplines of biology or psychology. Insofar as the social sciences do provide a distinctively
effective set of analytic resources for systematically analysing and explaining
this medium, they should hold considerable promise among those of us who

would hope to bring a more robust understanding of the loss of self-control to the scientific study of addiction.

Bibliography

Becker, H S (1953) 'Becoming a Marijuana User' **59** *American Journal of Sociology* 235–42

Becker, H S (1967) 'History, Culture and Subjective Experience: An Explanation of Social Bases of Drug-Induced Experiences' **8** *Journal of Health and Social Behavior* 163–76

Davies, J B (1992) *The Myth of Addiction* (Amsterdam, Netherlands: Harwood)

Denzin, N K (1993) *The Alcoholic Society* (New Brunswick NJ: Transaction)

Gardner, E L (1992) 'Brain Reward Mechanisms' in J Lowinson et al. (eds), *Substance Abuse: A Comprehensive Text* (Baltimore MD: Williams & Wilkins)

Gawin, F (1991) 'Cocaine Addiction: Psychology and Neurology' **251** *Science* 1580–6

Haraway, D J (1991) *Symians, Cyborgs and Women* (New York: Routledge)

Kirk, S A and H Kutchins (1992) *The Selling of DSM* (Hawthorne NY: Aldine de Gruyter)

Koob, G F (2006) 'The Neurobiology of Addiction' **101** *Addiction* 23–30

Koob, G F, L Stinus, M LeMoal and F E Bloom (1989) 'Opponent Process Theory of Motivation: Neurobiological Evidence from Studies of Opiate Dependence' **13** *Neuroscience and Biobehavioral Reviews* 135–40

Lindesmith, A R (1938) 'A Sociological Theory of Drug Addiction' **43**(4) *American Journal of Sociology* 593–609

Mol, A and J Law (2004) 'Embodied Action, Enacted Bodies: The Example of Hypoglycaemia' **10**(2–3) *Body & Society* 43–62

Moran, R (2002) 'Frankfurt on Identification: Ambiguities of Activity in Mental Life' in S Buss and H Overton (eds), *Contours of Agency* (Cambridge MA: MIT Press), pp. 189–217

O'Brien, C P, N Volkow and T K Li (2006) 'What's in a Word?: Addiction versus Dependence in DSM V' **163**(5) *American Journal of Psychiatry* 764–5

Peele, S (1989) *Diseasing of America* (Lexington MA: Lexington Books)

Ray, M (1961) 'The Cycle of Abstinence and Relapse Among Heroin Addicts' **9** *Social Problems* 132–40

Szasz, T (1961) *The Myth of Mental Illness* (New York: Hoeber-Harper)

Weinberg, D (1997a) 'Lindesmith on Addiction: A Critical History of a Classic Theory' **15**(2) *Sociological Theory* 150–61

Weinberg, D (1997b) 'The Social Construction of Non-Human Agency: The Case of Mental Disorder' **44**(2) *Social Problems* 217–34

Weinberg, D (2002) 'On the Embodiment of Addiction' **8**(4) *Body and Society* 1–19

Weinberg, D (2005) *Of Others Inside: Insanity, Addiction and Belonging in America* (Philadelphia PA: Temple University Press)

West, R (2006) *Theory of Addiction* (Oxford: Blackwell)

Winick, C (1962) 'Maturing Out of Narcotic Addiction' **14**(5) *Bulletin on Narcotics* 1–7

Section 5
Law, Morality and Science

13
Addiction and Responsibility

Alan Bogg and Jonathan Herring

Introduction

Early in 2011 there were press reports that a new law in Malawi intended to make farting in public a criminal offence (BBC News, 2011). One reason why such an offence would appear absurd is it would contravene a fundamental principle of criminal law: defendants are not responsible for their involuntary acts. Where the defendant is acting involuntarily the primary purposes of conviction and punishment through the criminal law are not capable of being fulfilled: involuntary acts cannot be deterred; there would be no wrongdoing that requires retribution; the use of a conviction to mark censure would be seriously unjust. But a parallel principle runs through the criminal law: defendants are responsible for their not-involuntary acts. In the absence of an established defence of automatism, which is defined incredibly strictly, defendants are taken to be responsible for their actions. Hence, in nearly all cases addicts are held to be responsible for their addiction and for crimes they commit as a result of addicted intoxication. We do not think of addicts as automatons. On the contrary, addictive behaviour is usually considered to be conscious and goal-directed.

In this chapter we explore the relevance to the criminal law of a defendant's claim to be addicted to a substance which had intoxicated him at the time of the offence. We seek to emphasize the dangers of reductive thinking which can be found in both the legal and medical literature. Hence a sharp line is too often drawn between the voluntary and the involuntary; the responsible and the not responsible. This is found too in the philosophical and medical literature on addiction with the well-known dispute between the medical or moral explanations for addiction. Very often, in reality, these concepts do not admit of bright-line binary distinctions. Instead, they involve sensitive judgments of degree.

We will examine the reasons why the criminal law rarely allows addicted defendants to have any defence based upon their intoxicated state. We seek to go on to justify the law's reluctance to provide such a defence, by relying on the perception of addicts themselves to their situation. Most discussion of legal approaches to addiction has focused on the view of medical experts or academic philosophers. Sometimes well-meaning experts assume that the marginalized groups such as drug addicts constitute communities beyond the reach of the criminal trial's language of responsibility and blame. Such assumptions can be patronizing. The self-understandings of addicts themselves provide, we argue, a useful and profound way of analysing the responsibilities of addiction. We do that through the 12 Step Approach developed by Alcoholics Anonymous (AA), a very widely respected and used programme of recovery from addiction.

Criminal law and addiction

There are two main ways that addiction may be relevant to criminal law. The first is that the defendant may claim that the addiction rendered intoxication involuntary and so the normal rules under which an intoxicated defendant is deemed to be reckless should not apply (see Williams, this volume). Essentially, this permits the defendant to rely upon the absence of *mens rea* (the mental element) for the crime. The second is that the defendant may raise a defence claiming that the addiction or the involuntary intoxication caused by the addiction, was such that she was not responsible for her actions. In legal terms this is likely to involve relying on a defence of automatism (involuntariness), duress or diminished responsibility (a partial defence which is only available to murder). We will be exploring the possibility of these defences shortly, but for now it is sufficient to note that addicts have had little success in the law to date relying on either of these kinds of arguments.

Indeed, the issue of addiction has received little attention in the criminal law. There are plenty of cases where it seems to go unmentioned. A notable example is the leading case of *R v Kennedy* [2007]. Their Lordships were asked to consider an appeal typical of a series of cases which had been troubling the courts. A drug dealer supplied a client with drugs who took them and died. Could the drug dealer be convicted of manslaughter? Their Lordships thought not. They confirmed the general principle that if someone acts in a free, voluntary and informed way they and they alone are responsible for the consequences of their actions. As the victim had freely injected himself, he and not the dealer caused the death. Their Lordships added:

> The criminal law generally assumes the existence of free will. The law recognises certain exceptions, in the case of the young, those who for any reason are not fully responsible for their actions,

and the vulnerable, and it acknowledges situations of duress and necessity, as also of deception and mistake. But, generally speaking, informed adults of sound mind are treated as autonomous beings able to make their own decisions how they will act, and none of the exceptions is relied on as possibly applicable in this case. (para. 14)

What is extraordinary about this case is that it is assumed, without argument, that the victim in this case in taking the drugs was acting in a voluntary way. This reflects the criminal law's position that 'not-involuntary' conduct is invariably equated with responsible conduct.

This lack of attention to addiction is not surprising. A superficial analysis would suggest that an addict seeking to claim that their intoxication is involuntary is going to face an uphill task. Involuntariness is generally only accepted in the law in cases of a complete loss of awareness or control. A partial loss is insufficient (*Attorney-General's Reference (No 2 of 1992)* [1993]). The possibility of duress, which might be raised, is readily dismissed on the grounds that that defence is only available where the threat facing the defendant is not one of death or serious harm. In short, the addict faces the dual difficulty that the impact of their condition is not sufficiently severe to mean they are not responsible for their actions and even if it was they have brought about the condition upon themselves and so should not be entitled to rely on any defence. These difficulties reflect the sharp divide that is drawn between those who are voluntary and those who are not, allowing no room for a defendant who was partially responsible (Horder, 1993). But might such a sharp divide be justified?

John Gardner on excuses

By far the best explanation for why the law is reluctant to allow a claim of involuntariness is found in the writing of John Gardner. In his influential role-based account of excuses, to be excused is to assert responsibility for what was done and, further, to assert that one lived up to the proper normative standards and expectations of the role one inhabits. The sober person of reasonable firmness, who plays a central role in the law on defences, reflects the standards and expectations that arise in virtue of our common humanity. By contrast, allowing a denial of responsibility is to deny self-respect.

It is worth setting out his views at length:

Self-respect is an attitude which everyone ought to have if they deserve it, and which, moreover, everyone ought to deserve. The self-respecting person aspires to live up to the proper standards for success in and fitness for the life she leads, and holds herself out to be judged by those standards. It follows that it is part of the nature of self-respect that a self-respecting person wants to be able to give an intelligible rational account of herself, to be able to show that her actions were the actions of someone who aspired to live up to the proper standards for success in her life and fitness to lead it. She wants it to be the case that her actions were not truly wrongful, or if they were wrongful, that they were at any rate justified, or if they were not justified, that they were at any rate excused. A denial of responsibility rules all of this out, and there is, accordingly, the line of defence which counts as an admission of defeat for any self-respecting person. (Gardner, 2007, p. 133)

Under Gardner's approach, a claim of lack of responsibility is a defeat for a self-respecting person. It follows that not only should the law severely restrict its access, but defendants should be reluctant to seek to rely on it (Macklem and Gardner, 2001).

We are not convinced by Gardner's argument. There is plenty to question about the extent to which a lack of capacity amounts to a lack of respect or a defeat. That shows a rather limited acknowledgment of the richness of humanity that can be found in those who lack mental capacity (Herring, 2009). It also suggests a somewhat inflated vision of our capacities accessible only to those heroic souls who occupy a philosophical Olympus (Herring, 2011). But the point that we wish to question in this chapter is whether a self-respecting person must accept the option of either full capacity or no capacity. Is there not room for a self-respecting person to claim partial capacity?: 'I have *some* responsibility for my actions.'; 'While I could comply with the law it is much harder for me to do so than most people.' Surely, under Gardner's approach a self-respecting person might accept responsibility for their actions, but also seek some acknowledgment that it would have been significantly harder for them to meet the standard expected than other people?

Conceptions of addiction

Turning to the philosophical and psychological literature, we find a fierce debate between those who emphasize a medicalized model of addiction and those who prefer a moral model.

Medicalized model

The medicalized model regards addiction as a disease (Buchman et al., 2010). Substance dependence is listed in the widely respected American Psychiatric Association's *Diagnostic and Statistical Manual of Mental Disorders (DSM-IV-TR)* (2000). Addiction is said to be caused by and lead to long-lasting changes in brain function (Ersche, this volume). Seeing addiction as a disease leads to a number of practical and ethical consequences. In practical terms, drugs are used to combat the addiction (Wood, 2010) and hospitals are regarded as the appropriate place for treatment. In the context of public policy, it leads to calls to regard addiction as a health issue, rather than a criminal justice one (Boseley, 2010). Indeed, to some, part of the appeal of the medicalized model is that it deflects blame from the addicted. Referring to studies suggesting that unconscious brain activity directs behaviour in addicts provides a route to deny moral accountability (Soon et al., 2008; Smith, 2011). However, the medicalized model carries with it dangers. First, it removes not only blame but also responsibility for the person's condition and for combatting it. The power is transferred to the doctors to treat and solve the problem of 'the patient'. Paternalistic responses to the 'patient' then become readily justified. Second, it opens up the danger of a separation between those addicts who have the symptoms which justify classification under the medicalized model, and those who do not and are therefore fully blameworthy.

The moral weakness model

For others, addiction is a moral weakness. Like all mortals the addict faces the temptation to do wrong, but lacks the moral fibre to resist the temptation. The addict therefore deserves no sympathy and certainly no excuse. The best that might be said is that the addict faces a harder job than others facing temptation as the craving may be particularly strong. Satel and Goodwin (1998, p. 21) argue:

> The fact that many, perhaps most, addicts are in control of their actions and appetites for circumscribed periods of time shows that they are not perpetually helpless victims of a chronic disease. They are instigators of their addiction, just as they are agents of their own recovery…or non-recovery. The potential for self-control should allow society to endorse expectations and demands of addicts that would never be made of someone with a true involuntary illness.

This view has received relatively little support in the academic literature, although a version of it has recent support from some philosophers (e.g. Fingarette, 1988, and particularly Foddy and Savulescu, 2010). They argue that addiction is simply having a strong appetite. The addict differs from 'the normal person' not because they lack the strength of will to resist the temptation, but because of the strength of the appetite for the addictive substance/ behaviour. The view sees the choice of the addict as therefore impaired. There is a partial responsibility. To Foddy and Savulescu (2010) the flaw with the scientific approach is to assume that addicted behaviour is abnormal.

All pleasurable behaviour alters brains. The addict is in essence no different from anyone who chooses to engage in pleasurable activities.

They therefore reject claims that an addict lacks autonomy. Although addicts may prefer imprudent outcomes that is not evidence of a lack of capacity. If the selection of only prudent choices described the mark of autonomy, none of us would be autonomous! The addict prefers the substance over other priorities when she makes the decision to take it. The immediate desire (craving) may be given greater priority than a longer-term goal (achieving sobriety/non-addiction), but that is no different from the common preference for the immediate pleasure over long-term benefits which is an all too common propensity. Indeed, they argue that the very fact that addicts are able to overcome their addiction through self-will indicates that the medicalized model is misguided.

This view has its critics. There seems little evidence from neuroscience that addicts face stronger desires than others (Wilkinson, 2010; and see Regan, this volume). Further it does not explain the impact of withdrawal symptoms when an addict ceases to take the substance in question. Facing these different views on addiction, the difficulties in formulating a legal response in part can be found in identifying the cause of and degree of responsibility for addiction. If the correct view is that addiction is a complex interplay between drug actions, impaired choice, social factors and personal circumstances, then it is unsurprising that it does not neatly fit into one of law's pre-prepared boxes for defences: the mental impairment is insufficient to amount to insanity; the degree of responsibility makes automatism inappropriate; the degree of pressure experienced is insufficient to amount to duress; and so on. Yet those arguing for the defence based on the addict's compulsion may claim that although understood individually, they fail to constitute a defence and the combination of these factors is such that there is a sufficient defect of will to justify a defence. We move now to developing our suggestions as to how the issue should be approached.

Developing a new response

In the literature it is easy to hear the voices of lawyers, philosophers, psychologists and ethicists on how to understand addiction. We suggest that one voice that has not been heard enough, and could usefully be heard, is that of addicts themselves. What sense of responsibility do they have?

We find much to learn from understanding addiction from the perspective of the addict and in particular the 12 Steps suggested by AA (2002). The ascent involved in the 12 Steps suggests a kind of journey. What kind of journey might this be? The journey seems to be a moral one. Step 4 envisages a 'searching and fearless moral inventory' followed by a step 5 admission of 'the exact nature of our wrongs'. Once that 'exact nature' has been identified, steps 6 and 7 envisage a morally transformative process encompassing the removal of 'defects of character' and the corresponding 'shortcomings' that impede the realization of the virtuous life. Steps 8 and 9 then envisage a process whereby the recovering addict reaches a willingness to make amends to all of those persons and institutions 'harmed' by the addict, and the making of such direct amends where appropriate. Let us pause to reflect upon the remarkably rich and subtle account of moral responsibility that is embedded in this call to the addict to engage in a moral transformation as a journey to a 'spiritual awakening' in step 12.

The 12 Step programme is famously aligned with a 'disease' conception of addiction (AA, 2002, p. 18). Rapid advances in the scientific understanding of genetics, psychiatry and neuroscience have entrenched the understanding of addiction as a mental illness with neurological causes and treatments. However, as Stephen Morse (2000) has observed, the flipside of the rise of this 'brain disease model' of addiction has been an unappealing tendency for dichotomous categorization in this sphere (pp. 21–2). Addiction is either a moral failing *or* it is a diseased condition. It cannot be both. On this view, it follows logically that *if* we are to think of addiction as a disease then it cannot be appropriate to hold the addict criminally responsible for actions associated with her drug use. However, Morse points out that 'there is no reason that our thinking about addiction must be polar, that it is only brain disease or only intentional conduct, that it is best treated only medically or psychologically or only by criminalization' (pp. 21–2). Consequently, 'its assumption that behaviour symptomatic of brain disease cannot also be evidence of moral failure is question-begging' (p. 22).

Of course, the question begged is an extraordinarily complex one. However, what seems to emerge from the 12 Step disease model is a rejection of the reductive dichotomous thinking criticized by Stephen Morse. On a superficial reading of the 12 steps, it might be thought that the model draws a neat connection between 'disease' and denial of responsibility. For example, step 1 refers to the addict being 'powerless' over alcohol or addiction and step 2 the need for a restoration of the addict's 'sanity'. However, the overall tenor of the 12 steps is rooted in a call to moral responsibility for the addict. Step 5 envisages a moral inventory of 'wrongs' perpetrated by the addict while engaged in active addiction. This seems to be based upon an understanding of the addict as *responsible* in some way for those wrongs. This is reinforced by the structure of steps 8 and 9 where the addict must make restorative amends for 'harm' done while addicted. Again, that amends are owed to those persons and institutions harmed by the addict imply a responsibility for the harm caused. The addict is thus conceived as a moral agent with capacity (and indeed duty) for taking responsibility for the harms and wrongs that result from addictive behaviour. In the *Big Book*'s discussion of the process of making amends, the possibility that the recovering addict may need to be unflinchingly prepared to face imprisonment for crimes committed while in active addiction is explicitly countenanced: 'we may lose our position or reputation or face jail, but we are willing. We have to be. We must not shrink at anything.' (AA, 2002, p. 79) The AA founder Bill Wilson described how 'I ruthlessly faced my sins' as part of his path to recovery from alcoholism (p. 13). Strong stuff.

We would like to suggest that the 12 Step model deploys a highly sophisticated 'moralized' conception of the disease of addiction. We can make better sense of this by locating the moralized conception within a normative framework of virtue ethics. The starting point for understanding this location is the *Big Book*'s observation that recovery from alcoholism requires 'self-searching, the levelling of our pride, the confession of shortcomings' (AA, 2002, p. 25) This is because *alcoholism is characterized as a disease that is (partially at least) constituted by a complex of vices and character defects* that must be transformed in order to achieve recovery from the compulsion to drink. The vice that lies at the root of compulsive drinking ('our liquor was but a symptom') (p. 64) is selfishness. This leads to a seemingly strong claim about the alcoholic's personal responsibility:

> so our troubles, we think, are basically of our own making. They arise out of ourselves, and the alcoholic is an extreme example of self-will run riot...Above everything, we alcoholics must be rid of this selfishness. We must, or it kills us! (p. 62)

This paramount vice of selfishness is associated with a range of other vices and character defects, which are described as 'the flaws in our make-up which *caused* our failure' (p. 64). These include indifference to other's interests, cowardice (excessive fear), dishonesty and irascibility/resentment. The alcoholic's recovery lies in the shedding of these vices and character defects, and the corresponding cultivation of virtuous dispositions. Only then will the character-based causes of the *disease* of alcoholism be addressed and the compulsion to drink lifted.

We would strike a rather cautionary note at this juncture. With scientific advances it is clear that the aetiology of addiction is extraordinarily complex. There is a risk that if we go too far down the 'character vice' line then addicts might be routinely castigated as moral failures. Nevertheless, the language deployed in the AA model mirrors what Duff (2003, p. 154) has described as a 'wider movement into "virtue jurisprudence" and reflects the revival of interest in Aristotelianism in philosophical ethics'. This tradition offers a richly differentiated account of the ethical dimensions of human character. The virtuous person is, in Duff's words, marked by 'an integrated unity of reason and passion ... a virtuous person's emotions and appetites are oriented towards, and structured by her understanding of, the good, so that what she feels or wants is appropriate to her situation' (pp. 162–3). By contrast, the vicious person 'is wholeheartedly oriented towards evil rather than good; his reason and his passions mutually reinforce each other's *mis*direction' (p. 165). Thankfully, the distinction between the virtuous and the vicious does not exhaust the moral possibilities of humanity (Duff, 2003, pp. 163–5). Thus, the *continent* person acts correctly and for right reason though this requires her to overcome contrary desires and inclinations. She lacks that 'integrated unity of reason and passion' that is the mark of the virtuous. The *weak-willed* person, by contrast, yields to those contrary desires and inclinations despite the rational sense that what is being done is wrongful. It is striking how this Aristotelian understanding of human excellence chimes with the latent understanding of alcoholism (and recovery from it) in the 12 Step model. It envisages nothing less than a metamorphosis of the soul and the transformation from *vicious* to *weak-willed* to *continent* to *truly virtuous*. Of course, the drinking alcoholic is not truly vicious nor is the recovering alcoholic truly virtuous. However, the journey of recovery indicates a very clear ethical direction of travel. The 'spiritual awakening' achieved in step 12 reflects the Aristotelian sense of 'eudaimonia' that is characteristic of the truly virtuous life and that is what the alcoholic must strive for if she is to recover.

Of course, we should not lose sight of the central question with which we started: what is the relationship between alcoholism/addiction and criminal responsibility? While the *Big Book* offers some clues and insights into that relationship, we should not forget that the *Big Book* does not claim to be a philosophical treatise on the nature of responsibility and blame. It is a text designed to help alcoholics recover from their illness. Moreover, even once we locate the 12 Step model within an Aristotelian frame of reference, the connections between virtue ethics and criminal responsibility are keenly contested. It is undoubtedly true that this ethical tradition has been significant in recent influential theorizations of criminal inculpation (e.g. Huigens, 2007) and, more especially, exculpation (e.g. Gardner, 2007). However, there are also serious questions about the proper reach of virtue ethics in criminal doctrine and theory. Thus, Alan Norrie (2000, pp. 34–9) observes that the Aristotelian conception of well-being, while central to the work of some criminal theorists, seems not to have precipitated a deep reconfiguration of the 'Kantian' categories and apparatus of legal doctrine. From a different perspective, Duff (2003) is sceptical that Aristotelian conceptions of virtue and vice can have anything more than a very marginal impact on the conditions of criminal liability. Fundamentally, the criminal law is interested in *actions*, and as Hursthouse (2007) points out, 'given that a virtue is such a multi-track disposition, it would obviously be reckless to attribute one to an agent on the basis of a single observed action or even a series of similar actions'. Nevertheless, the moralized conception of disease at least provides us with a set of starting points for exploring criminal defences for crimes arising out of addictive behaviour.

Developing a legal response

To this end, there are three putative defences/limitations on criminal liability that we would like to explore: (i) addiction as duress; (ii) involuntary intoxication; and (iii) diminished responsibility/capacity. We think that the scope for extending defences for addicts on the basis of the AA disease model beyond the strict limits of the current law is circumscribed.

Addiction as duress

As Stephen Morse (2000) has observed, there is a danger of being seduced by metaphors in thinking about addiction. These metaphors often emphasize the utter destruction of the addict's will. Intoxication is said to be, quite literally, involuntary where the addict is concerned. As the previous section indicated, we should be sceptical about the claim that drinking or drug use is literally involuntary for the addict. The addict who uses drugs does not do so as an automaton. On the contrary:

> the addict desires, broadly, either the pleasure of intoxication, the avoidance of the pain of withdrawal or inner tension, or both. The addict believes that using the substance will satisfy the desire and consequently forms the intention to seek and use the substance. (p. 28)

The activity of acquiring and taking drugs will usually be highly purposive, goal-directed, and deliberated. Whatever else such activity is, it cannot be described as involuntary. However, if we understand the addict's choice to become intoxicated as *morally* involuntary then this points to a more perspicuous understanding of the addict's dilemma. The gist of this dilemma is the exercise of a choice in the face of a potent internal pressure to become intoxicated (and to do whatever is necessary to make that happen). According to Gary Watson (1999, p. 590), 'the most plausible way of understanding this pressure is to see addictions as creating circumstances of duress'. This concept of 'internal' duress is also viewed as a putative defence warranting serious consideration by Husak (1999) and Morse (2000). Ultimately, and for different reasons, Husak, Morse and Watson are sceptical that such a defence is viable. Rather than re-rehearse those arguments, we want to test the 'addiction as duress' defence against the criteria of 'duress by threats' under the current law. This exercise indicates the difficulties inherent in any attempt to rationalize addiction as a defence in this way. Nevertheless, we also think that the idea of overwhelming pressure correctly identifies the gist of why addiction might be thought worth considering as a putative defence. Duress is therefore the correct place to start. The paradigm situation would be where an addict, faced with a powerful compulsion to use a substance, commits a crime as a direct means to sating the appetite for the substance.

Duress by threats exhibits a relatively stable structure in English law that displays both a subjective and an objective component. The subjective component requires that D be faced with an immediate and unavoidable threat of death or serious bodily harm and that D commits the crime (other than murder or attempted murder) in order to avoid that threat. The objective component requires that a sober person of reasonable firmness would have been unable to resist the threat. How do the cravings and desires of addiction measure up to this? First, in no sense can the withdrawal symptoms associated with opiate-based drugs or alcohol be viewed as equivalent in kind to threats of death or serious bodily harm. On the contrary, and as Morse (2000, p. 36) points out, 'withdrawal from heroin is often likened to a bad flu'. While the anticipation of withdrawal might generate extreme psychological distress and anxiety, particularly given the addict's actual experience of intensifying physical withdrawal symptoms over time once physical withdrawal is underway, cases such as *Quayle* [2005] reassert the restrictive rule that only threats of physical harm or death will suffice. The argument for equivalence between addiction and duress is even less compelling in cases where the drug does not give rise to physical dependency. As a thought-experiment to make the point even more vivid, consider Morse's (2000, p. 19) example of the drug addict under a standing threat of death if she uses drugs. Where such a threat is capable of immediate execution it is highly unlikely that most addicts would yield to the compulsion to use the drug.

Secondly, for a defence to be successful it would be necessary to prove that the addict used the drug in order to avoid the extreme pain of withdrawal. However, it is just as likely that for most addicts on at least some occasions 'the primary motive is the pleasure or satisfaction of yielding... The possibility of pleasure seems more like an offer... and offers expand rather than contract freedom.' (Morse, 2000, p. 35) We might say that the defence should be withheld in a situation where the primary motive is pleasure. However, given the difficulties of deploying such a fine-grained test for evaluating the addict's practical reasoning on an episodic basis, this hardly seems promising as the basis for a workable legal test. Further, in *Rodger* [1998] the Court of Appeal held that internal pressures (in that case suicidal feelings) could not constitute a threat for the purposes of duress. In part this may reflect a broader point in the defence of duress that a person cannot rely on duress if a person is responsible for the circumstances in which the threat occurred.

But it also reflects an acknowledgment that the law can never truly assess what kinds of threat a person perceives if those are internal (Corrado, 1999).

Thirdly, the threat must be 'immediate and unavoidable' so that D has no effective opportunity of avoiding it. Once again, it is unlikely that this is the situation for many addicts. The most plausible pharmacological candidate for a defence of 'duress by addiction' is heroin, given the relative intensity of its physical withdrawal symptoms (Husak, 1999). However, even here methadone is widely available as a 'harm reduction' strategy for managing opiate addiction and its related withdrawal symptoms. Furthermore, there will be a wide range of crimes where there is an insufficient nexus between their commission and the avoidance of withdrawal pain. The nexus will likely be sufficient where the crime consists in the use of the drug itself. It is less plausible that the addict had no realistic alternative to stealing this purse or burgling this house *in order to* purchase drugs *in order to* use those drugs *in order to* avoid the pain of withdrawal symptoms. Here the nexus between the avoidance of withdrawal symptoms and the criminality is insufficient to satisfy the immediacy and unavoidability criteria. Fourthly, the tendency in recent cases such as R v *Hasan* [2005] is to reinforce the principle of prior fault as a method for imposing strict limits on the availability of the defence. These limits have been crafted within the context of individual participation in group crime, such as gangs or organized crime. According to Lord Bingham:

> If a person voluntarily becomes or remains associated with others engaged in criminal activity in a situation where he knows or ought reasonably to know that he may be the subject of compulsion by them or their associates, he cannot rely on the defence of duress. (para. 38)

This raises identical concerns to those explored in the previous section. It cannot be said that the addict has no voluntary control over whether she remains trapped in active addiction: in the words of the *Big Book* (AA, 2002), even on the disease model 'there is a solution'. In these circumstances, a principle best described as *continuing* fault might apply in the failure to undertake available opportunities to recover from the disease.

For these reasons, the subjective component of duress is very unlikely to be satisfied in most cases. It must be observed that the barriers to satisfying the subjective criteria are not insurmountable. There is nothing *intrinsic* to duress that limits it to threats of death or serious bodily harm; or immediate (as opposed to imminent) threats; or even a draconian application of the principle of prior fault. They represent judicial and legislative choices to limit duress in specific ways. We could choose to do otherwise. However, we want to suggest that the objective element of duress that, personified in the sober person of reasonable firmness, does render duress morally unsuitable as a defence for addicts. Simply because it is difficult to imagine what the relevant standards and expectations of the role of drug addict or alcoholic might be.

One way out of this difficulty might be to understand drug addiction in the following way. According to Gary Watson (1999, pp. 615–16):

> addictions do not necessarily erode moral character in some general way. And the likelihood that they will dispose one to loss of control is a contingent matter; whether and how often the addict's special vulnerability is indeed realized depends largely on social norms and her economic circumstances.

On this view, an otherwise reasonable and continent person could also happen to be addicted to drugs. Just like an otherwise reasonable and continent person could also happen to have a crooked toe or bad flatulence. If this were true, it would be perfectly intelligible to apply the sober person of reasonable firmness to the addict's predicament. However, the AA disease model suggests, *pace* Watson, that addiction does erode moral character. Moreover, it is a disease that is constituted by a range of character vices and defects that structure the addict's reasoning, affective capacities, perceptual frames and entire world view. The very idea of the *sober* addict/alcoholic of reasonable *firmness* is not just difficult to apply. It is unintelligible because the addictive disease saturates the entire character of the addict – it is not simply a condition that otherwise reasonable people happen to 'catch' or acquire. This leads into a broader difficulty with excuse-based defences for addicts and alcoholics if the Gardner position is considered persuasive. None of this should be seen as a denial that the defensive gist of addiction is the fact of compulsion. In that respect, criminal theorists have been looking in the right place. It does suggest, however, that duress is not the correct legal response.

Involuntary intoxication

In the infamous case of *R v Kingston* [1995], Mr Kingston's coffee was clandestinely laced with dis-inhibiting drugs. He had latent paedophilic tendencies that (we must assume) he had otherwise restrained in the past. Once Mr Kingston was drugged he was put in a position of temptation with an unconscious teenage boy, and in his dis-inhibited state he acted on his sexual desires and committed an indecent assault on the victim. The House of Lords upheld his conviction for indecent assault. The defendant knew what he was doing – in criminal law terms, he had the *mens rea* for the offence. The fact that he would not have committed the offence but for the involuntary intoxication procured by a malicious third party was regarded by their Lordships as insufficient to generate an excuse for Mr Kingston. Both Sullivan (1996) and

Tadros (2005) have argued that a character-based defence might be warranted in this kind of situation. According to Sullivan (1996, p. 151), 'conjoining the notion of lapse from good character with circumstances of destabilization but for which the agent would not have done what she did' yields a proposal for a defence that is morally attractive and capable of being kept within manageable bounds. Building upon Sullivan's earlier work, Tadros (2005) proposes two conditions for a successful defence of involuntary intoxication: (i) that the defendant is not responsible for becoming intoxicated; and (ii) that the action undertaken in that state does not reflect the defendant's settled character. The proper measurement of (ii) is whether or not the defendant has any previous convictions for the type of offence for which the defence is being pleaded.

As a proposal, this 'out of character' defence has undoubted attractions. However, its scope within the addiction context is likely to be very tightly circumscribed for three reasons. First, the requirement that the defendant not be responsible for becoming intoxicated is likely to filter out many putative defence claims by addicts, as Sullivan (1996, p. 146) himself recognizes. He suggests as a threshold that the first and subsequent drink/drugs are 'compelled'. He also acknowledges that:

> these conditions are so exclusionary that practically all, if not all, alcoholics would fail to meet them. Nonetheless, it would be problematic to describe as 'involuntary' those states of intoxication which are a regular feature of the lives of alcoholics and other addicts.

It may be that the first condition is too tightly drawn insofar as it insists on a strict equivalence between involuntariness and negation of responsibility. Indeed, it seems very likely that intoxication could be both voluntary and of such a nature that the addict's responsibility is *diminished* if not negated. However, this points towards a different kind of defence that is not excusatory in nature (and which we will deal with in the next section). Secondly, the moralized disease model that we have deployed also suggests a limited sphere of operation for the defence. As we have seen, it is central to the self-understanding of addicts and alcoholics in 12 Step recovery that their malady is rooted precisely in a complex of vices and character defects, and that their recovery necessitates a transformation of character and the cultivation of virtue. This makes the forensic identification of the addict's 'settled' character (and the *point* of recovery is to unsettle that character!) a very delicate exercise indeed. It may be that in many cases the addict's criminality is simply a reflection of the vices that are constitutive of her addictive illness. Finally, the criminal law must attend to its own institutional concerns with systemic integrity and practical authority. As Simester and Sullivan (2010, p. 795) observe of an excuse of involuntary intoxication, it is 'exceptional, bounded, and forensically manageable'. Alas, if this excuse was reconfigured so as to include addicts and alcoholics within its scope, these criteria would not be met such is the extent of addictive behaviour within society and the criminal justice system.

Diminished responsibility/capacity

The one area of the criminal law where defendants have had some very limited success in utilizing addiction as a defence is in the area of diminished responsibility, a defence which is only available to murder and even then, if successful, reduces the conviction from murder to manslaughter (s. 2 of the Homicide Act 1957). The defence is only available if the defendant suffered from an abnormality of mental functioning which arose from a recognized medical condition. That abnormality must substantially impair the defendant's ability to do one of three things: understand the nature of her conduct, form a rational judgment or exercise self-control. Finally, the defendant needs to show that the abnormality provides an explanation for the killing.

The courts have been clear that being intoxicated does not amount to an abnormality of the mind (although brain damage induced by alcohol might). However, suffering from alcohol dependency syndrome might be. The most sophisticated discussion of the issue is found in the case of *R v Stewart* [2009] where the Court of Appeal considered a case where a man with alcohol dependency syndrome killed another man while heavily intoxicated. The Court of Appeal noted that in such a case a defendant may be able to escape a conviction for murder simply by arguing that he lacked an intention to kill or cause grievous bodily harm. This case involved a sustained violent attack and so such a claim seemed unlikely. More plausible was the defence of diminished responsibility. This required proof that the defendant suffered an abnormality of the mind. In this case that was the alcohol dependency syndrome. What is interesting about this case is the willingness of the court to go further and accept that if the syndrome caused the defendant to become involuntarily intoxicated, then the effect of the intoxication could be included as an abnormality of the mind. The Court of Appeal explained:

> This depends on the jury's findings about the nature and extent of the syndrome and whether, looking at the matter broadly, his consumption of alcohol before the killing is fairly to be regarded as the involuntary result of an irresistible craving for or compulsion to drink. (para. 31)

In taking this approach, the court rejected the suggestion in *R v Tandy* [1989] that the consumption of alcohol was involuntary if the defendant lacked control over all of the drinking, including the first drink of the day. The court went on to explain that in considering whether the defendant's responsibility for his or her actions was substantially impaired:

> In answering their questions, the jury should be directed to consider all the evidence, including the opinions of the medical experts. The issues likely to arise in this kind of case and on which they should be invited to form their own judgment will include (a) the extent and seriousness of the defendant's dependency, if any, on alcohol, (b) the extent to which his ability to control his drinking or to choose whether to drink or not, was reduced, (c) whether he was capable of abstinence from alcohol, and if so, (d) for how long, and (e) whether he was choosing for some particular reason, such as a birthday celebration, to decide to get drunk, or to drink even more than usual.
>
> Without seeking to be prescriptive about considerations relevant to an individual case, the defendant's pattern of drinking in the days leading to the day of the killing, and on the day of the killing itself, and notwithstanding his consumption of alcohol, his ability, if any, to make apparently sensible and rational decisions about ordinary day to day matters at the relevant time, may all bear on the jury's decision whether diminished responsibility is established in the context of this individual defendant's alcohol dependency syndrome. (para. 34)

There is an acknowledgment here that the defendant's responsibility for the intoxication is diminished as a result of the addiction (Corrado, 1999). It is to be remembered we are discussing a very limited defence here, and in particular that it is a partial defence that still leads to the conviction of the defendant. The defendant is still responsible for the death of the victim and deserves punishment for it. However, the law acknowledges that the censure that the defendant deserves is less. The defence is compatible with Stephen Morse's proposal that we develop a verdict of 'guilty but partially responsible', thereby preserving the formal denouncement of guilt, with an acknowledgment that the case is more complex than that. This could recognize that addicts are responsible for their behaviour, but in some cases it affects the agent's ability to grasp and be guided by reason (Morse, 2000). In our view, this provides the appropriate technique for partially exempting addicted defendants from full criminal liability in situations that, on the face of them, look like they might fall within the scope of an excusatory duress claim.

The benefit of this approach is that it recognizes the addict as a moral being: a person (partially) responsible for her actions and accountable for them. This is a central theme of the 12 steps. And with responsibility comes hope: the control over the addiction. And with that comes dignity and self-respect, where the addict can take a full place in the moral universe that other citizens inhabit. In John Gardner's view, to lack responsibility for one's actions is a pitiable state, not one to seek out. Perhaps this is true where responsibility is entirely destroyed by incapacity. Yet the use of *diminished* responsibility acknowledges another aspect of the 12 steps: that battling addiction is hard work, very hard work. Even where responsibility is diminished, it is not negated, and it is still being asserted by the addict as a moral agent. The loss of the battle is a moral failure, and one deserving of some blame, but blame tempered by a compassionate acknowledgment of the difficulty of the situation facing the defendant.

Wider social responsibility

We are painfully aware that the analysis of the legal issues has largely put to one side the social aspects of addiction: the social causes of addiction and the extent to which addiction is an interpersonal behaviour is put to one side in the analysis of criminal responsibility. Of course, it plays a major role in the AA's 12 steps. Central to recovery is the notion of fellowship. The move from the fellowship of addiction to fellowship of recovery from addiction is part of the journey of the 12 steps. But, as we have seen, responsibility and accountability are part of that journey. The failure of the criminal law to attach weight to the broader social and interpersonal aspects of offences is well recorded (Norrie, 2000). It is best justified, if at all, on the practical limitations of a courtroom and our human limitations of assessments of blame. What, however, we argue can be taken is that our response to addiction cannot lie in accountability alone, but in support, fellowship, education and the like. The criminal law's holding to account must lie alongside a more supportive social response to addiction. The holding to account by the criminal law is not incompatible with that, but rather we suggest an essential aspect of it.

Conclusion

In this chapter we have sought to outline the reasons why the criminal law has been reluctant to allow addiction as a basis for a defence to a criminal charge. We have sought to support the general approach of the law. Our justification for this has differed from the standard models of analysis within the legal literature. Too often those seeking to promote a medicalized model and well-meaning critical lawyers have patronized addicts. Reducing addiction to simply a sickness for which no responsibility attaches fails to accord respect for the agency, albeit limited, that addicts have. But an assumption of full responsibility fails to captures the constraints on agency that addiction creates. In this chapter we have identified an organic discourse, generated by a community of addicts themselves, that speaks a cognate language of responsibility for wrongs with a virtue ethics slant. This means that the communicative dimension of the criminal trial is not necessarily lost on drug addicts and alcoholics.

Our approach rests on the understanding of addicts about their own condition. It has relied on the 12 Step programme developed by the AA to explore a complex acknowledgment of responsibility and accountability, alongside an awareness of the difficulty of the task of overcoming addiction. For the 12 steps, the notion of accountability and responsibility is a central aspect of the appropriate response to and recovery from addiction. We have argued that this approach fits well into academic legal analysis resting particularly on a virtue ethics approach to law. However, we have also emphasized, as does the 12 Step programme, that a holding to account must be placed alongside supportive and affirming social structures.

Bibliography

Alcoholics Anonymous (AA) (2002) *Big Book* (London: Hazelden Information & Educational Services)

American Psychiatric Association (2000) *Diagnostic and Statistical Manual of Mental Disorders* (DSM-IV) (Arlington VA: American Psychiatric Association)

BBC News (2011) 'Malawi Row over Whether New Law Bans Farting' www. bbc.co.uk/news/world-africa-12363852

Boseley, S (2010) 'Leading doctor urges decriminalisation of drugs', *The Guardian*, 16 August

Buchman, D, J Illes and P Reiner (2010) 'The Paradox of Addiction Neuroscience' *Neuroethics*, 22 June

Corrado, M (1999) 'Addiction And Responsibility: An Introduction' **18** *Law and Philosophy* 579

Duff, A (2003) 'Virtue, Vice, and Criminal Liability: Do We Want an Aristotelian Criminal Law?' **6** *Buffalo Criminal Law Review* 147–65

Fingarette, H (1988) *Heavy Drinking: The Myth of Alcoholism as a Disease* (Berkley CA: University of California Press)

Gardner, J (2007) *Offences and Defences* (Oxford: Oxford University Press)

Foddy, B and J Savulescu (2010) 'A Liberal Account of Addiction' **17** *Philosophy, Psychiatry and Psychology* 1–22

Herring, J (2009) 'Losing It? Losing What? The Law and Dementia' **21** *Child and Family Law Quarterly* 3–29

Herring, J (2011) 'Vulnerability and Childhood' in M Freeman (ed.), *Law and Childhood Studies* (Oxford: Oxford University Press)

Horder, J (1993) 'Pleading Involuntary Lack of Capacity' **52** *Cambridge Law Journal* 298–318

Huigens, K (2007) 'On Aristotelian Criminal Law: A Reply to Duff' in C Farrelly and L Solum (eds), *Virtue Jurisprudence* (Basingstoke: Palgrave Macmillan)

Hursthouse, R (2007) 'Virtue Ethics' in *Stanford Encyclopaedia of Philosophy* http://plato.stanford.edu/entries/ethics-virtue/

Husak, D (1999) 'Addiction and Criminal Liability' **18** *Law and Philosophy* 655–84

Macklem, T and J Gardner (2001) 'Provocation and Pluralism' **64** *Modern Law Review* 815–40

Morse, S (2000) 'Hooked on Hype: Addiction and Responsibility' **19** *Law and Philosophy* 3–49

Norrie, A (2000) *Punishment, Responsibility and Justice* (Oxford: Oxford University Press)

Satel, S and F Goodwin (1998) *Is Drug Addiction a Brain Disease?* (Washington DC: Ethics and Public Policy Centre)

Simester, A and G R Sullivan (2010) *Criminal Law* (Oxford: Hart Publishing)

Smith, K (2011) 'Taking Aim at Free Will' **477** *Nature* 23–5

Soon, C, M Brass, H-J Heinze and J-D Haynes (2008) 'Unconscious Determinants of Free Decisions in the Human Brain' **11**(5) *Nature Neuroscience* 543–5

Sullivan, G R (1996) 'Making Excuses' in A Simester and A Smith (eds), *Harm and Culpability* (Oxford: Oxford University Press)

Tolmie, J (2003) 'Alcoholism and Criminal Liability' **64** *Modern Law Review* 688–709

Tadros, V (2005) *Criminal Responsibility* (Oxford: Oxford University Press)

Watson, G (1999) 'Disordered Appetites: Addiction, Compulsion and Dependence' in J Elster (ed.), *Addiction: Entries and Exits* (New York: Russell Sage)

Wilkinson, D (2010) 'Demedicalizing and Decriminalizing Drugs' *Practical Ethics*, 17 August 2010

Wood, E (2010) 'Evidence Based Policy for Illicit Drugs' **341** *British Medical Journal* c. 3374–5

Cases

Attorney-General's Reference (No 2 of 1992) [1993] 3 WLR 982

Quayle [2005] EWCA Crim 1415

R v Hasan [2005] UKHL 22

R v Kennedy [2007] UKHL 38.

R v Kingston [1995] 2 AC 355
R v Rodger [1998] 1 Cr App R 143
R v Stewart [2009] EWCA Crim 593
R v Tandy [1989] 1 All ER 267

Legislation

Homicide Act 1957

14

The Current Law of Intoxication: Rules and Problems

Rebecca Williams

Introduction

The current approach of English and Welsh criminal law to the problem of intoxicated defendants is governed by the so-called *Majewski* rules (first discussed by Loughnan in Chapter 3). *Majewski* was concerned in a pub brawl, during which he assaulted the landlord, customers and the police officer who arrested him. The following morning he also assaulted a police inspector in a cell at the police station. He was thus charged with three offences of assault occasioning actual bodily harm and three offences of assault on a police officer in the execution of his duty, contrary to s. 51 (1) of the Police Act 1964, but sought to defend himself on the basis that he had been suffering from the effects of alcohol and drugs at the time. The courts deciding *Majewski*'s case were thus faced with the same dilemma as all courts that deal with intoxicated defendants; on the one hand those who are intoxicated are in general more likely to do more harm, but in each specific case the individual's culpability in creating the harm may be less than if they had been sober at the time of the offence (see Maguire and Nettleton, 2003; Loughnan, Chapter 3 of this volume).

The decision of the House of Lords (*DPP v Majewski* [1977], at 474–5, per Lord Elwyn-Jones) was that:

> If a man of his own volition takes a substance which causes him to cast off the restraints of reason and conscience, no wrong is done to him by holding him answerable criminally for any injury he may do while in that condition. His course of conduct in reducing himself by drugs and drink to that condition...supplies the evidence of mens rea, of guilty mind certainly sufficient for crimes of basic intent. It is a reckless course of conduct and recklessness is enough to constitute the necessary mens rea in assault cases: see *Reg. v. Venna* [1976] Q.B. 421, *per* James L.J. at p. 429.

> The drunkenness is itself an intrinsic, an integral part of the crime,
> the other part being the evidence of the unlawful use of force
> against the victim. Together they add up to criminal recklessness.

As a result, the decision in *Majewski* has been taken as laying down the following series of propositions relating to the criminal law's treatment of intoxicated offenders:

1. Intoxication is never a defence to a criminal charge in the technical sense (Simester 2009).
2. In the context of what are known as 'offences of specific intent' the defendant can use evidence of his/her intoxication in order to deny that he/she had the necessary *mens rea* at the time of committing the offence (*Sheehan* [1975]).
3. However, in the context of 'offences of basic intent', as Lord Elwyn-Jones suggests in the above passage, not only can a defendant not use evidence of his or her intoxication to deny *mens rea*, in fact a defendant's 'course of conduct in reducing himself by drink and drugs to that condition ... supplies the evidence of mens rea, of guilty mind'.

In addition to these principles, others have been established by subsequent case law:

4. In cases where the intoxicants were taken for therapeutic reasons, the defendant can use evidence of his/her intoxication in order to deny that he/she had the necessary *mens rea* at the time of committing the offence, even if the offence in question is one of basic intent (*Hardie* [1984]).
5. Similarly, the defendant can use evidence of his/her intoxication in order to deny *mens rea* in instances where the intoxication was involuntary (*Kingston* [1995]).
6. On the other hand, if the defendant in fact had the *mens rea* for the offence, then regardless of the nature of the offence and regardless of the nature of the intoxication, the defendant will be guilty of the offence (*Kingston* [1995]).

These rules are, however, problematic for several reasons.

The specific–basic distinction

First, the *Majewski* rules require a distinction to be drawn between so-called 'offences of specific intent' and those of 'basic intent'. As Lord Simon's judgment in *Majewski* ([1977], at 477) makes clear, there are several different potential senses in which the specific/basic distinction might be understood.

One is to regard an offence of 'specific intent' as one of 'ulterior intent' in the sense that the defendant 'contemplat[es] consequences beyond those defined in the actus reus'. This approach was more recently adopted in the decision of the Court of Appeal in *Heard* [2007], which suggested that the intentional or reckless causing of criminal damage being reckless as to whether life was endangered, contrary to s. 1(2)(b) Criminal Damage Act 1971 would count as an offence of specific intent, even though recklessness would suffice for the ulterior element. However, as Lord Simon goes on to point out, the ulterior intent approach is not wholly satisfactory for the purposes of the intoxication rules since it does not fit some of the offences which actually are regarded as being specific intent offences. For example, murder is an offence of specific intent for the purposes of intoxication, and yet it is not necessary for the *mens rea* for murder even to extend *as far* as the *actus reus*, never mind extending beyond it. Thus it is sufficient that the defendant intends grievous bodily harm (GBH): he/she need not intend that the victim should die. Instead, therefore, Lord Simon in his decision in *Majewski* preferred the definition of specific intent given by Fauteux J in *R v George* ([1960], at 301):

> In considering the question of mens rea, a distinction is to be made between (i) intention as applied to acts considered in relation to their purposes and (ii) intention as applied to acts apart from their purposes. A general intent attending the commission of an act is, in some cases, the only intent required to constitute the crime while, in others, there must be, in addition to that general intent, a specific intent attending the purpose for the commission of the act.

Lord Simon in *Majewski* ([1977], at 480) then went on to elaborate this distinction between specific and basic intent offences as follows:

> a crime of specific intent requires something more than contemplation of the prohibited act and foresight of its probable consequences. The mens rea in a crime of specific intent requires proof of a purposive element. This purposive element either exists or not; it cannot be supplied by saying that the impairment of mental powers by self-induced intoxication is its equivalent, for it is not.

However, as various academic commentators (e.g. Simester et al., 2010, p. 689) have pointed out, this explanation does not fit particularly well with the current law either, since murder is, as noted above, an offence of specific intent, and yet a defendant can be guilty of murder without any purposive element at all, provided that he or she foresees that death or GBH will be 'virtually certain' as a result of his/her actions (*Woollin* [1998]). A person with such foresight can thus be guilty of murder even if he/she could not care less whether or not such GBH or death in fact results.

The difficulty of establishing the difference between offences of specific and offences of basic intent could be, and indeed in practice is, resolved by simply having lists of offences for each of the two categories. Thus, for example, murder (*Sheehan* [1975]), GBH contrary to s. 18 of the Offences Against the Person Act 1861 (OAPA) (*Bratty v AG for Northern Ireland* [1963]), theft (*Ruse v Read* [1949]), burglary (*Durante* [1972]), and handling stolen goods (*Durante* [1972]) are all crimes of specific intent, as is recklessly causing criminal damage being reckless as to whether life is endangered, if the Court of Appeal in *Heard* [2007] is to be followed. However, such an approach is unhelpful both in terms of certainty regarding offences which have not yet been classified, or indeed new offences, and in terms of intellectual coherence. If we cannot satisfactorily establish the criteria for deciding whether an offence is specific or basic, why do we maintain that distinction in the first place?

Attempts have been made to provide more normative support for the distinction, by Horder (1995), Gough (1996) and Simester (2009) who argue in various ways that offences of specific intent are those in which the mental element is somehow *constitutive* of the wrong, rather than additional to it. Thus, for these authors, whereas, for example, any act of actual bodily harm is in itself a wrong and the question is simply what level of mental culpability is necessary before the law will make the defendant criminally liable for having caused it, the taking of another's property is not inherently wrong unless the defendant was also dishonest and had an intention permanently to deprive the victim of that property. I have argued elsewhere (Williams, 2013), however, that this argument rests on certain assumptions being made about what precisely is to be regarded as the wrong in each offence, and if these assumptions are not shared then there will still not be agreement on the location of the specific/basic divide. This in turn means that, as a means of predicting or dictating the location of that divide, even this more principled approach still leads to uncertainty and is thus unsatisfactory.

The basic intent rules only work for reckless result crimes

In fact, as I have argued elsewhere (Williams, 2013), closer examination of the precise operation of the rules for basic intent offences reveals that in fact those rules can only apply to offences which have one particular form of *actus reus* and one particular form of *mens rea*, namely reckless result crimes. This is because in practice juries asked to apply the rules of basic intent are asked whether the defendant *would* have foreseen the relevant harm had he/ she not been intoxicated, a test also favoured by the Court of Appeal in *R v Richardson and Irwin* [1999]. However, as can easily be appreciated, this question assumes that the prohibited wrong (*actus reus*) takes the form of causation of a particular form of harm, and assumes that foresight of that harm (i.e. subjective recklessness) is the relevant form of *mens rea* required by the offence. If the offence were one of *intentional behaviour* it might be thought that the question of what *harm* a sober person might have *foreseen* would be irrelevant. And yet in practice it is not the case that offences of basic intent are all reckless result crimes. On the contrary, in the case of *Heard* [2007] the Court of Appeal held that an offence of sexual assault contrary to s. 3 of the Sexual Offences Act 2003 was an offence of basic intent, despite the fact that this offence in fact requires an intentional touching. Of course, in many cases of offences involving intentional behaviour it may well be the case that the behaviour was in fact carried out intentionally, despite the defendant's intoxication, and indeed this was true of Heard himself. Nevertheless, as Ormerod (2007) has pointed out, it would be difficult now to know what to do with the example raised briefly by the Court of Appeal in *Heard* ([2007], at 22) concerning a 'Defendant who intends to avoid (just) actual physical contact, but realizes that he may touch and is reckless whether he will', or a defendant who deliberately touches *something*, but believes, intoxicatedly, that what he/she is touching is not a human being. Neither of these issues can be satisfactorily resolved by asking what *results* the defendant would have *foreseen* if sober, because that question is entirely beside the point. The question is whether the defendant in either of these scenarios should be regarded in law as having the *intent* to *touch* another human being.

Voluntary intoxication, contrary to the views of Lord Elwyn-Jones and the Law Commission, does not in fact necessarily equate with the *mens rea* normally required for offences of basic intent

As is exemplified by the quote from Lord Elwyn-Jones given above, the assumption that evidence of voluntary intoxication equates with the evidence of *mens rea* that would usually be required for conviction appears to underlie the approach taken by the House of Lords in *Majewski*. A similar approach has also been taken more recently by the Law Commission (2008, para. 2.14) report, arguing that the 'underlying policy' of the current intoxication rules is that:

> an offence will be regarded as one of 'basic intent' if the judi-
> ciary conclude that the commission of its external element in a
> state of voluntary intoxication (without the fault required by the

definition of the offence) is the moral equivalent of committing it
with the fault required by the definition of the offence.

If this equation were a valid one, it would certainly explain why a defendant
charged with a basic intent offence cannot use proof of his or her voluntary intoxication to deny liability for that offence as outlined in what I have
labelled rule 3 above.

In fact, however, proof of voluntary non-therapeutic intoxication differs
from the normal requirement to prove *mens rea* in several 'morally different' ways. The first is that to equate intoxication with the normal *mens rea*
(usually recklessness) required for offences of basic intent is to ignore problems of contemporaneity; D's decision to get drunk may precede his/her
harmful actions by some hours. Second, there are problems of substantive
mismatch; the decision to get drunk hardly constitutes foresight of, for example, physical harm. Third, there are problems of causation in cases where the
failure to foresee the harm was independent of the intoxication and would
have occurred even had the defendant been sober. Even if, as is the Law
Commission's second argument, the current rules on voluntary intoxication
are viewed as a kind of *prior* fault principle, there is still a significant moral
difference between the argument that D ought to have foreseen in advance
an increased risk of harm to persons or property and the argument that he/
she did in fact foresee it at the time of the offence, and of course nowhere is it
laid down *how* drunk D must be before his or her intoxication could be taken
to constitute the recklessness required for a finding of, for example, assault
occasioning actual bodily harm on either a prior or a contemporaneous fault
basis (Law Commission, 1993). Thus, while it would be convenient if the
view of Lords Edmund-Davies and Elwyn-Jones were correct, the conclusion
must be that voluntary intoxication does not equate to the usual *mens rea*
requirements for criminal liability.

No doubt it was precisely this conclusion which led Hughes LJ, giving the
decision of the Court of Appeal in *R v Heard* ([2007], para. 30) to hold that:

> there were…many difficulties in the proposition that voluntary
> intoxication actually supplies the mens rea…if that were so the
> drunken man might be guilty simply by becoming drunk and
> whether or not the risk would be obvious to a sober person,
> himself or anyone else. That reinforces our opinion that the prop-
> osition being advanced was one of *broadly equivalent* culpability,
> rather than of drink by itself supplying the mens rea.

However, this in itself raises two further difficulties. First, if the House of
Lords in *Majewski* did substantively equate voluntary intoxication with *mens
rea* in that case, it is not clear what authority the Court of Appeal had in
Heard to reach the conclusion that they are only *broadly* equivalent. Second,

'broad equivalence' seems to be neither one thing nor the other. Either voluntary non-therapeutic intoxication constitutes the *mens rea* of a crime of basic intent or it does not. Either proof of voluntary intoxication constitutes or equates with the usual *mens rea* requirements for criminal liability, thereby alleviating the prosecution of the burden of proving that *mens rea*, or it does not. And for the reasons given here, and apparently accepted by the Court of Appeal, it does not.

This in turn leads us to a fourth problematic conclusion.

The intoxication rules for basic intent crimes effectively criminalize the intoxication itself to some extent

The reasons for reaching this conclusion are as follows. As noted above, a defendant accused of a basic intent offence cannot use evidence of his/her intoxication to deny that he/she had the requisite *mens rea* for the offence. This cannot be simply a rule of evidence, because s. 8 of the Criminal Justice Act 1967 provides that 'a court or jury in determining whether a person has committed an offence...(b) shall decide whether [that person] did intend or foresee [the relevant] result by reference to *all the evidence*' (emphasis added). It would therefore not be compatible with s. 8 for the courts simply to exclude evidence of intoxication in establishing the defendant's *mens rea* or lack of it. However, instead, as also noted above, juries asked to apply the rules of basic intent are in fact asked whether the defendant *would* have foreseen the relevant harm had he/she not been intoxicated. Taken literally, of course, this would require juries to consider what would have happened in an alternate, parallel universe which never existed, but in fact it is arguable that instead, in practice juries will ask themselves what a *reasonable person* would have foreseen in the circumstances, given D's other subjective characteristics (such as mental or learning disabilities). It is true that this approach conflicts with *dicta* of Clarke LJ in *Richardson and Irwin* [1999] itself, but it is difficult to see how else the jury could be expected to go about answering the hypothetical question.

If the 'reasonable person' test were to be applied to determine *mens rea* throughout criminal law, this would at least bring the intoxication rules into line with the rules applicable to sober defendants, and indeed many of those who support the current *Majewski* intoxication rules do so on the basis that they essentially criminalize inadvertent conduct (see e.g. Gardner, 1994). However, outside the intoxication context, in the case of *R v G and R* ([2003], at 463), the House of Lords referred to a 'new or renewed, emphasis on the subjective nature of the mental element in criminal offences', as a result of which the court in that case removed objective recklessness (based on the reasonable person standard) from its last major stronghold in the offence of criminal damage, holding instead that a defendant could only be guilty of criminal damage contrary to the Criminal Damage Act 1971 if he/she had actually personally foreseen some damage to another's property. Lord Steyn's view was that this change would

> fit in with the general tendency in modern times of our criminal law. The shift is towards adopting a subjective approach. It is generally necessary to look at the matter in the light of how it would have appeared to the defendant. (para. 55)

The conclusion must therefore be that we are now in a situation where the threshold for *mens rea* is much lower for intoxicated defendants than it is for sober ones; for a sober defendant the prosecution must establish that the defendant him/herself foresaw the relevant harm, while for intoxicated defendants it is apparently sufficient for the jury to be satisfied that a reasonable person would have done so. In other words, we are permitted to convict intoxicated defendants of inadvertence, but not sober ones. All of which provides direct support for Lord Birkenhead's statement in *Beard's* case [1920] that 'the cause of the punishment is the drunkenness which has led to the crime, rather than the crime itself'. Had that drunkenness been the direct moral equivalent of the usual *mens rea* requirements, this conclusion would not have been so problematic. But as noted above, it is not. If we are, then, to criminalize the intoxication itself, arguably we should do so directly in a manner which recognizes at both the conviction and sentencing levels that this is what we are doing, and that the liability of intoxicated defendants is indeed different from the liability of sober ones (see further Williams, 2013).

The rules on therapeutic intoxicants are not wholly clear, and are based on the same problematic theory underlying the rules of voluntary, recreational intoxication

As noted above, in cases where the intoxicants were taken for therapeutic rather than recreational reasons the defendant can use evidence of his/her intoxication in order to deny that he/she had the necessary *mens rea* at the time of committing the offence, even if the offence in question is one of basic intent. However, the precise scope of these rules in practice is unclear, and in any case they are subject to the same criticisms as have just been levelled at the rules concerning voluntary, recreational intoxication.

In *R v Bailey* [1983], the appellant hit a man with an iron bar and was charged with wounding with intent to cause GBH contrary to s. 18 of the OAPA, or alternatively with wounding under s. 20 of that Act. He was a diabetic and argued that he had acted in a state of automatism caused by hypoglycaemia as a result of failing to take food after a dose of insulin, but at first instance this was rejected on the basis that self-induced automatism would not constitute a defence, and here the automatism was self-induced by the appellant's failure to take sufficient food after his dose of insulin. The Court of Appeal, however, held, on the contrary, that:

> In our judgment, self-induced automatism, other than that due to intoxication from alcohol or drugs, may provide a defence [even] to crimes of basic intent. The question in each case will be whether the prosecution have proved the necessary element of recklessness. In cases of assault, if the accused knows that his actions or inaction are likely to make him aggressive, unpredictable or uncontrolled with the result that he may cause some injury to others and he persists in the action or takes no remedial action when he knows it is required, it will be open to the jury to find that he was reckless. (at 765)

It was common knowledge, held the court, that:

> those who take alcohol to excess or certain sorts of drugs may become aggressive or do dangerous or unpredictable things, they may be able to foresee the risks of causing harm to others but nevertheless persist in their conduct. But the same cannot be said without more of a man who fails to take food after an insulin injection. If he does appreciate the risk that such a failure may lead to aggressive, unpredictable and uncontrollable conduct and he nevertheless deliberately runs the risk or otherwise disregards it, this will amount to recklessness. But we certainly do not think that it is common knowledge, even among diabetics, that such is a consequence of a failure to take food and there is no evidence that it was known to this appellant. (at 764–5)

Similarly, in *R v Hardie* [1984] the defendant was asked to leave the flat of the woman with whom he had been living. He then took a Valium tablet belonging to her in order to calm himself, but when this had little effect she informed him that the tablets were old stock and he could therefore take as many as he liked and it would do him no harm. He later returned to the flat in an intoxicated state, apparently caused by his having by then taken five Valium tablets. Having fallen asleep in the bedroom of the flat, he was discovered there later with a wardrobe in the bedroom on fire. Since he had been the only person in the room he was also the only person who could have started the fire, although he had no recollection of having done so. The judge directed the jury that the voluntary self-administration of the drug was irrelevant as a defence and that it could not negative *mens rea* for the purposes of the offence of arson contrary to s. 1(2) and 1(3) of the Criminal Damage Act 1971. However, the Court of Appeal (at 69–70) held that:

> There was no evidence that it was known to the appellant or even generally known that the taking of Valium in [that] quantity would be liable to render a person aggressive or incapable of appreciating risks to others or have other side effects such that its self-administration would itself have an element of recklessness. It is true that Valium is a drug and it is true that it was taken deliberately and not taken on medical prescription, but the drug is, in our view, wholly different in kind from drugs which are liable to cause unpredictability or aggressiveness. It may well be that the taking of a sedative or soporific drug will, in certain circumstances, be no answer, for example in a case of reckless driving, but if the effect of a drug is merely soporific or sedative the taking of it, even in some excessive quantity, cannot in the ordinary way raise a conclusive presumption against the admission of proof of intoxication for the purpose of disproving mens rea in ordinary crimes, such as would be the case with alcoholic intoxication or incapacity or automatism resulting from the self-administration of dangerous drugs.
>
> In the present case the jury should not, in our judgment, have been directed to disregard any incapacity which resulted or might have resulted from the taking of Valium. They should have been directed that if they came to the conclusion that, as a result of the Valium, the appellant was, at the time, unable to appreciate the risks of property and persons from his actions they should then consider whether the taking of the Valium was itself reckless.

These cases are consistent with the underlying theory of intoxication adopted by the courts in cases of voluntary, recreational intoxication, in that in both cases the defendant's liability would depend on the extent of his prior fault in becoming intoxicated in the first place. Thus in *Bailey* the court reiterated the view of Lords Edmund-Davies and Elwyn-Jones in *Majewski* ([1977], at 764) that:

> Automatism resulting from intoxication as a result of a voluntary ingestion of alcohol or dangerous drugs does not negative the mens rea necessary for crimes of basic intent, because the conduct of the accused is reckless and recklessness is enough to constitute the necessary mens rea in assault cases where no specific intent forms part of the charge.

Whereas the Courts in *Bailey* and *Hardie* distinguished the cases in front of them on the basis that it was not 'common knowledge' that hypoglycaemia could increase the risk that the defendant would perpetrate violence, and nor was it 'generally known that the taking of Valium in [that] quantity would be liable to render a person aggressive or incapable of appreciating risks to others', and thus there was no reason automatically to assume that the defendants in those two cases had been reckless in becoming intoxicated. However, as explained above, it is by no means clear that the prior fault principle provides a satisfactory basis for liability in situations of voluntary, therapeutic intoxication, and thus it is equally questionable whether it is desirable in this context. Indeed, the prior fault theory is arguably even more problematic here because not only is its fundamental assumption (that voluntary, recreational intoxication equates with the requisite *mens rea* for the relevant offence) inherently flawed, it is not even clear precisely when the theory will apply in this context. How common must the knowledge be that a particular form of therapeutic intoxication will lead to aggression and violence before the prior fault principle would be triggered? After all, diabetics are not generally completely unaware of the potential problems associated with becoming hypo- or hyperglycaemic. Why is 'common' knowledge rather than the defendant's own knowledge relevant? Which drugs would be 'commonly' regarded as 'soporific' as in *Hardie* [1984], as opposed to liable to cause aggression?

And even if the case of *Hardie* [1984] can be explained on the basis that he at least was trying to make himself *less* liable to cause harm, the same cannot, of course, be said of *Bailey*. However, *Bailey* [1983] opens up another problematic question in this context. If the basis of liability is the prior fault of the defendant in becoming intoxicated, then should not account be taken of the fact that, whereas for most people without a particular medical condition, the default position is one of sobriety, for diabetics the reverse is true? In its natural state a diabetic's blood sugar will be imbalanced, and thus for such a person maintenance of 'sobriety' necessitates constant, positive action, unlike those without such a condition. And if this is true of diabetics, then what about other mental conditions which might dispose a person more naturally to violence but for which medication is available? If Bailey could be regarded as being potentially reckless for failing to maintain a correct level of blood sugar, could other such people equally be regarded as inherently reckless for failing to medicate themselves properly? Both the prior fault principle and the fact that our intoxication rules effectively criminalize the intoxication itself are problematic, as explained above, even in the voluntary, recreational intoxication context. But if applied to their logical conclusions in the case of therapeutic intoxicants (or indeed, failure to use therapeutic substances to maintain sobriety), their desirability becomes even less apparent.

Arguably, even where the defendant is permitted to use evidence of intoxication to deny *mens rea* in principle, the law may be too harsh

As noted above, even in instances of therapeutic intoxication where the defendant is not found to be reckless, or in cases of involuntary intoxication or those involving offences of specific intent, intoxication still does not provide a defence. The most that can happen in these three instances is that the defendant will be allowed to use the evidence of his/her intoxication in order to deny that he/she had the requisite *mens rea* for the offence of which he/she is charged. If, despite that intoxication the defendant nevertheless formed the requisite *mens rea*, he/she will be found guilty of the offence, and the fact that he/she would never have formed that *mens rea* or acted in that particular way were it not for the intoxication will be regarded as completely irrelevant.

In the context of involuntary intoxication this rule can have some disturbing effects, as demonstrated by the decision of the House of Lords in *Kingston* [1995]. Kingston, who was described as having 'paedophiliac tendencies', was in a business dispute with a couple. The couple then employed Kingston's co-defendant, Penn, to obtain damaging information which they could use against Kingston in the dispute. Penn therefore drugged Kingston and a 15-year-old boy and Penn and Kingston then 'indulged in gross sexual acts' with the boy. As part of the plan, Penn made a recording of what was going on and took photographs. As Lord Mustill explains:

> In ordinary circumstances the respondent's paedophiliac tendencies would have been kept under control, even in the presence of the sleeping or unconscious boy on the bed. The ingestion of the drug (whatever it was) brought about a temporary change in the mentality or personality of the respondent which lowered his ability to resist temptation so far that his desires overrode his ability to control them. Thus we are concerned here with a case of disinhibition. The drug is not alleged to have created the desire to which the respondent gave way, but rather to have enabled it to be released. (at 364)

In the light of this the Court of Appeal (*Kingston* [1994], 82–3) had held that:

> the question can be answered by turning to first principles. The importance of ensuring, under a system of law, that members of the community are safeguarded in their persons and property is obvious and was firmly stated in *Reg. v. Majewski*; see, for example, the speech of Lord Edmund-Davies, at p. 495. However, the purpose of the criminal law is to inhibit, by proscription and by

penal sanction, antisocial acts which individuals may otherwise commit. Its unspoken premise is that people may have tendencies and impulses to do those things which are considered sufficiently objectionable to be forbidden. Having paedophiliac inclinations and desires is not proscribed; putting them into practice is. If the sole reason why the threshold between the two has been crossed is or may have been that the inhibition which the law requires has been removed by the clandestine act of a third party, the purposes of the criminal law are not served by nevertheless holding that the person performing the act is guilty of an offence. A man is not responsible for a condition produced 'by stratagem, or the fraud of another.' If therefore drink or drug, surreptitiously administered, causes a person to lose his self-control and for that reason to form an intent which he would not otherwise have formed, it is consistent with the principle that the law should exculpate him because the operative fault is not his. The law permits a finding that the intent formed was not a criminal intent or, in other words, that the involuntary intoxication negatives the mens rea. As was pointed out in argument, there is some analogy to be found here in the rationale underlying the defence of duress. While it is not necessary for the decision of this case, it appears to us that if the principle applies where the offence is one of basic intent, it should apply also where the offence is one of specific intent.

However, although supported to some extent by Sullivan (1994), this conclusion was regarded by other academics (e.g. Smith, 1993) as 'surprising, dangerous and contrary to principle', and the House of Lords ultimately concluded that, while it would be worth the Law Commission giving some attention to the problem, the common law was not a suitable vehicle for creating a new defence in these circumstances. Thus, since the defendant had formed the requisite *mens rea*, the fact that he had done so only as a result of intoxication brought about by a third party would not afford him any defence.

From the point of view of practicality it is easy to see why this conclusion was reached; were such a defence to exist there would be difficult questions of proof, as Lord Mustill points out (at 376–7), and it would be relatively easy for defendants to argue that they would never have acted in the same or a similar way but for someone else's actions in intoxicating them. There would be obvious policy concerns if such arguments were to be accepted too readily. Nevertheless, if the facts in *Kingston* are taken literally, as they must be, there must be real concerns associated with the decision reached by the House of Lords in that particular case.

First, from a theoretical point of view, the interrelationship of this decision with the decision reached in *Majewski* [1977] gives something of a 'heads I win, tails you lose' impression. Evidence of prior fault in becoming intoxicated is supposed to be sufficiently culpable that it will replace even an absence of *mens rea* at the time of the offence. But conversely, prior *lack* of fault in actually forming that *mens rea* is irrelevant. Of course, Lord Mustill did deal in *Kingston* ([1995], at 370) with the interplay between that case and the rules in *Majewski*, concluding that:

> where the intoxication is involuntary, *Majewski* does not *subtract* the defence of absence of intent; but there is nothing in *Majewski* to suggest that where intent is proved involuntary intoxication *adds* a further defence.

And, of course, the two situations are not perfectly symmetrical; *Majewski* dealt with situations in which D wishes to deny *mens rea*, not situations like *Kingston* (1995) in which the *mens rea* is unquestionably present. But, arguably, the logic and policy of prior fault behind *Majewski* mean that more ought perhaps equally to be made of a prior absence of fault.

Second, if it is to be assumed that Kingston really was capable in normal circumstances of controlling his paedophilic tendencies and genuinely did only act on them because of the disinhibition brought about by a third party, it is difficult to establish what deterrent purpose the House of Lords' decision is intended to have. What precisely is the law suggesting that Kingston should have done in this instance that he did not do? As the Court of Appeal concluded, it is difficult to see how the 'purposes of the criminal law' are to be served by the decision.

As for the other two scenarios in which intoxication can be used to deny *mens rea* (namely, voluntary recreational intoxication for offences of specific intent and therapeutic intoxication), the concerns are naturally less serious. Nevertheless, as noted above, at least in some instances of *non*-ingestion of therapeutic substances, intoxication may also be regarded as being perhaps partly involuntary, and even in situations of apparently voluntary, recreational intoxication there may be reason to question the complete irrelevance of that intoxication, as Bogg and Herring (Chapter 13 in this volume) demonstrate. The conclusion must therefore be that, as with the other rules examined above, the correctness of the law's conclusion on this point is far from self-evident.

Conclusion

The current rules of criminal law regarding intoxication are the result of an uneasy compromise. On the one hand, there is an obvious and understandable desire to protect society from the clear dangers posed by intoxicated defendants, while on the other hand an intoxicated defendant might be regarded as being less subjectively culpable than one who committed a similar offence in a sober and calculating manner. If the arguments above are accepted, it appears that to a large extent it is the first half of the balance that currently has the upper hand. This in itself is problematic, in that the law apparently criminalizes the intoxication itself to some extent, without doing so openly. But in addition, as also outlined above, many of the rules themselves are neither clear in practice nor readily explicable in theory. Two successive examinations of the issue by the Law Commission (1993; 2008) both resulted in the conclusion that the current rules cannot be much improved, but if the problems surrounding the current rules are examined carefully, it arguably becomes more difficult to conclude that they are really the best we can do.

Bibliography

Gardner, S (1994) 'The Importance of *Majewski*' **14** *Oxford Journal of Legal Studies* 279

Gough, S (1996) 'Intoxication and Criminal Liability: The Law Commission's Proposed Reforms' **112** *Law Quarterly Review* 335

Horder, J (1995) 'Sobering Up? The Law Commission on Criminal Intoxication' **58** *Modern Law Review* 534

Husak, D (2012) 'Intoxicants and Culpability', available at www.law.upenn.edu/academics/institutes/ilp/actiolibera/papers/secure/HusakIntoxicantsandCulpability.pdf

Law Commission (1993) *Intoxication and Criminal Liability* Consultation Paper No 127 (London: TSO)

Law Commission (2008) *Intoxication and Criminal Liability* Report No 314 (London: TSO)

Maguire, M and H Nettleton (2003) *Reducing Alcohol-Related Violence and Disorder: An Evaluation of the 'TASC' Project* Home Office Research Study 265, available at www.homeoffice.gov.uk/rds/pdfs2/hors265.pdf

Ormerod, D C (2007) 'Comment on *R v Heard*' *Criminal Law Review* 654

Simester, A (2009) 'Intoxication is Never a Defence' *Criminal Law Review* 3

Simester, A, J Spencer, G R Sullivan and G Virgo (2010) *Simester and Sullivan's Criminal Law: Theory and Doctrine* 4th edn (Oxford: Hart Publishing)

Smith, J (1993) 'Commentary' *Criminal Law Review* 784

Sullivan, G (1994) 'Commentary' *Criminal Law Review* 272

Williams, R (2013 forthcoming) 'Voluntary Intoxication – A Lost Cause?' *Law Quarterly Review*

Cases

Bratty v AG for Northern Ireland [1963] AC 386
DPP v Majewski [1977] AC 443
R v Bailey [1983] 1 WLR 760
R v Beard [1920] AC 479
R v Durante [1972] 3 All ER 962 (CA).
R v G and R [2003] UKHL 50
R v George (1960) 128 Can CC 289 at 301.
R v Hardie [1984] 3 All ER 848.
R v Heard [2007] EWCA Crim 125.
R v Kingston (CA) [1994] QB 81
R v Kingston [1995] 2 AC 355
R v Richardson and Irwin [1999] 1 Cr App R 392
R v Sheehan [1975] 2 All ER 960
R v Woollin [1998] 3 WLR 382.
Ruse v Read [1949] 1 KB 377 (DC)

Legislation

Criminal Damage Act 1971
Criminal Justice Act 1967
Offences Against the Person Act 1861
Police Act 1964

15
The Addicted Self: A Neuroscientific Perspective

Ciaran Regan

One of the charms of drunkenness unquestionably lies in the deepening of the sense of reality and truth which is gained therein. In whatever light things may then appear to us, they seem more utterly what they are, more 'utterly utter' than when we are sober. (James, 1890)

Introduction

Intoxicants are remarkable; they arouse us and incite us to action. This emotional excitement gives us pleasure and a greater belief in the intoxicant and the reality of the pleasure it provides. This primary self-consciousness is provided for by the brainstem and the limbic, or hedonic, system that act in tandem to regulate bodily functions concerned with consummatory and defensive behaviours. It is a value system; a system whose extensive connections adjust the response of hormones and the autonomic nervous system to emotional demands. It responds slowly, in seconds to minutes. Unlike the cortex, which has discrete functional regions designed to deal with signals from the exterior, the limbic-brainstem loop system has evolved to match the body. Heart rate, sweating, appetite, digestion, sex and sleep are all regulated by this system; it deals solely with the interior and maintains our state of well-being. This is homeostasis, the mechanism that maintains stability within the physiological systems and holds all parameters of our internal milieu within limits that allow us to survive (Sterling and Eyer, 1981).

Intoxicants not only alter our primary self-consciousness; the emotional context of their use can unknowingly influence our judgments of their effects. For example, the whole history of witchcraft and early medicine involves human belief in intoxicants; any remedy is a relief once accompanied by emotional circumstance such as the laying on of physician's hands or the rhythmic chanting of the shaman (Vitebsky, 2001). It would seem that normal responses become separated from information based on our learning and memory of prior associations and inferences. The amygdala is a brain structure believed to be involved in such post-perceptual processing and is closely located to brain regions involved in information processing, such as the hippocampus. The amygdala also receives visual information stored in the cortex and uses this to influence perceptual processing in other brain areas. In this way, the social significance of stimuli being processed by the amygdala influences our memory, decision-making and other more general cognitive functions (Damasio, 1994; LeDoux, 1996).

Sensory signals from exterior environments are delivered to our cortex by a second major system termed the thalamocortical system, a structure within the centre of the brain. The thalamus delivers signals, in milliseconds to seconds, to regions that are discretely mapped on the cortex and simultaneously deal with our sensory modalities such as sight, sound, touch and taste. In addition to controlling signals from the cortex to our voluntary muscles, the thalamus orchestrates the extensive connections of the cortex to all other brain regions, such as the striatum and amygdala and hippocampus, that primarily deal with timing of motion, emotion and memory. The

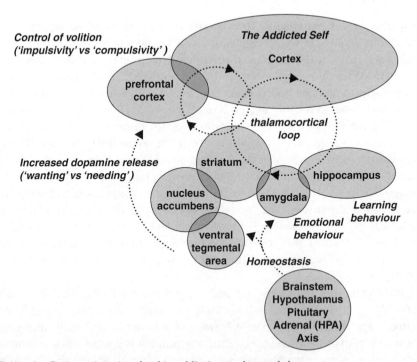

Figure 1:   Brain regions involved in addiction to drugs of abuse

thalamocortical system categorizes our environment and the limbic-brain-stem system applies value adjustments to physiological needs. This is crucial to the learning and behaviour necessary to adapt to increasingly complex environments of our exterior (Edelman, 1992) (see Figure 1).

Finally, it is important to note that the patterns of behaviour that we adapt to the signals emerging from these complex and ever-changing environments are specific to each individual. We are gregarious individuals who desire to please and attract. We pursue individual intellectual, moral and spiritual ideals. We have, it seems, as many selves as there are individuals who recognise us and carry images of us in their minds. Such images are frail and can be altered by memory loss, false recollections and insane delusions. Indeed, sometimes, our moral and spiritual convictions are more profound on some occasions than others and we seem able to suspend our self-beliefs in the presence of a more emotionally exciting experience. Intoxicants can provide such exciting experiences and in extremes of intoxication, as William James puts it, *'every man's soul will sweat with conviction, and be all the while unable to tell what he is convinced of at all'*.

Behavioural plasticity

Humans and other animals readily learn to take addictive drugs; this requires the specific recognition of drug-associated cues and the performance of specific, often complex, actions. This process of associative learning, by which the drug abuser connects specific cues, such as a particular place, with drug-induced states leads to the consideration of drug addiction being an aberrant form of learning, perhaps mediated by maladaptive recruitment of certain memory systems of the brain (Torregrossa et al., 2011). The notion that certain events promote change in behaviour cannot be considered a unitary process but one comprised of several independent functions, some or all of which can be active simultaneously. Therefore, understanding learning and memory processes is essential to the analysis of changes in behaviour produced by different addictive drugs.

The remarkable array of repertoires of behaviour in each individual suggests that they are subject to the laws of genetic variation and natural selection, a process by which genes and traits propagate or are lost by differential mortality and reproductive success. In truth, however, genes do not alter behaviour, they act in complex ways to alter the physical nature of brain and body which, in turn, alters behaviour. Song birds, for example, have an innate vocalization pattern yet they require to hear the song of conspecifics before they acquire the mature song necessary for successful mating (Nottebohm and Liu, 2010). This requires structural change to occur in the song-generating motorneurons and this leads to extraordinary behavioural consequences.

This is an example of epigenetics, the word being derived from the Greek *epi* meaning 'upon' and genetics.

The idea that complex behaviours are formed from both genetic and epigenetic components was originally proposed by Conrad Waddington (1957) and later expanded to include the phenomenon of plasticity by Mary Jane West-Eberhard (2003). Epigenetics, West-Eberhard argues, gives rise to alternative phenotypes which are the observable features and behaviours of an organism. She further suggests alternative phenotypes to be important as they can give rise to traits that are novel and that these traits might lead to genetic divergence and so give rise to speciation. As in the example given for songbirds above, the environment can induce alternative phenotypes and thereby take a lead in genetic evolution. This is a facet of Darwinian evolution that remains to be more fully explored.

The phenomenon of plasticity implies that experience impacts on the neuronal network in a manner that modifies the efficacy of information transfer beyond that which is innate. It also implies that the synapse, the connection among neurons and ultimate element of the neural system, can be modified by experience and result in changes that are both structural and behavioural. The brain, therefore, may be considered to be a highly dynamic organ in permanent relation with the environment as well as the individual and their acts.

Such neural representations of the environment have been described in the work of O'Keefe and Nadel (1978). They have identified 'place cells', neurons that exhibit greater activity whenever an animal is in a specific location in a given environment. Moreover, they have demonstrated that the firing patterns and locations of these neurons change when the animal is placed in a different environment. Similarly, Wolf Singer (1993) has used brain-imaging techniques to demonstrate that visual perception is mediated by neurons within different neuronal assemblies that fire in synchrony to unite different features of neuronal representations. These features can include shape, motion, colour, depth and other aspects of perception. The synchronous activation of these neuronal assemblies for a few milliseconds binds aspects of external reality into a single neural representation or perception.

Neuronal assemblies are formed during early development through directed migrations of newborn cells to their eventual position in the cortex by the dynamic regulation of cell and substrate adhesion molecules, cell process extension and activity-dependent matching of connections. This idea has been elegantly encapsulated by Gerald Edelman in his theory of neuronal group selection (Edelman, 1987). In the first tenet of his theory, Edelman argues that the formation of neuronal cell assemblies involves selection of specific neurons from populations engaged in topological or spatial competition, that the genetic code does not provide a specific wiring pattern but a

set of constraints that regulate the epigenetic selection of the primary repertoire of neurons. The second tenet assumes that, during behaviour, synaptic connections in the assembly are selectively strengthened or weakened by
specific biochemical processes, a mechanism that underlies memory, to form
a variety of functioning circuits by selection, the so-called secondary repertoire. The third tenet requires that the primary and secondary repertoires
form maps, functionally segregated (e.g. for colour and movement in the case
of the visual system) but with reciprocal connections that allow interaction
by a process called re-entry whereby widely distributed groups of neurons
achieve integration through synchronized firing. This underlies how brain
areas co-ordinate with each other to yield new functions and, importantly,
link psychology to physiology. The unit of selection is not the individual
nerve cell, but is a rather closely connected collection of cells called a neuronal group.

These cortical maps are dynamic, not static. The acquisition or learning of
new behaviours, for example, produces structural and functional changes in
the neurons of these maps that lead to alterations in their pattern of inter-
connections between the various systems associated with the learning of a
task. Thus maps in the adult cortex can continually change in response to
increased activity arising from change in the extent of their use. Given that
we are all reared in different environments and, later, acquire our perceptual
and motor skills through exposure to unique combinations of environmental
stimuli, our brain architecture will be modified in unique ways. This diversity
sets the biological basis for our individuality.

This notion has been elegantly supported by Michael Merzenich and
colleagues (1983) who have demonstrated neuronal groups to undergo
competition for interaction with neighbouring neurons by strengthening
their synaptic connections in map boundaries of cortical regions that control
the sensation of touch. Merzenich encouraged monkeys to use their middle
three fingers at the expense of other fingers to rotate a disk for the purpose of
obtaining a food reward. This resulted in the area of the cortex devoted to the
middle finger becoming greatly expanded. Practice, or continual exposure to
the task/stimulus therefore, may act on pre-existing patterns of connections
and strengthen their effectiveness. The mechanisms involved in the creation
and interlinking of these neuronal groups can re-occur at certain times and
places by changing synaptic strengths and, even in a developed brain, sprout-
ing can occur in which new neural processes form additional synapses.

Thus, in summary, there are two components, parallel but different: a
genetic component and an environmental or behavioural component, which
are linked in a special way in the phenomenon of plasticity. The internal environment of the body also influences plasticity. The tendency towards stability in the body is called homeostasis and this is controlled by the brainstem-

limbic system which also regulates emotional behaviour. Emotions reach consciousness and thought and, conversely, higher cognitive functions affect emotions. Not surprisingly, therefore, the brainstem-limbic system has recip-rocal connections with the cortex. The hippocampus and amygdala are also involved through reciprocal connections between the cortex and brainstem-limbic systems as these regions are necessary to process information acquired during learning, particularly for behavioural responses that require co-ordi-nation of information from different sensory modalities or, in the case of the amygdala, the association of a stimulus and an emotional response. The inter-play between the neural activity of the brainstem-limbic system and the activ-ity of higher cortical centres results in emotional experiences that we describe as fear, anger, pleasure and contentment. There is not only recall of our percep-tual representations, emotional awareness also accompanies perception. These are the feelings saved up along with their perceptual representations. Antonio Damasio (2000) terms these feelings as being somatic markers, a body memory of some sort. Further, we are not always aware of the somatic states that may accompany the evocation of a perceptual representation.

The activation of this limbic-brainstem system by the sensory cues in our environment provides us with a survival mechanism that allows us to learn to discriminate between dangerous and harmful stimuli and those which provide us with pleasurable and strengthening behaviours associated with natural reinforcers such as food, water and sexual contact. The crucial point is that addictive drugs activate this neuronal circuitry by chemical means, so bypassing the need for evolutionarily useful behaviours.

Addiction and the dysregulation of bodily homeostasis

Many now accept that addiction arises from a progressive malfunctioning of the brain reward system that ultimately leads compulsive drug use and loss of control over drug intake, an eventual state that renders the individual vulner-able to relapse long after drug taking has ceased (Koob and LeMoal, 2001; Everitt and Robbins, 2005; Koob and LeMoal, 2006). This is based on the idea that the constancy of the internal environment of the body is the result of a system of control mechanisms that limit the variability of body states. As was mentioned above, this tendency toward stability in the body is called home-ostasis. The key neuronal mechanisms relating to maintaining homeostasis are located in the brainstem-limbic system that receives information directly from the internal environment. This control system regulates all variables within a certain range, a desired value or set point.

In addiction there is a spiralling dysregulation of the brain reward system in which many, if not all, physiological functions become increasingly acti-vated, or suppressed, as the initial hedonic effects of the intoxicant become masked overtime. As the individual becomes increasingly addicted, motivation and drive for drug taking behaviour changes from one of positive reinforcement arising from the euphoric effects of the intoxicant to the negative reinforcement of the withdrawal state. This leads to further drug-seeking and drug-taking behaviours and these ultimately lead to craving and relapse. The latter is further exacerbated by the individual becoming sensitized to the effects of the drug whereby the increased effects of the drug add to its motivational value, lead to compulsive wanting of the drug, and increased salience of the drug and/or drug-associated stimuli. Koob and LeMoal (2001) describe this as an allostatic state in which normal body and brain physiological functions no longer operate around the set point critical for survival. The reward set point has been increased to a point in which the addicted individual is in a state manifested by compulsive drug taking and loss of control over drug taking. The addict seems to be enveloped by an unusual emotional state in which their compulsion to imbibe a drug is remarkably unencumbered by the negative withdrawal consequences of drug taking. Thus, it would appear that many brain and hormonal systems combine to produce the dynamic adaptation, or allostatic state, that underlies the pathology of addiction.

It is also worth noting that addiction is not a unitary process. Different drugs produce different patterns of addiction, individual differences in the stages of addiction, and different types of drug users (Regan, 2000). There are three major components in the addiction cycle – intoxication and bingeing, the negative effects of withdrawal, and preoccupation and anticipation of these actions and effects. Nicotine, for example, is not associated with intoxication but characterized by an intake pattern that is so compulsive that daily activities become constrained. Yet individuals exist who smoke regularly but do not escalate their intake – non-dependent 'chippers' in the American lexicon of Koob and colleagues (George and Koob, 2010). Opioids and alcohol, on the other hand, produce the most intense negative withdrawal effects that lead to compulsive drug seeking and drug taking. Marijuana addiction shares aspects of both nicotine and opioid addiction. Initially, there is intense bingeing and intoxication but this is then followed by a more titrated use of the drug. In all cases, use of these intoxicants can be associated with an intense dysphoria, anxiety and the loss of motivation for naturally rewarding stimuli (anhedonia). As such, these cognitive and affective representations, the essential qualities that constitute our uniqueness or self, become altered by the constant use of addictive substances.

Reward pathways

While the full diversity of drug effects is mediated by multiple neurotransmitters acting in different brain regions, most addictive drugs share the common property of increasing release of the dopamine neurotransmitter in the striatum from neurons emanating from the ventral tegmental area (VTA). The ventral striatum includes the nucleus accumbens which mediates the most rewarding effects of addictive drugs. Dopamine is not only important in mediating the instant pleasurable effects of addictive drugs, but also in the arousing effects that are predictive of the impending reward.

While the dopamine-containing neurons that emanate from the VTA may be centrally involved in early acute exposure to all classes of intoxicants, the later plasticity changes that underpin the addicted state engage many other discrete brain regions. Striatal dopamine levels set thresholds for action, they modulate behavioural reactivity. Loss of the dopamine input to striatum, for example, results in Parkinson's disease, a condition characterized by slowness in initiating actions. The striatum also exhibits a functional topography. The cortex projects mainly to more dorsal parts of the striatum, while other regions such as the hippocampus and amygdala project mainly to the ventral part of the striatum. As a consequence, the impact of intoxicants on this system not only has rewarding actions but can influence higher-order functions including cognition and memory. For example, the VTA can critically assess reward value and, through its connections with the hippocampus, control the entry of this information into long-term memory, perhaps by attaching the motivational connotation of the intoxicant experience. Moreover, human brain-imaging studies have shown the same neural circuits respond similarly to drug administration, or drug-related stimuli in abstinent abusers, suggesting these pathways are also key elements in drug craving and relapse.

Neurons from the VTA also project onto the cortex, especially the prefrontal cortex, which in turn sends projections to most cortical and subcortical structures. The prefrontal cortex plays a key role in decision-making and, based on its relation to processes of attention, working memory, long-term memory formation and emotionality, may reasonably be expected to be involved in the development of drug-taking behaviours. Individuals with strong neural activity in discrete regions of prefrontal cortex (dorsomedial area), for example, are risk-averse whereas those with strong activity in the ventromedial area are more likely to make risky decisions (Bechara, 2005). This defines individuals that may be vulnerable to the initiation and maintenance of drug self-administration. Thus, addiction has been argued to be a failure in self-regulation and that this relates to deficits in brain structures which regulate information processing, attention, planning, reasoning, self-monitoring, or inhibition of a specific brain function or behaviour.

Loss of control in addiction is often ultimately attributed to impaired regulation in the different cognitive systems that are under the control of the prefrontal cortex. An important role of the prefrontal cortex is the mobilization and integration over time of simpler units of behaviour into more complex ones. This integration develops a hierarchical structure for behaviour that leads to the pursuit and attainment of a goal. This single-minded drive towards a target can persist over long, discontinuous stretches of time and requires the suppression of numerous behaviours and the urge to respond to competing internal and external stimuli.

Susceptibility of individuals to drug addiction

The different neurobiological systems within this multi-system framework of discrete brain regions described above may equally contribute to inter-individual differences in susceptibility to addiction. Based loosely on the ideas of Jerry Fodor (1983), that significant parts of the mind, such as perceptual processes, are structured in terms of modules, Koob and colleagues have used this concept of modularity of mind to help understand the neural basis for individual differences in vulnerability to drug addiction (George and Koob, 2010).

Modules are groups of neurons that have separate classes of input and information processing and in principle cannot be influenced by activity arising in another module. Numerous studies have established modularity of cognition with classic examples being the high specificity of activation of cortical areas during the presentation of words, colours, faces, or places, as described previously. It is now generally accepted that sensation, perception, motor action and even different types of memories are represented by different cognitive modules with dedicated neural systems that are more or less independent in their functioning. Organizing, selecting and consolidating information that derives from different modules into a coherent and unified experience requires an adapted cognitive control system, such as that provided by the modules of the prefrontal cortex (Everitt and Robbins, 2005), to ensure flexible, goal-directed behaviours. Meshing the idea of self-regulation with the concept of cognitive function being organized in a modular manner has the potential to provide a neural basis for understanding how individual differences exist in terms of plasticity and vulnerability to drug addiction. Modularity of brain structure can, for example, explain the role of stress in the development of the addicted state.

Stress is associated with the activations of the hypothalamus-pituitary-adrenal (HPA) axis, a brainstem-limbic modular structure, and individual differences in the extent of HPA axis activation increases sensation- and novelty-seeking and the propensity for drug self-administration (Piazza and LeMoal, 1998). Increased activity in the HPA axis also drives the mesolimbic dopamine system arising from the VTA and this augments the positive reinforcing effects of drugs, increases their incentive salience, and leads to more profound drug-seeking behaviours. Further, the HPA axis can activate the amygdala which reinforces the emotional stimuli associated with gaining the drug reward, a drive that can ultimately lead to drug dependence. Importantly, these activations of the amygdala correlate with decreased activity in a discrete area of the prefrontal cortex, the ventromedial aspect. In some cocaine addicts, the structures of the fibre tracts between the cortex and the amygdala have been found to be abnormal (Lim et al., 2002). These fibre tract anomalies may be drug-induced or arise, for unknown reasons, in certain individuals during development. Such anomalies would explain how a specific dysfunction of the prefrontal cortex may lead to loss of control over a specific neurobiological response, such as activation of the amygdala during craving in one individual or to hyper-reactivity of the stress system in another. Brain region-specific mechanisms, therefore, can explain differences in vulnerability to drug addiction.

Cellular and molecular mechanisms of drug addiction

At a more basic level, brain modules can be viewed as networks of neurons connected to each other by specialized structures known as synapses and it has long been assumed that structural and functional changes in this complex circuitry provide the basis for the acquisition and long-term storage of sensory information. Numerous studies have provided evidence for the involvement of many neurotransmitter systems in addiction, however, the current best hypothesis for a common final pathway to drug dependence involves changes in synaptic strength between neurons within the modules that form the basic functional structure of the addicted brain. This change in synaptic strength is a phenomenon commonly referred to as synaptic plasticity.

The two best studied forms of synaptic plasticity are long-term potentiation (strengthening of synapses, LTP) and long-term depression (weakening of synapses, LTD). These two processes have long been proposed to be cellular models of memory, respective mechanisms for learning and forgetting (Bliss and Collingridge, 1993). It also seems that these molecular mechanisms of synaptic plasticity may be engaged in behaviours involved in the pursuit of rewards, such as those provided by drugs. As a consequence, these cellular mechanisms may operate in areas of the brain essential for processing of rewards and so be involved in generating the addicted state. Studies in animals have confirmed that exposure to drugs of abuse, such as cocaine, causes the neurons of the VTA to become potentiated. Moreover, the concomitant release of dopamine, which occurs in the VTA as part of the drug action, and is associated with its reward response, can further activate the neurotransmitter receptors involved in this form of synaptic plasticity. This results in a form of LTP that persists for months (Dacher and Nugent, 2011). Synaptic plasticity, therefore, could serve as an ideal substrate for reward-based learning and motivated behaviours and that the aversive and addictive properties of drugs of abuse might arise through their interaction with learning mechanisms, suggesting that drug-associated memories are critical parts of the addiction process. It is not unreasonable to suggest, therefore, that the brain 'learns' to crave drugs.

This longer-lasting form of LTP is associated with the synthesis of new proteins that are required for the structural and functional changes that occur at the synapse in this form of plasticity. These structural changes have given rise to the 'synapse tagging and capture' hypothesis which, among others, has been promoted by Richard Morris and colleagues (Redondo and Morris, 2011). This idea suggests that LTP identifies, or 'tags', synapses in a manner that allows directed delivery of plasticity-related proteins. In this manner, the synapses are strengthened, or 'captured', and incorporated into the newly activated neural network. Protein synthesis gives rise to increased size and shape of the synapses and even the growth of new synapses. In contrast, the induction of LTD prevents delivery of plasticity-related proteins and is associated with shrinkage of synapses and their possible retraction from the neural circuit.

In terms of neural modules, therefore, two types of synapse manipulation can be discerned. A form of plasticity in which the strength of existing cell synapses is retuned. This gives rise to the cell assembly hypothesis in which networks are distinguished by the composition of the cells that are co-activated. In the second discernment, the synapse assembly hypothesis suggests that new synapses are created by experience, incorporated into the network, and the redundant supernumerary synapses eliminated by a pruning mechanism. This allows the elaboration of a network of specific groups of novel synapses with a connectivity scheme that has been optimized for each experience.

Experimental studies in rodents have provided reasonable certainty that continued exposure to addictive drugs results in persisting structural change in the neuronal cells of brain regions associated with addiction and that these changes may be correlated to behavioural phenotypes associated with a drug-dependent state (Russo et al., 2010). One of the major types of structural plasticity observed in neurons is change in the extent of their branching, the dendritic arbor, and in the number and shape of synapses on these branches, the spine frequency. Morphine, for example, decreases the density of dendritic spines on neurons in the nucleus accumbens, a key brain reward region which is located in the striatum and receives input from the dopaminergic terminals arising in the VTA. This observation is consistent with a novel synapse assembly optimizing the functional response of the neural network to the presence of a drug. Moreover, the extent of this spine remodelling is much greater in animals which self-administer the drug, as compared to those who have the drug administered by the investigator, which suggests that intentional use of the drug is important in this form of plasticity and that the remodelling is likely influenced by other brain regions involved in aspects of volition. Consistent with this suggestion, opiates have also been found to decrease spine density on neurons of the medial prefrontal cortex and hippocampus, brain regions intimately involved in cognitive functions. Surprisingly, and in contrast to opiates, stimulants such as cocaine, amphetamines and methylphenidate, consistently increase dendritic complexity and spine density of neurons in the nucleus accumbens, VTA, hippocampus and medial prefrontal cortex.

The observation that stimulants and opiates induce opposite effects on the spine density in several brain regions is a conundrum, as both drug classes produce similar states of addiction. The same behavioural phenotypes associated with drug sensitization are observed with both drug classes and the same negative emotional states occur during their withdrawal. However, the devil may be in the detail. For example, several subtle differences in behavioural response exist in both laboratory animals and humans (Badiani et al., 2011). Rats, for example, when given unlimited access to stimulants develop an uncontrolled bingeing behaviour that is not seen when they are provided with an unlimited access to opiates. Human addiction to stimulants is associated with greater impulsivity as compared to that observed in those addicted to opiates and, further, imaging studies in humans indicate relapse to opiates and cocaine is controlled by different sub-regions of the prefrontal cortex. At the molecular level, we know that drugs of abuse exert their effects at different receptors. As a consequence, they activate separate signalling pathways that can lead to the regulation of different gene expression programs. This, in turn, has the potential to deliver plasticity-related proteins associated either with the elaboration of synapse structure or the retraction of synapses from the neural circuit. This idea is consistent with the separate and distinctive profiles of gene expression observed in nucleus accumbens post-mortem tissue of both cocaine and heroin abusers (Albertson et al., 2006). Indeed, in these studies, only a tiny fraction of gene transcript change (<0.05%) was common to both drug-dependent populations. The ability of opiates and stimulants to modulate spine and synapse structural plasticity also means they have the capacity to expand or compress networks in the immediate or more distant brain modules that they influence. In this manner they can strengthen or weaken connections with other brain areas and thereby drive distinct aspects of addictive behaviours that are controlled by these modules.

Finally, it is important to note that the majority of animal studies describing the effects of opiates and stimulants on synapse remodelling have been performed in juvenile rodents. In such animals, and in humans, the pruning of the excess synapses produced in early development continues into adolescence (Huttenlocher, 2002). It is, therefore, unlikely this process would have been complete in the animals used in these studies. This raises the question as to whether modulation of spine and synapse structural plasticity relates to impaired or excessive pruning of synapses during adolescence. This question requires being resolved. Adolescence is a period of increased vulnerability. It is a time when regions of the prefrontal cortex strengthen their connectivity with areas of the limbic system, regions that respond to risk and reward. This is a period governed by the affective systems of the brain and these are operating largely outside conscious awareness: 'gut feelings' of high emotional content (Steinberg, 2005).

Epigenesis and the mechanisms of addiction

Addiction is not an automatic outcome of drug use and only a small subset of individuals (about 20 per cent) experience the switch from controlled to compulsive drug use that defines the addicted state. The mechanisms that are responsible for the transition from initial drug use to chronic drug use and then to compulsive, relapsing drug abuse are significantly influenced by both the genetic constitution of the individual and the psychological and social context in which drug exposure occurs.

The genetic risk contribution for addiction is roughly 50 per cent and, as yet, the nature of the genes involved is almost completely unknown. For example, monozygotic, or single egg, twins share a common genotype yet most twin pairs are not identical and exhibit differences in their individual susceptibilities to disease, a wide range of other anthropomorphic features and drug addiction (Fraga et al., 2005). In addition, many individuals at risk of developing compulsive drug use often have distinct personality or psychiatric traits that are not only genetic but significantly influenced by environmental factors that include adverse life experiences, stress and the psychological and social context in which drug exposure occurs (Kendler et al., 2007). There are several possible explanations for these observations but one is the existence of epigenetic differences.

Although the cells of an individual contain essentially the same genetic complement they can differentiate during development to form distinct tissues and organs. This involves environmental cues and cell-to-cell signals that invoke change in the transcriptional activity of each gene. The transcription of the genome is highly regulated and involves the unfolding of specific chromatin proteins to reveal the DNA structure to be transcribed. This also involves the activation or repression of the controlling transcription factors, proteins that bind to regulatory elements of the gene and control its expression. This physical control of the genome relies on cellular signals that are dynamically regulated by the behavioural and subjective stimuli provided by environmental context. There is now evidence to indicate that the processes involved in early development continue to regulate cellular adaptation to environmental signals in the adult, such as those involved in social interaction, and that many of the regulatory events concern genes involved in synaptic plasticity (Zhang and Meaney, 2010).

Evidence from laboratory animal studies supports the idea that epigenetic mechanisms are directly engaged by drugs of abuse. Many view these dynamic adaptations to be the allostatic mechanisms by which drugs induce highly stable changes in the brain and form the addicted phenotype. Long-lasting expression of ΔFOSB, for example, a protein which forms a complex with other proteins to regulate gene transcription, is induced by chronic administration of virtually any drug of abuse. This drug-induced expression of ΔFOSB has been shown to be all that is necessary to account for the increases in dendritic spines in the nucleus accumbens that accompany chronic cocaine administration. Further, animals genetically programmed to overexpress ΔFOSB, specifically in the nucleus accumbens, exhibit behaviours that increase their vulnerability to drug addiction. Exposure of these animals to cocaine results in increased behavioural activation, such as increased locomotion, and a greater propensity for cocaine self-administration (Robison and Nestler, 2011). The mechanism of ΔFOSB remains to be established but is believed to alter the interactions of the chromatin proteins with DNA and, in the presence of cocaine, allow the expression of genes not otherwise transcribed.

Another form of epigenetic regulation involves the direct chemical modification of DNA through the addition of methyl groups onto cytosine bases in DNA. This modification has greatest impact when it occurs near gene transcription start sites as this effectively blocks gene expression. DNA methylation is a crucial event as it provides a more stable, if not permanent, state of gene expression (Zhang and Meaney, 2010). There are, however, few mechanistic insights into the processes that dictate where in the genome methylation is likely to be established and maintained and how this might contribute to states of addiction.

These epigenetic markings of DNA have been referred to as 'memorized states of gene expression' (Borelli et al., 2008) to describe how neural networks might collectively control the cognitive function and behavioural responses of each individual in a manner that endures for life.

Acknowledgment

The author wishes to thank Veronica Jane O'Mara for her most helpful critiques on an earlier draft of this paper.

Bibliography

Albertson, D N, C J Schmidt, G Kapatos, M J Bannon (2006) 'Distinctive Profiles of Gene Expression in the Human Nucleus Accumbens Associated with Cocaine and Heroin Abuse' **31** *Neuropsychopharmacology* 2304–12

Badiani, A, D Belin, D Epstein, D Calu, Y Shaham (2011) 'Opiate Versus Psychostimulant Addiction: The Differences Do Matter' **12** *Nature Review of Neuroscience* 685–700

Bechara, A (2005) 'Decision Making, Impulse Control and Loss of Willpower to Resist Drugs: A Neurocognitive Perspective' **8** *Nature Neuroscience* 1458–63

Bliss, T V and G L Collingridge (1993) 'A Synaptic Model of Memory: Long-Term Potentiation in the Hippocampus' **361** *Nature* 31–9

Borrelli, E, E J Nestler, C D Allis, and P Sassone-Corsi (2008) 'Decoding the Epigenetic Language of Neuronal Plasticity' **60** *Neuron* 961–74

Dacher, M and F S Nugent (2011) 'Opiates and Plasticity' **61** *Neuropharmacology* 1088–96

Damasio, A R (1994) *Descartes' Error. Emotion, Reason and the Human Brain* (London: Putnam)

Damasio, A R (2000) *The Feeling of What Happens: Body and Emotion in the Making of Consciousness* (London: Heinemann)

Edelman, G M (1987) *Neuronal Darwinism: The Theory of Neuronal Group Selection* (New York: Basic Books)

Edelman, G M (1992) *Bright Air, Brilliant Fire: On The Matter of the Mind* (London: Allen Lane, The Penguin Press)

Everitt, B J and T W Robbins (2005) 'Neural Systems of Reinforcement for Drug Addiction: From Actions to Habits to Compulsion' **8** *Nature Neuroscience* 1481–9

Fodor, J (1983) *The Modularity of Mind* (Cambridge MA: MIT Press)

Fraga, M F, E Ballestar, M F Paz, S Ropero, F Setien, M L Ballestar, D Heine-Suñer, J C Cigudosa, M Urioste, J Benitez, M Boix-Chornet, A Sanchez-Aguilera, C Ling, E Carlsson, P Poulsen, A Vaag, Z Stephan, T D Spector, Y Z Wu, C Plass and M Esteller (2005) 'Epigenetic Differences Arise During the Lifetime of Monozygotic Twins' **102** *Proceedings National Academy Science USA* 10604–9

George, O and G F Koob (2010) 'Individual Differences in Prefrontal Cortex Function and the Transition from Drug Use to Drug Dependence' **35** *Neuroscience Biobehaviour Review* 232–47

Huttenlocher, P R (2002) *Neural Plasticity* (Cambridge MA: Harvard University Press)

James, W (1890) *The Principles of Psychology* (Cambridge MA: Harvard University Press)

Kendler, K S, J Myers and C A Prescott (2007) 'Specificity of Genetic and Environmental Risk Factors for Symptoms of Cannabis, Cocaine, Alcohol, Caffeine, and Nicotine Dependence' **64** *Archives of General Psychiatry* 1313–20

Koob, G F and M LeMoal (2001) 'Drug Addiction, Dysregulation of Reward, and Allostasis' **24** *Neuropsychopharmacology* 97–129

Koob, G L and M LeMoal (2006) *Neurobiology of Addiction* (New York: Elsevier)

LeDoux, J (1996) *The Emotional Brain: The Mysterious Underpinnings of Emotional Life* (New York: Simon & Shuster)

Lim, K O, S J Choi, N Pomara, A Wolkin and J P Rotrosen (2002) 'Reduced Frontal White Matter Integrity in Cocaine Dependence: A Controlled Diffusion Tensor Imaging Study' **51** *Biological Psychiatry* 890–5

Merzenich, M M, J H Kaas, J T Wall, M Sur, R J Nelson and D J Felleman (1983) 'Progression of Change Following Median Nerve Section in the Cortical Representation of the Hand in Areas 3b and 1 in Adult Owl and Squirrel Monkeys' **10** *Neuroscience* 639–65

Nottebohm, F and W-C Liu (2010) 'The Origins of Vocal Learning: New Sounds, New Circuits, New Cells' **115** *Brain Language* 3–17

O'Keefe, J and L Nadel (1978) *The Hippocampus as a Cognitive Map* (Oxford: Oxford University Press)

Piazza, P V and M Le Moal (1998) 'The Role of Stress in Drug Self-Administration' **19** *Trends in Pharmacological Science* 67–74

Redondo, R L and R G M Morris (2011) 'Making Memories Last: The Synaptic Tagging and Capture Hypothesis' **12** *Nature Reviews Neuroscience* 17–30

Regan, C M (2000) *Intoxicating Minds* (London: Weidenfeld & Nicolson)

Robison, A J and E J Nestler (2011) 'Transcriptional and Epigenetic Mechanisms of Addiction' **12** *Nature Reviews Neuroscience* 623–37

Russo, S J, D M Dietz, D Dumitriu, J H Morrison, R C Malenka and E J Nestler (2010) 'The Addicted Synapse: Mechanisms of Synaptic and Structural Plasticity in Nucleus Accumbens' **33** *Trends in Neuroscience* 267–76

Singer, W (1993) 'Synchronization of Cortical Activity and Its Putative Role in Information and Processing and Learning' **55** *Annual Review of Physiology* 349–74

Steinberg, L (2005) 'Cognitive and Affective Development in Adolescence' **9** *Trends Cognitive Science* 69–74

Sterling, P and J Eyer (1981) 'Biological Basis of Stress-Related Mortality' **15** *Social Science and Medicine* 3–42

Torregrossa, M M, P R Corlett and J R Taylor (2011) 'Aberrant Learning and Memory in Addiction' **96** *Neurobiology of Learning and Memory* 609–23

Vitebsky, P (2001) *Shamanism* (Norman: University of Oklahoma Press)

Waddington, C H (1957) *The Strategy of the Genes: A Discussion of Some Aspects of Theoretical Biology* (London: Allen & Unwin)

West-Eberhard, M J (2003) *Developmental Plasticity and Evolution* (Oxford: Oxford University Press)

Zhang, T Y and M J Meaney (2010) 'Epigenetics and The Environmental Regulation of the Genome and its Function' **61** *Annual Review of Psychology* 439–66

Index